D0146550

Keeping the Dream Alive

THE SOUTHERN CHRISTIAN LEADERSHIP CONFERENCE

Dr. Martin Luther King, Jr.
Founding President 1957–1968

Dr. Ralph David Abernathy
President 1968–1977

Dr. Joseph Echols Lowery
President since 1977

Thomas R. Peake

Keeping the Dream Alive

A History of the Southern Christian Leadership Conference from King to the Nineteen-Eighties

PETER LANG

New York · Berne · Frankfurt am Main · Paris

Library of Congress Cataloging-in-Publication Data

Peake, Thomas R.
  Keeping the dream alive.

  Bibliography : p.
  Includes index.
  1. Southern Christian Leadership Conference--

History. 2. Afro-Americans--Civil rights--Southern
States. 3. Southern States--Race relations. I. Title
E185.61.P4 1987 323.42'3'06073 86-10439
ISBN 0-8204-0397-0

CIP-Kurztitelaufnahme der Deutschen Bibliothek

Peake, Thomas R.:
Keeping the dream alive: a history of the
Southern Christian Leadership Conference
from King to the nineteen-eighties / Thomas
R. Peake. - New York; Berne; Frankfurt am
Main; Paris: Lang, 1987.
  ISBN 0-8204-0397-0

Cover photo: Washington 1963 Courtesy of SCLC

©Peter Lang Publishing, Inc., New York 1987

All rights reserved.
Reprint or reproduction, even partially, in all forms such as
microfilm, xerography, microfiche, microcard, offset strictly prohibited.

Printed by Weihert-Druck GmbH, Darmstadt (West Germany)

To my parents Charles Bryan Peake and Mattie Jane Wells
Peake

LIBRARY
ALMA COLLEGE
ALMA, MICHIGAN

LIBRARY
ALMA COLLEGE
ALMA, MICHIGAN

Contents

Illustrations

Acknowledgements

If ever a book was the product of the work, faith, and co-operation of numerous people and organizations, this one is. The scope and complexity of the history of the Southern Christian Leadership Conference required input from many directions, and even with it there is much more that could have, and should have been included here. But this study is an effort to begin the process of bringing to the reading public the story of an organization that has been, and is, an important part of the development of contemporary American life and global awareness of the need for faith and nonviolent solutions to societal problems.

Since so many people made this work possible, I cannot adequately give credit where it is due. Nor can a few words of gratitude accurately reflect the profound intellectual and spiritual impact this research had on me as a person and a teacher. But I would be remiss not to mention the indispensable assistance and encouragement of several individuals who took me into their confidence and provided information, ideas, and inspiration. I am particularly grateful to C.T. Vivian and his wife Octavia for believing from the beginning that the project was viable and sharing with me much of their own insight. I am thankful also to Dr. Joseph E. Lowery, whose work as president of SCLC has been internationally recognized, for opening his offices and records to me and giving me the freedom to do serious historical research. His wife Evelyn also shared much vital information on her work as National Convener of SCLC/WOMEN and other aspects of SCLC's outreach. Former SCLC president Dr. Ralph David Abernathy, Reverend Fred Shuttlesworth, Reverend Hosea L. Williams, Mrs. Septima Clark, Reverend Fred Taylor, Reverend Albert Love, Reverend E.

Randel T. Osburn, Mrs. Bernita Bennette, the late Dr. Kelly Miller Smith of Vanderbilt, Leon Hall and Reverend James Lawson, one of the pivotal figures in the founding of the Student Nonviolent Coordinating Committee (SNCC), along with those mentioned above, were especially helpful in sharing their experience and providing hours of interviews that convinced me that many writers have inadequately treated the role of Christian faith in their analyses of the events, strategies, and results of the nonviolent movement.

The SCLC national staff in Atlanta was patiently helpful. Always busy with a wide range of tasks, they hardly had time for historical research. But they graciously accepted my many visits and helped me find my way among the documents and showed me the processes of the office. During the period of my research, Dr. Lowery, Reverend Love, Reverend Taylor, and Reverend Osburn were surrounded by a team of men and women who demonstrated dedication to their work but who also were willing to assist as time permitted with this book: Elaine Day, Bernice Alexander, Elaine Tomlin, Rick Dunn, Quentin Bradford, field secretaries Frederick Moore and Ralph Worrell, printer Eddie Mathes, administrative secretary Peggy A. Perry, Operation Breadbasket director Timothy McDonald, *M.L. King, Jr. Speaks* engineer Orville Lee (Skip) Marshall, James Orange, Michelle Alexander, Hattie Brooks, former field worker Lester Hankerson, and Claudette Mathews, who has been with the movement for many years and recently has served as Dr. Lowery's secretary. Scores of other people across the SCLC network outside Atlanta added to the input. And former SCLC officials Stoney Cooks and Representative Tyrone Brooks provided helpful interviews and suggestions.

I must add that young people were highly valuable to this research. The image that nonviolence is a dead issue and has no new supporters is quite erroneous. Even in the middle 1980s young blacks are picking up the themes of the nonviolent pioneers and adding their own creative contributions. Many young people who cannot be mentioned by name here reinforced the thesis of this book that the dream is still alive. I want to thank particularly Miss Brenda Davenport and Miss Kim Miller for

xii

intelligent, confident interviews which reflected their dedication to the Christian faith and to the ongoing work of nonviolence among the youth of the nation and other countries.

At King College, many individuals gave unselfishly to this effort. The confidence and support of President Donald R. Mitchell and former Dean of the Faculty John S. Gaines and his successor Douglas W. Boyce were vital to the completion of the research. My colleagues Dr. William J. Wade, Dr. Thomas Schroder and the other members of the social science division endured inconvenience and encouraged the research throughout. From the beginning, much needed inspiration came from Mrs. Elizabeth Ann Hay, Dr. and Mrs. Willis Wager, Dr. Jack Snider, Dr. and Mrs. George Winship, and board member Dr. Richard Ray, an accomplished pastor and editor who examined the manuscript and was otherwise helpful with publication. The library staff at King went far beyond normal duties to help: Director Mark Y. Herring, Mrs. Ann Peake, Mrs. Sharon Volkman, Mrs. Anna Slagle, and Mrs. Lila Ray, as well as student workers. Typing, editing, proofreading, and useful suggestions were provided by Mrs. Linda Henninger, Miss Fara Smith, Miss Julie Blackwell, William Roland Roark, and Mrs. Joan Shelton.

Valuable documentary sources, especially those at SCLC National Headquarters and the Martin Luther King, Jr. Center for Nonviolent Social Change, are the core of this study. I am inestimably grateful for their use and want to thank Dr. Lowery and Mrs. Coretta Scott King for opening them to me. At the King Center, Mrs. Louise Cook was a superb guide and adviser on the use of the materials on Dr. King, SCLC, and SNCC. She administers one of the finest archival centers in the world. I also want to acknowledge the personal help, use of documents and guides, and quotation permission of the King Center, Library of Congress, Morris Brown College, East Tennessee State University, Fisk University, Boston University, Howard University, Virginia Intermont College, and the University of North Carolina at Chapel Hill. I am grateful to Marion Reiner and Joan Daves of the Estate of Martin Luther King, Jr. for use of articles published in *Nation* and the "I Have a Dream" and "Mountain Top" speeches.

Special gratitude is due to Charles East, formerly of the University of Georgia press, for his skilled examination of the manuscript and suggestions for improvement, as well as for his confidence in the importance of the project. And there were other individuals and organizations that cannot be cited here but, in their own way, share in this history. Above all, I am grateful to my wife Peggy Ann Collins Peake and to my six children for their work, encouragement, and sacrifice.

Photographs were provided by courtesy of SCLC, Elaine Tomlin, Pamela Harvey, and Eddie Mathes. Photographic reproduction assistance was provided by Stewart Bartow Foulke, III. E. Randel T. Osburn was also helpful in securing photographs and taped historical material.

Financial assistance was provided by several organizations. The Lilly Foundation allowed me to participate in a course of study at Duke University that contributed to the conception of this book. The Southern Regional Education Fund, the American Philosophical Society, and King College made possible several of the 120 research trips between 1977 and 1986. To all of these and individuals who assisted, I am forever thankful.

It is my hope that what is presented here will help preserve in a coherent manner the essentials of SCLC's meaning and contributions. SCLC is one part of a larger community of thousands of men and women who, by their actions, wrote the story of nonviolent social change in our generation. But it is an important part that needs to be reviewed and analyzed. The errors of fact or judgment are mine alone and in no way should detract from the value or relevance of any of the people who helped with this study. The NAACP, PUSH, the King Center, the Martin Luther King, Jr. Movement, and more share in the story presented here. And in a real sense, we all do. How this legacy affects the future will depend ultimately on how much faith we have in the dream of a world of justice and peace.

Thomas R. Peake
Bristol, Tennessee
February 1986

Introduction

To many Americans, the Southern Christian Leadership Conference is more of a memory than a viable contemporary movement. As the organizational arm of Dr. Martin Luther King, Jr.'s nonviolent civil rights movement, it frequently received headline media coverage and had high public visibility from 1957 until his assassination in 1968. After that, the national press often referred to SCLC as "Dr. King's old organization," and began treating its conventions and campaigns in brief stories usually far from the front page. Occasionally, as with the 1968 Poor People's Campaign in Washington a few weeks after King's death, the major papers gave it first-page attention, but often with more emphasis upon divisions in the ranks of its leadership than upon the content of the program. Gone were the days when network correspondents and newspaper journalists eagerly followed SCLC's activities across the cities of the South at the height of the civil rights movement.

For more than a decade SCLC and King were inseparable. He was its principal founder and its president, as well as its philosophical spokesman and bridge to white America. Even after his break with the Johnson administration over the Vietnam War in 1967, Martin Luther King, Jr. remained the most quotable and most famous American black leader. It was inevitable that his death dealt a serious blow to the organization he led and to an already declining public commitment to the black movement. "No man, dead, living, or unborn," stated his friend and successor Ralph David Abernathy, "could have filled the shoes of Dr. King."[1]

Undoubtedly, Abernathy was correct. The peculiar qualities and circumstances that had made Dr. King a historical force

1

could not be duplicated. No one could succeed him without considerable difficulty, and certainly no other leader could meaningfully replace him. In many circles there was the feeling that his work had to go on, however, and SCLC, among others, determined to make an effort at continuity. With Abernathy as president from 1968 to 1977, the organization continued even though financial support declined and the black movement became more diverse and less dramatic. Meanwhile, Coretta Scott King began the development of the Martin Luther King, Jr. Center for Nonviolent Social Change as both a memorial to her slain husband and as an instrument of education in nonviolent theory and technique. Others linked to the King legacy established additional organizations not formally attached to SCLC.

It is important for a proper historical understanding of SCLC to see that although the organization and Martin King were inseparable, they were not identical. King himself was impressed in early 1957 at the inception of the organization with the degree of enthusiastic support he saw among dozens of southern black leaders, mostly ministers, for creating a coordinating leadership structure to link the various local movements spawned by, or intensified by, the Montgomery bus boycott of 1955–1956.[2] There was an incipient southern movement which King and SCLC amalgamated, but did not create. Nor did SCLC displace these local manifestations of black activism although at times there were tensions among leaders and some resentment of King's enormous public image. From C. K. Steele's work in Tallahassee to Joseph E. Lowery's in Mobile to Fred Shuttlesworth's in Birmingham, to mention only a few, the substance of southern activism existed before SCLC. Indeed, it was because of this phenomenon that SCLC was created.

Furthermore, SCLC was a relative newcomer to the American scene. The NAACP and the National Urban League had been founded before World War I, and CORE (Congress of Racial Equality) was already fifteen years old when the Southern Christian Leadership Conference began. SCLC leaders, including Dr. King, were cognizant of the historical debt owed to these organizations and to individuals like Asa Philip Randolph, James Farmer, W. E. B. DuBois, and Thurgood Marshall in recent years, as well as to more remote men and women who had articulated black demands for freedom long before the civil rights era. On both sides of Martin King's family, too, there were ancestors whose work in behalf of civil rights was quite influential upon him.

If SCLC stood in the midst of a historical movement and if it possessed a distinctive set of relevant goals, its continuance after 1968 was a possibility and, by its own standards, a necessity. Despite its relatively loose structure, SCLC had numerous ties across the South and in a number of northern areas, and several key programs operative in 1968. In view of its specific historical connections with the King legacy, these could not summarily be ended without calling into question the viability of his dream for American and global society. Many people still held to it as both right and possible. Thus, there was no serious hesitation among King's successors about going on with the work of the organization. Naturally, there were some defections and cleavages, but "keeping the dream alive" was soon a rallying symbol for the inner circle of SCLC leaders.[3]

The leadership-organizational question was a crucial one in 1968, and knowing this, most of SCLC's leaders rallied to Ralph David Abernathy, whom King had specifically chosen to succeed him. Despite detractors, a less friendly press, and the tremendous burden of moving from being King's close aide to being the president of SCLC, Abernathy acted quickly to attempt continuity in the Memphis march and the Poor People's March on Washington already in process at the time of King's death. But the fundamental character of SCLC's leadership needs was profoundly altered by King's absence.

Equally significant was the problem of retaining a distinctive identity in the wake of King's death, a challenge complicated by the fact that before April 1968 he had shifted his own public emphases more openly to issues that alienated some erstwhile supporters. Peace, housing, political participation, and economic justice had occupied King's mind after Selma and the 1965

Voting Rights Act, and these were issues that strained the limits of social liberalism far more than access to public facilities or the franchise had. They were less matters of racial integration than systemic factors that related to the permanent underclass status of many blacks and other minorities. They also more directly challenged prevailing norms of foreign policy and domestic social priorities.

Thus "keeping the dream alive" became an imperative for SCLC and an integral part of its identity as an organization. The historical paradigm, as well as the imagery, had been provided earlier by the direct-action, nonviolent tactics of the previous decade. King and SCLC had pierced the conscience of the nation by nonviolently moving cities like Birmingham and Selma to change their practices, if not always their attitudes, toward blacks. King's "I Have a Dream" speech at the Lincoln Memorial in late August 1963 encapsulated a vision of society that he felt was commensurate with the best of the American tradition. "I have a dream today," King said, "that one day this nation will rise up and live out the true meaning of its creed: 'We hold these truths to be self-evident, that all men are created equal'. . ." He went on to project the possibility that blacks and whites could live as brothers and sisters because all were children of God, that areas where racism abounded could become "oases of freedom and justice," and that people could learn to judge each other according to "the content of their character" rather than race.

Some 200,000 people, a quarter of them white, had come to Washington for the March and heard King's address in person while millions more listened to radio and television broadcasts. The Civil Rights Act of 1964 was still a year away, the Voting Rights Act two years. There was a high degree of interracial enthusiasm for what he was saying. Five years later, with King dead and an increasing number of Americans convinced that blacks had gotten everything they really needed in the federal acts of 1964 and 1965, SCLC shared with all civil rights organizations the problem of keeping the spirit of the dream alive. For millions of blacks, integration and the right to vote had made little difference in their standard of living or their ability to move upward in society. The years between 1963 and 1968 had brought scores of ghetto revolts and an even worsening poverty for many. With the Vietnam War escalating and public sentiment shifting toward law and order and fiscal restraint, the task of keeping the dream alive as a force for more social action was extremely difficult but crucial to SCLC's organizational identity.

A third problematical area was the altered coalitional basis of civil and human rights advocacy in the late sixties and beyond. Before Selma, King once wrote, whites and blacks moved together to rectify the worst abuses of discrimination, but after that they diverged "like a giant X" as the social and economic cost of full equality for blacks came into focus. White liberals had joined strategically in the financial and organizational support of integration of public facilities and the securing of the franchise, but they were less enthusiastic about the more strictly economic dimensions of the movement. Furthermore, the social upheavals of the Vietnam War period operated to redirect a substantial part of the youth movement toward anti-war projects and to bring about a conservative swing in public sentiment toward virtually all marches, demonstrations, and acts of civil disobedience. The economy waned, too, giving further reason to limit social programs at a time when black leaders were calling for more.

Among the major civil rights organizations, SCLC was not alone in decrying these trends and seeking closer alliances with labor, non-black minorities, and women. Nor was the post-1968 coalitional emphasis entirely new. King had increasingly attached himself to labor and was in fact supporting a strike in Memphis when he was killed. But it is clear that SCLC after his death increasingly underscored the plight of the poor, the underprivileged, and the politically powerless as its prime concern and did so with the view that such was always germane to SCLC's purpose. This meant that political alliances were most likely among such people, assuming that their collective potential could be translated into political influence and the nonviolent strategy be preserved. It was the pursuit of this "power for the powerless'' as an agent of continued socio-economic reform that shaped much of SCLC's outreach under Ralph Abernathy and, later, under Joseph E. Lowery.

As the Southern Christian Leadership Conference celebrated its Silver Anniversary in Birmingham in August 1982, it borrowed its theme from the distinguished black poet Langston Hughes: "Hold Fast to Dreams: Economic Justice, Political Justice, and Peace.'' Hughes wrote in one of his short poems, "Dreams":

> Hold fast to dreams
> For if dreams die,
> Life is a broken-winged bird
> That cannot fly.
>
> Hold fast to dreams,
> For when dreams go,
> Life is a barren field
> Frozen with snow.*

Although much had changed over the two decades since the Birmingham campaign that thrust SCLC into national prominence, the choice of this theme to express the organization's concern as it reached its 25th anniversary revealed feelings that much remained to be done. Birmingham now had a black mayor, Richard Arrington. Across the face of City Hall was a huge sign welcoming Dr. Joseph E. Lowery, SCLC's president, and the organization he led. Yet the tone of the conference was hardly complacent or suggestive of the notion that black Americans had good reason to feel secure.

Most Americans, whatever their racial identity, have never marched in a civil rights demonstration or been frightened by an inflamed mob. Such things have seemed remote and relevant only as peripheral events to many people. Nonetheless, they are a central part of recent American history and the story of the Southern Christian Leadership Conference. It is important to

---

* From Langston Hughes, *The Dream Keeper and Other Poems* (New York: Alfred A. Knopf, 1959, c1932).

review the struggles of black liberation and to engage them intellectually and morally, for they comprise one of the most decisive chapters in the development of contemporary America. It is SCLC's conviction that they represent a continuing challenge as well, that the dream must be kept alive.

This is not an official history of SCLC written internally or commissioned by its Board of Directors. But it would have been impossible to attempt this first comprehensive history of the organization without the cooperation of present and past leaders, as well as dozens of other men and women who were willing to give interviews, share documents, suggest possible lines of exploration, and otherwise contribute to the research. Nor would it be as complete without the many useful biographies of King and the various analyses of the civil rights movement that scholars have produced in recent years. Thus, what follows is a collective effort intended to provide a scholarly recounting of SCLC's history while giving due regard to the human story it relates.

There is much that can be learned from the historical development of the Southern Christian Leadership Conference and the evolvement of its social dream. Some of the events covered here are so recent that perspective is elusive, since many of their aspects are still openended. It seems that King's query in the last chapter of his first book, which he used as the title of a later work, is appropriate: "Where do we go from here?" King committed himself to the nonviolent method and the inclusive ethos of brotherhood because as he said, 'our end is a community at peace with itself.''[4] SCLC's story is largely one of crisis and struggle, but since it is also one of promoting peace and principles of justice and human brotherhood, it is a story more than worth the telling.

Three features have distinguished the historical role of the Southern Christian Leadership Conference. First, its relationship to Martin Luther King, Jr. is unique. He presided over the organization from its inception until his death in 1968. There was no real debate at the beginning over his election to the presidency and no serious challenge to his position over the following decade. King and SCLC were, in Hosea Williams' words, "inextricably bound." After 1968 the memory of King remained basic to its identity and its public relations. Certainly other organizations have derived at least in part from the King legacy, among them the King Center for Nonviolent Social Change, Andrew Young's organization known as Young Ideas, the Chicago-based People United to Save Humanity (PUSH) of Rev. Jesse Jackson, and the Martin Luther King, Jr. Movement led by Georgia State Representative Tyrone Brooks. But SCLC has the distinction that for the first eleven years of its history King sat in its executive chair and shaped its programs.

The second distinctive of SCLC is its strong ties to local churches and its specific orientation to Christianity. This is not unique, for religious faith has been vital to virtually all black organizations and movements. The idea that God is a liberator of the oppressed is as strong in the black tradition as it is in the Hebrew Exodus theology.[5] For SCLC, however, Christian churches of various denominations have been the organizational matrix and the basic link to grassroots support. This is not true in the same sense of the other major civil rights organizations. Too, all three of SCLC's presidents have been active pastors, King and Abernathy Baptists, and Lowery a Methodist. Andrew Young, Hosea Williams, C. T. Vivian, James Lawson, John Nettles, Fred Shuttlesworth, C. K. Steele and many more SCLC leaders have also served churches. There have been notable exceptions, of course, but the centrality of faith and ministerial leadership is obvious in SCLC's development.

Thirdly, SCLC emerged as the principal nonviolent direct-action organization in the South. NAACP, CORE, and the National Urban League began and operated primarily in the North. Furthermore, their strategies were quite different from SCLC's. Although these organizations have been significantly involved in nonviolent direct-action (CORE led sit-ins, for example, in the 1940's and again became quite activist in the 1960's), they were not predominantly marching, demonstrating direct-action groups. Closer to SCLC's model was the Student Nonviolent Coordinating Committee (SNCC), which began in

8

April 1960 and spearheaded numerous direct-action sit-ins and Freedom Rides across the South. SNCC provided many of the shock troops for southern direct-action and voter registration drives in several states. Some see SNCC as the cutting edge of the southern civil rights movement, but its historical role was shorter-lived than SCLC's and less closely linked with the nonviolent ethos. Although its young reformers were tremendously influential in the transformation of the South, SNCC's leaders eventually changed both its character and its name. SNCC ceased to operate after the heyday of the civil rights campaigns.

SCLC was basically southern in orientation although it had some meaningful connections in western and northern regions. Essentially, SCLC's hub was, and is, Atlanta and its programs have continued to focus on nonviolent direct-action such as pressuring communities and governments to implement laws against discrimination and violence, seeking better job opportunities for blacks, increasing the black voting population and dealing on a daily basis with appeals by individuals and groups facing problems because of race. There has always been a strong emphasis upon helping the dispossessed.

Although not as large today as several other civil and human rights organizations, the Southern Christian Leadership Conference continues to understand its role in basically those terms. As SCLC celebrated its twenty-fifth anniversary in 1982, it remained committed to these principles:

The Southern Christian Leadership Conference is a movement of people and for people, growing out of the deep tradition and long history of struggle for basic human rights.

This movement is grounded in the philosophy of nonviolent resistance based on the lives and teachings of leaders like Jesus Christ and Mohandas Gandhi.

It is a movement that also has roots in the larger history of liberation and struggles by black people and all oppressed people of the world. . .

Basic decisions made by the founders included the adoption of nonviolent mass action as the cornerstone of its strategy, the affiliation of local community organizations with SCLC across the South, and a determination to make the SCLC movement open to all, regardless of race, religion, or background. . .[6]

Ideologically, then, SCLC represents an inclusive movement with singular ties to the struggles of black Americans. The story of its origins, development, and contemporary involvements is not only an interesting, but also a challenging episode in the emergence of contemporary America.

Nor has SCLC's history ended. The Lowery years have witnessed the revitalization of a number of programs and more vigorous critique of foreign and domestic policy. Named one of the fifteen top black preachers in the United States by *Ebony Magazine* in 1984, Lowery has been visible in many parts of the world in recent years. He has visited several trouble spots like Lebanon, Nicaragua, and drought-stricken Africa and has established, according to Lerone Bennett, "a new Black presence in shaping American foreign policy." The 1982 Voting Rights Pilgrimage to Washington led by Lowery and his wife Evelyn was one of the most ambitious nonviolent undertakings since the Poor People's Campaign of the late sixties. President Lowery and his associates show no loss of faith in the principles that have shaped SCLC for more than a quarter century.

It seems particularly appropriate to produce this study at the time when Martin Luther King, Jr. is officially recognized with a national holiday and the nation ponders again the meaning of his life and the nonviolent movement. There is much popular interest in religion these days, and SCLC stands as a reminder that authentic religion is more a matter of doing than saying, of believing and acting than judging. As world tensions increase and leaders seek for ways to resolve them, SCLC reminds us that the nonviolent solution is not only morally compelling, but also within reach of those willing to sacrifice for it.

10

Part 1

Emergence of the Nonviolent Movement

"The only thing necessary for the triumph of evil is for good men to do nothing."
Edmund Burke

1

The Awakening of Hope

It is interesting to speculate on what the course of recent American history might have been had Martin Luther King, Jr. not gone to Montgomery, Alabama in 1954. But he did go, and the America he had grown up in was forever changed. The historic bus boycott that began there in late 1955 brought him national recognition and triggered a decade of direct-action protest that permanently altered the status of black Americans.

Andrew Young once said that Rosa Parks thrust greatness upon King. Certainly she shaped the setting in which he emerged as a national figure and challenged him to translate his theory of nonviolence into practice. King had no intention of initiating a major campaign in Montgomery, but Mrs. Parks' refusal to yield her bus seat to a white man on December 1, 1955 forced the first serious test of King's willingness to undergo personal sacrifice for the sake of Negro freedom. She has never claimed much credit for what happened in Montgomery, but Rosa Parks' action was a catalyst in King's rise to prominence and the emergence of the southern civil rights movement that dominated American social history for a decade.[1]

The circumstances that brought King to Montgomery were not particularly unusual for a young minister anxious to go to work. Nearing the end of his graduate studies at Boston University, he went to Montgomery in January 1954 for a trial sermon at Dexter Avenue Baptist Church. King flew to Atlanta, then drove to Montgomery, taking in the beauties of the countryside and listening to his favorite opera, Donizetti's *Lucia di Lammermoor*. It was his first trip to Montgomery, and his mind was full of the potential challenges of working there. Already he had turned down offers to teach, including one by Benjamin Mays to join the faculty at Morehouse College where he had done his undergraduate work. King felt that he should get more experience in the pulpit and engage a real pastorate on his own before entering the academic world. That was what Paul Tillich, Reinhold Niebuhr, and Walter Rauschenbusch had done, and the idea appealed to young King who had been deeply influenced by their thought.[2]

Preparation: King's Intellectual Pilgrimage

If King shared certain common feelings and aspirations with many other young ministers, he had more than the usual personal and academic preparation for leadership. His father, Michael Luther King, was pastor of one of Atlanta's leading black churches, the Ebenezer Baptist Church on Auburn Avenue, a position he took when Martin was only two years old in 1931. Martin's mother, Alberta, was the daughter of the distinguished minister Adam Daniel Williams, who had preceded King's father as pastor of Ebenezer. The family of Mike King (as he was known even after he changed his name and that of his infant son to Martin Luther King) enjoyed a middle class economic status and considerable prestige in the community.

In that sense, King's childhood was rather unusual for a black youth, but not unique. Atlanta has, and had in King's childhood, a sizable black middle class with considerable financial security. His better-than-usual economic comfort and opportunities were important to his development but were neither unparalleled nor the only important factor in his later emergence as a national black leader.[3] Equally significant was the spirit of opposition to racism and discrimination that characterized the King family. In his first book King recalls several instances when his father, for example, openly refused to submit to separate treatment in stores, racial slurs by public officials, or the general assumption of black inferiority.[4] As young King—known as Mike, or M. L.

to some, in deference to his father—grew up in northeast Atlanta, he escaped many of the cruder manifestations of racial discrimination but identified with blackness and the pride that permeated the family atmosphere. All evidence points to his being a vigorous, even exuberant, playful boy with more than typical interest in words, symbols, and ideas.

King's education profoundly affected his personal goals and his perception of racial relations and the principles of human community. Intending to study medicine, he entered Morehouse College in Atlanta in 1944 in an early-entry program that shortened his secondary studies at Booker T. Washington High School. King was only fifteen years old, but with his precocious ability to understand and analyze complex material he soon impressed his professors and Morehouse president Benjamin E. Mays, who had established the early-entry policy. A great man in his own right, Mays sensed in King an unusually gifted young man.[5] Dr. Mays was a sincere believer in nonviolence and the relevance of the Christian faith to race relations, basic concepts that helped shape the young student he would describe a few years later as "a prophet in the 20th century."[6]

Despite the war and limited financial resources, Morehouse College in those days reflected the changing mood of American blacks and was, in the words of one of its distinguished alumni, *Ebony* editor Lerone Bennett, "alive with political and social ferment."[7] Thus, the future civil rights leader entered the west Atlanta college, where his father and grandfather before him had studied, at a time when it was mirroring the broader questions of social reality in an intense way. King abandoned his interest in medicine for law, taking a major in sociology. But as the influence of Mays, Professor George D. Kelsey of the Religion Department, and others on the faculty increased, he decided during his junior year to reverse his course and commit himself to church ministry.

The Morehouse experience was very basic to King's development, both in terms of classroom work and his summer jobs which brought him more directly into contact with racism and the economic plight of Negroes. He began to probe the relationship between moral principles and social experience and to develop a deep interest in major currents of thought, both historical and contemporary. Though not widely visible in extra-curricular activities, King did excel in his academic work and enlarged his mental horizons. When he graduated in 1948, he bypassed a chance to work with his father at Ebenezer and chose to continue his education at Crozer Seminary in Chester Pennsylvania, near Philadelphia.

At Crozer (1948–1951) and later at Boston University (1951–1954), King became more than superficially acquainted with the major thought currents of modern times, from Hegel and Marx to the thinkers who formulated contemporary nonviolent theory. Gandhi's thought and actions were especially attractive to him. The famous reformer's concept of *Satyagraha* (force of truth in the soul, or soul force) and his nonviolent strategy against the caste system and British colonial rule in his native India gave young King a tangible basis for much of his own reform philosophy.

It is sometimes overlooked, however, that King was neither then nor later a thoroughgoing Gandhian. He recognized the distinctive features of the British colonial rule over India and knew that Gandhi's strategy was not fully appropriate for American blacks who faced something quite different from a colonial mentorship by a foreign power. What impressed King most about Gandhi was his linkage of nonviolence and social reform. "Gandhi was probably the first person in history," wrote King, "to lift the love ethic of Jesus above mere interaction between individuals to a powerful and effective social force on a large scale."[8]

It is obvious that King was less an original thinker than a searcher during his studies at Crozer and Boston. For the first time, by his own admission, he began a "serious intellectual quest for a method to eliminate social evil." Yet this quest was grounded in some basic concepts nurtured earlier. Already he was strongly opposed to racism and its various discriminatory results. Significantly, too, King was convinced even before he went to Crozer of the linkage between racial discrimination and economic problems. As he saw it, "the inseparable twin of racial injustice was economic injustice."[9] The view that King came much later to this linkage of issues is simply incorrect and distorts the evolution of his political philosophy.

During this period of post-baccalaureate study the basic essence of King's thought took shape. Though it would change somewhat in later circumstances, the nucleus was present from his seminary and graduate school days. Three fundamental elements of that philosophy continued throughout King's life to be the major distinctives of his reformism: 1) the moral basis of all human affairs, including politics; 2) the necessity and possibility of human community; and 3) the imperative of nonviolence. King could not separate morality from politics because, in his view, all reality ultimately must be judged in the light of eternal moral principles. This included the laws that govern political order. In the tradition of Aquinas, King was convinced that laws—if they are to be just and valid—must correspond to eternal law. "A just law is a man-made code that squares with the moral law or the law of God," he wrote.[10]

By the early 1950s King had read enough and experienced enough to find profound relevance in the thought of theologian Reinhold Niebuhr, author of *Moral Man and Immoral Society* (1932), *Christianity and Power Politics* (1940) and other ruggedly realistic appraisals of public life in the light of Christianity. Neibuhr had underscored the effects of human sin on politics and the tension between privately held convictions and the moral compromises of collective evil.[11] Niebuhr was a gadfly to King, qualifying his early excitement with Walter Rauschenbusch's Social Gospel and its rejection of original sin as the fundamental emphasis in theology. Niebuhr reminded King of the evil in man and the realistic response it demanded.[12]

But this was only one side of the issue. King, like Rauschenbusch, believed in the possibility and necessity of improving conditions in the politico-social sphere. As one analyst of his political thought put it, "Otherworldly as religion may seem to some, to King it descends from the loftiest heights to the lowest valleys."[13] In short King set out to find a basis for working toward a better society shaped by the community-creating force of religious convictions.

It was at times a confusing and painful effort for King. There were many conflicting tugs on his mind: Hegel, Marx, Neitzsche, as well as Rauschenbusch, Neibuhr, Tillich, and others. At Crozer in 1950 King heard A. J. Muste, leader of the Fellowship of Reconciliation (FOR) speak on pacifism. FOR had been established as early as World War I, and the largely white pacifist organization had linked itself to civil rights and engaged in civil disobedience between the wars. Now under Muste it was beginning a revival of influence that would have considerable impact in the direct-action campaigns of the late 1950s and 1960s. Though King was not particularly moved by Muste's lecture, since pacifism presented some real problems for him, he did find Muste's ideas challenging.[14]

King never committed himself during his educational odyssey to any particular world-view espoused by a specific individual or school of thought. He qualified the various intellectual currents with his own synthesis. Obviously, certain ideas were distinctively valuable to him, including Gandhi's approach to love and reform, the Social Gospel of Rauschenbusch, Neibuhr's neo-orthodoxy, and above all his own Christian social reformism. In all this the rudiments of a view of community that King would apply in his civil rights activism were formed.

The society envisaged by King resembled the Beloved Community concept of Rauschenbusch, though there were some important differences. Rauschenbusch (1861–1918) was a German-American scholar and pastor who worked among immigrants in the Second German Baptist Church in New York at the turn of the century. His background in Germany and England, coupled with his intense Christian experience, gave him an intimate knowledge of Fabianism and Christian social reformism. In works like *Christianity and the Social Crisis* (1907), *The Social Principles of Jesus* (1916), and *A Theology for the Social Gospel* (1917), Rauschenbusch affirmed the essential inter-relatedness of man's spiritual life and his economic-social condition. He was opposed to purely *laissez-faire* government and unbridled capitalism, preferring an emphasis upon cooperative efforts for the welfare of all. "The finest public life," said Rauschenbusch, "will exist in a community which has learned to combine its citizens in the largest number of cooperative functions for the common good."[15]

Rauschenbusch's flirtation with the progress view of history disturbed King, but on the essential content of the Social Gospel he was in basic agreement. Both rejected materalism and the Marxist variety of communism but shared the conviction that religious experience was inseparably related to social life. God's Kingdom created community, a community sensitive to human suffering. King acknowledged an indelible impression left on his own thinking by Rauschenbusch. In his first book, *Stride Toward Freedom* (1958), he wrote:

> It has been my conviction ever since reading Rauschenbusch that any religion which professes to be concerned about the soul of men and is not concerned about the social and economic conditions that scar the soul, is a spiritually moribund religion only waiting the day to be buried. It well has been said: 'A religion that ends with the individual ends.'[16]

It was King's study of Rauschenbusch that led him to examine more deeply the ideas of great thinkers from Aristotle to the modern philosophers, including Marx.

To King, Marxism had both oversimplified social reality and imposed some false values on it. He belabored the point that he could never accept the materialism, secularism, atheism, or moral relativism of Marxism.[17] The major concession he made to Marx was to recognize that the founder of modern communism had raised some questions about which the church should also be concerned. After all, King noted, it was Jesus himself who associated his own ministry with the passage, "The spirit of the Lord is upon me, because he hath anointed me to preach the gospel to the poor; he hath sent me to heal the brokenhearted, to preach deliverance to the captives. . ." King's troubling awareness of the gulf between "superfluous wealth and abject poverty" caused him to ponder some of the same issues that prompted Marx's early emphasis upon human alienation, but

King's conclusion was that neither Marxism nor traditional capitalism was the real truth. "The Kingdom of God," he averred, "is neither the thesis of individual enterprise, nor the antithesis of collective enterprise, but a synthesis which reconciles the truth of both."[18] King called upon the church to face its "historic obligation" in the crisis of race relations.

King's view of the church's role in race relations derived from his belief that the race problem was, at heart, a moral one. The universal message of the Gospel, he stressed, meant that segregation was unjustifiable. "Racial segregation is a blatant denial of the unity we have in Christ." Specifically, he called upon the church to: 1) inform the popular mind on the realities of the Negro race, educating people on the myth of black inferiority; 2) clarify the real intentions of black people, calming irrational fears of the white community by showing that Negroes really wanted only to be first class citizens; 3) keep the focus on God, an emphasis that would diminish the fear so often involved in race relations; and 4) take the lead in social reform. This was an important feature of King's total vision of reform possibilities. That the church should take initiatives in the arena of social action was as imperative to him as its leadership in the realm of ideas. He saw a fundamental contradiction in segregated churches. "It is appalling," he wrote, "that the most segregated hour of Christian America is eleven o'clock on Sunday morning when many are standing to sing, 'In Christ there is no East nor West'."[19]

No idea has been more closely associated with the dream of Martin Luther King, Jr. than the concept of nonviolence, though he neither originated it nor brought it into the mainstream of the civil rights movement. Its roots lay in the great world religions, particularly the challenge of Jesus to love one's enemies rather than hate them or retaliate for wrongdoing. In modern times it had been promulgated by Tolstoy, Thoreau, Gandhi, and other seminal thinkers. King, as we have seen, was the intellectual heir of a number of earlier advocates of nonviolence.

The nonviolent approach was employed by the National Association for the Advancement of Colored People for many

20

decades before the 1950s. Founded in 1909 by Mary White Ovington, William English Walling, and others interested in uplifting blacks, the NAACP succeeded the short-lived Niagra Movement of W. E. B. DuBois. The famous Niagra leader and the NAACP he helped lead for many years went beyond Booker T. Washington's cautious self-help approach promulgated at Tuskegee. All-white primaries, discrimination in transit, inequities in the military, and many other important barriers to justice fell piecemeal to the program of litigation and lobbying carried on by this historic organization from World War I to the 1950s. It always rejected violence and pursued its goals largely in the courts and halls of legislatures. It relied on white-black cooperation.

Nonviolence in the Gandhian tradition was brought more fully into American black activism by the Congress of Racial Equality (CORE) during the early years of World War II. The early forties were a veritable watershed in race relations in the United States. Under the pressure of wartime needs, the Roosevelt administration could hardly afford to alienate the black population. Asa Philip Randolph, an experienced black labor organizer and an outspoken advocate of racial justice, threatened a march on Washington in 1941, causing Roosevelt to issue Executive Order 8802 which forbade discrimination on the basis of race, creed, color, or national origin in defense industries and federal agencies. This marked a change in the hands-off policy of the federal government, unbroken since the Supreme Court overturned the 1875 Civil Rights Act in 1883. The Fair Employment Practices Commission (FEPC) would preside over the reception and redress of complaints.

Randolph's bold action helped stimulate confidence in direct-action elsewhere. In 1942 at the University of Chicago, CORE was established by James Farmer and four others including two white divinity students. These young leaders infused the infant organization with Gandhian principles and adopted the direct-action technique. Here was a significant departure from recent tradition. Direct-action in the previous century was the shibboleth of anarchists and the often violent strategy of revolutionaries. In their opposition to authority, anarchists (literally, those who reject authority or rule) used direct-action to dramatize the need for change by engaging in 'propaganda by the deed', a euphemism for attacks of various kinds on prominent leaders and institutions. CORE's juxtaposition of 'nonviolence' and 'direct-action' elevated the strategy to one of challenging undesirable laws and mores through public refusal to comply with them. CORE's announced purpose was "to federate local interracial groups working to abolish the color line through direct non-violent action." CORE used the sit-in method at lunch-counters in 1942.[20]

Thus King's focus on nonviolence and direct-action was not new. What was distinctive in his case was the theological-philosophical basis that forged a mass movement, energized chiefly by nonviolence. He grounded it in love—first God's love for man, then the derivative love among human beings. His was no naive sentimentalism, a point lost to a number of contemporary scholars. The young civil rights leader was the first to recognize that his view was unnatural in a purely logical sense, but not when viewed in Christian terms. "It would be nonsense," he wrote in early 1957, "to urge men to love their oppressors in an affectionate sense. 'Love' in this connection means *understanding good will*." King distinguished between *agape* and other types of love. "Agape means nothing sentimental or basically affectionate; it means understanding, redeeming good will for all men, an overflowing love which seeks nothing in return."[21] It was, in short, the kind of love exemplified in Christianity.

Nonviolence to King was more than a strategy. It was a universal imperative of religious faith and the only viable approach for realistic reformers. He could not endorse violence for two reasons: it contradicted the idea of a moral universe, and from a practical point of view it would not work. Violence would produce counter-violence and hatred and thus destroy the very community envisaged in his dream. Problems were inherent in such a view and King did not completely resolve some of them. As Hanes Walton concludes, King's moral emphasis insofar as it

22

was expressed as a political philosophy had several apparent weaknesses. People have different perceptions of what God wills, for example. Segregationists could, and did, often justify their views by appealing to religious notions. Furthermore, the inherent flaws of human nature have sometimes produced situations wherein the state is compelled to use violence in the cause of justice.[22] In the final analysis, however, it is essential to keep in mind that Martin Luther King, Jr. never set his dream in concrete. It was a value system that he projected, rather than a specific political method. His dream broadened as he developed, always retaining the reference point of community brought about by nonviolent resistance to those social practices and attitudes that militated against it.

By the summer of 1953 the young man who would become the major spokesman of black America for more than a decade was nearing the end of his professional training. Numerous biographers have also shown the human side of his development. Just twenty-four years old at that time, he had hardly resolved all of the conflicts that come with young adulthood. With all his intellectual enthusiasm, Martin Luther King, Jr. had a playful and sensuous side that would significantly affect his career. He had by 1953 experienced his share of casual and more serious romantic attachments, including an ill-fated one with a white girl at Crozer. The one who would change his life and perpetuate much of his dream, however, was Coretta Scott, an attractive young black woman from Alabama.[23]

King met the aspiring singer in early 1952 in Boston where she was studying at the New England Conservatory of Music. A native of the Marion, Alabama area, Coretta knew first hand the problems blacks faced in the South. Although her family had done rather well after the trying Depression years, they had experienced a number of the cruelties of racism. Meeting Martin altered her career plans as well as the prospect of living in the North. After their marriage by King's father in June 1953 at her parents' home in Marion, Coretta's life was linked to a young man who, like herself, was torn between the seemingly freer air outside Dixie and the inner compulsion to return to help those less fortunate. Mrs. King recalled years later that, "Though I had been opposed to going to Montgomery, I realize now that it was an inevitable part of a greater plan for our lives. Even in 1954 I felt that my husband was being prepared—and I too—for a special role about which we could learn more later."[24]

Thus the young boy who had entered Morehouse nine years earlier was now a man with an unusual interest in and knowledge of social and moral ideology. He had witnessed several examples of racial prejudice, even in the North, and was all the more opposed to it. He had the substance of a distinctive philosophy of reform, but it was not yet fully synthesized or tested in real life. Running through his mind were the currents of influence from "meaningful others," most of them teachers like Benjamin Mays and George D. Kelsey at Morehouse; George W. David and Kenneth Lee Smith at Crozer; and Edgar S. Brightman and L. Harold DeWolf at Boston University. But others, too, had helped shape his mind, not the least of whom was Dr. Mordecai W. Johnson, president of Howard University, whom King heard speak in Philadelphia. Johnson's topic was his trip to India and the Gandhian philosophy.

As he responded to the call for a trial sermon at Dexter Avenue Baptist Church in early 1954, King was working on his Ph.D. dissertation: *A Comparison of the Conceptions of God in the Thinking of Paul Tillich and Henry Nelson Wieman*. King was still searching the world of ideas as he made his decision, after much discussion with his new wife, to accept the enthusiastic call to pastor the church in Montgomery. King began his pastorage at Dexter Avenue in May 1954, still commuting by air to Boston for several months while completing his dissertation, as the church had agreed. Coretta graduated from the Boston conservatory in June and saw Dexter Avenue Baptist Church for the first time in July 1954.[25] On September 1, the Kings moved into its redecorated manse.

Built during the Reconstruction period, the beautiful, but rather small Victorian church stands not far from the Alabama State Capitol, once the seat of the Confederacy. It was in those days largely an upper middle class church, but shortly after his arrival King planned for a broadening of its auxiliary ministries and some modification of its image as a church oriented to a particular class of blacks. King joined the local chapter of the NAACP and the Alabama Council on Human Relations and was soon busy with the broader problems of blacks in Alabama. He was elected to the NAACP's executive board and actively raised money and otherwise supported its efforts.[26] The Kings had been in Montgomery some fifteen months when Rosa Parks, an early middle-aged black seamstress, took her historic stand against the city's rigidly segregated bus system in December 1955. Committed to quality preaching, King spent much time preparing his sermons—full of literary allusions and spiritual challenges—but did not neglect his instincts for social activism. He urged his congregation to join the NAACP and register to vote, and he organized the men and women of his church in committees that busily attended to various needs in the community.

At times King was discouraged, though not surprised, by the degree of acquiescence he saw among blacks. Somehow, decades of discrimination had convinced many that there was little that could be done about the extreme poverty they faced or the ubiquitous presence of segregationists policies.[27] Even local ministers, who were the only professional group roughly equal in numbers to their white counterparts, seemed to ignore the blatant racism that hung over the old capital of the Confederacy. In a city of about 120,000 people, 50,000 blacks lived with a median income far below that of the whites and in houses lacking in plumbing, bathrooms, or other conveniences. Worse, all social life was segregated, so that even places to meet and talk were severely restricted.[28]

The Montgomery Boycott

Montgomery was in many ways a microcosm of segregated America. The difficulties blacks encountered there were typical of patterns across the South. The 1954 *Brown* decision on school desegregation had made little difference, despite the May 31, 1955 order by the Supreme Court for schools to desegregate "with all deliberate speed." Racist White Citizens' Councils committed to opposing the order were springing up in many communities, and segregated transportation was normative in the South. These were only the most visible signs of the hardships blacks faced. Economic deprivation and dehumanizing racist attitudes cut even deeper into Afro-Americans' self-image and hope for advancement, despite the impressive gains made by organizations like the NAACP. Furthermore, white-dominated churches of both the evangelical and Reformed traditions had little room in their theology or social practice for the issues of racial justice.[29]

It appeared that neither Montgomery nor the nation would ever really change. Divisions of opinion among blacks about whether an imitative accommodation of white culture or militant resistance was the more promising tactic, indicated that the barriers to progress were not simply legal. Memories of Harriet Tubman's heroic liberation of slaves, Frederick Douglass' bold affirmations, and the urgency of W. E. B. DuBois' claims on freedom were remote in the South of the 1950s. Even the historic cases methodically guided through the courts by the NAACP left the basic superstructure of racism and segregationism intact all over the South.

But there was a steadily growing number of blacks who were ready to challenge the system. Several black leaders in Montgomery were anxious for a catalyst, an occasion when they could combine their efforts in a unified mass stand against segregation. Among them were the hardy pullman porter E. D. Nixon and Jo Ann Robinson of the Women's Political Council. Mrs. Robinson, a native of Macon, Georgia, was a member of King's Dexter Avenue Baptist Church but was strongly attracted to mysticism. A graduate of Atlanta University and Columbia University in New York, the pretty divorcee, says Lawrence Reddick, blended "her metaphysical view of life with direct social action."[30] She often sparred with local officials, and when the Montgomery bus crisis broke out she was one of the first to sense its potential. Nixon, different in background and with much less formal education, was no less prepared to seize opportunities to challenge the status quo. He both admired and emulated Asa Philip Randolph, and his tall swarthy appearance accentuated his identification with workers. Nixon was active in the NAACP and was an official of the Brotherhood of Sleeping Car Porters which Randolph had organized in New York as early as 1925.[31]

There were others, like young attorney Fred Gray, and countless black workers, who were tired of the caste system in Montgomery. But the event that could spark a true conflagration did not occur until December 1, 1955 when Rosa Parks refused to yield her seat to a white man as local law and habit required. Despite the fact that blacks comprised 70% of the bus company's passengers, they were rigidly segregated. Negroes could not sit in the first four rows of seats even if this meant they were left vacant. There were, to be sure, occasional instances of black opposition to this, including three in 1955. One particularly dramatic incident occurred when a fifteen-year-old high school student, Claudette Colvin, was dragged from a bus and hand-cuffed. But each time officials charged the resisters with some minor infraction other than violation of the segregation statutes. Thus, the kind of case some black leaders wanted eluded them.[32]

But, as King noted, people "do get tired of being trampled by oppression."[33] And Rosa Parks was certainly weary of it. She was tired and her feet were hurting after a long day's work at the Montgomery Fair Department Store where she was a seamstress. An attractive, calm-tempered woman in her early forties, Rosa Parks was not looking for trouble. It is true that she was active in the NAACP, but on this occasion on Thursday, December 1, 1955, she was simply boarding the Cleveland Avenue bus to ride home. The early Christmas season rush had made it harder than a typical day, and she sat down wearily, but in compliance with the rules for "colored people" just behind the "white section." There were twenty-three other blacks on the bus, and for a while things went smoothly. Then several additional whites boarded the bus, and the driver ordered Parks and three other blacks to move to the rear. Since the bus was already filled, she would have been required to stand while a white male took her seat. The other three blacks complied, but Rosa Parks refused.

Police were called and Mrs. Parks was arrested. Significantly, this time authorities made a serious tactical mistake, charging her with violating the segregationist transit laws. When E. D. Nixon heard of the incident he knew that this could be the event blacks had waited for. News of the arrest spread rapidly in the black community, and with it an excitement rarely seen in the circles of black leadership in the city. Nixon phoned Jo Ann Robinson and by Friday morning the telephone lines buzzed with the idea of a bus boycott. Nixon also contacted Reverend Ralph David Abernathy, pastor of the black First Baptist Church, who agreed that a boycott would be appropriate. Nixon then called Martin King at his Dexter Avenue office. "We got it!" he cried excitedly. "We got our case. We got to boycott the buses!" Reinforced by news of Abernathy's approval of a boycott, King concurred and agreed to pursue further organization. Nixon arranged Rosa Parks' bail and received her consent to be the focal point of the bus boycott.[34] More than anyone could realize, a historical corner had been turned in Montgomery and the nation.

That same Friday evening, December 2, Montgomery blacks gathered at King's church. The young Dexter Avenue pastor was in a quandary, not knowing how much support to expect or what his own role should be. But when he saw the impressive turnout, he marvelled at the scope and variety of response. There were teachers, doctors, attorneys, workers, clergy. . . everyone seemed to be there after a day of circulating leaflets to communicate the news about Mrs. Parks arrest and the proposed boycott. "I was filled with joy," King recalled, "when I entered the church and found so many of them there, for then I knew that something unusual was about to happen."[35]

Since E. D. Nixon was out of town on his regular railroad run, Rev. L. Roy Bennett, president of the Interdenominational Ministerial Alliance, was selected as chairman of the meeting. Bennett reported the latest news of the bus incident and urged a massive boycott. "Now is the time to move. This is no time to talk; it is time to act." That was the essence of what was happening in Montgomery. Action would now replace speculation and talk. The meeting was not without its disagreements, but after all was said, a consensus emerged. The black ministers present agreed to support the boycott in their pulpits on Sunday. That was crucial in view of the past pattern of acquiescence.

On Monday, December 5, the moment of truth arrived. King had spent a troubled weekend pondering the implications of the boycott. Was it any different from what White Citizens' Councils were doing? Was it fair to make the bus company suffer economically for a racist practice created by a social system? Finally he concluded that the boycott was morally appropriate. "What we were really doing," he felt, "was withdrawing our cooperation from an evil system, rather than merely withdrawing our economic support from the bus company."[36] That King worried about such things mirrored his conscientious approach to reform. He had to be sure in his own mind that what he was doing was in harmony with his religious values and that it would not unjustly hurt anyone. But as he saw the tangible signs that the boycott was working his misgivings paled before the challenge it thrust upon him. Coretta was the first to notice. Looking out the window at the nearby bus stop, she cried, "Martin, Martin, come quickly! Darling, it's empty!" The South Jackson bus did not have the usual crowd of blacks on their way to work. This marked the genesis of a 381-day boycott of Montgomery's segregated buses and a transformation of both King's life and the status of blacks in the United States.

A New Prophet of Nonviolence

Later that morning, Mrs. Parks was tried, convicted, and fined $10 plus court costs. King could only marvel that officials had made such an error. Now they were vulnerable in the courts on constitutional grounds. This realization fueled continuing organizational efforts to keep the boycott going beyond its proposed one-day life. An afternoon meeting was held at the Mt. Zion A.M.E. Church and yet another in the evening at Holt Street Baptist Church where black people would know, as Abernathy recalled, that "something was going on." The afternoon session was largely organizational. In it the Montgomery Improvement Association (MIA) was created. Abernathy provided the name and was chosen vice president. Martin King was elected president, a job he took with some reluctance mixed with excitement.[37] It was an extremely busy afternoon, and King arrived home at 6:00 PM with the task of telling Coretta about his election and of preparing to address the mass rally at the Holt Street church.[38]

In retrospect, what King said to the December 5 evening meeting appears as one of his most pivotal speeches. Ironically, it was not carefully prepared. There was no time for that. Nor was King quite sure what to say. On the one hand, he wanted to appear "militant" in the sense of being agitated about the issues, so as to stir the crowd. On the other, he feared saying anything that would be out of line with his nonviolent Christian perspective. Somehow he had to balance militancy and moderation, or more precisely, activism and Christian love. Long fascinated at the way ministers could use words to move people to action and repentance, King had always wanted to articulate ideas in a compelling way. On this particular occasion, that passion was more than academic. A crowd was waiting to hear words of inspiration and guidance. And as he took the pulpit, young King condensed years of spiritual and intellectual searching into a provocative political sermon. He reviewed the long history of abuse of blacks and proclaimed:

> But there comes a time when people get tired. We are here this evening to say to those who have mistreated us so long that we are tired—tired of being segregated and humiliated; tired of being kicked about by the brutal feet of oppression.

The demand of militancy was met. The crowd loved it and applauded vigorously. King went on with his scathing criticism of racism, the Ku Klux Klan, and violence. But he did not omit his concern for moderation. "Our method will be that of persuasion, not coercion. We will only say to the people, 'Let your conscience be your guide.' Emphasizing the Christian

30

doctrine of love, our actions must be guided by the deepest principles of our Christian faith. Love must be our regulating ideal. Once again we must hear the words of Jesus echoing across the centuries: 'Love your enemies, bless them that curse you, and pray for them that spitefully use you.' ''

As King thought later about his address that night, he was amazed that it had come off so well. Like some of the older preachers who counselled "open your mouth and God will speak for you," he was learning something about spontaneous preaching. He told the Montgomery audience that what God wanted was the crucial consideration in the proposed civil disobedience. For the rest of his career, that concern was a seminal force in the social philosophy that King called nonviolence. "If you will protest courageously, and yet with dignity and Christian love, when the history books are written in future generations, the historians will have to pause and say, 'There lived a great people—a black people—who injected new meaning and dignity into the veins of civilization.' This is our challenge and our overwhelming responsibility."[39]

The story of the 381-day boycott from December 5, 1955 through December 21, 1956 has been told elsewhere and cannot be recounted here. Yet its significance for the nonviolent movement must be underscored. Years of preparation by people like Nixon, Jo Ann Robinson, Fred Gray, and many others, made it possible. Reverend Vernon Johns, King's predecessor at Dexter Avenue Baptist Church, was a significant forbear of the movement, as were Mary Fair Banks, Rev. H. H. Hubbard, Rev. E. N. French, Rufus Lewis, Roy Bennett, A. W. Wilson, professor J. E. Pierce of Alabama State, A.M.E. Zion ministers W. J. Powell and S. S. Seay. Lutheran minister Robert Graetz, Mrs. Euretta Adair, and more paved the way for the boycott and sustained it on the streets of Montgomery and through the courts. Perhaps above all, the working men and women, the students, and the many who will remain unnamed in history books, made the unfolding events decisive for the nation. Professor C. Lamont Yeakey of Purdue University has graphically underscored the importance of the women who worked in common jobs in Montgomery and who made the resultant boycott a success.[40]

The Montgomery movement was more complex than anyone anticipated. Months of car pooling, court battles, walking, meetings, and financing were involved. But the very things that made it challenging increased its impact outside Montgomery. The NAACP aided in the legal struggle despite the organization's own difficulties. A concerted attack on the NAACP was launched in Alabama and several other states during the period. An Alabama circuit court judge tried to ban the NAACP in 1956, and similar moves were made in other southern states. But this did not deter its efforts to support what was happening in Montgomery.[41] Indeed, the NAACP worked with the MIA in filing suit in federal court in early 1956 to invalidate the segregationist transit laws. Nor was the NAACP the only organization to assist. The Fellowship of Reconciliation joined the effort, as did ministerial groups, students, and labor unions. Financial and moral help came from as far away as Britain, France, India, and Japan.

Violence accompanied the long boycott. Racist groups openly resisted and sneak attacks were made on some of the participants. King's home was bombed on January 30, 1956 while he was speaking to a rally and Coretta was in the living room chatting with a friend. The porch and windows of the house were demolished, a harbinger of many atrocities that lay ahead. King was deeply angered by the attack but managed to hold his temper by reminding himself of the nonviolence he was preaching. The real test of his commitment to the nonviolent way was beginning in earnest.

Other problems abounded. White city officials vigorously tried to counter the boycott. They launched a campaign to discredit the MIA, spreading rumors that funds were being misused by its leaders. They even provided false newspaper stories that the boycott had ended. Car pool drivers were charged with crimes, and eventually King and MIA were accused in court of interfering with private enterprise. It was in the midst of the trial that word came on November 13, 1956 that the U. S. Supreme Court had ruled against the Montgomery transit system. As the trial was resuming after a recess, an Associated Press reporter handed King a note that completely reversed the situation. King read it to the court.

> The United States Supreme Court today affirmed a decision of a special three-judge U. S. District Court in declaring Alabama's state and local laws requiring segregation on buses unconstitutional.

On the following evening blacks voted to end the boycott, and on December 21 the buses of Montgomery began to operate on an integrated basis.

This was more, in fact, than the boycotters had sought. Their demands were basically that whites would enter from the front, blacks from the rear of the buses and that each group would fill toward the center with no special privileges for either. Indeed, some outsiders who supported the Montgomery boycott thought that not enough was being sought. Mobile, Alabama, for example, already had such a first come first serve arrangement and its black leaders urged a more extensive set of demands in Montgomery.[42] When the Supreme Court smashed the foundations of Alabama's segregationist transit laws, it set in motion a larger movement among blacks to topple segregated transportation rather than seek amelioration within a racially differentiated system. The implications were profound.

One should not underrate the significance of the transportation question. Many blacks lacked private automobiles and thus depended upon public transit for their livelihood. Furthermore, segregated buses were negatively symbolic, adding to the psychological burden Negroes carried in the South. The essence of the segregation was non-communication and separation, implying that blacks were somehow not fully human or at best not worthy of the company of whites. In King's mind, such segregation was also a denial of the creation of all men by the same God who loved people without regard to race or class. Both from a practical and an ideological point of view, the Montgomery outcome was a turning point in the history of black American liberation.

Above all, the results of the Montgomery boycott vindicated the nonviolent approach. King and others had preached it for months, and in late 1956 it bore observable fruit. Already there was talk of a southwide nonviolent movement, and several local areas were witnessing intensified anti-segregationist drives. Martin Luther King, Jr. had become within the space of a few months a familiar figure in national media. His philosophy of Christian nonviolence became the mark of his leadership. And by 1957 he was a frequent guest speaker at rallies, churches, and colleges. Honors came his way, too, including his first honorary doctorate, bestowed by his *alma mater* in June 1957. At the ceremonies, his mentor Benjamin E. Mays lauded King's courage and values:

> You are mature beyond your years, wiser at twenty-eight than most men at sixty; more courageous in a righteous struggle than most men can ever be; living a faith that most men preach about and never experience. Significant, indeed, is the fact that you did not seek the leadership in the Montgomery controversy. It was thrust upon you by the people. You did not betray that trust of leadership. You led the people with quiet dignity, Christian grace, and determined purpose. While you were away, your colleagues in the battle for freedom were being hounded and arrested like criminals. When it was suggested by legal counsel that you might stay away and escape arrest, I heard you say with my own ears: "I would rather spend ten years in jail than desert the people in this crisis." At that moment my heart, my mind, and my soul stood up erect and saluted you. I knew then that you were called to leadership for just such a time as this. . . . On this our 90th anniversary, your Alma Mater is happy to be the first college or university to honor you this way.[43]

A few days later King received the NAACP's coveted Spingarn Medal for his service in the cause of racial justice. Previous recipients of this old and meaningful award inaugurated in 1914, were W. E. B. DuBois, George Washington Carver, Mary McCleod Bethune, Asa Philip Randolph, and many others considered to have made the "highest or noblest achievement by an American Negro." Martin Luther King, Jr. at twenty-eight was entering the company of the most respected of America's black leaders.[44]

The Montgomery struggle had given King his first opportunity to publicly articulate his nonviolent philosophy and to connect it to specific political objectives. Moreover, the year-long effort demonstrated the importance of organization. The Montgomery Improvement Association had to manage a budget, and create special committees for transportation, finance, and other aspects of the boycott. By the end of the confrontation, a number of black leaders felt that the Montgomery victory might be duplicated in other cities across the South. Coretta King has written that the idea of a continuing and broader organization was discussed in their home in late 1956.

In other places, too, black leaders became excited about the prospect of sustaining the momentum of Montgomery. The seasoned civil rights advocate Bayard Rustin, whose reformist career reached back to the Randolph era and who would be attached to King's movement for several years, reports that:

> In practical terms, this meant that the movement needed a sustaining mechanism that could translate what we had learned during the bus boycott into a broad strategy for protest in the South. At the same time we felt it vital that we maintain the psychological momentum Montgomery had generated. If nothing else, we needed at least to appear to be moving ahead, attacking new targets, testing new tactics, and pressing the movement forward.[45]

Soon Tallahassee, Mobile, Birmingham, Atlanta and other cities would reflect the sense of 'movement' engendered in Montgomery. Among the many figures who would act locally and in concert with the broader movement were the Reverend Fred Lee Shuttlesworth, president of the Alabama Christian Movement in Birmingham; the Reverend Joseph E. Lowery of Mobile, Alabama; the Reverend C. K. (Charles Kenzie) Steele, leader of Tallahassee's desegregation efforts and pastor of the Bethel Baptist Church; and in Atlanta, the Reverend William Holmes Borders, pastor of the Wheat Street Baptist Church.[46] It would be only a few months until these and others would combine their energies in a southwide organization to perpetuate and broaden the reform effort. Steele, Rustin, and King were the prime movers in calling an organizational meeting in early 1957, but the idea struck a responsive chord in the minds of many others.

Perhaps the most significant aspect of this emergent southern movement was the rising hope that things could be changed more broadly and deeply than was previously believed. Although the record of the NAACP and other organizations was impressive, no black movement had ever substantially moved the South from its traditions of segregation. As black people saw what had happened in Montgomery, and took note of King's effectiveness, they began to believe that more could be done. C. Eric Lincoln wrote that "It may well be the final judgment of history that Martin Luther King's greatest contribution to black freedom was made in Montgomery when he helped black people free themselves from self-doubt and self-abasement."[47]

Even the very young were affected by the Montgomery boycott. Leon Hall, who would become one of the many young people who contributed strategically to the campaigns of the sixties, was drawn to the movement by the boycott. Although only nine years old at the time, he recalls that the campaign in his home town was the catalyst in his career in nonviolent activism. All over the South, something important was happening in black consciousness.

Nonviolence means taking the responsibility for aiding the direction of human communication and brotherhood.

Edward Guinan

2

Movement and Community
The Early Development of SCLC, 1957–1959

The "Montgomery way" had become a model by the end of 1956 for a new strategy in the South. If its dynamic could be harnessed, the results would likely be far-reaching. King predicted that blacks were "in for a season of suffering" after the Montgomery success, but at the same time he was solidly convinced that nonviolence was a viable strategy. It could reach beyond legal changes and "touch men where the law cannot reach them," that is, at the highest levels of their conscience. In this regard, he saw three categories of people in the South at that time: 1) a minority who resisted integration at all costs; 2) a majority who tacitly or openly supported segregation but "at the same time stand on the side of law and order." This second group was a potential ally in the black struggle since they gave high regard to principles of constitutional legality and order; and 3) a growing minority of people, black and white, who were "working courageously and conscientiously to implement the law of the land: because they believed "in the morality as well as the constitutionality of integration."[1]

It was essential, King thought, not to distort what had actually happened in Montgomery. Despite his own pivotal role, he attributed the legal victory there to the throngs of supporters who made the boycott work, and to the providence of God. It was a human movement, to be sure, but not simply that. The 50,000 determined people who "were willing to substitute tired feet for tired souls, and walk the streets of Montgomery until the walls of segregation were finally battered by the forces of justice" were the indispensable human element. But ultimately, he argued, "There is a creative power that works to pull down mountains of evil and level hilltops of injustice. God still works through history his wonders to perform."[2]

King was not simply being modest or engaging in rhetorical double talk. Montgomery had been a collective effort by the local stalwards like Nixon, Robinson, and Gray, whites such as the Reverend Robert Graetz, outside financial supporters, and more. Religious faith and language had permeated the dialogue throughout the campaign, and ministers and their parishioners had provided much of the organizational matrix. King saw that as more than circumstantial. God was working in Montgomery, he believed, to begin something larger than the scope of any local black demands. In the final analysis, the most important thing that happened in Montgomery in King's estimation was that blacks acquired a "growing self-respect" that inspired them "with a new determination to struggle and sacrifice until first-class citizenship becomes a reality. . . . One can never understand the bus protest in Montgomery without understanding that there is a new Negro in the South, with a new sense of dignity and destiny."[3]

The Birth of the Southern Christian Leadership Conference

If there was a new Negro emerging in the South, there was also a new concept of leadership inspired by the Montgomery example. King was at its center because of the strength of his intellect and his ability to articulate the nonviolent philosophy forcefully. SCLC's historian Lawrence D. Reddick noted early that "Martin Luther King was the spokesman, the philosopher, and the symbol of the Montgomery bus boycott. In these roles he was without peer and gave the additional dimension to the movement that helped make the struggle epic.''[4] Naturally, King realized that his personal role was pivotal and, like Gandhi, he felt responsibility for the actions of his followers and worried about the dangers direct-action protest presented. He well knew that he had to set an example, and for that reason he boarded the first desegregated bus in Montgomery on December 21, 1956. Riding with Abernathy, white supporter Glenn Smiley, and E. D. Nixon, King heard racist slurs from incensed white passengers. And this was only one rather tame reminder that all was not over in Montgomery. Blacks still moved by habit to the back of buses, and the Ku Klux Klan rode in defiance of the court orders. Violence erupted again in the city in early 1957, and what King called a ''reign of terror'' brought bombings, shootings, and verbal confrontations.[5] There were also personal attacks on King designed to impugn his character and thus draw away some of his following.[6]

Nonetheless, King remained the symbol and spokesman of the new movement, and with the emergence of the idea of an organizational framework for continuing the Montgomery-style protest he was considered its natural leader. He did not, however, singlehandedly conceive of or create the organization he would lead for more than a decade. Its genesis lay in the convergence of three salient factors which, while separate, were interrelated. The first was King's own personal commitment hammered out during the Montgomery boycott.

As early as January 1956, King was on the verge of ending his involvement in the MIA. Threats by the Ku Klux Klan upon himself and his young family, mysterious phone calls, and overtly hostile anti-integrationists brought him to the brink of despair. One night he could hardly stand the strain. Exhausted from an intense MIA meeting, he found sleep elusive and comfort far away. A telephone call interrupted his introspection. The angry voice warned ''Nigger, if you aren't out of town in three days, we gonna blow your brains out and blow up your house.'' King was dismayed. Then, instinctively, he cupped his bowed head in his hands and prayed. ''Oh Lord, I'm down here trying to do what is right. But, Lord, I must confess that I'm weak now. I'm afraid. The people are looking to me for leadership, and if I stand before them without strength and courage, they too will falter. I am at the end of my power. I have nothing left. I can't face it alone."

With that, King was beginning to find a new strength, born of apparent weakness. With Daddy King far away in Atlanta, with his wife and young daughter depending on him—not to mention all those who relied on him for leadership in the boycott—inner resources were all he had. Suddenly, Martin King joined the company of Christians who, since the early days of the church, had thrown themselves totally on the power of God.

> At that moment I experienced the presence of the Divine as I had never experienced Him before. It seemed as though I could hear the quiet assurance of an inner voice saying "Stand up for righteousness, stand up for truth, and God will be at your side forever." Almost at once my fears began to go. My uncertainty disappeared. I was ready to face anything.[7]

Indeed King did face much more opposition. The bombing of his home occurred less than a week later. He went on trial in the spring, and many other ordeals accompanied the completion of the campaign. There is no doubt that his spiritual wrestlings in January 1956 prepared him more deeply for assuming an ongoing role in the southern nonviolent movement and steeled his determination to go beyond purely local efforts. He was receptive to suggestions for an organization to link blacks all over the South in a cooperative endeavor, and in fact often discussed that possibility with close friends and associates throughout 1956. Through it all he shared his inner feelings with his friend Ralph Abernathy, who would long remain the person King could most readily lean on in crises.

The other two causal factors in the formation of a southwide organizational structure were the proliferation of nonviolent campaigns in other southern cities, and the specific plans of small groups of people who felt that the time was right for a regional assault on segregationist practices. Various writers have attributed the conception of the organization to particular individuals. Most frequently mentioned are Bayard Rustin, white attorney Stanley Levison, Ella J. Baker, C. K. Steele, and the inner circle of MIA leadership.[8] On balance, the evidence shows that no single person can be identified as the one who initiated the process that led to the formation of the Southern Christian Leadership Conference. To take that approach is misleading, for the SCLC concept was spawned by a new mood triggered by the Montgomery experience and mirrored in many local situations where blacks were prepared to protest more openly.[9] Recollections by the principal participants in the shaping of SCLC vary, but much of the story is recoverable.

Bayard Rustin was apparently the first to make a specific proposal. A long-time activist with the Fellowship of Reconciliation (FOR) and even with the Gandhi movement in India, Rustin knew well the importance of organization. He came to Montgomery during the boycott and offered King some much appreciated assistance. A pacifist and a socialist, Rustin was different from many of the MIA leaders in social philosophy, but he shared their basic commitment to desegregation and proved to be quite influential in organizing the Southwide movement. As early as February 1956, Rustin proffered to the Kings in Montgomery the idea of a national nonviolent movement based on a southern coordinating organization.[10]

Meanwhile, extensive discussion of a possible southern organization began in the family circles of the Kings and Abernathys, who had grown closer during the difficult boycott. They often talked into the early hours of morning, sometimes at the Kings' home, sometimes at the Abernathys'. There were not many places, recalls Abernathy, where blacks could meet for lengthy discussions in segregated Montgomery.[11] Coretta, Martin, Juanita, and Ralph pored over the weighty questions of protest organization while sipping coffee around dining room tables. As the circle broadened, the parleys included Joseph Lowery from Mobile, Fred Shuttlesworth from Birmingham, C. G. Gomillion from Tuskegee, and others. C. K. Steele of Tallahassee and T. J. Jemison of Baton Rouge were part of this seminal "think tank" and influential protest organizers in their communities. The long distances between them militated against regular discussions, but they managed by personal meetings and letters to give rough shape to a possible organization and to compile a list of strategic contact persons.[12]

A more specific step was taken in December 1956 after the Supreme Court decision on Montgomery's bus system. With King's approval Rustin, along with Ella J. Baker, met with white liberal attorney Stanley Levison in New York to plan a benefit concert in behalf of the black struggle. These meetings gave them opportunities to discuss the possibility of a larger cooperative framework in the South and perhaps beyond. From this point onward the controversial Levison would be a key figure in the southern civil rights movement, often raising large sums of money to finance protest activity. Ella Baker brought to the planning many years of experience in working with the New School for Social Research in New York and as a field secretary for the NAACP. A native of Virginia who studied at Shaw University in North Carolina, Baker knew firsthand the barriers to black advancement, and she was eager to help organize the post-Montgomery movement.[13]

Calls by Rustin to Steele and Shuttlesworth initiated implementation of the plans. In conjunction with King, Reverends Steele and Shuttlesworth signed a roundrobin invitation to selected civil rights activists across the South to attend an organizational conference in Atlanta on January 10 and 11, 1957.[14] About sixty people, mostly black ministers, traveled to the two-day conference at Ebenezer Baptist Church where King was slated to open the proceedings.

But a frightening reminder of the seriousness of the issues at hand prevented King from carrying through with his plans and left Coretta with the task of welcoming the delegates. Around 2:00 A.M. on January 10, Abernathy received a call from his wife in Montgomery giving him the grim news that their home had been bombed along with several other houses and churches. Angry opponents of the bus desegregation decree had vented their wrath in an orgy of violence that destroyed considerable property and endangered the lives of a number of people, including Juanita Abernathy (who was pregnant at the time) and her young daughter Juandalyn.[15] King and Abernathy rushed to Montgomery to view the destruction and try to comfort the victims.

Despite this ominous beginning, the Atlanta gathering proved to be the tangible start of the nonviolent southern movement. The renewed violence in Montgomery did not deter King or Abernathy, but seemed to inspire them to get on with the business of the Ebenezer conference where Steele presided.[16] Violence was one of the principal issues in the movement and this latest example underscored the need for action. As they returned to Atlanta by plane on January 11, King and Abernathy were tired but encouraged by the good turnout.

Many of the concerns of SCLC's founders were political in nature, but they were discussed in the context of nonviolent strategies and Christian values. Extant working papers for the Atlanta conference indicate that the founders were aware of the psychological dimensions of racial solidarity. Much emphasis was placed upon group pride and a sense of community-in-action.[17] One can see in their deliberations the distinctives of the organization's identity among older civil rights groups like the NAACP and CORE. This new organization would orient itself candidly to the church, "the most stable social institution" and give credence to the concept that blacks acting directly and in concert to improve their lot would be the most effective means of change.[18]

It is possible for a casual observer or even a serious scholar to miss what happened in Atlanta in January 1957. It must be kept in mind that most of the participants were church ministers, men who prayed and preached and led local congregations. As writers have often observed, this gave the infant organization a ready-made base of operation in local black churches. Rustin, one of the pivotal figures in the early history of SCLC has said, "This close identification with the Negro church proved a source of strength at the outset," although in his view it later caused some problems.[19] Lacking both the historical continuity and the resources of a well-organized body like the NAACP, this new group relied heavily on local congregations.

This relationship affected the structure of the organization as well, in the sense of giving it a relatively small, pastoral kind of leadership pyramid. But it went much deeper. In addition to financial support, leaders, and an independent forum for dissemination of ideas, the tie to the church gave these people their fundamental values. Rustin went on to say about the church link, "Ultimately, however, it contained the seeds of the SCLC's destruction."[20] That observation fails to grasp what Coretta King saw in the early organization. To her the church orientation defined the nonviolent ideal that shaped it. In her view, nonviolence was "a spiritual concept in deep accord with the American Negro's Christian beliefs."[21] Rustin's point was that the peculiarly authoritative pastoral function in black churches, and the evangelistic style of campaigning were out of step with later conditions. However accurate that may be, it is necessary to see that the Atlanta meeting was held in a church and its deliberations were set in the context of values that permanently influenced the organization which it fostered.

The name they chose was the Southern Leadership Conference on Transportation and Nonviolent Integration. Accordingly, the leaders gave much attention to further bus protests defined by the precedent of Montgomery, feeling that additional successes were both possible and necessary to keep the movement going. Successful campaigns would also give blacks a better self-image and a sense of making progress. King and his associates knew that 10% of the American population could never win by force, but through nonviolent, orderly, and concerted action they could change the prevailing order. Ultimately, such a transformation could not be accomplished without the enfranchisement of millions of blacks. Noting that the legislative branch of the national government had failed to pass any civil rights acts since 1875, they set out to enlarge the black electorate. But until that was accomplished they would have to rely on direct-action as the "one realistic political weapon at their disposal."[22]

A mixture of specific issues and broader contextual matters, the deliberations of the Atlanta conference shaped the future direction and character of SCLC. There were three foci of attention: 1) future actions by blacks; 2) the attitudinal framework of further reform efforts; and 3) the potential role of the federal government. On the first point the Atlanta delegates were convinced that the Montgomery victory was penultimate. If they could not carry through effectively on that model, not much would have been gained. ". . . There is a question as to whether Montgomery or any other campaign can succeed unless many more areas of protest spring up."[23] But they would not simply spring up. Cadres of disciplined nonviolent volunteers would be necessary to serve as "shock troops" to ride in the front lines and be "prepared to go to jail if necessary."[24] Their function would be totally nonviolent, serving as an example whose "courage would inspire the community and shame those who might resort to violence."[25] Those committed volunteers, it was hoped, would elicit larger groups of volunteers who also accepted the nonviolent strategy.

The matter of attitude operated in two directions. First there was the question of the attitudes of blacks. Could they maintain a nonviolent frame of mind even if confronted with violence? What response should be made if people were hurt in direct-action protests, and should innocent whites such as bus drivers who might have nothing to do with a hostile confrontation be included in any collective nonviolent reaction?[26] Beyond this, there was the larger issue of white acceptance of integration. These black leaders who formed the new southern organization knew that ultimately white response was crucial. They realized that future successes, if based on nonviolence and political realism, could have a positive impact on the white population. If, on the other hand, present and future protests failed, the general public would likely "move towards reaction."[27] While this issue was not resolved during the Atlanta conference, the broad outlines of a consensus took form.

The third focus of the Atlanta conference was shaped by the political situation of 1957. The first term of the Eisenhower administration was ending, and already the famous President had been re-elected in a second victory over Democrat Adlai

Stevenson. So far he had taken a very cautious approach to civil rights, and black leaders were determined to move the federal government into a more active role. Under Eisenhower's immediate predecessors, Franklin D. Roosevelt and Harry S. Truman, the federal government had edged away from the traditional *laissez-faire* policies of the post-Reconstruction era, providing at least a limited degree of governmental involvement in civil rights guarantees. Truman had appointed a civil rights committee shortly after World War II, and he agreed basically with the thrust of its classic report of 1947 entitled *To Secure These Rights*. In it the committee affirmed that the "national government of the United States must take the lead in safeguarding civil rights of all Americans" and argued that the international influence of the country was tarnished by the racial inequities that existed in the United States.[28]

Eisenhower's philosophy of government was socially conservative, and he was not comfortable with the notion of the national administration's becoming an advocate of civil rights. Race relations were basically a personal matter to him, and he preferred a limited federal role in guaranteeing constitutional principles while depending on steady growth of a better informed and more tolerant public. He did, though, see the need for further civil rights legislation. When he delivered his fifth State of the Union Message to Congress in January 1957, he urged the legislators to pass the administration's proposed civil rights package sent to Capitol Hill in 1956. It was a moderate set of proposals by most standards, but it included establishing a bipartisan commission to investigate alleged civil rights violations, creation of a civil rights commission in the Department of Justice, enactment of new laws to enforce voting rights, and an increase in federal authority in civil rights litigation.[29]

On matters of school desegregation and integration of other public facilities, Eisenhower had little to say. While he objected to the tactics of the White Citizens' Council and publicly condemned racial violence, he was not willing to push any further. Evidence suggests that the President felt that the Supreme Court had acted too hastily in its desegregation judgments and should have taken a more gradual approach. He even opposed a strong civil rights plank in the 1956 Republican Platform, arguing that "leaders must be encouraged to appeal to the moral obligations of our people rather than refer only to the law."[30]

Ironically, Eisenhower was pushing for his civil rights bill on the same day the Ebenezer conference opened in Atlanta. And the founders there wanted a great deal more than what the President was prepared to give. They appealed to Eisenhower and Vice-president Nixon to come to the South and speak out directly and boldly against the violence blacks were encountering and make a straightforward endorsement of integration. Nixon had shown sympathy for revolution-battered Hungarian refugees in 1956, they pointed out, and now it was time for him to "make a tour of the South" in behalf of American blacks. Furthermore, the conference delegates asked for a meeting between black leaders and Attorney General Herbert Brownell to discuss the responsibilities of the Justice Department in situations where both blacks and whites who stood up for justice "feared for their lives."[31]

When the Ebenezer conference adjourned on January 11, it was understood that there would be follow-up meetings. The lack of positive response from the White House or Justice Department underscored the need to continue that emphasis, and there was still the business of electing officers, initiating programs, and financing to consider. On February 14, a second meeting was held in New Orleans and from it emerged the basic organizational structure of the movement. This time, ninety-seven delegates attended, representing about three dozen communities in ten southern states. Again, ministers were at the forefront.

The New Orleans meeting was a short one-day session devoted primarily to urging the Eisenhower administration to get involved in the southern struggle. Numerous messages to the White House and other federal offices were drafted, including a long cable to the President renewing the January invitation to visit the South.

While we are sensitive to the burdens of your responsible office, we believe that human life and the orderly, decent conduct of our communities are at stake. Their imperative considerations leave us quite reluctant to accept as final that a speech by you in the South cannot be scheduled. It is our sincere belief that action on your part now can avert tragic situations by cooling passion and encouraging reasonableness. In saying this we are not unmindful of the immense responsibility of your office in the conduct of our national and international affairs. However, morality, like charity, begins at home. Here at home, as we write, we are confronted with a breakdown of law, order and morality. This sinister challenge and threat to our government of laws drastically calling for attention and remedial action.[32]

They also asked Eisenhower to convene a White House conference on civil rights and warned that if "effective remedial steps are not taken, we will be compelled to initiate a mighty Prayer Pilgrimage to Washington. . ." Cables were also sent to Nixon and Brownell, but again without results. For a full month after the New Orleans conference the black leaders waited for a positive sign from Washington, only to discover that none of the principal administration leaders was available to tour the South or willing to make a bold initiative on civil rights at that juncture.

As the New Orleans meeting ended, the new leadership conference was still not fully organized. The name was changed from the cumbersome original to the 'Southern Negro Leadership Conference' after consideration of "Southern Negro Leaders Conference' and others. They would finally settle on its permanent name at a third meeting in Montgomery later in 1957. For the moment, there were more pressing matters, with the resurgence of violence, uncertainty about the administration's policies, and King's own personal problems.

It was a tense period for King, and those around him recognized that he needed a break. The opportunity came with an invitation from Prime Minister (and later President) Kwame Nkrumah to witness the March 5, 1957 ceremonies celebrating the formal termination of Britain's colonial rule in Ghana. Martin and Coretta left in late February, funded by the Dexter Avenue congregation and friends within the MIA. It proved to be an uplifting experience for them, not only because it was their first trip abroad, but also because it underscored the trend of liberation that was assuming global dimensions. In Ghana, also, King met Vice-president Nixon, who invited him to confer with him at the White House later.[33]

Shaping a Program

Returning from his African trip, King stopped in New Orleans on March 25 to confer with Asa Philip Randolph and Roy Wilkins about the forthcoming march on Washington. It would be known as the Prayer Pilgrimage and would mark the third anniversary of the 1954 *Brown* decision in May. It was an interesting spectacle to see these three men, so different in temperament and age, sit together in dialogue. King was impressed that he was in such prestigious company, but the truth is that both Wilkins and Randolph had profound respect for the young man who had just led the Montgomery campaign.[34] The trio met again on April 5 at the Metropolitan Baptist Church in Washington and each energetically supported the march.

There were detractors to be sure, but generally the Prayer Pilgrimage engendered widespread support. Some blacks questioned it, and the Klan and White Citizens Councils resisted it, but the planners of the march had lofty expectations. The principal leaders hoped for 50,000 participants, and Ralph Abernathy felt that 100,000 was possible.[35] The actual turnout was about 25,000 to 30,000, an impressive figure nonetheless. Along with about 3,000 whites, blacks from 33 states converged on the nation's capital on May 17, 1957 to hear an array of dignitaries including Congressman Adam Clayton Powell, A. P. Randolph, C. K. Steele, Fred Shuttlesworth, and the Reverend A. L. Davis. Singer Mahalia Jackson stirred the crowd with her Gospel music.

King delivered the closing address, his first speech before a national audience. Standing in front of the Lincoln Memorial, he began to speak in the rhythmic tones for which he would become famous. "So long as I do not firmly and irrevocally possess the right to vote, I do not possess myself," he said. "So our most urgent request to the President of the United States and every

member of Congress is to give us the right to vote." The crowd
began to respond with applause and repetition of his phrase
"Give us the ballot."

> Give us the ballot and we will no longer plead—we will write the proper
> laws on the books. Give us the ballot and we will fill the legislatures with
> men of goodwill. Give us the ballot and we will get the people judges who
> love mercy. Give us the ballot and we will quietly, lawfully, implement
> the May 17, 1954 decision of the Supreme Court. Give us the ballot and
> we will transform the salient misdeeds of the bloodthirsty mobs into the
> calculated good deeds of orderly citizens.

The decorum and restraint of the Prayer Pilgrimage to Washington impressed many observers. It was basically an orderly
group headed by civil rights activists as well as prominent
entertainers like Harry Belafonte, Sammy Davis, Jr., and Sidney
Poitier. Much of the local preparation had been spearheaded by
pastors including Joseph Lowery, William Holmes Borders,
Ralph Abernathy, and Thomas Kilgore, Jr. The march was
inter-organizational in structure, with the funding provided
largely by the NAACP. If King gained the limelight, it is also
true that the Prayer Pilgrimage was a cooperative endeavor.

Even at that, there was some tension among black leaders
who, consciously or not, were entering a period of competition
for supporters and prestige. No doubt, some of the more
seasoned black spokesmen worried somewhat when the *Amsterdam News* in Harlem proclaimed a few days after the event that
King had become the "number one leader of sixteen million
Negroes" and that. . ."the people will follow him anywhere."[36]

Actually King made no effort to upstage other civil rights
leaders. Rather, he entered a number of cooperative ventures
with them, and in his own decision-making took several people
into his confidence and listened to their suggestions. Rustin,
Levison, Shuttlesworth, Lowery, and Steele were certainly in
this inner circle in varying degrees, while Abernathy remained
his closest confidant. Group dialogue was the hallmark of the
formative stages of the leadership conference.[37]

Political trends of the summer provided the framework for the completion of the organizational process. On June 13, King and Abernathy met with Labor Secretary James P. Mitchell and Vice-president Nixon in the latter's office. Nixon had been slow in carrying through with his promise made in Ghana that he would talk with King. When it finally materialized, the two black spokesmen were ready for the discussion, carrying a carefully worded set of proposals which they, Rustin, and Levison had prepared. The emphasis was upon the need for federal help in resolving the tremendous and worsening problems of blacks in the South. Echoing the appeals from the Atlanta and New Orleans conferences, King urged Nixon and Eisenhower to get more directly involved and to travel in the South to see conditions there and lend their prestige to resolving them.[38] It was also essential that the civil rights bill pending in Congress be passed despite the growing opposition it was encountering.

Very little resulted from the meeting with Nixon. The Vice-president defended the administration's record on civil rights and said that Eisenhower was doing as much speaking as he could. Nixon did say that he expected the civil rights bill to pass, but he demurred on the question of visiting the South. The truth is that Nixon knew that southern conservatives feared passage of a strong bill and that political wisdom dictated not countering them directly. The administration had voiced its disappointment over the 1956 "Southern Manifesto" by which about 100 southern Congressmen and Senators had pledged to resist the school desegregation order by "every legal means," but neither then nor in 1957 was the Eisenhower government prepared to do what black leaders had in mind. Both the President and Nixon, however, did want to see passage of the administration's bill without the watering down measures southern conservatives were attempting.[39]

If nothing concrete came of the June 13 meeting, worse problems attended the fate of the civil rights bill in Congress. On July 16 the Senate began debate on the version that had passed the House. Rarely has a proposed piece of legislation engendered as much tension. Southern conservatives spearheaded by Senators Richard Russell of Georgia and Strom Thurmond of

South Carolina were as determined to stop passage as they were to resist the school desegregation order. Particularly divisive was Section III, which enlarged the Justice Department's authority and raised the specter of armed intervention in the South, at least as Russell saw it. Eisenhower steadily backed away from his original support of the whole bill, which after all was more the product of the Justice Department than the White House. Section III was eliminated by the Senate on July 24, and by August 1 the bill was further weakened by the addition of a jury-trial amendment which tended to ameliorate the fears of some southern legislators by providing the likelihood that a jury of native whites would balance off other provisions of the act. Senator whip Everett Dirkson of Illinois convinced Eisenhower that the jury-trial provision was necessary for passage.[40]

The eventual result was a set of compromises disappointing to the bill's opponents as well as the advocates of strong civil rights legislation. Majority leader Lyndon B. Johnson of Texas pushed the bill through in its final form.[41] On August 7, after a 24-hour filibuster by Senator Thurmond, the bill as amended passed by a vote of 72 to 18. Eisenhower signed it into law on September 9, 1957, ending a vacuum of civil rights legislation that began in 1875. Certainly it was a landmark, despite its limitations. The *Civil Rights Act of 1957* did give the Attorney General considerable authority in local cases, and it contained some provisions on voting rights. Its major feature was the establishment of a Civil Rights Division within the Justice Department and a Civil Rights Commission. Perhaps John Hope Franklin was correct when he observed that "The real significance of the legislation lay not so much in its provisions as in its recognition of federal responsibility and its reflection of a remarkable and historic reversal of federal policy of hands-off in matters involving civil rights.[42]

In any case the intense opposition civil rights legislation encountered in the summer of 1957 stimulated completion of the organization of the southern protest movement. Blacks knew better than before that their own actions would be essential to any genuine improvement of their condition. At King's invitation, the Southern Negro Leadership Conference met in Montgomery on August 7 and 8. There the name of the group was changed to the Southern Christian Leadership Conference, although not without some difficulty. Since Levison was a Jew and Jewish support for the black movement was regarded as important, some wondered whether a specifically Christian title would alienate him. It did not, recalls Abernathy, and the organization that began in Atlanta seven months earlier assumed its present name.[43] Thus, SCLC officially began in the city where the historic boycott had occurred less than two years earlier. In a sense the new organization was an extension of the MIA, which continued to operate. But it was also a much more comprehensive body with broader participation and vastly larger potential resources.

After some debate over whether Martin King or C. K. Steele should be SCLC's first president, the conference decided on King and elected Steele first vice-president. Activist ministers were chosen for most of the offices. The other two vice-presidents were the Reverend A. L. Davis, a leader in the desegregation of buses in New Orleans, and Reverend Samuel W. Williams, professor of philosophy at Morehouse College. The chaplain of SCLC was Kelly Miller Smith, a minister from Nashville. Dr. Lawrence D. Reddick, a historian by profession and later a biographer of King's early career, was named official historian. SCLC's first executive director, Dr. John L. Tilley, was chosen in the spring of 1958 after months of searching. He was followed in that post by his tireless associate, Ella J. Baker, from 1959 to 1960.

Altogether, eleven states were represented in SCLC's initial leadership, and its headquarters were established at 208 Auburn Avenue, N.E. in Atlanta, not far from the present location and the Ebenezer Baptist Church. Ralph Abernathy was chosen as treasurer, and he administered SCLC's financial affairs for many years. But Abernathy's role was more central than this would suggest, as will be seen as SCLC's history is examined.

The goals of the early Southern Christian Leadership Conference were not unlike those of NAACP and CORE. All three of these believed in the importance of integration and an essentially nonviolent approach to improving the status of black Americans. Indeed the SCLC leadership relied on the Legal Defense Fund and other resources of the NAACP as a protective device as they engaged in direct action tactics. What was special about the Southern Christian Leadership Conference was its unification of blacks and white sympathizers around the central philosophy of nonviolent direct-action and Christian faith.

SCLC channeled its movement into a loosely organized, but centrally led system of mass mobilization. With close ties to black churches and an ever-enlarging group of 'affiliates' it set out with certain coherent, if somewhat general, objectives. The Preamble to its Constitution is informative:

> *Our nation came into existence as a protest against tyranny and oppression. It was created upon the fundamental assumption that all men are created equal and endowed with inalienable rights. The government exists to protect the life and liberty of all without regard to race, color, or religion.*
>
> *The Federal Government has announced this principle and pledged repeatedly in its basic documents equal protection under the law. The Declaration of Independence, the Constitution of the United States, particularly the Bill of Rights and the 14th and 15th Amendments, the Federal Civil Rights Laws, and many recent decisions of the United States Supreme Court, proclaim unequivocally that all American citizens shall be accorded full citizenship rights and opportunities without discrimination.[44]*

From this nucleus of constitutional principles, SCLC defined its goals. It was particularly interested in achieving full citizenship rights for blacks, including the right to vote and to be educated in integrated schools. SCLC promised not to "cooperate with evil, appealing to the conscience of man, and working for social change but always in a spirit of good will and nonviolence." It pledged itself to being a service organization to facilitate coordinated local action and to "assist in the sharing of resources and experiences."[45] Basic to its purpose was the provision of Christian guidance in efforts to improve political, economic, and social conditions, especially in the South, but also nationwide. More specifically, it committed itself to inter-racial harmony, improvement of opportunities for individuals, and education of citizens in their rights and duties in society. Significantly, these aims were to be achieved "through non-violent direct action, lectures, dissemination of literature and other means of public instruction."[46]

Crusading for Full Citizenship

The first major campaign of the young SCLC was what it called the Crusade for Citizenship, a massive project to at least double the registration of black voters in the South. Conceived in 1957, it was officially launched in early 1958 after the passage of the Civil Rights Act. Undertaken with the support of Roy Wilkins, executive director of the NAACP since 1955, the Crusade for Citizenship was SCLC's primary focus until the sit-in movement of 1960. The Crusade was important for King's organization for a variety of reasons. First, it was a timely undertaking. The momentum of Montgomery and the Civil Rights Act could not sustain the black movement without a much larger electorate. "The constructive program ahead," wrote King, "must include a campaign to get Negroes to register and vote." Accomplishing that would entail not only changes in laws and attitudes among whites, but also displacing apathy among blacks with confidence and participation. Whereas apathy in the past, King concluded, was a moral failure, "Today it is a form of moral and political suicide."[47]

Secondly, the citizenship campaign had immediate practical relevance to broader issues of integration. The desegregation of schools was a heated and divisive issue. Just four days after the enactment of the Civil Rights Act, a major confrontation began in Little Rock, Arkansas, where Governor Orval Faubus tried to block the integration of Central High School. As White Citizens' Councils prepared to resist desegregation the Governor threw the weight of his office behind their efforts, forcing President Eisenhower to call upon the National Guard to protect NAACP leader Daisy Bates and the black children who tried to exercise their legal right to enter the school. Eisenhower told the nation

Chronological Table No. 1: Principal Movements for Racial Advancement 1895 to 1957

Part I: 1895–1942

1880	1890	1900	1905	1910	1915	1920	1925	1930	1935	1940
					World War I (1914–1918)			*Great Depression*	Franklin D. Roosevelt (President 1933–1945)	*World War II* (1939–1945)
1877 end of Reconstruction Disenfranchisement and Segregation of blacks						League of Nations begins 1920				
Frederick Douglass Protests against racism, peonage		1895 Booker T. Washington's Atlanta Exposition Address								
									"Double V" (victory) sought by blacks, over Nazism in Europe, racism at home	
			TUSKEGEE MOVEMENT (Booker T. Washington) Education/Self-Help							
				NIAGRA MOVEMENT (W.E.B. DuBois) Voting Rights/ Equality Now						
					NAACP (founded 1909) Legal and constitutional Rights/advancement of blacks on all fronts/court battles					
						Great Migration of blacks to northern cities *Harlem Renaissance*				
						Marcus Garvey leads Black Nationalism movement/ "back to Africa"				
						UNIA (United Negro Improvement Association) (founded 1914 in Jamaica/ spreads widely in U.S. by 1919)				
										Asa Philip Randolph threatens March on Washington 1941
										Roosevelt issues Executive Order 8802 (June 25, 1941) banning racial discrimination in by defense industry
										CORE (Congress of Racial Equality) (founded 1942) Gandhian direct action

Part II: Formation of the Southern Christian Leadership Conference (SCLC)

1955	1957

Dwight Eisenhower (President 1953–1961)

May 1954
Brown v. Board of Education (Topeka) overturns *Plessy v. Ferguson* (1896)

Local efforts to desegregate schools and public facilities meet strong resistance by Citizens' Councils and Congressmen

Montgomery Bus Boycott (1955–1956) sparked by Mrs. Rosa Parks

Montgomery Improvement Association (MIA) created

Other local desegregation movements in Tallahassee, Mobile, Birminghan, New Orleans, *et al.*

November 1956
U.S. Supreme Court overturns Montgomery segregated bus system

January 1957
Atlanta meeting creates Southern Leadership Conference on Transportation and Nonviolent Integration

February 1957
New Orleans Meeting petitions federal government for desegregation stand/name changed to Southern Negro Leadership Conference

May 17, 1957
Prayer Pilgrimage in Washington, D.C.

August 1957
Montomery Meeting formally establishes SCLC

September 9, 1957
Civil Rights Act Signed by Eisenhower Civil Rights Commission created

that "mob rule cannot be allowed to override the decisions of the courts."[48]

But federal force was not the ultimate answer. What was needed most was more political strength for blacks and nonblacks who supported the goals of the civil rights movement. Voting rights were basic to that objective. And in concert with the NAACP, SCLC set out to begin the process of voter registration and training in the fundamentals of participatory citizenship. The challenges were greatest in the South where evidence of almost unmovable resistance to integration, not only in the schools but in transportation and public facilities, was abundant. By the fall of 1957 only 350,000 black children were attending nominally integrated schools in the South, while more than two million were going to totally segregated institutions.[49] This squared with indications of negative southern attitudes toward "mixing the races." A Gallup Poll of October 1957 indicated that about 59% of all Americans approved of school integration, while a high 72% in the South disapproved.[50] Most jobs, many public facilities, and virtually all social interaction showed marks of segregationist attitudes.

Furthermore, the Crusade for Citizenship was a cooperative endeavor, which placed King and the new Southern Christian Leadership Conference in a position of learning from, and informing other groups like the NAACP and various support organizations. It infused new vigor into the black movement and furthered the maturation of black reform strategy. The historic work of the NAACP in the courts and in its own programs of citizenship extension found common ground with a direct-action movement spawned by the growing activism of southern black leaders. That there were some tensions between SCLC and the NAACP was inevitable. They were different in structure and philosophy, but basically they shared common goals.

Fittingly enough, Abraham Lincoln's birthday marked the beginning of the Crusade for Citizenship. On February 12, 1958, approximately 13,000 people assembled in rallies held simultaneously in twenty-two southern cities to dramatize the voter-registration drive. Although it happened to be the coldest night in the South in fifty years, the shivering crowds would not be deterred as they came to hear ministers and civil rights workers speak out for the vote and full citizenship. King's father spoke to a rally in Nashville, while the SCLC president addressed a crowd in Miami. "Let us make our intentions clear," King told the Florida gathering. "We must and will be free. We want freedom now. We can't wait another hundred and fifty years." He was adamant in condemning the negative image projected by denial of black suffrage. Only if the United States became unified across racial lines could it make a believable case for democracy in other parts of the world. What was needed, King argued, was "examples of democracy in action," not voteless victims of the "denial and corruption of our heritage."[51]

King's speech and the other rallies brought more pressure on the White House, where there was much uncertainty, if not confusion, about what to do. Assistant to the President, E. Frederick Morrow, a black, noted many frustrations he experienced in attempting to get the administration to act.[52] As for Eisenhower, he was still opposed to the excesses of white backlash but persistent in his belief that more time and patience were needed.

In May 1958, Eisenhower aired his views at a Negro Summit Conference sponsored by the National Newspaper Publishers Association. Racial problems, said the President, "have their roots in the human heart and in human emotions." They could not be resolved by logic, he argued. "We must depend more on better and more profound education than simply on the letter of the law." With that, he essentially turned the racial issue over to local communities and to patience and forebearance.[53] Rebuttals abounded. The 400 black leaders at the Summit had different views from the President's. Asa Philip Randolph spoke of the losing battles blacks were fighting against racism and the "corrosive spirit of despair and creeping paralysis of faith among Negroes." Thurgood Marshall, who had been the key attorney in the *Brown* case, and Lester B. Granger joined the chorus of disagreement.[54] The mood favored more direct federal effort, not less.

At the end of the month, SCLC held a conference in Missississippi and again articulated its demands in an urgent appeal to Eisenhower to call "an immediate conference" with black leaders.[55] This time the President felt compelled to act, and on June 23 he received King, Wilkins, Randolph and Granger in the Oval Office. He had no concrete program to offer the black leaders, but the symbolism of the high level meeting was impressive. King was a comparative newcomer, but no longer simply regional in influence. Wilkins and Randolph were the old hands of the black movement, and Granger was an educator and former adviser to civil and military officers and had served as head of the National Urban League since 1941. Eisenhower knew that he was in the company of influential black spokesmen whose demands could not be easily ignored.

Randolph spoke for the group, presenting the nine proposals similar to the ones King delivered to Nixon the previous year. Randolph asked Eisenhower to make a nation-wide statement that the law would be vigorously enforced with all the resources at his disposal. Randolph also requested a White House conference on peaceful compliance with the Supreme Court's rulings and new executive directives to government agencies to provide information and guidance on integration in local communities. The other six demands included a new civil rights law to strengthen the Attorney General's authority, and more extensive Justice Department involvement in the ongoing Little Rock case and in protecting voting rights. There were specific requests also for extension of the Civil Rights Commission which was due to expire in 1959, federal action against those who had bombed churches, homes, and community centers, and a bold request that the President oppose the use of federal money to support any agency, service, or business that practiced racial discrimination.[56]

If these black leaders expected some clear sign of support from Eisenhower on this program, they were surely disappointed. The President referred to the weight of world problems like the crises in Algeria and Lebanon, but he responded only mildly to the proposals. According to Coretta King, her husband

60

came away from the meeting unruffled, but now convinced that Eisenhower's conservatism was "fixed and rigid, and any evil defacing of the nation had to be extracted bit by bit by a tweezer because the surgeon's knife was an instrument too radical to touch this best of all possible societies."[57]

For the Southern Christian Leadership Conference as well as the King family, difficult and unexpected trials began in the late summer of 1958 and continued throughout the next year. After a short vacation in Mexico, King returned to the work of the movement and the completion of his first book, *Stride Toward Freedom*, which told the story of the Montgomery boycott. It also presented his basic views on society, reform, and faith.

In early September 1958 King was drawn into a legal bout in Montgomery after Ralph Abernathy was attacked in his church office on August 29. Abernathy pressed charges and was soon in a court hearing. King's effort to see one of the attorneys at the courthouse brought his arrest on September 3 for "loitering." He was handled roughly by the police officers. As it turned out, King was given the choice of paying a fine or going to jail. Emulating Gandhi, he chose jail. Although someone paid King's fine and prevented his incarceration, the SCLC president took the opportunity to make one of his most cogent statements of his philosophy of civil disobedience. To the judge, King said:

> Let me assure you, your Honor, that my position at this point is not some histrionic gesture or publicity stunt, for moral convictions never stem from the selfish urge for publicity. Neither am I motivated by a desire to be a martyr, for without the love even martyrdom becomes spiritual pride. My action is motivated by the impelling voice of conscience and a desire to follow truth and the will of God wherever they lead. . .[58]

The Montgomery episode was trivial compared to the trauma King experienced two weeks later in New York. On September 20, he was in a Harlem department store promoting his new book, when a forty-two year old black woman, Mrs. Izola Ware Curry, stabbed him with a razor-sharp Japanese letter opener. The deranged woman almost punctured King's aorta as she plunged the improvised weapon deeply into his chest. By the painstaking efforts of surgeons, and as King and his family would see it, a kind providence, the young civil rights leader survived. Outpourings of sympathy from many people deeply moved and encouraged the Kings. But even more meaningful to them were the many intimate conversations they had at bedside about their future and the value of the work they were doing.

As King was released from the hospital on October 3, it was a time of introspection and adjustment, rather than an in-stride resumption of old patterns. In February 1959, with financial support from concerned friends, he decided to accept an invitation from the Gandhi Peace Foundation to make a speaking tour of India. A long-time dream was fulfilled as he, Coretta, and Lawrence Reddick flew to India to visit the places where Gandhi once walked and taught.

Seeing Gandhi's homeland was an almost mystical experience for the Kings and led to Martin's feeling that he fell short of his great Indian mentor's example. There was some disillusionment as they viewed the starving masses still present in India more than a decade after Gandhi's assassination. Nevertheless, the trip was a refreshing and inspiring experience and a prelude to an even more vigorous commitment to the cause of nonviolent social change in the United States.[59]

Upon returning home, King concluded that the time had come for him to leave his pastorate in Montgomery and give himself more completely to the work of SCLC. On November 29, 1959, a tearful King announced his resignation to an equally saddened congregation at Dexter Avenue Baptist Church. It would become effective at the end of January 1960, when he would return to Atlanta to work with his father at Ebenezer Baptist Church and be closer to the center of SCLC.

Meanwhile, the Southern Christian Leadership Conference faced the new challenges of the voter registration campaign and the diversification of its activities. By 1959 its organizational structure was largely in place and regular meetings of the Board twice a year planned its general programs. Annual conventions in the early fall continued the sequence begun in Atlanta and

New Orleans in 1957. The first two were in Norfolk, Virginia (1958) and Columbia, South Carolina (1959).

There was some encouragement from the first report of the Civil Rights Commission that was made public in the fall of 1959. The report began with a vigorous endorsement of civil and human rights and affirmed the "fundamental principles of the Founding Fathers." Its evidence of black disenfranchisement in the South was devastating. In some areas where blacks represented a quarter or more of the potential electorate, they comprised only three or four percent of the registered voters. Despite an increase from about 595,000 black registered voters in 1947 to roughly 1,200,000 in 1956, the vast majority of Negroes remained voteless.[60]

None of this was news to the NAACP, SCLC, or CORE, but to have it officially confirmed after more than a year of investigative hearings, added substance to the appeals of the Crusade for Citizenship. Furthermore, the Commission recommended specific changes similar to those urged already by black leaders, including several related to federal enforcement of voting rights. With little surprise these recommendations were received negatively in the South. Coming near the end of the Commission's statutory life, several southern politicians used them as further reason to end it at that point. The issue of states' rights and the specter of undue federal interference again were aired in the Congress. However both the House and the Senate voted overwhelmingly to extend the life of the Commission for two more years.

In its Third Annual Convention in Columbia, South Carolina in September 1959, SCLC commended the Civil Rights Commission for its report but urged further action. Specifically the convention wanted federal registrars to assure voting rights for blacks and favored a constitutional amendment on universal suffrage. SCLC also strongly favored integration of schools where the 1954 decision was still not implemented, calling for federalization of schools where local officials refused to provide open facilities.[61]

The Columbia convention also demonstrated a growing

awareness of longer-range political involvements as it resolved to place its case "squarely and dramatically" before the upcoming 1960 party conventions.[62] Recognizing the increasing importance of King's public influence, the delegates also voted a resolution calling upon the SCLC president to "seriously consider giving the maximum of his time and energies to the work of the Southern Christian Leadership Conference."[63] As we have seen, that was precisely what King was planning.

Our lot is irrevocably cast, and whatever fate awaits America awaits the Negro; whatever fate awaits the Negro, awaits America.

Louis E. Lomax

3

The Crisis of Nonviolence, 1960–1962

As the new year and the new decade began in 1960, King completed what he could of the unfinished business in Montgomery and settled in Atlanta. He had told the Dexter Avenue congregation that he needed a break from the "giving, giving, and giving and not stopping to retreat" and a chance to think through the tasks history had thrust upon him. It would be no easier in Atlanta but at least he would be close to Ebenezer and to the Auburn Avenue national headquarters of SCLC where he felt he could give himself more broadly to the movement.

Actually, there was not enough to work with effectively. The staff was tiny, although capable, and funds were distressingly short. Ella Baker and MIA secretary Maude Ballou helped King administer the office. Baker was a very able person, but was not comfortable with the way women were often treated as somehow out of place in leadership roles.[1] In any case her tenure as executive director would be short-lived but strategically important. She helped give the national office a professional style and a continuing visibility among affiliated churches and groups.[2]

King lived modestly in Atlanta, with an inexpensive car and a rented house near his offices. He received only $1.00 per year as SCLC president and approximately $6,000 from his pastoral work. Most of the royalties from his writings went to SCLC at a time when large-scale outside support was not yet coming in.[3] He spent much of his office time at Ebenezer rather than SCLC and refrained, somewhat grudgingly, from launching any campaigns in segregated Atlanta. The kind of *de facto* balance of forces among the white establishment, black businessmen, and the larger community left no room, for the moment, for a confrontation there. Elsewhere King and SCLC could challenge the *status quo*, but Atlanta was off limits.

The SCLC Dilemma: Movement vs. Organization

Those who have written about SCLC as if it were simply and totally Martin Luther King, Jr. have missed something essential to a proper historical understanding of both. The thousandfold repetition of the notion that SCLC was "but the lengthened shadow of a man" named King veils as much as it conveys.[4] By temperament and circumstances, King was not an organization man. He spoke in broad, almost eschatological terms about the goals of the movement, and his own personal time was consumed by demands for speeches, conferences, and public appearances of one kind or another. Yet, he was concerned that SCLC be something visible, capable of carrying on a routine as well as engaging in direct-action protest when it was necessary. He made the final decisions, but SCLC had a collegial aspect.

The history of SCLC after 1959 was the story of the interaction of campaigns and organizational development. Both were important to its identity, and neither in itself explains the essence of the organization. Its loose structure sharply contrasted with the NAACP. SCLC had no membership, but rather affiliates which paid a small fee of about $25 to $50. The activities of SCLC were local in nature rather than guided meticulously from Atlanta.[5] But the organization depended upon King's visibility and upon a sense of active movement. Without that sense of carrying on what began in Montgomery, there would have been no Southern Christian Leadership Conference.

As the sit-in movement revitalized the black revolution in early 1960, it became even more imperative that SCLC enlarge its facilities, increase its operations, and broaden its base of support. Ella Baker became directly involved in the youth movement and left her post at SCLC in 1960. Replacing her was

Wyatt Tee Walker, a lean bespectacled young activist from Petersburg, Virginia. Walker brought with him from his Virginia staff Dorothy Cotton and James R. Wood. Miss Cotton became Walker's secretary and later the director of the incipient citizenship education program. James Wood was director of public relations.

When King invited Walker to head the executive office of SCLC in July 1960, he knew what he was getting. Walker was a tall man with a commanding style who could joke about being amiable but expecting perfection from those who worked with him. A graduate of Virginia Union College, he was also an intellectual and a Baptist pastor. The same age as King, he was born in Massachusetts in 1929. In Petersburg he had been involved in school and public facilities desegregation and brought to Atlanta the fervor that was sweeping the youth of the nation in 1960. As King's "nuts and bolts" man he was somewhat tougher than the SCLC president in dealing with people and often shielded King from some of the less pleasant tasks of leadership. He also had a sense of the necessity for SCLC to be an activist organization with well-tuned operative machinery.[6] The presence of Walker, Cotton, and Wood at SCLC national headquarters was a harbinger of an influx of young talent that marked its history in the early sixties.

The Sit-In Movement

The sit-in movement and the presidential election that brought John F. Kennedy into the White House were the two most important external events bearing on SCLC's development in 1960. The first infused the black movement with a potent new vibrancy and the latter shaped the political context within which King's organization had to work. As Kennedy began his campaign for nomination in the early primaries, snatching victories from the older Democratic leaders like Hubert Humphrey and Stuart Symington, four young black students in Greensboro, North Carolina opened the door to the most influential desegregation effort since Montgomery. John Hope Franklin was not alone in describing the resultant resurgence of black liberation as "the most profound, revolutionary changes in the status of black Americans that had occurred since emancipation."[7]

The sit-ins caught everyone, including King, by surprise. Like the Italian unification leader Camillo di Cavour in 1860, black leaders learned that their resurgence had more support at the grassroots than they realized. It is not that the sit-in technique was new. As we saw, it was used by CORE some twenty years before 1960, and the NAACP had sponsored sit-ins in the late fifties in Kansas and Oklahoma.[8] Dr. Kelly Miller Smith, a local NAACP president, had also worked with Fisk students in similar activities before February 1960.[9] But the scope of the 1960 sit-ins and related stand-ins, pray-ins, etc. was gargantuan. They caught the attention of all the media, and immediately affected the strategic thinking of many black advocates.

The catalyst was an incident in Greensboro on February 2, 1960. In the bustling F. W. Woolworth's store on that day; the four North Carolina A & T freshmen—Joseph McNeil, David Richmond, Franklin McCain, and Ezell Blair—went to the lunch counter for service. They anticipated resistance and thus a pretext for a local boycott, but not the kind of social explosion that resulted. When the waitress would not serve them because they were black, they refused to budge. Soon other students joined them, and the sit-in spread to other stores in Greensboro. Then other North Carolina cities witnessed sit-ins, and rapidly the tactic spread across the South, Southwest, and Midwest with white and black students joining in. Sympathizers came southward from northern colleges, and the civil rights movement experienced its most important boost since the Montgomery boycott.

Though generally nonviolent, the sit-ins sometimes triggered violent reaction. At times too, militant blacks led the sit-ins, as they did in Columbia, South Carolina in March 1960. In Chattanooga, Tennessee street fighting accompanied the sit-ins and marches that erupted there in late February. Some state and local governments were quick to pass emergency statutes to restrict the sit-ins, often in the form of anti-trespassing laws. Virginia, Georgia and South Carolina were among the states that acted legislatively to restrict this new strategem of black reformers.[10] More courtroom and street battles lay ahead.

Reactions to the sit-ins ranged from the angry resentment of conservatives who saw them as disruptive and arrogant intrusions of public order, to the praise of enthusiastic devotees who viewed them as harbingers of a new age of human relations. Black writers and white civil rights activists almost invariably praised the sit-ins and the youth who participated in them. Lerone Bennett saw the sit-inners as "mirrors reflecting the reality of American life; they were clocks telling America what time it was historically, they were bridges spanning the abyss between two mutually hostile and mutually hateful communities." Bennett argued that the youth movement was directed as much against the slow pace of progress under the integrationist organizations as it was against the white community. It marked a crisis of leadership, and sense of purpose, in the black community. It was not integration they wanted, he said, "they wanted freedom."[11]

Langston Hughes credited the sit-ins with crumbling walls of segregation from North Carolina to Texas. Roy Wilkins, who announced a more extensive direct-action program for the NAACP in the spring of 1960, concluded that the sit-in students "forced the nation to take a new look at the old race problem."[12] In a similar vein—from the white liberal point of view—Anne Braden, editor of the *Southern Patriot*, stressed the moral challenge of direct-action to what she spoke of as the "evils of segregation." To Braden the new social eruptions indicated that "a new society is struggling to be born."[13] Yet, more than they realized, one should add, the sit-in youth were beneficiaries of earlier work by the older civil rights organizations and the paradigm of Montgomery. Progress made before 1960 enabled the sit-in youth to enjoy some legal protections, although not effective in all cases, for their protests. Furthermore, the psychology of resistance had already been anticipated by Rosa Parks. When Joseph McNeil was refused service at the bus depot restaurant in Greensboro just before the historic sit-in, he told his friend Blair that "we ought to have a boycott."[14]

On the other hand, the youth movement was more independent than many older blacks saw at the time and more influential upon them than they realized. "There is little doubt," wrote two scholars who made an in-depth study of the nature and effects of the sit-ins, "that a new mood of impatience and militance was sparked in Negro adults by the sight of their youngsters being heckled and beaten up by white people."[15] While the press emphasized the dramatic violent aspects of the youth protest, many older blacks were moved emotionally by the display of courage it embodied.

The youth themselves were, in part, demonstrating against the established black leadership. Some of the civil rights organizations sought to claim the sit-ins for themselves, or at least give them direction.[16] But the youth maintained their own autonomy as much as they could. "We wanted to sort of destroy the old idea," said Ezell Blair later, "that Negroes had to be told everything to do by the NAACP or CORE."[17] However, the sit-in youth were essentially in harmony with American values as they understood them, and they had considerable respect for King and the nonviolent protest movement. Clayborne Carson has demonstrated that the sit-inners began with modest goals and did not depart radically from tradition. "Quite inadvertently," he concluded, "the four students had set in motion historical forces which they and most of their fellow activists were unable to forecast or even comprehend. . . In the spring of 1960. . . few students would have disagreed with the view that they were motivated by conventional American values."[18]

However conventional their views were, the sit-in students were less patient with segregation than the older blacks were. Interestingly, King was forbidden to eat in the white section of an Atlanta airport restaurant just a few days before the Greensboro incident. He had struck up a conversation with a white man on the plane flying into the city and wanted to continue it over coffee after landing. But the hostess refused and sent King to the "colored section" behind a curtain. The SCLC leader walked out angry and hurt.[19] In contrast, Franklin McCain suddenly realized in Greensboro that "maybe they can't do anything to us. Maybe we can keep it up."[20] King's approach was more comprehensive, more systemic, and less immediate.

Nonetheless, King was a hero to the sit-in young people and to some a kind of pastor. Tradition has it that Blair and McNeil had been influenced by a FOR comic book about King and the Montgomery boycott, although this is not certain.[21] Certainly the nonviolent approach was the model most influential upon the sit-ins. "The movement started out as a movement of nonviolence and as a Christian movement," said McCain, "and we wanted to make that very clear to everybody, that it was a movement that was seeking justice more than anything else and not a movement to start a war. . . . Martin Luther King was a hero. . . but he was not the individual that we had upmost in mind when we started the sit-in movement.[22] Presumably, Gandhi was that person. But to these youth Gandhi and King were closely related.

SCLC participated in the first serious effort to organize the sit-in youth, though the initiative was taken by the students themselves. A conference at Shaw University in Raleigh, North Carolina on Easter weekend, April 16–18, 1960 was the decisive step in organizing the youth movement. It was called by Ella Baker, SCLC's outgoing executive director who was soon to be replaced by Wyatt Tee Walker. Baker arranged for the use of the facilities at her alma mater and served as the principal organizer of the gathering of about 200 people, mostly students.* With $800 she borrowed from SCLC, Baker provided the setting for these young people who came from fifty-eight southern communities and nineteen northern colleges to discuss ways to find a "more unified sense of direction for training and action in nonviolent resistance." The letter which announced the meeting was signed by both Baker and King and promised that the youth themselves would be the center of the discussions, although

* Delegates to the Shaw conference included 126 black students from 56 high schools and colleges in a dozen southern states and the District of Columbia. There were also 12 southern white students, more than 50 northern students and several observers from the National Student Association, Students for a Democratic Society (SDS), and other student and reform groups. It was a meaningful cross-section of American activist youth.

71

there would be adult advisers present.[23] It is generally held that Baker was more inclined than King to encourage the youth to be independent from organizations like SCLC. Actually, King did want to influence the sit-in movement, but he refrained from interfering with the students' wishes.[24]

In the parlance of the sixties, the Shaw conference had features of "a happening," in the sense that spontaneous feelings, romantic notions, youthful idealism, and impatience with the *status quo* converged to lift them emotionally and inspire them to act. Music was deeply influential in the civil rights movement, and Shaw was no exception. They joined hands and sang "We Shall Overcome," helping to establish the song as one of the most familiar rallying choruses of the nonviolent movement. More and more verses would be added over the following months to the song that began:

> We shall overcome, we shall overcome,
> We shall overcome some day.
> Oh, deep in my heart, I do believe
> We shall overcome some day.

Jane Stembridge of Virginia, a white girl who soon became secretary of the organized students, said that the singing of that song was "the most inspiring moment" for her at the conference.[25]

On the other hand, the Shaw conference had been well planned by Baker and several other organizers. Knowledge that King was coming helped draw a sizable crowd, but the painstaking preparatory work was invaluable. Black minister Douglass Moore of Durham contributed to the planning and enlistment of delegates, and James Lawson was pivotal. Lawson was part of the influential Nashville group which did much to shape both the conference and the subsequent course of youth activism. Among them were Marion Barry and Diane Nash of Fisk, John Lewis of the American Baptist Theological Seminary, and others who would make deep marks on the history of the youth movement. They were committed to nonviolence, careful planning, and to King personally. John Lewis, one of several who had been influenced by the Montgomery movement, saw in King a "Moses, using organized religion and emotionalism with the Negro church as an instrument, as a vehicle, toward freedom."[26]

Ella Baker addressed the students and encouraged them to persist in their cause and affirmed the value of the fellowship she saw emergent among them. Already in her fifties, Baker was highly regarded by the youth and was considered by a number of them as their "spiritual mother."[27] She was more inclined than King to encourage their independence, but it does not follow that she opposed cooperation between the young people and older adults.[28]

King's presence was strongly felt at the conference. He gave a press conference before its opening, suggesting an agenda for the students that included selective boycotting, adherence to nonviolence, and organizational planning. Obviously, the SCLC president hoped that the students would emulate the Montgomery pattern and dedicate themselves to fundamental beliefs of the southern Christian movement. His address on Saturday decried the view that the students were radical or communist inspired. "I didn't need Nikita Khrushchev," he said, "to come to the United States to tell me someone's standing on my neck." King urged the students to organize more formally so they could deliberately direct their energies and he offered them SCLC aid and advice. He again encouraged them to use selective buying and to be willing to go to jail in resistance to segregation.[29]

If King was the spiritual mentor of the Shaw student delegates, it was the other keynote speaker, James Lawson, who most influenced the process of organization. His personal bearing, ideological depth, and practical experience made him stand out even in the company of the unusual number of influential Nashville youth of the early sixties. A graduate student at the Vanderbilt School of Divinity studying for the Methodist ministry, Lawson had been an activist for several years by 1960. He had been the Southern secretary for the Fellowship of Reconciliation since 1957 and before that a missionary and a conscientious objector during the Korean War. Lawson's background was in pacifist activism and faith-related social reform.[30] In Nashville his association with Dr. Kelly Miller Smith and the young activists like Diane Nash, Marion Barry, C. T. Vivian and James Bevel was mutually influential. Vivian recalls that Lawson was the spiritual mentor or 'Guru' of the group.[31] Despite what has been termed his "mystical bent," Lawson was basically practical and emphasized the political forces that shape society.[32] Active in the sit-ins in Nashville, he had been expelled from the Vanderbilt Divinity School for his presumed radicalism.

Lawson saw the need for affiliation with older adults to provide "continuity and stability" since student generations rotated every four years or so. He was accustomed to working with older adults in the Nashville Christian Leadership Conference (NCLN), an affiliate of SCLC, and while he did not always agree with them, Lawson recognized the value of association with ministers, teachers, and other adult partners.[33] His was a deliberate approach that had regard for spontaneity such as the Greensboro sit-inners evinced, but in his mind the key was planning and organization.[34]

Yet Lawson was no carbon copy of the civil rights organizational leadership. He decried the view that the present youth generation was "silent" or "uncommitted." Young people, he argued, were waiting for "that cause, that ideal, that event, that 'actualizing of their faith' which would catapult their right to speak powerfully to their nation and world." He went on to deny that the student movement was simply a fad. To him it was a substantive expression of resistance to a too slow pace of integration and lack of clarity on the real issues. For too long, he insisted, blacks and whites had "pretended that all was well" when in fact real community had not been realized. Repeatedly, Lawson referred to the Christian faith and its radical demands and methods. He closed by observing that "The extent to which the Negro joined by many others apprehends and incorporates non-violence determines the degree that the world will acknowledge fresh social insight from America."[35]

From the Raleigh conference emerged the organizational base

of the Temporary Student Nonviolent Coordinating Committee, later revised to Student Nonviolent Coordinating Committee (SNCC).* Over the following months SNCC was organized more fully. Meeting at Atlanta University in May with King, Lawson, and Baker, it made plans for offices, newsletters, and further direct-action activities. SNCC met again in Atlanta in October and put the organization on a permanent footing. It was at this point that 'Temporary' was dropped from the name. Although not a formal subsidiary of SCLC, it would adhere to the nonviolent philosophy and maintain close relations with that organization. SCLC wrote SNCC into its budget and provided legal defense funds, as did the NAACP and CORE, for those arrested during sit-in demonstrations.[36] Marion Barry was elected chairman.

The statement of purpose drafted by SNCC in 1960 graphically illustrated its adherence to a philosophy of nonviolent love-in-action:

> We affirm the philosophical or religious ideal of nonviolence as the foundation of our purpose, the presupposition of our faith, and the manner of our action. Nonviolence as it grows from the Judaic-Christian traditions seeks a social order of justice permeated by love. Integration of human endeavor represents the first step towards such a society. . . . Such love goes to the extreme; it remains loving and forgiving even in the midst of hostility. It matches the capacity of evil to inflict suffering with an even more enduring capacity to absorb evil, all the while presisting in love.
>
> By appealing to conscience and standing on the moral nature of human existence, nonviolence nurtures the atmosphere in which reconciliation and justice become actual possibilities.[37]

This seemed to confirm what the *Christian Century* had said in March: that Negro young people "have begun to learn from Martin Luther King, Jr., who learned from Gandhi, the power of truth, love and self-respect.[38] That same editorial, on the other hand, warned that infiltration by advocates of violence and hatred could damage the movement.

* In 1969 as it took a more nationalistic and less nonviolent course, SNCC was renamed the Student National Coordinating Committee.

For several months after the Shaw conference, SNCC depended upon the support of SCLC, the National Student Association, and other organizations for financing, office space and equipment, and other necessities. "Despite such backing," wrote Carson, "SNCC would probably not have survived its first summer had it not been for the energy and skills of (Ella) Baker and (Jane) Stembridge."[39] These two worked with the growing inner circle of committed SNCC leaders to give it a focus and an organization with which to work. The sit-in movement was already showing signs of waning at the time of the October 1960 meeting in Atlanta. Renewal came with the Freedom Ride movement that began in May 1961. From that point, SNCC became a vanguard of the deepening black revolution, paralleling a similar resurgence in the older CORE organization which sponsored the initial Freedom Rides.

SCLC and the New Wave of Protest

How did all this affect King and SCLC? The simplest answer is that the youth protest movement caught King by surprise, put him in an awkward position, and opened the door for rifts between him and the activist youth. And, to be sure, there is some truth in this. But for a clearer picture we must recall the decisive factors in the SCLC situation: King's personal circumstances, organizational plans already in place, and the sit-ins' impact upon the political context. It is the interaction of these elements that provides the best answer.

As 1960 began, SCLC's focus was on continuing the boycott or selective buying tactic as a means to force further desegregation and fair hiring practices for blacks, and on voter registration. With the elections approaching in the fall of 1960, the second was becoming more pressing. Projected numbers of new black registrants were not materializing, indicating that more was needed to get blacks interested in the democratic process. On top of this, there was a concerted effort by anti-integrationist whites to resist increases in the black electorate. The public was aware of Congressional resistance to voting rights legislation, but this was only the most visible manifestation. At local levels, blacks who showed interest in politics ran the risk of losing their jobs, and those who tried to educate them in that direction also often met reprisals.[40] The new Civil Rights Act signed by Eisenhower on May 6, 1960 was hailed by the President as "an historic step forward in the field of civil rights," but its provisions on voting rights were weak.[41] Although it did strengthen the authority of the FBI in investigating violence and provided for federal voting referees and mandatory retention of voting records for five years, the new law fell far short of black demands and the goals of the Civil Rights Commission.[42]

Thus, SCLC joined the NAACP and SNCC in putting pressure on the political conventions and selected presidential candidates to support strong voting rights and civil rights planks. King met with candidate John Kennedy on June 22, 1960 to urge the Massachusetts Senator to take a strong stand on better voting rights policies, control of violence, and a number of other pressing issues. Kennedy had not been viewed by black leaders in a positive light in the past, partly because he voted with the conservatives on the jury trial amendment in the 1957 Civil Rights Act. Furthermore, Kennedy had considerable southern support, which did not seem to be a propitious sign. But Kennedy was deliberately seeking to improve his image among blacks, and by mid-1960 King and others were beginning to see in him a possible ally.[43] Still, King would not endorse Kennedy. The SCLC head wanted to retain some leverage in making direct appeals to both political conventions as they shaped their platforms in July and August.

Even after Kennedy's nomination, it was not clear to black leaders just how far he or any other candidate would go in pushing for civil rights. In general, the Kennedy-Johnson ticket ran well ahead of the Nixon-Lodge Republican slate among black Americans, but it was well known that Kennedy depended upon his key southern support and could not be counted on to make a radical departure in executive action in behalf of minorities.

Meanwhile, King's personal trials, Walker's efforts to enlarge SCLC's programs, and presidential politics began to converge in such a way as to draw King and SCLC more deeply into the resurgence of black protest. Legal battles with the state of Alabama were not new to King, but this round was perhaps the most disturbing ever. In February 1960, King was arrested in his church office at Ebenezer and charged with falsifying his 1956 and 1958 income tax returns. Behind this plot lay Alabama officials' allegation that King had dishonestly taken money from the MIA and SCLC and had failed to report over $30,000 to the IRS. Priding himself in his impeccable honesty in matters of money, King was deeply offended. To make matters worse, he was charged with perjury during the trial. Not until May 28 did the all-white jury acquit him of the charges. With obvious relief, King told his Ebenezer congregation the next morning that "Something happened to that jury." Perhaps, King speculated, it could happen more broadly in the nation.[44]

The worst was yet to come, however. The legal bout in Montgomery had been difficult and expensive. Stanley Levison had garnered a corps of attorneys to defend King, but the task was not easy even for that capable group which included Fred Gray, S. S. Seay, Jr., Arthur Shores of Montgomery, and two other prominent lawyers. Then on May 29, some King supporters placed a lengthy advertisement in the *New York Times* to help raise money for King's defense.[45] The city of Montgomery and state of Alabama sued those who had signed the ad and demanded a public retraction of their "lies and crude slander." The *New York Times* did retract statements made in the controversial advertisement, but this did not end the matter. Eventually, the state of Alabama won a $2 million judgment, and several of SCLC's key leaders sustained heavy financial losses. To carry the case to the Supreme Court required a $4 million bond, half of which had to be raised by King's supporters, the other half by the *New York Times*. Ralph Abernathy, Fred Shuttlesworth, and Joseph Lowery all lost considerable property and money.[46]

During that same eventful summer of 1960, Walker and his associates worked at length on a comprehensive blueprint for SCLC program development. Conceived in broad outline while Ella Baker was still in office and refined in the light of unexpected events in 1960, the General Program was slated for presentation to the annual convention in Shreveport, Louisiana in October. The plan was cast in fairly broad terms but reflected some concrete goals of the Walker administration and King's broadening interests. For the plan to have any chance of success, more personnel and a much larger income would be required. SCLC's working budget for 1959–1960 was about $57,000, and although it climbed to over $100,000 in fiscal 1960–1961, much more was needed.[47] White opposition was not the only barrier SCLC encountered. There was also illiteracy among blacks, lack of motivation and experience in citizenship, and indifference that would yield only to massive propaganda efforts. These things were costly.

The General Program would be implemented in what were called "phases," although they were to be basically coterminous. Phase I would concentrate on the Action Program of "coordinated, simultaneous, Southwide, nonviolent mass action against segregated public facilities. Included were lunch counters and transportation terminals, an emphasis already agreed on before the Greensboro sit-ins. Accompanying the demonstrations would be economic boycotts and voter registration drives.

Phase II marked an enrichment of SCLC's outreach and demanded vastly increased funding. With it, the organization envisaged an educational program providing short concentrated seminars on citizenship and voting. This would become one of SCLC's distinctive contributions to the southern movement, although the press rarely covered these seminal efforts to raise the literacy and political consciousness of southern blacks and poor whites. Much of the inspiration and technique of SCLC's training seminars came from the Highlander Folk School in Monteagle, Tennessee and specifically from a black teacher, Septima P. Clark, who had worked with the Highlander school for several years after being ousted from her teaching post in Charleston, South Carolina in 1955 because of her anti-segregationist efforts there. Septima Clark's involvement with the Highlander adult teaching program began as early as 1953 when she attended a workshop on school desegregation sponsored by the school.[48] From that began her work on Johns Island, the largest of the Sea Islands off the Charleston coast. The Johns Island work among the Gullah-speaking blacks established a new base for the kind of adult training Highlander had been involved in since 1932 under Myles and Aimee Horton, a white couple deeply interested in integrated education and labor leadership.[49]

The educational outreach that grew out of SCLC's contact with Septima Clark and the Highlander Folk School will be treated in more detail in the following chapter, but it is necessary to note here that in 1960 Dorothy Cotton, King, and other SCLC leaders had already made contact with Monteagle and were preparing to develop their own citizenship educational program operating through local, regional, and national conferences, a correspondence institute, and summer youth and adult educational seminars. The cost would be met, it was projected, by SCLC resources, special contributions, and nominal participation fees.[50] To that end, SCLC began to seek large foundational grants, a task that carried over into 1961 and beyond.

Phases III and IV dealt with fund-raising and public relations. SCLC would seek to become financially stable, building a list of donors and grant sources that would relieve the pressure of constant appeals to individuals. Walker tightened bookkeeping procedures and the national office began to approach systematically its mailings, follow-up thank you letters, and accounting, but even at that there were moments of confusion and certain questionable procedures for some years. SCLC was learning that to raise money one had to spend money. All of this would require a larger staff, more field workers, and additional equipment for printing and distribution. King's unexpected legal battles aggravated the problems involved.

Above all, the best possible image had to be projected to prospective supporters. Since King was already widely known and identified with certain strong qualities, he was to be treated as the symbol and substance of SCLC. As leader of the nonviolent movement, King would be presented in terms of moderation: "devout, reverant but not pious; humble, determined, modest but not retiring; dedicated but not fanatical; courageous, but not intimidating." These were honestly held estimations of King, no doubt, and should not be taken as pure propaganda, but they were set forth as the essence of SCLC as a whole. Publicity, choice of personnel, and all of the workings of SCLC it was felt, "must reflect the qualities of the leadership symbol."[51]

Walker was an insider, a true believer in the King mystique. Others were less generous, and just as the General Program was being discussed at the annual convention in Shreveport, forces were working in another direction. The presidential election was in its last month, and King was quite concerned now with the outcome. The political conventions had made some concessions to black demands, at least in wording of certain platform planks, but it was still imperative that whoever was elected be more than a passive President on civil rights. By now Kennedy was well ahead among black voters, but the election was too close for any comfort.

At the same time, the sit-in movement spread to Atlanta, and its leaders were appealing to King to help them. He was, after all, the overreaching symbol of the nonviolent movement. They needed him, and it was with much personal pain that King rejected their initial pleadings. He had agreed not to disturb Atlanta, and there were political risks with the Presidential and Congressional elections so near. There were the older local blacks to think about, too. What if the youngsters drew too much support from the masses and undermined their own role as spokesmen in the community?[52] An earlier sit-in effort in the city in the spring had dwindled with the beginning of the students' summer vacation, but this time it might be more disruptive. King was pulled in several directions.

When the "second battle of Atlanta" began on October 19, King did join in, and was arrested in the first wave of protests against the huge Rich's Department Store. Along with him, some fifty others were jailed, including Lonnie King, who had strongly appealed to King for help, as well as Otis Moss, Ruby Doris

Smith, Fred C. Bennette (the "commandant" of the protest), and many more who were committed to "jail, not bail." Even King's father thought the move unwise. And King himself thought that it was unfortunate to protest against Rich's since the Rich family had been very generous to blacks and black colleges.

Worse than the political dilemmas of the Atlanta skirmish was the serious danger it presented to King's life. He had pledged to stay in jail for years if necessary, and as it turned out that was a distinct possibility. Most of the protesters received suspended sentences, thanks to the intervention of Mayor William Hartsfield. But King remained in jail. And suddenly, a ghost returned to haunt him in what was to be a parody of justice. Earlier, he had been arrested for not having a Georgia driver's license—a detail he forgot to attend to after moving from Montgomery. Now he was suddenly spirited away to DeKalb county jail. He was sentenced harshly. . . four months at hard labor in the state penitentiary. The incredible drama deepened when the SCLC president was secretly moved to Reidsville a week later. He and his family feared that he might never be seen again. When the press learned of it, newspapers, including the *Atlanta Constitution*, spoke out candidly against the abuse of King's rights, and NAACP branches all over the country communicated their disapproval to the Governor.[53]

It was the decision of Kennedy and his aides to step into the Georgia crisis that seems to have broken the logjam and, at the same time, endeared him to many black voters just a few days before the election. Both President Eisenhower and candidate Nixon refused to take action, or even issue a clear statement of opposition. Rather, Kennedy's brother and campaign manager, Robert, telephoned Judge Oscar Mitchell in Georgia asking about King's right to bail. Senator Kennedy himself phoned Coretta King, assuring her of his concern for her husband and empathizing with what she and the family were going through.[54] On the next day, October 27, King was released on bail.

It is impossible to tell just how much all this affected such a close election as that of November 1960. But it certainly moved

Dr. King, Sr., to make a frank endorsement of Kennedy, and in all likelihood it contributed to the large margin of victory Kennedy enjoyed among blacks in states where the overall vote was close. In his provocative study of the election, *The Making of the President 1960*, Theodore H. White notes that in Illinois Kennedy won by only 9,000 votes while an estimated 250,000 blacks voted for him, and in Michigan another quarter of a million blacks supported him as he gained only a 67,000 vote margin over Nixon. Several other states revealed a similar pattern. White concludes that Kennedy's move was crucial to his victory.[55]

If King owed much to Kennedy, it is also true that the President was indebted to the many black voters who gave him the slim margin of victory over Nixon. King did not let up on his pressuring Kennedy for more assertiveness in civil rights. In early February 1961, he challenged the new administration in an article in *The Nation* entitled "Equality Now." This was the first of a long series of articles which focused on the need for federal assistance. King wanted far-reaching legislation on voting rights and integration, "moral persuasion" by the young President, as well as executive orders to guarantee basic rights and a deliberate alliance between the White House and those "citizens who are crusading for their freedom within our borders."[56]

Kennedy did take certain steps to associate his administration with a positive civil rights image. He appointed blacks to high federal jobs, including former New Deal participant Robert C. Weaver as Housing Administrator. On March 6, 1961, just one month after the appearance of King's article, Kennedy issued Executive Order 10925 which established the President's Committee on Equal Employment Opportunity. He also ordered a full study of current government employment practices and of the status of minorities in "every department, agency, and office of the federal government."[57]

It was a good beginning, and certainly marked a noticeable break with previous laissez-faire policies. But the Kennedy administration did not completely satisfy even the more conservative black leadership. The same pressures that worked against integration at the local level also militated against a comprehensive voting rights bill and other reforms. Preoccupied with the recent Bay of Pigs fiasco, the President delegated the main efforts in civil rights to his brother, Attorney General Robert Kennedy, and to Assistant Attorney General Burke Marshall, who decided to use negotiations with local officials as their front-line strategem, with court action as a reserve pressure.[58] Hardly had they begun to function in this area when the Freedom Ride movement was launched in May 1961.

Although fewer people participated in them than in the sit-ins, the freedom rides had a more powerful impact on the nation and upon black consciousness. The freedom rides raised blacks' awareness of their identity and added pressure upon the federal government to guarantee rights. They also mirrored, and increased, the intense feelings within SNCC, CORE, and other organizations that the federal government was contradicting its pronouncements about democracy in the world by failing to guarantee it at home.[59]

The Freedom Ride movement began in May 1961 under the aegis of CORE and its newly chosen national director, James Farmer. Unlike the sit-ins, the freedom rides did not come as a surprise. CORE's Rock Hill, South Carolina movement of 1960 stimulated interest in a ride through the deep South to test discrimination in interstate travel and to engender support for a broader frontal assault on segregation in general. The concept was not unprecedented. As early as April 1947, eight blacks and eight whites left Washington, D.C. on a 'Journey of Reconciliation' sponsored by CORE and FOR shortly after the *Morgan v. Virginia* (1946) case against segregation in interstate transit. Among the participants in this prototype journey through Virginia and North Carolina were Bayard Rustin and white liberal and pacifist James Peck.

The 1961 freedom rides were much larger and more explosive than the 1947 precursor, although they began inauspiciously. On May 1 a group of seven blacks and six whites met in Washington for orientation, including training in nonviolence.[60] Three days later they set out for New Orleans via Atlanta and other intermediate sites. They encountered resistance in Danville, Virginia and other points en route to Georgia. John Lewis and his associate Albert Bigelow were beaten in Rock Hill, South Carolina.[61]

The worst was yet ahead. The two buses, one a Trailways carrier and the other a Greyhound, left Atlanta on Mother's Day (May 14). As they crossed into Alabama, the Greyhound bus, running about an hour ahead of the other, was attacked by a white mob near Anniston. Tires were slashed, windows smashed, and a fire bomb was thrown abroad. Several passengers suffered smoke inhalation as the bus was burned, and others were beaten. The Trailways bus did not stop as its stunned passengers looked back at the carnage. When it arrived in Anniston, that bus also was attacked and the riders were beaten with tire irons and sticks. Arriving too late to restrain the violence, local police were of little help in either case.[62]

Meanwhile Fred Shuttlesworth sent cars from Birmingham to pick up the stranded freedom riders. He had warned of further mob violence in Birmingham, and the Anniston attack was indeed a prelude to more resistance there as another white group met the riders with verbal insults and beatings. James Peck was abused so severely that fifty-three stitches were required to patch his battered head and face. Several others were also hurt, but again there was no help from police.[63]

Finally on May 17 the first freedom ride arrived in New Orleans on the anniversary of the May 1954 *Brown* decision. This was not the original plan. They had expected to go on to Montgomery, but no bus drivers would take the riders from Birmingham. Air travel was also blocked. Thus, the trip was truncated somewhat as the group flew to New Orleans aboard a special flight arranged by the Justice Department.[64] On the same day, however, another group of riders, sponsored by SNCC and including SCLC affiliated students, left Nashville for Alabama. Among them were Diane Nash and James Lawson. The Nashville riders also confronted violent opposition as they journeyed to Birmingham and Montgomery. Promising to keep order on the highways, Alabama governor John Patterson adamantly refused succor for the riders or to escort "the agitators."[65]

Further attacks came when the second group reached Montgomery. Twenty-one-year-old James Zwerg, a white student from Wisconsin was beaten into a bloody mess in Montgomery and others were battered severely and jailed. SCLC felt it had to act quickly, and so King flew from a speaking engagement in Chicago to try to help after unsuccessfully attempting to telephone President Kennedy and the Attorney General. The administration was aware of the situation, however, and sent federal marshals to Montgomery. President Kennedy appealed for calm, but it did not materialize. Ku Klux Klan marchers angrily confronted the riders, and many other local citizens cried out against them. As King spoke in the First Baptist Church where Abernathy pastored, the violence mushroomed. Windows of the church were broken, and before the melee ended federal marshals hurled tear gas to subdue the mob.

This was a trying experience for King. The freedom rides, which had begun so violently, forced him to face realities more pointedly. Some militants were beginning to charge that King did not have the personal courage to participate in a ride himself. A cleavage opened in black circles between those who wanted to continue this strategy regardless of the consequences and those who feared that more harm than good would ensue. The Montgomery crisis did not halt the rides; in fact, it triggered more. Riders soon set out for Mississippi, whose Governor Barnett expressed sympathy with Governor Patterson of Alabama. Not surprisingly, freedom rides encountered serious resistance in Mississippi and more people were hurt and jailed.

In Washington Attorney General Robert Kennedy called for a "cooling off" period, but it was rejected both by the freedom riders and SCLC, as well as the NAACP and CORE.[66] King would not pursue the freedom ride technique nearly so forcefully as SNCC or CORE since he was counting more than they on the possibility of federal action to end segregation in transportation. Yet, he would not agree to restrain the movement either. Before the end of the first month of freedom rides, he and his organization acted to assist them. SCLC worked with CORE and SNCC to provide guidance to the freedom riders and training in nonviolence.

A Freedom Riders Coordinating Committee was formed at a meeting in Atlanta on May 26. Called by King, the gathering included representatives from SCLC, the Nashville Christian Leadership Conference, SNCC, the National Student Association, and CORE. There they determined to support the rides until interstate transportation was safe and equally available to all people. In fact, they decided to enlarge the freedom ride effort in order to focus national attention on the "denial of legal rights of interstate travelers by certain citizens and public officials in hard-core Southern states."[67] Wyatt Walker of SCLC, Diane Nash of the SCLC affiliate NCLC, Edward King of SNCC, and Gordon Carey of CORE formed a permanent coordinating committee, and CORE joined SCLC in depositing funds to be used by the freedom ride movement.[68]

SCLC continued to support the freedom ride technique throughout the summer. In late September, the conference held its annual convention in Nashville, the starting point of the more militant freedom ride group of May. Under the theme 'The Deep South in Social Revolution," SCLC delegates gathered to map strategy, hear speeches, and above all to be invigorated—as was by then the SCLC custom—by intense sessions on the movement. The freedom riders were honored, and James Lawson delivered a spirited keynote address on the vigorous pursuit of reforms. By then Lawson had finished his theological studies at Boston University and was a pastor in Shelbyville and an SCLC staff director of workshops.[69]

King spoke to a Freedom Rally attended by some 2,000 people at War Memorial Auditorium on September 27. He told the audience that blacks could "not slow up" their integration efforts because "they had a date with destiny." They could not slow up, King averred, because they had their "self-respect to maintain. . . and the welfare of America to maintain. The state of the world will not allow us anemic democracy."[70] Interrupted about twenty times by applause, the SCLC president praised the freedom riders and noted that many cities, including Nashville, had desegregated lunch counters in response to the riders' bold actions. But King knew that integrated lunch counters were only a small beginning. "Not only have we come a long, long way," he said, "but we have a long, long way to go."

Just how true that was became more apparent over the following months as SCLC became involved in a major campaign in Albany, Georgia. Viewed generally as a setback for SCLC, the Albany campaign was critically important for King's organization for a number of reasons. Many things went awry in the Albany confrontation. More than any single event to that time, it called into question the viability of nonviolence and the strength of King's leadership. The campaign also opened deeper rifts between SCLC and SNCC.

Setback in Albany

SCLC did not initiate the Albany campaign and was never in control of it. A small group of reform-minded blacks led by attorney Chevene King came close to opening the door to change in the city in the late fifties by considering a suit against segregated polling stations. But nothing came of it. Most of the black establishment in Albany was inactive in civil rights and even the local NAACP was relatively quiet until after the September 1961 Interstate Commerce decree ordering integration of buses and depots. Then in the fall the NAACP challenged Albany's segregated bus stations, and from that came further legal action and the involvement of SNCC. Two young SNCC field workers, Charles Sherrod and Cordell Reagan, both experienced sit-inners and freedom riders, did much of the preparatory surveillance and organizational work for a campaign while NAACP continued its pressure upon officials. Sherrod and Reagan bused into Albany in October 1961 but received little help from the black population, even from ministers, who worried about church bombings or attacks upon their homes. After several weeks of patient work the SNCC workers put together a front, but even then there was more than a small degree of local black resentment of the "outsiders".[71] Dr.

Chronological Table No. 2: Early Development of SCLC's Programs 1957 to 1962

President: Martin Luther King, Jr. (1957–1968)

Executive Director:

1957	1960	1962
vacant (1957–early 1958)	Ella J. Baker (1959–1960)	Wyatt Tee Walker (1960–1964)
John L. Tilley (1958–1959)		
		Civil Rights Act (May 1960)
		CITIZENSHIP EDUCATION PROGRAM (CEP) begins on large scale
		Dorothy Cotton
		Septima Clark
		Andrew Young
		Wyatt Walker
		James Wood
	King moves to Atlanta	
	Selective buying campaigns	
CRUSADE FOR CITIZENSHIP (with NAACP)	Pressure on political candidates	
Voter registration	GENERAL PROGRAM presented at Shreveport convention	
Encourage voting		
Educate voters	SIT-IN MOVEMENT begins in February 1960 (Greensboro)	
	STUDENT NONVIOLENT COORDINATING COMMITTEE founded in Raleigh (Shaw Conference) (with support by Ella Baker, King) in April 1960	
Local Affiliates established, linked loosely to SCLC		ALBANY CAMPAIGN (1961–1962)
	FREEDOM RIDES begin May 1961 (CORE)	
	Sit-ins spread to Atlanta, King arrested (candidate John Kennedy helps with release)	
	King pressures the new President, John Kennedy, for strong support of civil rights in 1961–1962	

89

William G. Anderson, a black physician, was the most responsive to SNCC's appeals.

When the September ICC decree went into effect on November 1, it was put to the test in Albany. During October and November a coalition took shape: the Negro Voters League, CORE, SNCC, local NAACP branches, the Criterion Club, the Ministerial Alliance of Albany, and the Federation of Colored Women's Clubs being the principals. Dr. Anderson became the president of the Albany Movement and businessman Slater H. King, brother of attorney Chevene King (but no relation to Martin) was chosen first vice president.[72] If, as some say, the Albany Movement was created to cushion the impact of the students Sherrod and Reagan led, this did not mean it had no substance.[73] As these groups came together on November 17, 1961, they pledged themselves to end segregation and discrimination in the city. The statement of purpose that was hammered out committed the group to "totally desegregate all city facilities and secure equal educational and economic opportunities for every citizen."[74]

The Albany campaign developed in such a way that it combined the seemingly paradoxical elements of mass arrests on the one hand, and, on the other, an official nonviolent response to the demonstrators by Police Chief Laurie Pritchett. By his own admission this was more pragmatic than ideological. Pritchett had researched King's nonviolence and was ready to meet the Gandhian method with his own inverted form of it.[75] The die was cast on November 25, 1961 when five blacks who staged a sit-in at the local bus terminal restaurant were refused service. Events snowballed over the next three weeks. By December 10, freedom riders, including Bernard Lee, SCLC's youth director, came into Albany. Hundreds of demonstrators and freedom riders were jailed, and Mayor-elect Asa Kelley asked that the Georgia National Guard be mobilized. Anderson, against the wishes of several SNCC workers, then telephoned Martin King on December 15, asking him to come to Albany at least for one speech.[76] The SCLC president thus entered a campaign he did not plan, at a time when he was busy with efforts to move the

Kennedy administration to more forceful action, and without full support from the Albany leaders.

But come to Albany he did. And with his presence, the campaign gained more national attention and an aura of greater significance. Some locals apparently resented the 'intrusion' by SCLC, especially that of Wyatt Walker, who traveled to the city with King.[77] But probably too much has been made of this since the real problem in Albany was the inadequate preparation and insufficient unity for direct-action in such a tightly segregated region. In any case, problems attended many aspects of the Albany campaign. "De Lawd," as some SNCC critics referred to King, found it hard to exercise effective unifying influence among divided leaders.

King spoke at Shiloh Baptist Church on Saturday evening, and to the large crowd he cried, "Keep moving. Don't get weary children. We will wear them down by our capacity to suffer." Others spoke, seeming to give the effort a focus. Ruby Hurley, NAACP's Southeastern regional director, emphasized the economic and voting pressure blacks could bring. Anderson called for a march the next morning beginning at the church and preceeding to the court house. He urged the audience to eat a good breakfast, put on warm clothes and "walking shoes" for the encounter.[78]

Few were there the next day, and when the march did begin only 250 were present, though others joined later. Leaving the church later than expected, around 4:30 in the afternoon, they set out singing "We Shall Overcome." Chief Pritchett's policemen met the crowd. Pritchett warned the demonstrators to disperse and then proceeded to arrest the marchers. At that point over 700 people had been arrested in Albany. King, Abernathy, and Dr. Anderson were among them. Newspapers all over the world picked up the story, and it seemed that the presence of King was about to bring another turn of the historical page. But it did not, at least not in any decisive way. King refused to pay bail and expressed the hope that thousands of people would support the Albany campaign. Abernathy went so far as to call for a crusade to Albany by people from all over the country. Some local black leaders resented that.[79]

In response to these appeals dozens of white ministers made plans to go to Albany, and the white community acted to head off the influx of outsiders.[80] Asa Kelley, acting in concert with Governor Vandiver, telephoned Robert Kennedy for Justice Department assistance in halting outside agitators. City officials began to negotiate again with the Albany Movement leaders and by Monday, December 18, had put together terms for agreement. Although not in writing, it was agreed that all except the freedom riders would be released on property bonds, that bus and train facilities would be desegregated, and that no further marches or demonstrations would be staged until after January 23. The city promised to hear complaints by blacks once the new city commission began to function. King was released on bail. So were the freedom riders from Atlanta, but charges were still in effect and a trial would be necessary.

The terms of the agreement were disappointing. The Interstate Commerce Commission ruling on desegregation of transit had been in effect since November, so that this was really only an acquiescence on the part of Albany in its enforcement. It saved the city money not to contest it.[81] King lost many of the youthful militants at this point. He appeared too conservative, too quick to take bail and be released after he had pledged to stay in jail through Christmas and had called upon others to join him.

But the struggle was not over in Albany. Movement leaders, including Reagan and Sherrod, anticipated a premature settlement and were prepared to push ahead. They wanted King and his associates out on bail and a truce that would last until King and SCLC were back in Atlanta. They did not trust the commitment of Anderson and King and knew that segregation went much deeper than train stations. What about libraries, parks, and schools, not to mention employment and social segregation? Was Albany the site of racial oppression or not? Something strange had happened with the release of King and the compromise of December 18. Coretta King says that the Albany Movement leaders "had tasted victory, and they wanted to continue, and Martin encouraged them to do so.''[82] King seemed surprised and disappointed, and one could surmise, embarrassed, by his release. "Looking back over it," he said later, "I'm sorry I was bailed out. I didn't understand at the time what was happening. We thought that the victory had been won. When we got out, we discovered it was all a hoax. We had lost a real opportunity to redo Albany, and we lost an initiative that we never regained.''[83]

King and SCLC then helped organize a selective boycott of stores and the bus company, still segregated despite the federal transit regulations. Little was accomplished, however, since blacks in Albany did not have decisive purchasing power. They were more important as bus passengers, but even there trouble came early. In January a young black female passenger was jailed after responding curtly to a driver who tried to move her to a back seat. More trouble, and more arrests followed. Even in courtrooms there was violence and segregation.

In the early months of 1962 the situation in Albany deteriorated. On February 27, King and Abernathy were found guilty of the December charges, but sentencing was deferred until July. In the intervening months, there was more injury and even death. A black cafe operator was shot and killed for resisting arrest. There were many other skirmishes and arrests before the two SCLC leaders returned on July 10 for sentencing. King in these months was troubled by the Albany situation and apparently knew that it was highly risky for his image and the viability of the nonviolent movement. A boost to the movement came in the spring as he came to know and confide in Harry Wachtel, a wealthy Jewish attorney who helped to establish in May 1962 the Gandhi Society for Human Rights to raise money for the cause.[84]

But Albany beckoned King and Abernathy back to the city on July 10 to hear their sentence. It smacked of a setup. The judge was strikingly lenient, giving them the choice of a small monetary fine of $178.00 or forty-five days in jail at hard labor. They quickly chose jail, but someone, presumably a black man, paid their fines and they were released on July 13. Thus King and Abernathy lost another opportunity to use jail to their advantage. This unexpected development occurred as high ranking national figures protested the latest jailing of King. "I've been thrown out of a lot of places," Abernathy said wittily, "but never before have I been thrown out of jail."[85] King returned to Atlanta but was back within a few days ready to "turn Albany upside down." That would be an elusive goal, and there was no small amount of confusion in SCLC circles.

A week later, on July 20, a recent Kennedy appointee, Judge J. Robert Elliot, issued a forceful injunction against further demonstrations, specifically naming King and his associates. After wrestling with the hard question of compliance, King decided to honor the injunction, a fact that displeased SNCC. Although the injunction was overturned four days later by a federal appeals court after Chevene King filed suit, many blacks had already resumed demonstrations in anything but a nonviolent mood. Aggravating the situation was the fact that on July 24 Slater King's pregnant wife Marian was kicked by officers as she tried to bring food to a prison camp. Later her baby was stillborn.[86] Approximately 2,000 enraged blacks began to hurl objects at police officers. Upset by this non-Gandhian turn of events, King called for ending demonstrations. This displeased the militants and widened the gulf between them and King.[87]

King, Abernathy, and Anderson were jailed again on July 27 because of the new outbursts, and they spent two weeks behind bars, pending trial on August 10. Congressional leaders, ministers, and other public figures spoke out against this and tried to pressure Kennedy to act. The President, however, did not intervene, and King's misgivings about the administration were intensified.[88]

In early August, Coretta King and the children Marty and Yoki came to Albany to visit Martin. Other wives were ready to head a march in behalf of jailed demonstrators, and go to jail themselves, among them Juanita Abernathy, Jean (Mrs. Andrew) Young, Ann Walker, and Diane (Nash) Bevel, who was expecting a baby at any time.[89] But as it turned out, again rather anticlimactically, King and his friends were found guilty, given suspended sentences, and were free. Would they leave Albany?

King did leave, but he was back in a few days with about six dozen ministers of various faiths. Some of them participated in demonstrations. Students came also, but would soon have to return to classes. The Ku Klux Klan struck with fury. Around Albany, several towns witnessed the burning and blasting of black churches. King wept. "No matter what we seek," he wrote in the *SCLC Newsletter*, "if it has to do with full citizenship, self-respect, human dignity, and borders on changing the 'Southern Way of Life,' the Negro stands little chance, if any, of securing the approval, consent, or tolerance of the segregationists of the white South."[90]

There was no way to salvage the Albany campaign after September 1962. The city was still segregated and unwilling to negotiate on anything like an equal basis with blacks. The campaign had lacked focus and unity. It had faced an intransigent city government and a clever police chief who had prepared himself for meeting nonviolence with nonviolence. The FBI, King noted, had acquiesced and offered no real assistance, and he openly critized J. Edgar Hoover's organization. It appeared to King that the FBI relied too much on southerners and had only served to confirm the biases of a segregated society.

King was criticized severely for the Albany campaign, some major newspapers arguing that he had retreated. A few writers, like Louis Lomax, implied that in Albany King had failed to follow Gandhi by deciding to get out of jail and out of town.[91] Others, including Bennett, saw some progress within the apparent failure. Blacks had suffered together and despite differences, had shown some courageous resistance and were forced to think about their situation. King admitted that the effort was less than successful, but he too looked for redeeming features. In his *Why We Can't Wait* (1963) he looked back upon Albany like a leader who recognized it as a setback but not a total failure. As King put it, "Our movement had been checked in Albany, but not defeated."

To the reflective SCLC president, the Albany crisis gave his organization valuable experience for what lay ahead. With philosophical perspective he said that human beings must "taste defeat as well as success, and discover how to live with each other.''[92] At least in Albany, local officials had been checked to some degree. They closed libraries and parks in order to avoid integration. Their options had been limited, too, and that brought some consolation. At a deeper level King realized as never before some of the limitations of nonviolence and its concomitants like 'jail not bail'. Blacks could not afford literally to fill the jails, leaving their homes and jobs. There were limits to practicality and options. Injunctions against marches now loomed large as barriers to direct-action.

The crisis of nonviolence that occurred between 1960 and 1962 was not necessarily an indictment of its integrity. Part of it was the birthpangs of a complicated revolutionary surgence that had disparate roots. King and SCLC viewed the youth movement as an expression of some of the same motivations that had prompted the creation of the Southern Christian Leadership Conference a few years ago. There was a sense of community among several black organizations, despite their differences. To ignore the crisis of leadership in the early 1960s would be naive, but to exaggerate it would be superficial.

If Albany was a failure as many writers have judged, it was not simply that for SCLC. Rather it was a learning experience in regard to the need for specific focus instead of a broad "shot-gun" approach in a campaign. The Albany experience also raised the important question of whether to obey judicial injunctions and led SCLC to the policy of breaking them when they were barriers to constitutional rights. At a deeper level still, the Albany campaign underscored the true meaning of nonviolence. In the final analysis Laurie Pritchett had not met nonviolence with nonviolence. As understood by Gandhi and King, nonviolence was not simply the equivalent of avoiding hostility. It was a community-building activism premised on the need for change. Pritchett totally missed that in Albany and only served to confirm SCLC in its own quest for reform.

Part 2

SCLC and the Second Reconstruction

"It takes a fairly strenuous course of training to attain to a mental state of nonviolence."

Mahatma Gandhi

4

Forging the Dream
From Albany to the March on
Washington

The significance of the Albany Movement can easily be distorted by focusing only on its failures and not its larger contributions. As an episode in SCLC's organizational history the Albany experience obviously had its discouraging aspects. For a while after Albany, King was tempted to quit the civil rights movement. As the rifts revealed in Albany came into sharper focus in his mind and the formidable prospect of facing legal injunctions, intransigent racism, and federal immobilism weighed upon him, he wondered whether he should go on. But he worked his way through the difficulties, as well as lucrative job offers in other fields, reports Andrew Young, and made an irreversible commitment to the black movement.[1] Others in SCLC had a similar experience. Albany, after all, had been the first city-wide desegregation effort, and they had learned from it. What was needed now was a campaign victory elsewhere to offset the image of failure.

The Student Nonviolent Coordinating Committee, moreover, emerged stronger in certain respects. It is clear that the student organization had been inspired by the fellowship, the practical experience, and perhaps especially the songs of Albany, to plunge into larger undertakings. "Ain't gonna let nobody turn me 'round. . ." became more than musical poetry to SNCC. It expressed a growing urge to move forward. Furthermore, SNCC after Albany sensed that it had arrived as a force equal, if not superior in potential to the older and more traditional civil rights organizations.[2]

Perceptions of what happened in Albany were quite important for the black movement of the sixties. The apparent failure notwithstanding, Albany signalled a shift of expectations, as well as a sharpening of awareness. Among those who saw King and SCLC as too conservative or too inclined to take over the leadership of a campaign they did not create, the experience heightened their need to distinguish between themselves and his kind of movement. Much the same can be said about such critics' views of the NAACP, an organization which appeared to Louis E. Lomax, for example, to be dedicated to "strict legalism" and lacking a genuine connection with popular reform. Lomax accused King of self-contradiction, if not outright hypocrisy, and blasted the NAACP for being out of step with the times. "We now want our major civil rights organization to look beyond the courts to the people themselves as the final and quick arbiters of public policy."[3]

King and SCLC could not accept this kind of narrowly focused analysis. Nor could the NAACP. Both organizations became more convinced of the necessity for a complex approach to civil rights. They saw Albany as a catalyst that moved blacks toward a more comprehensive view of freedom. The *Crisis* argued in early 1963 that "the lasting significance of Albany may be that there a Deep South Negro community glimpsed the possibility of a truly free America. . ."[4] King was thinking along the same lines and appears to have refined his sense of strategy for achieving more complete freedom. While in jail in Albany in July 1962, he became convinced that a "four-pronged approach" was necessary: legal action, direct action, selective buying, and voter registration. Each of the prongs had importance, but only in concert would they bring the desired ends.[5]

King, then, saw a composite approach as the only workable

100

one. This cost him some influence among more militant blacks, though perhaps not as much as was thought at the time. His approach also necessitated a comparatively patient stance toward the systemic dimensions of segregation and inequality. King still strongly believed in the need for federal action, and this further qualified his attitude toward sit-ins, demonstrations, and other direct-action techniques. Desegregating lunch counters or even schools would bring only partial freedom.

For SCLC as an organization, Albany meant that a successful campaign elsewhere was needed to assure credibility and internal confidence. That the disappointments in the Georgia city inspired key SCLC leaders to go into Birmingham in 1963 with vigorous, well-formulated strategies is undeniable. While Shuttlesworth is appropriately credited with initiating the Birmingham Campaign by inviting SCLC to aid the efforts of his Alabama Christian Movement for Human Rights, it is also true that SCLC leaders were anxious to reverse their image of failure in Albany.[6]

Educating the New Black Citizen

It was only as a setback to the momentum of public movement, then, that the Albany campaign was a failure. During the campaign SCLC was moving ahead on several organizational fronts and was already having discussions with Shuttlesworth about a major campaign in Birmingham. King also kept up his pressure on the White House in 1961 and 1962 and did not veer from his basic notions of nonviolence. His "dream," as he would express it during the 1963 March on Washington, focused on a set of ideas directed toward creating a society marked by justice, freedom, and peace.[7] These were elusive concepts, to be sure, but they were basic to the evolving SCLC program.

Success would depend on both politics and black self-help. After a year in office, President Kennedy had not yet altered traditional federal policy, and his administration's weak showing in Albany did not help his image among blacks. In the second of his *Nation* articles, King let it be known that he was not pleased with the President's first year. He seemed "cautious and defensive" rather than creative toward civil rights, King surmised, and the country was facing the "chilling prospect of a general administration retreat" in this area.[8] King did credit Kennedy with being a vigorous leader with good intentions, but the President needed to emulate Lincoln by moving from hesitation to forcefulness, and to put civil rights matters ahead of domestic political opposition and foreign policy concerns.[9] On May 17, King marked another anniversary of the *Brown* decision by again calling Kennedy to task. The President had enough power, the SCLC head argued, to end (by executive orders) most of the overt discrimination in the nation. Kennedy did issue some orders, but the chorus of black critics grew in 1962.[10]

The other side of the equation was blacks themselves. Too many remained indifferent to citizenship and unfamiliar with its language and techniques. Leadership was especially deficient. Many blacks still could not vote in 1962, but many also lacked motivation, information, and even basic writing and reading skills. No amount of presidential or judicial action could in itself compensate for this deficiency. Thus SCLC, like some other organizations, set out to provide the necessary leadership and to try to undo quickly the cultural effects of centuries of discrimination, at least insofar as they militated against blacks' participating in the democratic process.

As we have seen, SCLC was moving into citizenship education by 1960. Indeed this arena of activity was an outgrowth of SCLC's early emphasis upon voting rights and participation. King had met Septima Clark in late 1956, and he had known about and visited the Highlander Folk School years before that. He was interested in the type of intensive adult education practiced there, but at first was slow to move in that direction because of the cost and his cluttered schedule. Education, in fact, was a topic of discussion at the Atlanta conference in 1957 and at the annual conventions of the late fifties.[11] And in the early sixties this interest became a tangible program.

For almost thirty years, since the depths of the Great Depression, Myles and Aimee Horton had trained labor leaders and other adults who needed remedial education. Their residential workshops and outreach programs like that at Johns Island were paradigms for projects undertaken by SNCC, CORE, the NAACP, and the MIA, among others. King's organization, as it turned out, used these methods extensively in its work.[12] Despite rumors that Highlander was a breeding ground for radicals, SCLC defended it and sought its help in implementing a citizenship education program. Highlander had never made social or racial distinctions and had been a pioneer in educational integration.[13] For that reason it was naturally attractive to black leaders from Montgomery and other cities where nonviolent protests were carried on.[14] As early as 1959 SCLC voted a resolution in support of the school, arguing that the allegations that it harbored communists were premised on racial prejudice.[15]

King's reluctance to get involved in a large educational effort was steadily eroded by Septima Clark's arguments and the street wisdom SCLC had acquired in its desegregation campaigns. Unemployment, poor education, and inexperience with democracy were visible everywhere the organization tried to function. Thus, by 1959 King was ready to look closely at freedom school material from Highlander and, in late 1960, to issue a widely distributed memorandum asking for volunteers to be trained as citizenship leaders:

> Through Myles Horton and Septima Clark, professional educators, a method to train individuals. . . was developed and tested for a period exceeding five years. This program was designed to equip persons for citizenship starting with the teaching of reading and writing in order to become registered to vote. The addition and inclusion of other areas of training took place as the need presented itself. The complete success of this training method. . . has met fully and successfully the objectives and requirements. It is the good fortune of the Southern Christian Leadership Conference to have been offered the use of this educational program in the development of its activities and social action. . . . SCLC has accepted this invitation. . . and considers its unique advantages in filling the need for developing new leadership. . . and providing the broad educational base for the population at large through the establishment of citizenship schools conducted by these new leaders throughout the South.[16]

Thus began the meshing of the work carried on for many years by a progressive white couple in Monteagle, Tennessee with that of the Southern Christian Leadership Conference. Highlander continued its own educational programs, but SCLC now developed its CEP with the help of Septima Clark. Interestingly, the Highlander connection brought to the SCLC both Clark and also one of the most influential figures in the nonviolent movement, a twenty-nine-year-old minister named Andrew J. Young. Reverend Young, who was a native of New Orleans and educated at Dillard University in New Orleans, Howard University, and Hartford Theological Seminary in Connecticut, brought to SCLC years of experience in pastoring, working with interracial groups, and the youth council of the National Council of Churches.

Septima Clark and Andrew Young joined SCLC through an arrangement made with Myles Horton. Young had applied for a position as director of Highlander's educational program, and Horton informed King. In turn, King contacted Stanley Levison in New York, and he interviewed Young, who was working at the time in the city. Levison was favorably impressed. And in view of Highlander's legal problems, it was decided that Young would be hired but be based in Atlanta with SCLC. Thus, he, Septima Clark, and Dorothy Cotton became jointly involved in launching SCLC's Citizenship Education Program (CEP). Clark formally joined the SCLC staff in July 1961 as director of workshops. Cotton was named general director of the CEP. This trio, along with James Wood, became the pivotal figures in the incipient program.

Highlander officials' decision to alter the formal structure of their educational outreach program and at the same time to broaden it, brought closer contacts with SCLC. A Citizenship School Committee, which included Wood and Young, was set up. Meanwhile, SCLC and Highlander jointly applied for funds to the huge Field Foundation. Highlander's problems with image had made it difficult to receive funding, so the connection with SCLC proved mutually beneficial. The Field Foundation grant committee responded positively and provided $100,000, of which $40,000 went to SCLC's citizenship program. The funds were administered by a neutral body, the American Missionary Association and some of its subsidiaries. The Fellowship of Southern Churchmen and the United Church of Christ participated in overseeing the grants.[17]

By the summer of 1961, SCLC was ready to launch its experiment in leadership training and citizenship education. It was, both from a civil rights and a pedagogical perspective, one of the most creative endeavors of the period. Didactical methodology and goals were closely integrated in the training procedure. To help illiterates learn to read while acquiring some basic skills of citizenship, Septima Clark and the other teachers used voter registration materials as their textbook. Cotton used protest and inspirational songs for the same purpose. The repetition and emotional appeal of the lyrics helped to convey word meanings and spellings. Impressively, SCLC began to turn out dozens, then hundreds of adults able to help others. Many of the participants in the early schools were people brought to SCLC's training centers by the efforts of Cotton, Clark, and Young, who traveled widely across the South in the early months of the program.[18]

Implementation of the training program coincided with the Kennedy administration's decision to encourage voter registration. After his May 1961 request for a "cooling off" period of the Freedom Ride movement, Attorney General Robert Kennedy tried to channel the youths' enthusiasm into this presumably less volatile activity. Not only did Kennedy hope that voter registration would be more orderly than protests—which was not always the case, as it turned out—but he also expected that funds would be easier to acquire if the protesters engaged in what many foundations already favored. With these things in view he called together leaders of civil rights organizations in mid-June and assured them that financial support would be available from foundations. While this caused a rift within SNCC between advocates of a strictly direct-action emphasis and those, like National Student Association vice president Timothy

Jenkins, who favored voter registration projects, the idea was more comfortably accepted by CORE, NAACP, and SCLC.

The result of this was a cooperative inter-organizational effort called the Voter Education Project (VEP). After heated debate, SNCC decided to participate and created two separate organs within its organization, the Voter Registration Division under Charles Jones and a Direct Action Projects Division led by Marion Barry, Diane Nash, and James Forman. Ella Baker arranged this compromise after a SNCC meeting at Highlander in August 1961 which came close to breaking up the organization. King, who also attended the Highlander meeting, listened to various points of view and tried to calm the dissension.[19]

VEP was in place by April 1962 under the overall sponsorship of the Southern Regional Council, which had worked since 1918 "to improve economic, civil and racial conditions in the South" and had the support of both whites and blacks. It was respectable in foundation circles and thus able to secure the necessary money to launch the first phase of the operation which ran from 1960 to 1964. The Taconic and Field foundations contributed over $800,000 to the project. One of CORE's freedom rider counsellors, Wiley Branton of Arkansas, administered the first VEP, which was a non-partisan, non-profit undertaking endorsed by both Democrats and Republicans. Augmented by additional drives led by the individual civil rights organization, VEP had favorable results. By the time of the 1964 elections, black voters had increased from 1.4 million in 1960 to 1.9 million.[20]

It would be a serious mistake, however, to attribute the increase in black voters entirely to the Voter Education Project. Furthermore, there were at times intense disagreements between VEP and the voter registration organizations. SNCC and CORE encountered difficulties in securing funds for some of their efforts, and generally there was a feeling among the leaders of the local projects that the federal government was contradicting itself by encouraging voter registration but not providing protection for the field workers.[21]

The truth is that registration of blacks in the South was a

difficult, dangerous, and often painful undertaking. SNCC and CORE were on the front lines of the struggle in several states and encountered deep-rooted resistance. One should keep in mind that there was no federal guarantee of voting rights until 1965, so that all of this work was done with little direct help from the government. Only a few foundations, furthermore, were willing to fund these efforts.

SCLC regarded the citizenship aspect of its program as vital to its entire operation. King was less directly involved than others because of his numerous public engagements, but he strongly supported CEP and saw to it that the project had good leaders.[22]

In its voter registration drives, SCLC relied heavily on local churches. Well before VEP began, SCLC administrators opted to link their efforts to ministers and congregations who could influence people in a given region. Reverend Joseph E. Lowery pushed for this approach as early as 1961, and the administrative council agreed.[23] With more than $900,000 from the Taconic Foundation, SCLC was able to augment greatly its campaign for voter registration begun in 1958.

Meanwhile SCLC's educational program expanded, building on the early contact with Highlander Folk School. With part of its Field Foundation grant of 1961, SCLC opened a training institute in an abandoned academy at Dorchester, Georgia near Savannah and Brunswick. There SCLC leaders and support personnel trained a handful of teachers, and as the work matured, a growing number of nonviolence-oriented black adults then spawned numerous local programs. Cotton led the first seminar at Dorchester in July 1961, and by 1963 the Dorchester Institute had a central place in the educational program of SCLC. Andrew Young administered the Field grant, and Wyatt Walker worked closely with the development of the Dorchester center. In Atlanta, a Citizenship School augmented the work of training leaders.

Underlying SCLC's educational program was the conviction that much could be done to raise the consciousness of blacks. Cotton felt that since blacks were often at the bottom of the social ladder, special efforts had to be made to raise their political consciousness while educating them in the fundamentals of participation citizenship.[24] Therefore, the Citizenship Education Program taught not only reading skills, but confidence and elemental political 'savvy' as well. By the spring of 1963, she could see meaningful results as more than 200 teachers had been trained by SCLC's version of the Highlander method. By the end of the summer when the Birmingham campaign catapulted SCLC to new heights of visibility, CEP could claim over 600 graduates of its citizenship training seminars.[25] In 1963, the Citizenship Education Program was beginning to be a major operation which would attract additional leaders like Annell Ponder, the Reverend Hosea Williams, and Dr. Robert L. Green of Michigan State University's department of psychology. Countless others would work in rural towns and counties, and major cities across the South.[26]

In the meantime SCLC began to give more organizational unity to its economic concerns. To that end, it launched Operation Breadbasket, so named, according to Abernathy, because "we would be operating in order to bring bread, money, and income into the baskets of blacks and poor people."[27] This program focused on helping blacks to raise their economic standards. An outgrowth of earlier selective buying campaigns and modelled after the program led by the Reverend Leon Sullivan in Philadelphia in 1959, Operation Breadbasket was the principal economic arm of King's movement and one of SCLC's most successful and durable undertakings. Operation Breadbasket began in September 1962 in Atlanta, where it pressured businesses to adopt fair hiring practices, and, King reported, it brought an increase of over 750 jobs and more than $20 million annually in income for blacks.[28]

Under the national direction of the Reverend Fred C. Bennette, Jr., "Le Commandant" of the 1960 sit-ins in Atlanta, Operation Breadbasket had wide influence as it allied with businesses, clergy, labor unions, and supportive individuals. Bennette was highly conscious of the fact that black families lived on less than half the income of a typical white family, causing serious deficiencies in nutrition, housing, health care

108

and other basics. It was not a welfare program he posited, but an upgrading self-help effort combined with pressure on businesses and governments to reciprocate with fair provision of opportunities and compensation. In addition to more and better jobs, Operation Breadbasket sought to promote black-manufactured products, help blacks pool their economic resources, support the use of black-controlled banks, and solicit patronage of black businesses. Though never as large a budgeted item as the citizenship and registration programs, Operation Breadbasket functioned well in the sixties in Louisville, Charlotte, Birmingham, Jacksonville, and more than forty other cities and towns. Chicago's program, under the direction of Jesse Jackson, became the best known and one of the most successful.[29]

The Battle of Birmingham

As SCLC delegates met in Birmingham in September 1962 for their annual convention, these kinds of programs were very much on their minds. Wyatt T. Walker reported to the convention that he had spent his first full year as executive director "charting the course" for SCLC and noted the centrality of the citizenship programs in those plans. Voter registration and training, he said, were rather like a farmer's planting seeds. Time had to pass before results could be seen, but in Walker's view "harvesting" was near. In Alabama, Tennessee, Virginia, and elsewhere he could see signs of progress. At least in a limited way, CEP was beginning to compensate, he felt, for educational deficiences resultant from many decades of inequitable treatment of blacks in the United States.[30]

Walker, though, was no gradualist. The movement needed a crisis, he believed, in order to regain momentum and to reach new plateaus.[31] At this same Birmingham convention where he lauded the seed-planting of citizenship training, he and others were looking toward a major campaign in that city in 1963. Walker, who would be the key logistical planner of the Birmingham campaign, was convinced that "We've got to have a crisis to bargain with. To take a moderate approach, hoping to get white help doesn't work. They nail you to the cross, and it saps the enthusiasm of the followers. You've got to have a crisis."[32]

Indeed, a local crisis was already brewing, and white leaders feared that the choice of Birmingham as the site of SCLC's sixth annual convention was the prelude to the influx of SCLC demonstrators. Since January some city businesses had been hurt by a selective boycott engineered by Dr. Lucious Pitts and students at Miles College, but no progress had been made in negotiations until news came of SCLC's forthcoming convention there. Fred Shuttlesworth's people had battled against discrimination for years with only short-lived costly gains, or "pyrrhic victories," as he called them, and as of September 1962, the white establishment had never negotiated face to face with the Alabama Christian Movement for Human Rights. As soon as a park or other facility was desegregated, it would close or revert to segregation.[33] The white Senior Citizens' Committee had met with the ACMHR in August and agreed to remove discriminatory signs from restrooms, water fountains and the like in return for a moratorium on the boycott. As Shuttlesworth had warned, however, the signs were back up as soon as the SCLC convention ended.[34]

Actually, the convention was not intended as an immediate precursor of the SCLC campaign in Birmingham. The decision to support Shuttlesworth's ACMHR had been made by the Board at their spring meeting in Chattanooga in May 1962 when the Birmingham minister requested help.[35] The Albany campaign had not yet reached its climax, and was only beginning to when the convention met in September. Furthermore, SCLC leaders knew that only the most deliberate planning and preparation would enable them to break through the deeply entrenched segregationism in Birmingham, so they set the target date for the pre-Easter buying season in 1963. While their fears were understandable, the white leaders in Birmingham had no idea how much work remained before SCLC would begin to confront the city.

Furthermore, King still held to his belief that the Kennedy administration could act boldly and thereby obviate possibly destructive confrontations. The time seemed perfect for such a move as the centennial of the Emancipation Proclamation neared, and the SCLC president found yet another way to attack federal inaction as he asked for a "Second Emancipation Proclamation" to mark the 1963 celebrations.[36] Too many black children had grown up with the debilitating effects of discrimination, and time was running out. Blacks, King said, could not wait indefinitely for freedom.[37]

King knew, of course, of the political barriers to bold executive action and of Kennedy's concerns about fiscal problems expected for 1963. What he was not fully aware of, he acknowledged later, was the degree to which an American-Soviet crisis over the placing of intercontinental nuclear missiles in Castro's Cuba had "understandably tended to dwarf all other issues."[38] At any rate, uncertainty about federal action was another reason for making the best possible preparations for Birmingham.

Scholars by now have amply demonstrated what Birmingham blacks knew all along. As an industrial hub of the South, Birmingham had many assets and great potential for the future, but its social structure was rigidly segregated. "Everything in Birmingham was segregated," recalled one who lived there in the sixties. . ."Everything from top to bottom."[39] No one expected an easy desegregation effort. Even Police Commissioner Eugene "Bull" Connor bitterly resisted desegregation. Shuttlesworth, who had been attacked many times and had his home bombed on Christmas day in 1956, warned SCLC leaders that the barriers to integration in Birmingham were virtually insurmountable. Having been jailed "twenty-five or thirty times" before he stopped counting, Shuttlesworth knew that resistance would be formidable. As early as August 1961, he had accepted a call to pastor a Baptist church in Cincinnati and was flying between the two cities during the 1963 campaign.[40]

Why, then, would SCLC choose Birmingham for a campaign? King has answered the question this way:

First, Birmingham is the home of our strongest affiliate, the Alabama Christian Movement for Human Rights, led by the most courageous civil rights fighter in the South, Fred Shuttlesworth; secondly, Birmingham represented the hard-core, recalcitrant, segregationist South, a veritable bastion of injustice and immorality; thirdly, the loss of vital industry coupled with the ugly image created by the Bull Connor philosophy of race relations had thrown the South's largest industrial center into an economic demise from which it was struggling to survive.[41]

True, King penned these words some months after the inauguration of the Birmingham campaign, but they undoubtedly give an accurate reflection of the premises upon which it was undertaken. By all accounts the Birmingham effort was a deliberately engineered crisis intended both to revitalize the nonviolent movement after Albany and to strike a damaging blow to the whole structure of southern segregationism. It appears, too, that it marked a change in the relationship between the nonviolent movement and the federal government. King's continuing personal efforts to move Kennedy to action notwithstanding, the Birmingham campaign was designed to take the black movement more directly to the nation and thus influence the government with a more effective kind of pressure. That aspect of the campaign broadened as events unfolded in Birmingham, and it is misleading to stress it too much at the outset. Nonetheless, the nature of the planning for Birmingham indicates that King and SCLC were from the beginning counting on gaining the political clout not only to bring changes in Birmingham but also to influence national policy on the problems of blacks elsewhere.

In the strictest sense this was a finesse. If the Birmingham nonviolent campaign worked, it would accomplish much. If, on the other hand, it failed and brought an internecine confrontation with only injuries and damage to show for it, it would expose the evils of racial oppression "before the court of world opinion," and thereby force the federal government to act. In that respect the thinking of King and several others in SCLC at this point reflected what a number of scholars have identified as a modification in the nonviolent strategy.[42] It seems that King was thinking in terms of provoking reaction, even if at heavy cost.

This shift was not as basic a revision of King's thought or SCLC's policies as some recent scholars have argued. It is true that from this point through the Selma campaign of 1965, King would place more emphasis upon the national political aspect of the nonviolent movement, but primarily because of conditions rather than re-evaluation of the strategy *per se*. As early as 1958 King had written that when "the mass movement repudiates violence while moving resolutely toward its goal, its opponents are revealed as the instigators and practitioners of violence if it occurs. Then public support is magnetically attracted to the advocates of nonviolence."[43] In 1963 the stakes were higher and the focus was on national policy, but the principle and the strategy were the same. At the Birmingham convention on the eve of the campaign King spoke more of the possibilities of change within the system through voting than of any shifts of policy in nonviolent reform.[44]

Nor was there any departure from SCLC tradition in the theme of the Birmingham convention: 'Human Rights, the Continuing Struggle.' Speakers emphasized the necessity and meaning of nonviolence. White liberal Anne Braden of the Southern Regional Council, for example, focused on "the deeper meaning of nonviolence" and stressed the counter productive character of hostile resistance to social change.[45] Reverend Otis Moss, baseball star Jackie Robinson and several more speakers underscored the urgency of change while simultaneously appealing for more involvement by both blacks and whites in the nonviolent pursuit of reform. Robinson urged blacks outside the South to become aware of the "disgraceful living conditions" in the southern states and try to rectify them by their support of the civil rights movement.[46]

On the other hand, there were reminders both at the convention and just afterward of the stubborn persistence of racism and hostility. At the Birmingham convention King was attacked by a young self-styled Nazi who jumped to the stage and punched the SCLC leader in the face. King insisted that the young white man be allowed to return to his seat and hear the rest of the session. Later, King said he was not interested in pressing charges but in changing the system that "produced that kind of man." The young Nazi, however, was arrested.

A few days later a court order allowed James Meredith to enter the University of Mississippi at Oxford. But as this young black matriculated, violence erupted. It troubled King to see Governor Ross Barnett standing at the door personally trying to block Meredith's entrance. King wondered whether recently nominated segregationist George C. Wallace would be elected governor of Alabama and do the same sort of thing there.[47]

Then on October 16, as he returned to confer with Kennedy, King met a rebuff in Washington. The President was still talking about black voter registration while King continued his appeals for suitable observance of the Emancipation Proclamation centennial. With the truce broken in Birmingham and the Jim Crow signs going back up, Kennedy's suggestions seemed quite inadequate. When the two met again in January 1963 nothing had changed and King felt that he had no choice but to go on with the planned campaign in Birmingham.[48]

Meanwhile preparations for the Birmingham campaign continued. Much of the preliminary work was done discreetly without conferring with very many local black leaders. This would cause difficulties later when these people learned how advanced the plans were. They felt left out and threatened by the negative economic consequences that could result. That was an important issue to King, and he would hold several meetings with them just before the campaign to explain why SCLC had been secretive and why it targeted the Easter season to initiate the effort.[49]

Questions of exact timing, focus, and various logistical matters were discussed at a December meeting of King, his SCLC staff, certain Board members and advisers at the Dorchester center. Since security and facility of communication were important, the entire project and its personnel were coded. The campaign would go under the code name 'Project C' (for confrontation). King was designated 'JFK', Abernathy was 'Dean Rusk', Shuttlesworth, amusingly enough was to be 'Bull', and Walker was dubbed 'RFK'. Demonstrators would be referred to as 'baptismal candidates' and 'going to a baptism' would indicate moving to a planned demonstration.[50] Although there was joking about this, the atmosphere was quite serious in view of the dangers the campaign presented. Some of them could die, as they knew all too well.

If the focus in Albany had been too imprecise, the Birmingham campaign would be more particularized. The business community would be the prime target, and the Easter buying season the time to exert the pressure. Since Easter fell on April 14 in 1963, the demonstrations and selective buying would begin in early March. Six weeks would give ample time to effect some significant changes. In the meantime, King could seek aid from groups known to be sympathetic toward SCLC, from other civil rights organizations and SCLC affiliates, and from Belafonte, Levison and other individuals who had raised large sums for SCLC in the past. Levison's involvement, as usual, caught the attention of the FBI.

In early January 1963 SCLC set up a command post in Room 30 of the Gaston Motel near Kelly Ingram Park in Birmingham. A. G. Gaston was a wealthy black who did not fully agree with the proposed obstruction of downtown businesses. Like insurance broker John Drew and other principals in the Birmingham black establishment, Gaston worried about the possible repercussions. He had always been less than enthusiastic about some of Shuttlesworth's actions, and now that SCLC was entering the struggle, he could not fully concur with the planned boycotts. But he did provide command headquarters, and this was appreciated. King would spend a great deal of time in early 1963 trying to get the local black upper class behind him despite their reluctance.[51]

Inertia was a problem among the working class as well. Birmingham blacks had lived so long in poverty and segregated lifestyles that it was not easy to move them to participate. SCLC brought in seasoned nonviolent activists like C. T. Vivian, James Lawson, Bernard Lee, Andrew Young, and James Bevel to hold workshops on nonviolence and to stir up interest. Dorothy Cotton and a number of other skilled organizers helped mobilize demonstrators, providing timetables, shifts of participants, and overall guidance. Those who were not qualified by SCLC's standards to demonstrate were asked to make telephone calls, type, or perform a host of other voluntary tasks.[52]

As it turned out, the starting date had to be delayed. Birmingham had changed from a city commission system to a mayor-council government in 1962, and a special mayoral election was slated for March 5. Because they did not want inadvertently to help Eugene "Bull" Connor in his bid for the post of mayor, SCLC decided to wait until after the election. Bull Connor could be more harmful to the movement in the mayor's office than as police chief. B (Birmingham) day was thus moved back two weeks.[53] But once again the timetable was interrupted when no one won a majority on March 5 and a runoff election was scheduled for April 2. In the runoff, comparatively moderate Albert Boutwell defeated Commissioner Connor.

The *Birmingham News* hailed Albert Boutwell's election as mayor with the headline: "New Day Dawns in Birmingham." But King and SCLC felt differently, although they did prefer him to Connor. King's people turned down a request from Boutwell to postpone the campaign until his administration had a chance to demonstrate its good faith by bringing some needed changes. And if all these developments were not enough to sap enthusiasm, the situation was further complicated by Connor's refusal to relinquish his job because under the old constitution his term ran until 1965. Incumbent Mayor Arthur Hanes took the same stand, and although they were expected to lose their case in the courts, it would be at least April 15 before that situation could be cleared up. Thus, SCLC decided to go ahead on April 3 with B (Birmingham) Day.

As the campaign began approximately 250 people were pledged to follow the guidelines set down by SCLC. All of the volunteers were expected to be willing to go to jail, as King himself was despite advice from associates to avoid incarceration until the campaign was well underway. King had come to Birmingham to "stay until Pharaoh let his people go," as he put it, and he expected commitment from volunteer participants. The pledge card each had to sign was rather demanding, calling for daily meditation, prayer, sacrifice of personal wishes, refraining from any violence "of fist, tongue, or heart," and more.[54]

To mark the official beginning the Alabama Christian Movement for Human Rights issued a manifesto on April 3 explaining the campaign and asking for support:

> We appeal to the citizenry of Birmingham, Negro and White, to join us in this witness for decency, morality, self-respect, and human dignity. Your individual and corporate support can hasten the day of "liberty and justice for all." This is Birmingham's moment of truth in which every citizen can play his part in her longer destiny.[55]

This first public pronouncement was followed the next day by King's presentation of the six goals agreed upon by the organizers: 1) to desegregate lunch counters and other public-facilities in the downtown area; 2) to force the implementation of fair hiring practices by stores; 3) to move the city to adopt similar fair hiring policies; 4) to get all charges against sit-inners and demonstrators dropped; 5) to reopen Birmingham's public recreational facilities on a desegregated basis; and 6) to form a bi-racial committee to facilitate further desegregation.[56]

While these were sweeping demands considering Birmingham's traditions, they were neither radical nor beyond realization. But unless the campaign evoked enough reaction to have any political clout, Birmingham would probably not be changed. In that regard the first few days were disappointing. The few sit-inners taken into custody were treated gently, and little seemed to be happening. Even in the arrest of forty-two demonstrators on Saturday, April 6, Bull Connor's officers acted, as King later admitted, "with amazing politeness."[57] It seemed as if Laurie Pritchett's tactics in Albany were being used again, and indeed Connor had consulted Pritchett in hopes of learning how to disarm the demonstrators politically.

Easter was only a few days away. Soon it might be too late to make the selective buying tactic work, and as yet there was no massive participation by blacks. So SCLC organizers held nightly rallies to raise emotions and enlist new demonstrators, and these continued even after the campaign picked up momentum. King attributed much of the success of these rallies to Abernathy, Walker and Shuttlesworth, each of whom exhibited distinctive personality traits. Abernathy, King wrote, had the unique ability to combine humor and inspiration. "When he plants himself behind the lectern, squat and powerful, his round face breaking easily into laughter, his listeners both love and believe him." Of Walker, King observed: "Youthful, lean and bespectacled, he brought his energetic and untiring spirit to our meetings, whose members already knew and admired his dedicated work as a behind-the-scenes organizer of the campaign." Shuttlesworth, wrote King, "had proved to his people that he would not ask anyone to go where he was not willing to lead."[58] Shuttlesworth, one should note, led the first street demonstrations in April and was among those arrested.

But dedicated leaders and rallies were not enough. By the end of the first week in Birmingham, SCLC had little to show for all the meticulous preparation. Deprived by unexpected developments of the desired six weeks of pre-Easter boycotting, they now faced charges by mayor-elect Boutwell that they were "outside agitators," and a number of local black leaders seem to have concurred in that view.[59] And that was not the full extent of the problems. Weapons were found among the demonstrators, and SCLC group leaders had to remind the over-zealous marchers that they were not there to strike down white people but to follow in the steps of Gandhi.

Nonetheless, the campaign slowly but surely picked up. King's argument that "Birmingham was the testing ground" for the whole black movement may not have convinced a large number, but the crowds did grow, augmented by many outsiders like blind singer Al Hibbler, who was among several arrested on April 9 during downtown demonstrations. On Wednesday, April 10, the second week of demonstrating began with increased enthusiasm. The jails were getting fuller.

But on that same day another ghost of Albany appeared in Birmingham, presenting SCLC's efforts with more difficulties than did Connor's policy of restrained force. The police chief received his anticipated trump card when Judge W. A. Jenkins issued a state injunction barring further demonstrations. King and his aides had to face what had been up till then a hypothetical question: would they defy a court injunction? They had chosen not to in Albany, and Connor was counting on their abiding by the injunction in Birmingham. What he did not know was that King and SCLC felt they had no choice this time, and the SCLC president told an eager young reporter the next day that the marches would continue.[60]

At a less demanding time for ministers than an Easter weekend, this would have been a simpler matter. But King, Abernathy, Shuttlesworth, and several more of the key figures were preachers who would be expected and would want to be in their pulpits on Sunday morning for one of Christianity's major holy days. That issue weighed on King as he anticipated arrest if he and the others carried out their commitment to continue the marches.[61] Beyond that there was another crucial consideration. If King went to jail, this might truncate the fund-raising effort to supply bail money for the many jailed demonstrators.

In less than happy circumstances then, two dozen of the Birmingham campaign leaders met at Gaston Motel on Good Friday, poring over the possibilities and weighing their options. Among them was King's father. King felt pressures from several directions. He understood the importance of bail money, but he was also aware that some were questioning his willingness to go to jail as he had said he would.[62] It took him what seemed to be a long time to make up his mind, and he retired to another room to meditate. Later he wrote that:

> I sat there conscious of twenty-four pairs of eyes. I thought about the people in jail. I thought about the Birmingham Negroes already lining the streets of the city, waiting to see me put into practice what I had so passionately preached. How could my failure now to submit to arrest be explained to the local community? What would be the verdict of the country about a man who had encouraged hundreds of people to make a stunning sacrifice and then excused himself?[63]

When King finally emerged from the other room he said he was ready to defy the injunction and invite arrest. Once he had worked through it, he felt good about the decision and began to tie it to the obvious Good Friday symbolism. Looking at Abernathy, he said, "Ralph, I will understand if you don't go with me today. Because you are a pastor of a church, you deserve to be with your congregation on Sunday morning, but I have to go." With that the close bond between the two veterans of Montgomery was too strong to ignore. "If you are going, Martin," Abernathy recalls answering, "I am going."[64] The twenty-four men joined hands and sang "We Shall Overcome." Then King hugged his father and they went out.

This broke open the Birmingham campaign. From the Gaston Motel they drove to Zion Hill Church where a large crowd waited to see King's commitment in action. His sermon focused on suffering for God's purposes. Referring to Jesus' crucifixion on a Good Friday almost two thousand years earlier, King said he wanted to be a good servant and follow Christ's example of dedication. As he walked out the audience did not miss the opportunity to underscore the symbolism. "There he goes," someone shouted, "just like Jesus."[65] As expected, Connor was waiting. There were no more reservations. King, Abernathy, and some four dozen others were quickly arrested and taken to jail.

King was isolated in a dark cell and Abernathy was also separated from the other prisoners. King worried about bail money for fellow prisoners, about whether anything positive would result. He felt the loneliness that came with solitary confinement. "You will never know the meaning of utter darkness," he wrote later, "until you have lain in such a dungeon, knowing that sunlight is streaming overhead and still seeing only darkness below." Some comfort resulted from a visit by two SCLC attorneys, Arthur Shores and Orzell Billingsley, who informed King that his friend and lawyer Clarence B. Jones would be coming from New York the next day. But their message was essentially negative. There was no money and little prospect of securing any. However, when Jones arrived he informed King that Harry Belafonte had raised some $50,000 and would seek more as needed. This display of his friends' loyalty gave King more succor than the money itself. "I don't know whether the sun was shining at that moment. But I know that once again I saw the light."[66]

There was less to be pleased about when he was shown a copy of the *Birmingham News* which carried an open 'Appeal for Law and Order and Common Sense' signed by eight prominent white Christian and Jewish clergymen. It criticized the timing of the campaign and made the familiar charge of "outside agitators" against King and SCLC. The words hit hard and prompted one of King's few lengthy responses to criticism. He wrote it on paper smuggled to him by Walker. The campaign leaders had agreed that all statements would be jointly issued, but in these circumstances it seemed appropriate to King to make an individual statement.[67]

In his "Letter from a Birmingham Jail" King denied that he was an outsider, or that it was possible for anyone to be such in the Birmingham setting. All communities, he argued, are interrelated. "I cannot sit idly by in Atlanta and not be concerned about what happens in Birmingham. Injustice anywhere is a threat to justice everywhere. We are caught in an inescapable network of mutuality, tied in a single garment of destiny." King also answered their criticism of the demonstrations. He wondered why they did not have as much concern about causes as they did about the manifestations of discontent. It was unfortunate that there were demonstrations in Birmingham, but "even more unfortunate that the city's white power structure left the Negro community with no alternative."

He pointed out that a nonviolent campaign went through four basic stages or steps. It began with investigation to determine whether injustice existed. The next step was to negotiate with the local officials. Both had happened in Birmingham, King said. The third step was self-purification, in which potential activists would examine their own lives, determining the purity of their own motives and raising basic questions about their commitment to undergo jailings and other sufferings if necessary. Fourth, King pointed out, was the stage of direct action. That was justified by the necessity for creative tension in order to bring change. Alluding to Socrates' assumption that tension in the mind was conducive to liberation from myths and half-truths, he spoke of nonviolent reformers as "gadflies" creating social tension. This would help people "rise from the dark depths of prejudice and racism to the majestic heights of understanding and brotherhood."

Perhaps the most important line of political argument in the Letter was its justification of opposition to unjust laws. Citing Niebuhr, King expanded on the idea of collective evil in society. Freedom, the cornerstone of the nonviolent movement, was difficult to acquire in the aggregate complexity of traditions, discriminatory laws, and social biases. King argued that freedom had to be won, and that it entailed taking active opposition to laws that were unjust. On this issue the SCLC president turned to Thomas Aquinas and his thirteenth century exposition on law. To St. Thomas, law was derived ultimately from the Eternal Law of God. In nature and human order Divine Law was expressed through Natural Law. Human Law, or law enacted by human institutions, in Aquinas' view, was legitimate only insofar as it was in harmony with God's natural order. Actually, Aquinas was at odds with the negativistic Augustianian view of the state that considered human political systems as a kind of "dike against sin" necessitated by human imperfections. Aquinas had a more Aristotelian understanding of politics in which the state and social order are natural and positive elements of human development.

Like Aquinas, King saw human laws as 'just' or 'unjust' according to their conformity with God's laws. But he applied the distinction in terms of the qualification that any law that uplifted human personality was just, while any degrading law was unjust. "All segregation statutes are unjust," said King, "because segregation distorts the soul and damages the personality." Such laws, which implied the superiority of some people, denied the essential personal links of society. King stated emphatically that he had the "highest respect for law." But he believed that history from Shadrach and Abednego to Adolf Hitler demonstrated that being "legal" was not necessarily the

122

same as being right. Civil disobedience, therefore, was an obligation rather than an abuse of one's legitimate function.

Above all in his Letter, King kept the Christian view in focus. He told his critics, fellow clergymen, that the "judgment of God is upon the church as never before," and warned that if it did not recapture the early church's sacrificial spirit it would be "dismissed as an irrelevant social club with no meaning for the twentieth century." While expressing some hope that the organized church would respond to the challenges of justice, King was hopeful chiefly because of the rightness of what he was doing and its consistency with the American goal of freedom. Negroes' destiny, he averred, was "tied up with America's destiny." If slavery could not stop black people, neither could the opposition they faced in Birmingham.

King ended his letter, his longest ever, with a conciliatory note. He apologized for any words that were overstatements of the truth, while at the same time asking God's forgiveness for any understatements of it. He said he hoped to meet his critics someday, "not as an integrationist or civil-rights leader but as a fellow clergyman and a Christian brother."

Meanwhile, Coretta King was painfully worried about her husband and attempted to telephone President Kennedy on Easter Sunday. Although she failed to reach the President, word of King's plight was relayed to him in Palm Beach, and the next day Mrs. King received a call from Kennedy. He assured her that her husband was all right and that the FBI had been sent to Birmingham. Within minutes, King called her and seemed safe. With that, the immediate crisis ended. On April 20 after eight days in jail, King and Abernathy were released.

Quickly the SCLC staff gathered to plan for continued demonstrations, but utilizing a new strategy, one that caused no small amount of controversy. Youth had been less involved in Birmingham than in previous campaigns and now Young, Cotton, Bevel, Lee and others began to enlist college and high school demonstrators. But they did not stop there. Small children, some as young as six, would be used in the third wave of marches planned for early May. To risk their safety in confrontation with police, trained dogs, and waterhoses was not an easy choice for King, but he justified it on the grounds that the children had never known freedom, but had acquired a real, if simple, understanding of racism. The very young were channeled into safer pursuits, as when Young sent a small group of black children to desegregate the city library. "In their own way," said King, the children "had struck a blow for freedom."[68]

He was correct. The use of children had a dramatic effect on the campaign. Bevel and the other youth recruiters combed the schools amassing a veritable army of 6,000 youngsters ready to march in small contingents of about 15 to 45. And on Thursday, May 2, or "D Day," they initiated what proved to be the most intense phase of the campaign. King spoke at length with the young people at the Sixteenth Street Baptist Church just before they set out. The first forty or so of the children held hands and sang "We Shall Overcome," while Connor's forces waited with dogs and high-powered waterhoses. Wave after wave of children, ranging in age from six to sixteen, marched in the streets. Connor lost his restraints and ordered the dogs and hoses to be used on the marchers, causing the press around the world to take note of the spectacle. This "Children's Crusade" had more impact than anything else to date in the Birmingham campaign.

Snarling dogs and waterhoses, turned indiscriminately on the demonstrators, moved the conscience of many outside observers, no doubt. And there were moments in Birmingham when city officials were also repulsed by the violence. On Sunday afternoon, May 5, Reverend Charles Billups led a band of adult marchers from the New Pilgrim Baptist Church on a prayer pilgrimage. As they reached the police barricades, they were almost overcome with fear. But as they fell to their knees to pray, a woman in the group began to hum. As she did, the frightened marchers began to hum with her, and their courage rose. When they got to their feet to resume marching, Connor ordered that the waterhoses be turned upon the demonstrators. "Turn on the hoses, damm it!" he repeatedly ordered. But no one could do it.[69] They were disarmed, wrote Mrs. King later, "by the moral pressure of a watching world and the spiritual force of that little band of blacks."[70]

In Washington the Kennedys were watching the televised events with deep interest. On May 4 the President said "I can well understand why the Negroes of Birmingham are tired of being asked to be patient."[71] That same day he dispatched Assistant Attorney General Burke Marshall to Birmingham to try to bring about negotiations.[72] In fact, talks had been going on quietly between the black leaders and city officials for several days, but nothing yet had been accomplished. Nor was there much confidence that Marshall could do anything. King feared that he was coming simply to get blacks to cool off, but as Marshall arrived and began to work the SCLC president became convinced of his sincerity.

By then black demands had crystallized into four basic goals: 1) desegregation of lunch counters, restrooms, fitting rooms and water fountains in stores; 2) upgrading and hiring of blacks on a nondiscriminatory basis; 3) dropping of all charges against demonstrators; and 4) the creation of a bi-racial committee to establish a timetable for further desegregation.[73] Moderate as they were, however, these demands were unacceptable to the white leaders, and so the demonstrations continued.

Indeed, Birmingham was literally paralyzed by the mass of marchers that covered the downtown area on May 7. On that day Marshall was meeting with business leaders and Senior Citizens' Committee representatives when what King called a "veritable sea of black faces" transformed the deadlocked talks into serious dialogue. It was one of the most dramatic moments in the history of the black movement. The crowds were disciplined and nonviolent as the angry cries and rockthrowing that had plagued the previous week gave way to singing. Connor was poised for war, however, with dogs, hoses, and weapons in place. But his barricades were useless as students swarmed everywhere, tying up traffic and throwing the entire downtown area into confusion. The jails were overflowing with more than 2,000 demonstrators, and now the heart of the city was inundated by seemingly endless marching throngs.

SCLC leaders were then reminded that huge excited crowds can be dangerous. Even as white and black representatives sat to negotiate, violence resumed when rioters began hurling objects and hostile words at police. More people were hurt in this outburst, including Shuttlesworth, who was lifted off the ground by a powerful stream of water from a fire truck and slammed against a wall. His injuries were serious enough to require hospitalization, and Connor reportedly said when he learned of the incident, "I am sorry I missed it; I wish they had carried him away in a hearse."[74] Obviously, racial hatreds were deep-rooted in Birmingham.

It was during Shuttlesworth's stay in the hospital that an agreement was reached between King, his associates, and the white leaders of the city. Around-the-clock talks between May 7 and May 9 resulted in a compromise settlement. With Connor's forces bolstered by 250 heavily armed state troopers sent by the new Governor George Wallace, and eight hundred more troopers poised nearby for a military-style assault, it seems that a blood bath was narrowly averted by the settlement. Demonstrations were suspended, and plans were made for a May 10 public announcement in both Washington and Birmingham.

When Shuttlesworth learned of the suspension of marches, he became, as he told this writer, "as angry as I had ever been."[75] Too many times he had been misled into thinking that substantive agreements had been reached only to find that they were ephemeral. Although still too ill to be discharged from the hospital and somewhat hyperactive from the injections he had received, the indomitable Shuttlesworth nonetheless left and sought out King to confront him with his misgivings. He told King pointedly that "if you call off the demonstrations prematurely, your image will be damaged." Shuttlesworth reminded King that some people already felt that the SCLC president often came into a city, started a campaign, and then left it without getting a durable settlement. Although he did not want to hurt King, whom he deeply respected, Shuttlesworth nonetheless pulled no punches.[76] He pointed out that the leaders of the

126

campaign had agreed not to make any separate or premature settlement, and this one seemed to be just that.[77]

It took no small amount of effort by Ralph Abernathy and others to convince Shuttlesworth that the agreement was genuine and that the cessation of demonstrations was a necessary move of good faith. Emotions were heated in this exchange of views that took place that day in the home of John Drew. While Abernathy, Walker and the others insisted that the truce was necessary and Burke Marshall pointed out that he had made promises, the stalwart Shuttlesworth replied, "I have my own promises to keep." His followers in the ACMHR were looking to him for a real settlement, not another illusory compromise, and were ready to resume demonstrations with or without SCLC.[78]

After further debate and telephone conversations between Robert Kennedy in Washington and John Doar of the Justice Department in Birmingham, the truce was effected. Shuttlesworth's concerns abated, and on May 10 public announcements were made of the suspension of demonstrations and the beginning of desegregation. The Kennedys were relieved that a bloody confrontation had been averted, and King saw the agreement as positive. In *Why We Can't Wait* the fact that he entitled his chapter on the compromise "Black and White Together" reflects his optimistic estimation of the agreement. King said publicly at the time that "Birmingham may well offer twentieth-century America an example of progressive racial relations, for all mankind a dawn of a new day, a promise for all men, a day of opportunity and a new sense of freedom for all America."

If measured by the concrete substance and viability of the May 10 agreement, King's words appear overly optimistic. The settlement had little official standing since it was made privately without the involvement of the city's official representatives. And hardly had the announcement been made when violence returned to the city. The next day, May 11, a bomb was hurled at the home of King's brother, A.D., while his family slept. They escaped unharmed, but another explosive device damaged the

127

Gaston Motel, the nerve center of the campaign and a source of precious bail money. In that blast people were injured. Some blacks again rose in violence, overturning police cars and assaulting officers. King came close to endorsing these reprisals, and Birmingham officials voiced angry criticisms. "That nigger King," said Mayor Hanes, "ought to be investigated by the Attorney General." Although he would soon be removed from office by court order, Hanes got in one final official blow at the blacks by ordering the expulsion of more than a thousand students from city schools for their participation in the rioting.

With help from the NAACP Legal Defense and Educational Fund, Hanes' expulsion order was reversed by a federal court, and he finally lost his office in late May. Blacks then celebrated what King called "another victory in the titanic struggle."[79] Perhaps most dramatic of all, however, was the clear reversal of Kennedy's position. On May 18 the President spoke out vigorously at Vanderbilt University in behalf of the rights of blacks. And a few weeks later, in a June 11 national telecast, Kennedy made clear how he felt about the black cause:

> We preach freedom around the world, and we mean it. And we cherish our freedom here at home. But are we to say to the world—and much more importantly, to each other—that this is the land of the free. . .except for Negroes; that we have no second-class citizens. . .except for Negroes; that we have no class or caste system, no ghettos, no master race. . .except with respect to Negroes? Now the time has come for this nation to fulfill its promise. The events in Birmingham and elsewhere have so increased the cries for equality that no city or state or legislative body can prudently choose to ignore them.

Eight days later Kennedy sent a comprehensive civil rights bill to the Congress, marking the beginning of a legislative battle that would change the status of black Americans by 1964. Kennedy had known all along that such a proposal would meet strong opposition, but he was now willing to take the stand SCLC had sought from Eisenhower in 1957 and from Kennedy himself since early 1961. That black leaders were far from believing that the civil rights act would soon pass or that circumstances had changed much is evinced by the fact that many of them were already preparing for a massive demonstration in Washington to dramatize both civil rights and the economic plight of black Americans.

Strictly speaking, this March on Washington was separate from the events in Birmingham. It had been conceived months before the May 10 truce. Yet the two were related historically and ideologically. Asa Philip Randolph, leader of the threatened march on Washington in 1941, served as chairman of the committee which planned the march. At 74, Randolph had been an influential activist for forty years and was the most revered of the mainstream civil rights advocates who participated in the march. He and Bayard Rustin conceived the idea of a march in late 1962. Reflecting on what was transpiring in the southern black movement, they were convinced that the time was right for a huge demonstration in the nation's capital to link political rights and economic needs. Soon a group described by the press as the "Big Six" began to organize the march. In addition to Randolph and Rustin, the group included King, Whitney Young of the National Urban League, John Lewis of SNCC, CORE's James Farmer, and NAACP head Roy Wilkins.[80]

President Kennedy opposed the idea of a march on Washington. Preferring to direct his major efforts toward getting his civil rights proposals passed, the President thought a march would be counter-productive. Kennedy met with the march planners on June 22, 1963 at the White House, where he tried to talk them out of it. In what Arthur Schlesinger called "the best meeting I attended in my years in the White House," the black leaders and Kennedy aired their views. The President argued that "a big show at the Capitol" might make some of the legislators feel coerced.[81] Randolph rebutted, insisting that "Negroes are already marching. It is very likely impossible to stop them."[82] And Farmer added a note of realism by observing that if demonstrations were not continued, and the civil rights bill failed, the "result would be that frustration would grow into violence and would demand new leadership."[83]

At that juncture, the black movement had reached a significant new plateau. Certainly, the situation in Birmingham was little cause for rejoicing, but the fact that white leaders and black activists had come face to face with a larger measure of reality indicated that the *status quo* was reeling under the impact of powerful forces of change.

The Southern Christian Leadership Conference had proven its effectiveness in Birmingham. While neither the organization nor King was beyond criticism, they had emerged from the confrontation with more influence and experience. Furthermore, as the March on Washington would show, the "dream" had been refined by the give and take in Birmingham. SCLC's leaders had fewer illusions about the problems nonviolent strategy faced. Yet they also had more determination to express the deeper implications of nonviolence as a way of life.

The two months before the March on Washington were not easy for King personally. Critics of the May 10 truce abounded. As he toured the country coast to coast to promote the march, King sometimes encountered an unexpected kind of opposition. To some militant blacks he was beginning to look like an accommodationist in new garb. In Harlem, for example, Black Muslims pelted his car with rotten eggs. King was not hurt, but he was angered and discouraged by this kind of treatment. They just did not understand what he was trying to do.[84] Unwittingly, these angry blacks were transferring to him their "bitterness toward the white man," King wrote.[85] In his view, anger would accomplish nothing and a few weeks later the beleagured SCLC leader would stand before the crowd of more than 200,000 at the Lincoln Memorial and cry out "I still have a dream".

5

Broadening Horizons of the Middle Sixties

The March on Washington

If King was discouraged by the negative reactions of the Black Muslims in Harlem, he was not surprised by them. Nor did he attribute the Muslims' hostility entirely to their peculiar political views. King knew that the frustrations of urban blacks were near explosive levels and that his nonviolent approach had thus far meant little to them. Somehow he had to reach them with the message that life could become better if the force of nonviolence could be translated into first, attitudinal changes, and then, substantive social reform. This had happened to some degree in the South. It could also occur nationally. That was the essence of the dream King had developed by late summer 1963. And within a year, he would expand it into a larger vision of national transformation as important to whites as to blacks.

King first used the specific "I have a dream" reference on June 23, 1963 in Detroit, less than a week before his unpleasant encounter in Harlem. The occasion was a huge demonstration called the Walk for Freedom which the Detroit Council for Human Rights sponsored in response to racial problems in the city. Over 125,000 people, whites and blacks, assembled for the march to be headed by the SCLC president. It was the largest group King had ever led, and most of them crowded into the massive Cobo Hall to hear him speak. There was an urgency in

131

his voice, even more so than usual. The Negro is through with segregation "now, henceforth, and forever more."[1] And as he defined the goals of the black movement, he appended to each one "I have a dream." The audience responded warmly with applause and cheers as King asked people of all races to take a stand for justice and to do so with infrangible commitment. "I submit to you that if a man hasn't discovered something he will die for, he isn't fit to live." Thousands were on their feet by then.[2] King had found his most potent verbal imagery since the "Give us the ballot" speech of 1957.

In Washington on August 28, King again used the "I have a dream" phrase, but to a larger audience and in a more carefully prepared address. Some 200,000 people, including 60,000 whites, had assembled for the march. Many had arrived early in the morning, and by the time of the actual walk to Lincoln Memorial, march leaders had difficulty staying ahead of the enthusiastic demonstrators. It was a very hot day, but the excitement was high and the throng of marchers managed to sit through more than two hours of speeches and songs with few signs of weariness. Asa Randolph led the long list of dignitaries who addressed them, underscoring the theme of the march 'For Jobs and Freedom' and calling for steps to elevate the economic condition of the poor.

Most of the other speakers followed suit, insisting on political and economic reforms but without attacking President Kennedy personally. The march leaders had agreed to avoid negative references to Kennedy in view of his importance to the black movement and the delicate balance in Congress. It was clear to most people that the underlying purpose of the march was to urge passage of Kennedy's civil rights package. It is true that John Lewis made critical remarks about the Kennedy bill the previous day, but he did so, he says, because he wanted to "say something truly relevant" and not simply be part of a show.[3] Several of the speakers, including Whitney Young and Roy Wilkins, gave suggestions for improving the Kennedy-sponsored legislation pending in Congress.

Finally, with notes in hand, Martin King took the microphone about 3:00 P.M. The heat was taking its toll by then, and people were distracted from the platform proceedings. Then Asa Randolph introduced the young president of SCLC as "the moral leader of the nation," and applause steadily spread across the audience. King began slowly and deliberately, "I am happy to join with you today in what will go down in history as the greatest demonstration for freedom in the history of our nation." Quickly he called attention to Lincoln's Emancipation Proclamation and the fact that even after a full century "the life of the Negro is still sadly crippled by the mannacles of segregation and the chains of discrimination. . . and [he] lives on a lonely island of poverty in the midst of a vast ocean of material prosperity." What they had come to do that day, King said, was to "dramatize a shameful condition." From there he went on to call the nation's attention to its collective failure to deliver on the "promissory note to which every American was to fall heir."

The crowd began to quicken as the SCLC president reviewed the national deficits of responsibility toward blacks and the poor and insisted that "it is time to make real the promises of democracy." Everything in his speech thus far pointed to full realization of the American dream of equality and democracy. He had words of criticism for white leaders, but he did not neglect telling blacks candidly that the answer to their problems did not lie in hostility or violence. To his own people who stood, King said, "on the warm threshold which leads into the palace of justice," he proposed a nonviolent approach. They must not, he urged, be guilty of satisfying their "thirst for freedom by drinking the cup of bitterness and hatred." Their struggle had to be conducted on a higher plain than that. It was "soul force" that must meet "physical force," he insisted.

For several minutes King spoke this way, looking closely at his text, making sure that all points were covered, including the bodily and mental suffering many had gone through because of racial prejudice and hatred. He demanded removal of segregationist signs and barriers to voting rights. "We will not be satisfied," he cried, "until justice rolls down like waters and righteousness like a mighty stream." He noted that many had come to Washington from recent ordeals in jails, from frightening confrontations in hostile crowds, and from other "storms of persecution."

Then, the magic of King's preaching locked the crowd in a rhythmic chord of response as they seemed to hang on every phrase. Looking away from his text now, he continued:

> I say to you today, my friends, so even though we face the difficulties of today and tomorrow, I still have a dream. It is a dream deeply rooted in the American dream. I have a dream that one day this nation will rise up and live out the true meaning of its creed: "We hold these truths to be self-evident; that all men are created equal."

With that King tied the objectives of the nonviolent movement to the historic dream of the United States, whose foundational documents taught equality of personhood under God.

His words swept across the panorama of southern life: "the red hills of Georgia," the states of Mississippi and Alabama, and all places where racism had marred the lives of blacks and whites. He dreamed that the time would come in Georgia when "the sons of former slaves and the sons of former slave-owners will be able to sit down together at the table of brotherhood." For his own children, King envisaged the day when they "will not be judged by the color of their skin but by the content of their character." The many thousands in the audience were meeting each declaration of the now flowing speech with words like "Tell it!" He continued the message of potential brotherhood, looking to the time in Alabama when "little black boys and little black girls will be able to join hands with little white boys and little white girls and walk together as sisters and brothers. I have a dream today!"

But King did not stop there. His dream, he told the audience, was one of victory for principles of religious truth.

> I have a dream that one day every valley shall be exalted, every hill and mountain shall be made low, the rough places will be made plains, and the crooked places will be made straight, and the glory of the Lord shall be revealed, and all flesh shall see it together.

134

This was the faith, he said, that he would return to the South with, and which he hoped would be the faith of all Americans. A better day was coming, King averred. It had to "if America is to be a great nation."

> So let freedom ring from the prodigious hilltops of New Hampshire; . . . from the mighty mountains of New York; let freedom ring from the heightening Alleghenies of Pennsylvania; . . . from the snow-capped Rockies of Colorado; . . . from the curvaceous slopes of California. But not only that. Let freedom ring from Stone Mountain of Georgia; . . . from Lookout Mountain of Tennessee; let freedom ring from every hill and molehill of Mississippi. From every mountainside, let freedom ring.

If "all of God's children" would join hands: Jews, Gentiles, whites, blacks, Catholics, Protestants, they would be able to sing together in the words of an old Negro spiritual, "Free at last! Free at last! Thank God Almighty, we are free at last!"[4]

As King finished, the audience fell silent for a moment, then burst into thunderous applause. The dream had been expressed in its most intense and comprehensive form ever. He felt good about it as he was wisked away by marshals to cars waiting to carry the top ten leaders of the march to the White House for a conference with Kennedy. The crowd nearly mobbed King as they tried to touch him. Mrs. King grabbed his arm, determined this time to be with her husband. She rode with him to the White House gate and then took a taxi to their hotel where she waited hours for the chance to celebrate the victory. Mrs. King wrote later that she "felt that the tremendous response to his great speech—perhaps his greatest—had completely restored the people's faith in the principle of nonviolence, and that it had established Martin beyond doubt as what A. Philip Randolph had named him, the moral leader of the nation."[5]

Not everyone shared Mrs. King's estimation of the speech or the march. Among the detractors were the militant blacks who viewed the whole affair as histrionic. Black Muslim leader Malcolm X called the demonstration "The Farce on Washington," and thought of it as being engineered more by Washington officials than by the black people of America. "Hollywood couldn't have topped it," he said.[6] The list was long of those blacks who either out of jealousy, sincere disagreement, or strategic politics, criticized what King did and said on August 28.

The FBI did not miss the opportunity to tighten its surveillance as Hoover's organization quickly set up devices and spies to watch King's activities and made tapes of a party where King allegedly engaged in immoral actions. More than ever King was marked by the FBI as both hypocritical and pro-communist. Soon the bureau would be tapping his telephones and watching his every move.[7]

Even more sobering were the events that surrounded the march. Both before and after August 28, the summer of 1963 was scarred by violence. In addition to the hostilities in Birmingham, there were hundreds of instances of racial conflict in dozens of cities. The most dramatic case was the murder of NAACP activist Medgar Evers, who was shot and killed as he stepped out of his car in Jackson, Mississippi on June 12. The young attorney had a promising career before he was cut down by what Wilkins called "a cold, brutal, and deliberate killing in a savage, uncivilized state."[8]

King's speech had no discernible effect on such atrocities, at least in the short run. Just two weeks after the Washington demonstration, violence hit with lightning-like fierceness in Birmingham during a Sunday School session at the Sixteenth Street Baptist Church. On September 15 while black children were reading about Jesus' teaching on loving one's enemies, a group of white men in a moving car hurled dynamite into the classroom, injuring several, and killing four young black girls. Stunned and disillusioned, King delivered a eulogy for three of the children at a joint funeral service. It was one of his hardest tasks, but he attempted to use the tragedy for good, noting that all who espoused hatred had contributed to it. Of the four little children whose lives had been snuffed out he said: "They did not die in vain. God still has a way of wringing good out of evil. History has proved again and again that unearned suffering is redemptive. The innocent blood of these little girls may well serve as the redemptive force that will bring new light to this dark city."[9] Except for a few ministers, white representatives of the city were glaringly absent from the funeral. As some blacks, like writer John Killens, were urging their race to carry guns for protection, King was still insisting that there were white people of good will in Birmingham, but they had to stand up and be counted.[10]

And in St. Augustine, Florida in September, the dream's content seemed very remote to black dentist Robert Hayling when he and three other blacks were kidnapped by the Ku Klux Klan. As president of the local NAACP branch, Hayling had been leading desegregation efforts in the historic Florida city and the Klan was seeking to stop him. Although he narrowly escaped death in the incident, Hayling went on with his work, only to have his home blasted a few weeks later.

It is not surprising that King's address did not deter such violent disregard for human life, or that the March was not the immediate prelude to a transformation of American race relations. The problems it focused on were too deeply rooted to be so readily resolved. It was, after all, an unrealized dream that King projected. Many of the variables that would determine whether it could be historically realized were matters of conscience. The speech was intended to touch American moral sensitivity to racial and human injustice. As King said in his closing remarks, it was faith in the rightness and viability of the dream that he would carry back to the South as he hoped others would to their home towns.

In the "I Have a Dream" address there was much continuity with King's earlier speeches and writings. A close comparison of its content with the "Letter from a Birmingham Jail" reveals that King continued his emphasis upon the inseparability of issues of human suffering and societal responsibility. That "whatever affects one directly, affects all indirectly" was reaffirmed in broader terms in the "I Have a Dream" speech. The economic dimensions of black freedom which King underscored in the Birmingham letter were again emphasized in the Washington speech. From his Birmingham jail in April King had written to the critical ministers that the black finds it impossible to explain racial segregation to his children, especially when he sees "the vast majority of his twenty million Negro brothers smothering in an airtight cage of poverty in the midst of an affluent society." In Washington he told the huge throng that even though a century had passed since the Emancipation Proclamation, "the Negro lives on a lonely island of poverty in the midst of a vast ocean of material prosperity."

Neither was there anything new in King's call for a collective multi-racial effort to end injustice and discrimination. With faith in the dream, he said in Washington, "we will be able to work together, pray together, to struggle together, knowing that one day we will be free." A few months earlier, he had tried to reach the Birmingham ministers with the idea of an "inescapable network of mutuality" that binds us all "in a single garment of destiny." One can see echoes, furthermore, of King's appeals in *Stride Toward Freedom* in 1958 for whites and blacks, especially those who claimed to believe in God, to "take the lead in social reform" rather than remain passive or afraid to act.[11]

Much progress had been made in that regard since the beginning of the nonviolent movement. The Kennedy administration was now openly pushing for strong civil rights legislation, people of all races had shown sympathy for the March on Washington, and all of the major civil rights organizations were growing in effectiveness and enthusiasm. But two glaring difficulties obstructed the path: continued violence and hostility in racial relations and the lack of a comprehensive civil rights act to guarantee basic rights.

At SCLC national headquarters and throughout its network of affiliates, the glow of the Birmingham success and Washington march engendered an overt confidence that these could be rectified. "Birmingham has transmitted a new sense of courage to Negroes everywhere," wrote Wyatt Tee Walker in 1964. "No longer was the Negro paralyzed by the fear of what might happen if he stood up like a man against segregation."[12] It had done more than that, as Walker saw it. The Birmingham struggle had literally filled the jails and marked a new plateau in the effectiveness of the nonviolent civil rights movement. The movement had come of age in a sense that had not been true of the campaigns in Montgomery or Albany. Not only had it affected blacks but it had moved the federal government as well, and things could never be the same after Birmingham and the March on Washington.[13]

King, too, felt that what had happened in the spring and summer of 1963 represented a watershed in the evolution of black political consciousness, especially in the area of self-perception. Even after the child killings at the Sixteenth Street Baptist Church he expressed confidence that "In the summer of 1963 the Negroes of America wrote an emancipation proclamation for themselves. They shook off three hundred years of psychological slavery and said: 'We can make ourselves free'. "[14] To both of these SCLC leaders that was important, for they shared the view that ultimately the freedom of blacks depended more upon themselves than any outside agency or group.[15]

In truth, blacks were moving to secure freedom, and because of the militancy of some manifestations of this effort, SCLC was placed in a complicated position. Its leadership knew that the heightened publicity of 1963 was valuable, but was not in itself the substance of real change. Tangible, specific steps had to be taken to increase black freedom and mobility, or the country could soon face violent black uprisings against the prevailing social order. SCLC leaders did not view that as a happy prospect, but they fully shared the sense of urgency some blacks were expressing by their words and actions. King warned that "the whirlwinds of revolt will continue to shake the foundations of our nation until the bright day of justice emerges." Yet he could neither endorse violent methods nor accept the notion that they were inevitable. In that sense, his nonviolent strategy was facing double-edged pressure from discontent black America and the political establishment.

One month after the March on Washington, SCLC met for its seventh annual convention in Richmond, Virginia. The theme, "Freedom Now," and the prevailing mood of the gathering reflected these tensions. Walker blasted the partial freedoms of blacks and cautioned against self-deceiving confidence that freedom had arrived. "We have been duped," he declared, "or we have duped ourselves, into believing the chains have been broken, when in truth we have only been chained more securely. Half-freedom has in many instances been worse than no freedom at all."[16]

King's speech to the convention was hardly more positive. The child killings in Birmingham just days earlier still troubled him, and while he expressed no doubts that "nonviolence will redeem the soul of America," he warned of obstacles ahead and called for continued vigilance.[17] He was losing no time glorying over Birmingham or Washington, but rather was considering bolder steps to push for fundamental changes in America's treatment of minorities. King was contemplating the possibility of supporting a nationwide strike or civil disobedience campaign, marked by marches, work stoppages, and other demonstrations. He heard Walker give the idea a trial run at the convention, and still had mixed feelings about it. "It is quite possible," Walker told the delegates, "that in the next few months on some appointed day, at some appointed hour, the nation will be literally immobilized by widespread acts of civil disobedience. That day may not be far off if the nation does not act swiftly on the Negro's plea for justice and morality."[18]

Partly on the advice of some of his aides and more because of his own uncertainty about the wisdom of a national strike, King decided to reject the work stoppage. For one thing, a nationwide strike might not elicit sufficient support, and it also ran the risk of backfiring to the detriment of the pending civil rights bill. In any case, King was realistic about the potential for black rebellion with or without a sanctioned strike. "I hope that civil disobedience will not be necessary," he told reporters, "but if something is not done quickly, if Congress filibusters the civil rights bill and does not pass the public accommodations section, Negroes will engage in massive civil disobedience."[19]

SCLC's expectations, therefore, were not unqualified. Even King's increased popularity contiued to be a mixed blessing. Militants stepped up their verbal barrage, describing King in

140

increasingly negative terms. Malcolm X said in a televised interview after Birmingham that King subsidized white people so that he could "teach the Negroes to be defenseless." In Malcolm's view, Birmingham was not a victory and King was only "a twentieth century Uncle Tom."[20] To the Muslim spokesman the answer lay in black self-defense, and a revolution "by any means necessary," rather than accommodating the white power structure and seeking federal support.

Furthermore, the FBI carried its surveillance of King a step further and was apparently seeking to discredit him as a national black leader. Already the Kennedy administration was concerned about the possible connections of some of SCLC's supporters with communism and was urging King to get rid of Levison, Jack O'Dell of the SCLC New York office, and others. Both John and Robert Kennedy were clearly convinced that passage of the civil rights bill was less assured as long as people of questionable political connections were associated with King's movement.[21]

FBI investigations turned to lower methods as SCLC headquarters, King's home, hotel rooms of SCLC officials during their travels, and other points of contact were electronically bugged. Telephones were tapped and even some of the most private actions of King and his staff were recorded and reported to Hoover. They could not jokingly allude to communism, or embrace a friend without the assumption that they were doing something unpatriotic or immoral. The Justice Department and White House soon amassed much information and misinformation about King and his organization.[22]

These were indeed difficult months for King as he sought effective strategies after the March on Washington. No doubt, as his biographers have demonstrated, King was going through much personal agony. The long days away from his family, the endless schedule of speeches, flights, conferences, and lack of privacy brought fatigue to the very human King. Nor was it easy for him to decide on his own future role or the scope and nature of SCLC operations. It is of the utmost importance to see King in perspective. Whatever his personal shortcomings revealed by

FBI secret investigations or the comments of some of his intimate aides, he painfully struggled with his "lower self" and took a Pauline view of his human tendencies to yield to it. Sexual temptations were profoundly troublesome to him but one can readily see that his Christian convictions were brought to bear on them. "I am conscious of two Martin Luther Kings," he said, and he meant more than the obvious dichotomy between the King of public image and his private self. He spoke in several sermons of the tension between one's best self as a Christian and the lower self so vulnerable to sin.[23]

Serious errors can be made in this regard in the name of objectivity. King was hardly the saintly superman that some have seen him to be. But true objectivity cannot be content with stressing the minor over the major or underrating the fact that King remained, despite his real and imagined flaws, the hero of the vast majority of young reformers and a respected leader among the major spearheading people in the black movement. James Lawson, who knew him well, has said that throughout the middle sixties King "by and large was still the fundamental symbol for the vast, vast numbers of people."[24] In its January 3, 1964 edition, *Time Magazine* named King man of the year for 1963, the first black American to be so honored.

SCLC also gave evidence of potential for greater impact, although it still had some very real limitations. By the end of 1963 its staff had grown to sixty-one and its budget to $735,000 for fiscal 1962–1963.[25] It would soon lose its ablest administrator, Wyatt Tee Walker, who would depart in 1964 to work with the development of the Negro Heritage Library of Education Heritage. King was reluctant to let him go, but was willing to give the project his blessing. But before long, Andrew J. Young, who would become one of SCLC's best known leaders, succeeded Walker. Furthermore, SCLC could still attract new personnel, sometimes from other civil rights organizations, but also literally from the streets. The capacity of SCLC to draw young people from lives with little sense of direction and give them something to work for, was a quality remembered by many former SCLC workers.[26]

142

Into SCLC's ranks in 1963 and 1964 came an additional number of capable and experienced people, including Willie Bolden, Ben Clark, and Lester Hankerson. Hosea Williams, a fiery frontline activist whom King would use to initiate campaigns and who refers to himself as "the Castro" and the "bad guy" of the movement, came from Savannah.[27] C. T. Vivian, a veteran of Kelly Miller Smith's Nashville campaigns and an associate of James Lawson, John Lewis, Diane Nash, became director of affiliates. Vivian worked in the St. Augustine campaign of 1964 and then led the affiliate department over the following years. A deep believer in nonviolence and the importance of a meaningful program of action, Vivian added much to SCLC's planning and organizational efforts.[28] There was also Randolph Blackwell, who came to SCLC from the Voter Education Project and served as field director from January 1963 to August 1964.

The last few months of 1963 gave SCLC much to do. King continued to hammer away in behalf of the civil rights bill in a strongly-worded article in the *New York Times Magazine* just after the Richmond convention.[29] Without slowing his pace he spoke to churches, civic groups, labor unions, and clubs, all the while working on his new book, *Why We Can't Wait*, which would appear the following summer.

Meanwhile other SCLC people were involved in conferences and programs, emphasizing the need for more jobs for blacks, political participation, and protection against violence. In September Abernathy spoke at the first anniversary of Operation Breadbasket and urged more pressure on businesses to hire blacks. Then in early October King and others were back in Birmingham pushing for the hiring of black policemen, more official protection, and proper legal action against the killers of the four children at Sixteenth Street Baptist Church. However, there were no convictions, not even any indictments.[30]

Another involvement occurred in Atlanta on October 19 as SCLC, NAACP, and CORE met with civic and business leaders in the Atlanta Summit Leadership Conference. The black leaders presented the mayor and alderman an "Action for Democracy'' plan that demanded more jobs and other concessions to local black citizens. If these were not met by mid-November, they warned, there would be a Christmas season boycott of selected businesses. The boycott was called off as white leaders appeared to be complying, but by December 15, there was such disillusionment with lack of progress that SNCC and comedian Dick Gregory led a demonstration in downtown Hurt Park. As winds chilled the air, King spoke to the crowd of about 3,000 giving one of his unusually outspoken critiques of Atlanta's racial policies.[31] Among conservative blacks, this caused further erosion of respect for King, since again he seemed to be encouraging the radical element.

In the midst of this busy autumn came the biggest public trauma of the early sixties when John F. Kennedy was assassinated in Texas on November 22 as he rode in an open car in Dallas. This thrust Vice-President Lyndon B. Johnson into the presidency at a time when many of Kennedy's proposals, including the civil rights bill, were not yet implemented. The black reaction to Kennedy's death was strong. Coretta King wrote that ''Nothing had ever affected me as deeply as President Kennedy's death, not even the news that Martin had been stabbed in Harlem.'' Mrs. King had profound respect and affection for Kennedy, who had intervened to help her husband and had appeared ''kind and thoughtful to us. . ., a friend to be relied upon, as well as our President.''[32] King echoed these feelings. To be sure he had done his share of criticizing Kennedy, but he came to believe that Kennedy was more than he seemed and that the President was maturing into a fairminded, determined friend of minorities. In a *Look* article of November 1964, King wrote that Kennedy was ''at his death undergoing a transformation from a hesitant leader with unsure goals to a strong figure with deeply appealing objectives.''[33] In *Why We Can't Wait*, he gave Kennedy credit for a ''deep grasp of the dynamics of and the necessity for social change.'' The President's untimely death, in King's view, had revealed to the nation, as nothing else had in recent times, just how contagious violence was and how disrespectful it was of class or status.

Four little black girls in a southern church. . . now a wealthy and famous President. To King the disease ran deep in the society as a whole. "We were all involved in the death of John Kennedy," he mused. "We tolerated hate; we tolerated the sick stimulation of violence in all walks of life; and we tolerated the differential application of law, which said that a man's life was sacred only if we agreed with his views."[34]

The Civil Rights Act of 1964

One initial effect of the Kennedy assassination was uncertainty among civil rights leaders. Wilkins noted that "Everything is in a state of suspension for the moment." No one knew when or how the civil rights movement would be resumed after the period of mourning and the necessary adjustment to Johnson. Wilkins was confident that progress would continue, but King and his aides wondered whether Johnson, a wealthy Southerner, would be supportive of the black cause.[35] Later, King was relieved of some of his misgivings when he met with Johnson in early December 1963. "His emotional and intellectual involvement were genuine and devoid of adornment," King wrote about the new President. "It was conspicuous that he was searching for a solution to a problem he knew to be a major shortcoming in American life."[36]

In sharp contrast, many blacks took the assassination as confirmation that their hopes had little chance of fulfillment. Nineteen-sixty-three had already produced about 1,000 demonstrations, over 20,000 arrests, and outbursts of violence in scores of cities across the nation. With Kennedy's death came another visible sign that violence was not abating. Journalist Pat Watters, who over several years viewed much of the civil rights movement in the South, concluded that Kennedy's assassination was a major contributing factor in northern blacks' disillusionment with nonviolence. And in the South, speculated Watters, the assassination was "an important one of many causes of the deterioration of hope, of will, of redemptive love, within the southern movement."[37]

But Johnson made contact with black leaders immediately

after the Dallas tragedy and continued to consult with them for several months. He strongly urged Congress to pass the Kennedy civil rights bill and in general to carry through with the slain President's programs.[38] In his State of the Union address on January 8, 1964, Johnson appealed to Congress to seize the historical moment and help him create what he called the Great Society. Included in Johnson's approach was considerable emphasis upon rights for minorities and indeed all Americans facing unusual difficulties or abridgement of rights. A few months later the President published *My Hope for America*, a short book in which he underscored the imperative of basing the Great Society on liberty and prosperity for all. He assumed that growth of the economy, elimination of poverty, and guarantees of basic rights were essential for achieving a more equitable society in the United States.[39]

Apparently Kennedy's death and Johnson's strong stand—indeed stronger than Kennedy's—helped move the Congress to act. On February 10, 1964, the House passed H.R. 7152 and sent it to the Senate. The act had provisions for banning discrimination in virtually all public facilities, some increased federal authority to enforce voting rights, as well as guarantees of basic constitutional rights, fair employment practices, and denial of federal financial assistance to programs or institutions practicing discrimination. Its weakest section was the voting rights provisions, but overall it was a more comprehensive package than any bill passed since Reconstruction.

As expected, debate in the Senate lasted several months. Hubert Humphrey, true to his long record of supporting civil rights, nursed it through the whole course from February to July 1964. Senator Richard Russell of Georgia and other southern conservatives prepared for a filibuster while Humphrey, Johnson, and others tried to enlist support. King spoke out in March 1964 in another article in the *Nation* in favor of the bill and against the filibuster.[40] But it was Republican Minority Leader Senator Everett Dirksen of Illinois who largely broke the deadlock in the Senate with a series of amendments to the House bill. The Dirksen amendments weakened the House version in some respects, but they were the key to Senate passage.* On June 19, 1964 the southern filibuster was crushed, and the bill passed the Senate by a vote of 73 to 27.[41]

On July 2 President Johnson signed the *1964 Civil Rights Act* into law, with many black leaders attending the White House ceremonies. The President credited Kennedy with its conception and praised the legislators whose "careful debate and discussion" had produced the new law. Then, in looking to the future, he said "This Civil Rights Act is a challenge to all of us to go to work in our communities and our states, in our homes and in our hearts, to eliminate the last vestiges of injustice in our beloved country."[42]

The eleven Titles of the 1964 Civil Rights Act ranged from voting rights to public accommodations, public facilities, public schools, the Civil Rights Commission, federal aid, employment, statistics, courts, conciliation, and miscellaneous juridical procedures. Title VI was critical since it provided that federal funds would be cut off from state or local agencies that discriminated. Significantly, it extended the life of the waning Civil Rights Commission to January 30, 1968, and created (Title X) a Community Relations Service in the Commerce Department to assist in conciliating racial disputes.

Black reaction was generally favorable, but cautious. Roy Wilkins saw it as "the culmination of decades of efforts by the NAACP and many other organizations and individuals to secure Congressional recognition of and action in behalf of the Negro's basic citizenship rights." Wilkins, though, like many others, soberly recognized that the struggle was not over. This "Magna Carta of Human Rights," as he called it, was likely to meet "hardcore resistance" in some communities.[43] James Forman of SNCC was less optimistic, pointing out that he believed police brutality was the number one issue and that the bill would not

---

* The Dirksen amendments brought an increase to the voluntary compliance aspect and deferred federal action in employment disputes until a local Fair Employment Commission had used a ninety-day period to deal with complaints.

prevent that. Forman doubted, too, that it would produce more jobs or guarantee access to public facilities in many areas.[44]

King saw the 1964 act as marking an historic juncture in the struggle for freedom. It appeared to him as "legislative recognition of the so-called Negro revolution of 1963." What concerned him most was the question of compliance. Would the United States live up to it? King told the Republican Platform Committee just five days after the bill became law that if it were not enforced, blacks would continue to demonstrate, indeed to such a degree that the civil disobedience of 1963 would appear "infinitesimal" by comparison.[45]

In addition to the salient question of compliance, the weak voting rights provision (Title I) of the 1964 Civil Rights Act called the new law into question. President Johnson recognized this deficiency, but apparently wanted to defer any further proposals on voting rights until the 1964 Act had been given time for "digestion" in the states most directly affected by it. Some evidence suggests that the President made provisional moves toward a voting rights act in mid-1964, but it was early 1965 before he would send specific instructions to the Attorney General.[46]

At last the pendulum of federal policy seemed to have swung to the side of the black movement. As Congress passed the Civil Rights Act it provided the legal basis for integration of virtually all public facilities and some measure of redress of a wide range of grievances. But the civil rights picture in 1964 was more complicated than it had ever been, and a wave of reaction and violence accompanied the legislative victory. King was by no means secure in the thought that blacks had won their freedom or even committed themselves to the nonviolent philosophy. "While we can celebrate that the civil rights movement has come of age, we must recognize that the basic recalcitrance of the South has not yet been broken."[47] Nor, he continued, had most blacks or whites been deeply influenced by nonviolence in its broadest meaning. "The great masses have used it pragmatically as a tactical weapon, without being ready to live it."[48]

Meanwhile, SCLC leaders attempted to resolve some of their

internal conflicts and chart a course for future activity. In January 1964 they held a retreat at Black Mountain, North Carolina, both for some much needed rest and to spend some relatively unfettered time talking among themselves about future directions of SCLC's work. Perhaps more than they realized, the SCLC leaders were confronting issues that were thrust upon all of the direct-action organizations at that juncture. SNCC and CORE were also troubled by generic questions of strategy, goals, and even conceptual framework. What were the relative merits of voter registration and the quest for federal action on civil rights?[49] What kind of coalition would be most effective—a black-white liberal partnership working collectively to desegregate the nation or a largely black movement less indebted to the white system? And beyond this, there was the issue of cooperation among the various black reformist organizations. The March on Washington had temporarily brought them all together, but this was no guarantee of a continuing common front or even an assurance that such was desirable.

At Black Mountain SCLC did not find answers to its own versions of these questions, but it did explore them and take some steps toward keeping the momentum of the summer of 1963 going. Already there were signs of declining popular enthusiasm, which had to be countered if the movement were to make any further progress. It was obvious at the Black Mountain retreat that careful, extensive planning was necessary, so King's staff looked over the voter education and registration programs, eyed possibilities for action in southern rural areas, and examined the viability of broadening SCLC's national outreach.[50] Significantly, they decided to create an SCLC advisory body known as the Research Committee to serve as a 'think tank' on strategic planning. The committee would include Abernathy, Andrew Young and Walter Fauntroy, as well as historian L. D. Reddick, Bayard Rustin, Harry Wachtel, Stanley Levison and other advisers from New York, Chicago, and Cleveland.[51] The inclusion of Levison gave the FBI further cause to maintain surveillance of King and to bring other members of the planning body under scrutiny.[52]

Two weeks later Annell Ponder, who had worked extensively with SCLC's citizenship program, wrote to King about the possibility of SCLC's sponsoring a benefit for COFO (Council of Federated Organizations) to support its planned voter registration drive in Mississippi that spring and summer.[53] A 1962 offshoot of the Voter Education Project, COFO linked SNCC, CORE, NAACP and SCLC in cooperative use of VEP funds, and in early 1964 agreed to promote a massive SNCC voter registration drive in Mississippi. This Summer Project would become the most dramatic voter registration project of 1964, and King and SCLC were happy to work with COFO in this concerted effort to register black voters and promote black office seekers in Mississippi.[54] SCLC also continued to make plans for its own voter registration drive in the Selma, Alabama area.

At that point, SCLC's practice of responding to needs as they arose brought some modification of plans. As disquieting news came of worsening conditions in St. Augustine, an avant-garde of SCLC personnel was dispatched to the Florida city. Dr. Hayling's home had been attacked again, this time with shotguns, endangering the lives of his family and leaving their dog dead. Other black families were also under attack for attempting to integrate local schools. In his distress Hayling called King to appeal for assistance. With such things going on King wondered why the federal government did not intervene and how it could financially support St. Augustine's forthcoming four-hundredth anniversary. Then in a meeting with Hayling during an SCLC rally in Orlando, King promised help. Soon Hosea Williams arrived in St. Augustine to prepare for a larger SCLC effort there, and by late May 1964, SCLC field leaders were organizing night marches.[55]

With only 12,000 citizens in 1964 and mostly oriented to tourist trade, St. Augustine was hardly a southern metropolis like Birmingham. But it had for King and SCLC considerable symbolic and practical significance. According to the SCLC president, it was "one of the most segregated cities in America and a stronghold of the Ku Klux Klan and the John Birch Society."[56] St. Augustine would become a test case, both for

150

nonviolence, and as it turned out, the 1964 Civil Rights Act. The timing was appropriate too as the city celebrated its founding four centuries earlier by the Spanish. King felt that the festivities would be a fitting occasion for making the city a "nonviolent battleground."[57]

This reference to St. Augustine as a "nonviolent battleground" had more meaning than is apparent at first glance, for King and his SCLC associates were experiencing, in the wake of Birmingham and the mammoth demonstration in Washington, a crisis of self-perception as well as strategy. Criticisms of nonviolence were coming not only from militant activists but also from experienced intellectuals. As recently as November 1963 King had participated in a conference on nonviolent social change at Howard University, where speakers of the quality of psychology professor Dr. Jerome D. Frank of Johns Hopkins had described nonviolence as contradictory and escapist. Dr. Frank argued that "only groups that believe that they cannot hope to win by violence have adhered to nonviolent tactics," and he suggested in no uncertain terms that "nonviolent advocates" ultimately had to rely on outside help and threat of violence to accomplish their goals.[58] King disagreed, of course, and tried to make a strong case for his position when he addressed a session of the conference on youth, nonviolence, and social change. The SCLC leader spoke of "tremendous gains" made so far, especially the raising of civil and human rights issues to a high level of national consciousness.[59]

King meant what he said, no doubt, but he was beginning to see more clearly that aspects of his approach were inherently problematical when measured by historical substance. The intensified violence in the ghettos of Harlem and other northern communities where blacks were highly concentrated was the most glaring evidence that nonviolence was questionable as a strategy and possibly in need of revision philosophically. Even Atlanta, King's operational headquarters, was troubled by violence in early 1964 following the Christmas season confrontations between blacks and white merchants. Before the St. Augustine campaign reached its climax later in the summer of

1964, the ghetto upheavals literally dominated the black reform movement and confronted it with difficult new pressures.

Further complicating what would frequently be termed the "long hot summer" of 1964 was the simultaneous occurrence of the Mississippi Summer Project or Mississippi Freedom Summer, the St. Augustine Campaign, the ghetto riots, and presidential politics. Their confluence made it impossible for King and SCLC to give undivided attention to any one of them. King's comparatively low-key involvement in Mississippi further alienated some of his critics within and outside the circles of SNCC and CORE, and the apparent helplessness of the nonviolent strategists in trying to control, or even fully understand, the urban uprisings made even more difficult the effort to enlarge the appeal of nonviolence. Quite clearly, King's "dream" articulated so cogently in Washington seemed to many, especially those less committed than he to the broader spiritual implications of it, to be purely and simply a dream.

For SCLC as an organization, St. Augustine was the principal preoccupation of 1964. One feature that made the campaign fundamentally different from Birmingham was that the leaders of the segregationist opposition were private interest groups and individuals rather than city officials or policemen. There was no Bull Connor figure to serve as the epitome of the systemic evils. There was no dearth, however, of violence or hostility. Local segregationist Holsted ('Hoss') Manucy and his Gun Club, augmented by the Ku Klux Klan and anti-black outsiders who poured into the little city, physically and verbally attacked blacks.

The crisis worsened after May 28 when white SCLC representative Harry Boyte and his son were fired upon as they sat in their parked car. Also Boyte was knocked unconscious by white assailants. Then the sheriff banned night marches, opening a legal battle between SCLC attorney William Kuntsler and local officials. On June 9, with King then in St. Augustine, SCLC won its case when a Jacksonville federal judge declared the demonstrations legal and ordered noninterference by local officials. The next day, however, both King and Abernathy were arrested.

It did not go unnoticed by his critics that King was released on bail and traveled to Yale University to receive an honorary doctorate.[60] Was this a serious campaign or not? In truth it was, but the "public King" as he sometimes referred to his visible image was highly obligated to appear for such occasions. Nor should this be taken lightly, for SCLC's force was fundamentally dependent upon King's visibility. Furthermore, King thought it important to be involved in the 1964 presidential election and was planning appearances at both the Democratic and Republican national conventions. Preparing for them took time, as did the planning for the Selma campaign and some degree of participation in the Mississippi project.

SCLC leaders were not the only prominent people to be arrested in St. Augustine. Before King's arrival, Mrs. Malcolm Peabody, mother of the governor of Massachusetts, was arrested as she came to witness the crisis. And throughout the spring and summer, many locals were arrested and a sizable number were hurt. Andrew Young, who was then replacing Wyatt Walker as executive director of SCLC, was stunned by what he witnessed. "St. Augustine is really worse than Birmingham," Young said. "It's the worst I've ever seen."[61] Local officials ignored the federal court order to permit the demonstrations, and throughout the summer continued to obstruct them. Hundreds of whites openly resisted desegregation, and SCLC appealed for help from President Johnson.

Meanwhile, secret meetings between black and white leaders were held, prompted in part by news of the forthcoming Civil Rights Act. Again, political considerations affected the outcome. King felt compelled to move with caution, especially in view of Walker's departure and the tenuous balance of forces in relation to the Civil Rights Act. Johnson had failed to send federal marshals into St. Augustine, but his stance in the civil rights legislation had been crucial to its passage and King did not want to engage in oppositional tactics. On the other hand, people had been hurt in the struggle and had risked their jobs and even their lives. C. T. Vivian, one of SCLC's own, nearly drowned in one skirmish with state troopers, and a group of young swimmers were burned by acid when they took it upon themselves to integrate the swimming pool at the Monson Motel.[62]

The result was an uneasy truce in St. Augustine just before the July 2 signing of the Civil Rights Act. King promised to call off demonstrations but insisted that a truly biracial committee, including Hayling, be formed to work out details for desegregation. On June 30, the Governor did appoint such a committee. But the violence continued beyond July 2 despite the new federal law. And the NAACP made the first test of the Civil Rights Act by bringing suits against Manucy, several merchants, and other resisters. Although King left St. Augustine to prepare for the political conventions and other obligations, Hayling and his supporters pushed forward armed with whatever legal leverage they could find in the Civil Rights Act.

King and SCLC claimed victory in St. Augustine, but with reservations. In June he wrote in the *SCLC Newsletter* that change could come, "God willing," but only with much difficulty. Events of July and August gave little reason to alter his qualified hopefulness. Indeed, there were some signs of deterioration, the most grotesque of which was the murder of three young CORE workers, two of them white and one black, near Philadelphia, Mississippi. The two whites, Mickey Schwerner and Andrew Goodman, were Jews from New York, and their black colleague James Chaney was from Mississippi. They were in the state to investigate the bombing of a church in late June when they were arrested by Neshoba County Deputy Sheriff Cecil Price for alleged speeding. After they paid a fine and were released, they disappeared. Friends reported them missing, and six weeks later in August, the FBI found their bodies.[63]

In the meantime, King addressed the platform committees of both political party conventions in July and August, hoping to get political support for additional reforms, particularly in the area of economic development. "Of what advantage is it to the Negro," he asked the Republicans in San Francisco, "to establish that he can be served in integrated restaurants or accommodated in integrated hotels, if he is bound to the kind of financial servitude which will not allow him to take a vacation or even to take his wife out to dine?''[64]

In late August he placed the same searching question in altered terms, before the Democrats in Atlantic City. King also became involved during the Democratic convention in a delegate credentials controversy that developed from the Mississippi Summer Project. The all-white Democratic delegation to the convention was challenged by a group called the Mississippi Freedom Democratic Party. Led by Dr. Aaron Henry the MFDP delegation included sixty-four blacks and four whites. Henry, a moderate black dentist, was chairman of the MFDP as well as state president of the Mississippi NAACP. Supporting him were more militant activists like Bob Moses, a profoundly influential figure in SNCC, and Stokely Carmichael, soon to be the leading spokesman of ''black power'' ideology.

Interestingly, King supported the Mississippi Freedom Democratic Party's right to be seated at the convention in lieu of the official all white delegation. Some of the members and supporters of the MFDP were much more militant and separatist than King, but for the moment he was thinking more about black influence in the Democratic Party than any contradictions in his coalitional strategies. He had by then seen what was happening in Mississippi during the Summer Project, both negative and positive. Whatever its shortcomings, the summer drive had attracted over 1,000 highly trained people: doctors, nurses, ministers, and teachers, as well as young student volunteers. They had set up freedom schools and medical and nutritional centers to help the chronically poor. King described the MFDP delegation as ''saints in ordinary walks of life,'' and told the credentials committee that ''any party in the world should be proud to have a delegation such as this seated in their midst.''[65]

As it turned out, the MFDP delegation was not seated, and the resultant controversy nearly split the convention. The Republicans had nominated conservative Barry Goldwater in July, and President Johnson felt that he could beat the Arizona Senator if he could avoid alienating the southern states. The balance, however, was tenuous. If the MFDP delegation were rejected, this could alienate liberal support, whereas if it were seated, the South might be lost in the November election. Thus, a compromise was effected whereby the MFDP would receive two at-large votes in the convention, and steps would be taken to prevent racially segregated delegations from being seated in the future. While this was not acceptable either to the MFDP or the regular delegation, it did avoid a floor fight.[66] The all-white delegation walked out during a nationally televised session.

Despite this unusual turn of events, King was determined to help Johnson in the election against Goldwater, who was known to have voted against the Civil Rights Act and was staunchly conservative on many issues.[67] Virtually all SCLC leaders favored Johnson, and King personally spent considerable time campaigning for him. Disappointed that the Democrats rejected his idea of an "Economic Bill of Rights" which he suggested in Atlantic City, King nonetheless appreciated the $1 billion anti-poverty package Johnson pushed through the Congress in August and the fact that the President was already considering sponsoring a voting rights bill to strengthen the 1964 Civil Rights Act. A Goldwater victory might threaten those prospects, as well as increase the likelihood of international conflict at a time when relations with the Soviet Union were tenuous and the war in Vietnam was beginning to escalate.

Beyond Protest: SCLC after the Civil Rights Act

The Southern Christian Leadership Conference, in effect, declared a moratorium on further direct-action demonstrations until after the 1964 presidential elections. Several of the major civil rights organizations did the same, on the basis of an agreement among King, Wilkins, Randolph, and Whitney Young in late July.[68] To defeat Goldwater seemed a more pressing concern than other possible undertakings. Goldwater's conservatism, they felt, would obstruct further progress, and moreover, the violent atmosphere of the summer was damaging the "whole climate of liberal democracy" in the United States.[69] The time had come to take the proverbial cooling off period and think carefully about the future while exploiting as much as possible the momentum of the Civil Rights Act. John Lewis of SNCC and CORE's James Forman disagreed and rejected the cooperative suspension of demonstrations.

The moratorium on direct-action campaigns was a tactical move, but it coincided with some major readjustments of thinking by black leaders on the future efficacy of demonstrations. Although James Farmer could not support that particular moratorium, he too was modifying his views and would soon suggest changes in CORE strategy. Farmer envisaged less reliance on demonstrations and more upon building a base of political power.[70]

In truth, that was a fundamental necessity for all of the activist organizations. Passage of the Civil Rights Act, the volatility of racial relations in the summer of 1964, and a number of other subtle changes in the political atmosphere marked another watershed in the black movement. The techniques that had succeeded in Montgomery and Birmingham and which had propelled the entire nonviolent movement from 1957 to 1964 would now bring, as Farmer aptly expressed it, "diminishing returns."[71] This did not mean that demonstrations were no longer relevant or potentially efficacious. The SCLC campaign in Selma in 1965 would illustrate that direct-action demonstrations could still have impact. But no longer could they be the salient emphasis of the movement as it broadened its expectations into other areas, notably economic improvement of blacks.

SCLC's seventh annual convention in Savannah in September 1964 reflected this important change in nonviolent strategy. In an hour-long presidential report to the delegates, King observed that "demonstrations can call attention to evil, arouse the conscience of the community, but such demonstrations are not a program for removing evil itself." With his mind now more specifically on seeking substantially better economic conditions for blacks, he proffered the idea of broadening the coalitional base of the leadership conference. It was time, King felt, to develop functional coalitions with various religious, political, and economic groups to bring about systemic changes. Knowing that this idea would meet some resistance, King urged the delegates to be openminded about new ideas and strategies. Although he claimed a central role for SCLC in bringing about the recent civil rights legislation, he understood that cooperation among several groups and thousands of individuals had been the driving force and would be even more indispensable to reforms beyond basic citizenship rights.[72]

King's comments were evidence of his broadening vision of the dream concept. If he largely spoke in terms of the full realization of the historic "American dream" in 1963, he was transcending it by the summer of 1964. Passage of the Civil Rights Act was a two-edged sword, heightening the potential for expansion into socio-economic spheres while contributing to political inertia against further change. The traditional American dream was one of equality before the law, freedom to realize one's potential for self-fulfillment within a democratic system. A large cross-section of American society had favored the Civil Rights Act, but it was quite another matter when the objectives were broader. Racial identity became a major consideration, since both blacks and whites worried about racial intermarriage, loss of distinctive heritage, and the uncertainties of integrated social relationships.

Consequently by 1964 there was no small degree of concern among blacks about integration. A sizable portion of black leaders viewed it as neo-accommodationism and King as a victim of his own popularity, unable to be truly black since he was trying to make blacks acceptable to the white majority. For his part, King believed that cultural pluralism was the answer. While he acknowledged the fears among blacks that they would be "swallowed up" in the white culture, he believed that such was not inevitable.[73]

Whatever the possible outcome of enlarged cultural interaction between blacks and whites with the coming of integration, SCLC leaders were convinced that the direct-action strategy would need to be augmented in order to carry the process of reform beyond desegregation of facilities. "After the Negro emerges in the desegregated society," King said in a 1964

158

interview, "then a great deal of time must be spent in improving standards which lag behind to a large extent because of segregation, discrimination, and the legacy of slavery. The Negro will have to engage in a sort of Operation Bootstrap."[74] This comment mirrored the essence of the implications of King's position in 1964 and beyond. A freer society would bring increased obligations to the black American to help himself and simultaneously demand much of the white majority. The entire society would have to work toward real community, and the church would have to examine the social implications of its theology.[75] Although radical in potential effects, King's views at that point were definitely not radical in terms of the usual political connotations of radicalism. If that point is missed, the whole thrust of the SCLC movement after passage of the Civil Rights Act is distorted.

One important failure of this transitional period was SCLC's inability to establish a strong independent identity in the public mind, for King far outstripped his organization in public visibility. SCLC was less known than the NAACP and several other organizations, and its programs only vaguely understood.[76] Some efforts to offset this would be made after 1965, but by then King himself was more controversial, complicating the necessary public relations efforts.

King's full entry into the international community in late 1964 probably contributed to the expansion of his dream, but this should not be overly emphasized. The main lines of his thinking about post-Civil Rights Act strategy were sketched before his busy autumn schedule of European travel or his reception of the Nobel Peace Prize. It is safe to conclude, however, that the global implications of nonviolence increasingly occupied King's thought from this point onward and that his international contacts definitely heightened his consciousness of world issues, especially war and hunger.

In September 1964, shortly after the Savannah convention, he accepted an invitation from West Berlin Mayor and future Chancellor Willy Brandt to speak at a memorial ceremony for

John Kennedy. Along with Ralph and Juanita Abernathy, King and his wife toured Europe. In the course of the long trip, King spoke at a Protestant church in East Berlin, saw the Berlin Wall for the first time, and had an audience with Pope Paul VI. King and his party took the time to talk at length with religious and political leaders, learning much about concerns in Europe.

After a brief stop in Madrid for relaxation, King and his companions returned to the United States. Despite the enjoyable trip, King was exhausted and entered an Atlanta hospital for rest. It was there that he learned from Coretta that the Nobel Prize Committee had selected him to receive the 1964 Prize for Peace. It was a very meaningful honor to the SCLC president, and he donated the $50,000 prize money to SCLC and other organizations.[77]

The two months between his hospitalization and the formal reception of the Nobel Prize were marred by an overt bout with J. Edgar Hoover. On November 18, during a press conference with women journalists, the FBI chief blasted King with unrestrained criticism, calling him "the most notorious liar in the country." Although angered, King kept his composure. While he readily acknowledged his earlier criticisms of the FBI, King gave Hoover the benefit of the doubt in this latest assault. "I cannot conceive," he said in a prepared response, "of Mr. Hoover's making a statement like this without being under extreme pressure. . . . I cannot engage in a public debate with him. I have nothing but sympathy for this man who has served his country so well."[78] King, of course, did have other feelings than sympathy for Hoover, but the statement was conciliatory and served to mitigate the confrontation. In early December, just before his departure to Oslo, Norway to receive the Nobel prize, King, Abernathy, Andrew Young, and Walter Fauntroy, met with Hoover and Deke DeLoach, another FBI leader who had worked against SCLC.

King called the meeting "a quite amicable discussion," although it confirmed that profound differences separated King and Hoover. Hoover favorably reviewed the FBI's record of involvements in civil rights and made subtle references to the existence of extensive tapes that implicated SCLC personnel and supporters in subversive activities and personal improprieties. King found a place in the exchange to play down his criticism of the FBI and to deny that he supported communists. Young later described the meeting as 'completely nonfunctional.''[79] Interestingly, the FBI at one time considered seeking Young as a spy on SCLC from within.[80]

The experience in Oslo was altogether different. There on December 10, Dr. Gunnar Jahn of the Nobel Prize Committee hailed King as one who had succeeded in keeping his followers in the path of nonviolence and thus prevented much bloodshed. King responded to the honor by crediting others.

> I accept the Nobel Prize for Peace at a moment when twenty-two million Negroes of the United States of America are engaged in a creative battle to end the long night of racial injustice. I accept this award in behalf of a civil rights movement which is moving with determination and majestic scorn for risk and danger to establish a reign of freedom and a rule of justice.

King in his acceptance speech rejected the idea that "man is mere flotsam and jetsam in the river of life" and the negative assumption that "the bright daybreak of peace and brotherhood can never become a reality." He argued that it was not too audacious to assume that hungry people could be fed or that "dignity, equality, and freedom for their spirits" were unattainable. He also deplored war and called for greater efforts to make and preserve peace. King told the Nobel Committee that he thought Alfred Nobel would understand what he meant by accepting the 1964 Prize for Peace "in the spirit of a curator of some precious heirloom which he holds in trust for its true owners—all those to whom beauty is truth and truth beauty— and in whose eyes the beauty of genuine brotherhood and peace is more precious than diamonds or gold."[81]

With monarchs and other dignitaries looking on, King articulated his vision of a nonviolent world. Poetically, he challenged the world to take seriously the possibility that nonviolence just might work where historic patterns of war and hostility had not. A month later, he and the Southern Christian Leadership Conference would launch in Selma, Alabama, their campaign to complete the process of enfranchising blacks.

"A task without a dream is a drudgery;
A dream without a task is a fantasy;
A dream with a task is a victory!"

6

From Protest to Politics

"In truth," wrote King biographer Stephen Oates, "the Selma Campaign was the movement's finest hour, was King's finest hour."[1] And in some respects it was. The Selma campaign broke down the final barriers to a strong federal voting rights act by forcing Congress to act, thus confirming the effectiveness of the policy of political coercion tested first in Birmingham and refined in Selma. In a very real sense the Selma campaign brought to fruition the enfranchisement effort begun by SCLC and allied organizations in early 1958.

There was another side, however. A number of SNCC activists were further alienated from King and SCLC as a result of the Selma operations. Well before SCLC's arrival, SNCC was working in Selma under the direction of Bernard and Colia Lafayette, who initiated voter registration efforts as early as February 1963.[2] SNCC also operated in nearby Marion, without seeing the results hoped for in either city. When some SNCC people and other local black leaders sought SCLC help in 1964, not everyone was pleased. Some resented the tendency, as they saw it, for SCLC and King to steal the thunder of the foundational people. As the Selma campaign evolved, such feelings increased and left memories, in Julian Bond's words, of "SCLC's hogging all the publicity and all the money and doing very little to deserve it."[3] In that respect and others the Selma campaign aggravated the differences that deeply divided the black movement in the middle and late sixties.

When the Lafayettes returned to college, several more SNCC workers entered Selma to continue their work, including John Love, Worth Long, and by early 1965, Silas Norman. SCLC organizers also appeared, notably James Bevel. SCLC personnel came to promote voter registration and citizenship clinics, but SNCC and SCLC did not always agree on strategy. The SNCC plan was to build steadily, rather than stage a massive Birmingham-type demonstration. SCLC had a different view. King's organization had been planning a forceful voting rights campaign for months, and Selma seemed the likely focal point. Dallas County Sheriff Jim Clark was an avowed segregationist, like Bull Connor in Birmingham, and was expected to play a similar role as catalyst in Selma. He would likely react strongly to direct-action tactics and open the door to arrests, demonstrations, and eventual success for the campaign.[4]

King and several aides came into Selma on January 2, but there were few incidents at first as they sought to desegregate hotels, restaurants, and other public establishments. King was slightly injured by an attacker at a hotel at one point, but no crisis resulted. Clark did not disappoint SCLC for long, however, and on January 19 he delivered the expected reaction. A SNCC-SCLC march to the courthouse resulted in an order from Clark to disband. The angry sheriff grabbed a black woman and shoved her, and the incident was pictured in the *New York Times* and the *Washington Post* the next day.[5] King described it as "one of the most brutal and unlawful acts I have seen an officer commit." More confrontations followed in late January and February, as a determined group of blacks kept up a steady pressure. "We are going to start a march on the ballot boxes by the thousands," King had said at the outset. "We must be willing to go to jail by the thousands. We are not asking, we are demanding the ballot." On February 2, Abernathy and King led some 265 marchers from Brown's Chapel to the courthouse to protest against the slowness of black voter registration. With that, Public Safety Commissioner Wilson Baker arrested all of

164

them, sending the recent Nobel Peace Prize winner to jail. Depicted in newspapers around the world, that spectacle dramatically highlighted the Selma campaign.

While King was in jail, Malcolm X arrived in Selma on February 3 at the request of SNCC. The militant Muslim leader, who would be assassinated only eighteen days later at a rally in Harlem, spoke to a crowd in Brown's Chapel. The tone of his speech was anything but nonviolent as he told the audience to meet violence with violence. But in a private conversation with Mrs. King, he asked her to assure her jailed husband that he did not come to Selma to make the SCLC-SNCC effort harder, but rather, to help. When Malcolm was killed later in the month, it had a significant emotional impact on the Kings. Despite their differences, Malcolm X and King did share some common concerns and had a mutual respect for each other. Malcolm's message was one of freedom "by any means necessary" while King continued his nonviolent effort that put more emphasis upon the morality of the means to secure that freedom.

Both approaches experienced difficulty in Selma that month. On February 5, King was released from jail and was soon in Washington pushing for a voting rights bill and federal assistance in registration. Meanwhile Congress began to move. A delegation of fifteen legislators, led by black Michigan Congressman Charles Diggs, flew to Selma on the day of King's release. The next week they spoke out critically on the floor of the House about what they had seen. Had they stayed longer, they would have witnessed even worse confrontations.

King's visit to Washington brought assurances that a strong voting rights bill would be sent to Congress very soon. From the Selma jail he had written an open letter that appeared in the *New York Times*, asking for support and raising the question "Why are we in jail?," and answering, "We are in jail simply because we cannot tolerate these conditions for ourselves and our nation."[6] His conference with Hubert Humphrey and Attorney-General-designate Nicholas B. Katzenbach on February 9 encouraged King's belief that the administration was sincere, but he realized that time was critical in Alabama.

In both Selma and Marion there was violence, made even more chilling by news of Malcolm X's murder. One of the worst instances was the shooting of young Jimmie Lee Jackson by police on February 18 in Marion. The black youth died eight days later, causing an angry Mrs. King to call the shooting an "act of senseless white rage." Her husband had the painful task of helping with the funeral. Increasingly King was troubled by the mounting toll of violence in the United States: the black children in Birmingham, John Kennedy, now Malcolm X and young Jackson. Would it ever stop? James Bevel was beaten severely, and other nonviolent organizers were hurt. The strain even brought Sheriff Jim Clark to exhaustion, and he entered a hospital. With that, SCLC decided to send some 200 children to the hospital to offer prayers for the sheriff's recovery, "in mind as well as body."[7] This was not as cynical as some thought, for the purpose was to dramatize the inhumanity of the violence.

Washington began to take notice. On February 23, thirty-nine Republican leaders, including governors and Congressmen, criticized Johnson for lack of clarity on voting rights. Democrats also urged action, as Malcolm X's murder and the death of Jimmie Lee Jackson added to the momentum. But there was a sharp contrast between SCLC's desire for quick passage of a voting rights bill and the administration's political concerns in Congress. King returned to Washington in early March to confer again with the President, while plans were made to stage a massive voting rights march in Alabama. Governor George Wallace, meanwhile, was trying to head off the proposed demonstrations.

While the drafting process for the administration's bill went forward, the climax was coming in Selma. "I can't promise," King told his followers, "that you won't get beaten. I can't promise that you won't get your house bombed. I can't promise that you won't get scarred up a bit, but we must stand up for what is right." King was committed. . . and that commitment led him and hundreds of others to undertake a march from the Edmund Pettus Bridge to Montgomery.

The Selma to Montgomery March began in very dangerous

circumstances. Governor Wallace prohibited the march and sent state troopers to block it. On March 7, over 500 marchers met at Brown's Chapel to begin the fifty-mile trek. King and Abernathy were in Atlanta preaching. So Hosea Williams and John Lewis of SNCC walked at the front in bold defiance of officers who stood close together just across Pettus Bridge, blocking Highway 80.[8] The troopers put on their gas masks and readied their clubs. Major John Cloud ordered the marchers to halt as they came close enough for face to face staring. Williams asked for time to talk with Cloud, but it was denied. Sheriff Clark was there with his forces, as was Colonel Al (Albert J.) Lingo, whose state troopers had been ordered to Birmingham two years earlier. With night sticks, tear gas, and their collective power they pushed back the blacks, some of whom asked for mercy. Some fell to their knees to pray. All were stunned by the weight of the military-like force that blocked them, while side-line observers shouted angry profanities. Whips tore into the backs of the marchers on this "Bloody Sunday," as it was to be known in the annals of the Selma campaign.

King would not be denied. Upset by the events of Sunday, he slated another march for Tuesday, but a federal injunction prohibited the march, and President Johnson publicly requested a postponement. But hundreds of priests, pastors, and rabbis poured into Selma and the throngs of marchers grew. Johnson sent former Florida Governor LeRoy Collins to try to keep peace. Nonetheless on March 9, some 900 marchers, among them many white supporters, hundreds of black citizens, and even high-ranking society leaders, set out to break the unbreakable. "We've gone too far to turn back now," King cried. "We must let them know that nothing can stop us—not even death itself."[9] The marching crowd grew to about 1,500 with many more closing in, as they neared the same Pettus Bridge where the march aborted on Sunday. Up front this time was King, along with Fred Shuttlesworth, James Forman, and Methodist Bishop John Wesley Lord. By the same route along Sylvan Street they came. "We're on our way to Montgomery! We're on our way!

Ain't gonna let nobody turn me 'round!'' Soon, their enthusiasm would abruptly end.

What the marchers did not know was that an agreement, or at least a tacit understanding, had been reached by King and the authorities to stop the march just across the bridge, that is, short of a violent confrontation. This was a means of allowing some time for further dialogue. Thus when the marchers crossed the bridge, and the troop lines opened, it came as a surprise to many that King ordered the crowd to stop and turn around. The confused demonstrators followed King's instructions. Press interviews that followed were rather awkward, but violence had been averted, and President Johnson was relieved. But some journalists virtually crucified King for having accommodated the system.

That there was an actual march to Montgomery was due largely to the fact that subsequent events did not lead to a peaceful resolution. Three Unitarian ministers who had come to Selma to march were beaten, and one of them, Reverend James Reeb of Boston, was struck in the head and died. The Ku Klux Klan was accused of the violence. By mid-March the situation was deteriorating to intolerable levels of hostility.

Moreover, SNCC and SCLC were at odds over tactics, and King was accused by the students of capitulation in the March 9 aborted march. The idea that King had made a deal to halt the march just across Pettus Bridge was repulsive to many. King denied that he had made such a deal, but he did admit during court hearings on March 11 that he knew that the long march to Montgomery would not occur. The SCLC leader was, of course, under various kinds of pressure. He did not want to violate the injunction against the march, and he knew of the possibility of sniper fire from the Klan or possible bloody confrontations with the police. In any case it was not a good situation, and the events of March 15 came as a pleasant relief, qualified by deep-seated disappointment.

On that day a federal court declared Selma's ban on demonstrations invalid, and President Johnson spoke out vigorously to a special joint session of Congress. He was in no mood to demur on the Selma situation. Despite a visit by Governor Wallace to present his side of the story, Johnson laid his own approach on the line. Amist three dozen rounds of applause and two standing ovations, the President told the lawmakers:

> What happened in Selma is part of a far larger movement which reaches into every section and state of America. It is the effort of American Negroes to secure for themselves the full blessings of American life.
> Their cause must be our cause, too. Because it's not just Negroes, but really all of us who must overcome the crippling legacy of bigotry and injustice. And we. . .shall. . .overcome.

"No President," wrote David Lewis, "had ever spoken so feelingly of the overdue rights of the American black or pledged more unequivocally to cause their fulfillment than Lyndon Johnson."[10]

It was no coincidence that two days later, on March 17, Judge Frank M. Johnson authorized the march to Montgomery and ordered officials, including Governor Wallace, not to interfere. It was the same day Johnson sent his voting rights act to Congress. With that, many thousands of people, from entertainers to politicians and organizational leaders, gathered for the journey to the state capitol. SNCC would not officially approve the march, but many of its members participated as individuals. That James Forman marched was significant, for he had been deeply angered by what had happened so far and seemed to be planning militant action on his own.

As the march began on Sunday, March 21, the tables were entirely turned. Governor Wallace had no leverage against it, except to criticize Judge Johnson's "mock court". Now police forces were protecting the marchers rather than threatening them. Leonard Bernstein, Harry Belafonte, and other musicians entertained the marchers. King took a break on Wednesday to fly to Cleveland for a speech, and the arrival of the March in Montgomery on Thursday was more of a celebration than a victory. The 30,000 who participated were symbolic to King of a new era. He had told them as they left Selma, "Walk together, children; don't you get weary, and it will lead us to the Promised

Land. And Alabama will be a new Alabama, and America will be a new America." When they arrived in Montgomery, he said, "Last Sunday, more than eight thousand of us started on a mighty walk from Selma. . . They told us we wouldn't get here. And there were those who said that we would get here only over their dead bodies, but all the world together knows that we are here and that we are standing before the forces of power in the State of Alabama saying: 'We Ain't Gonna Let Nobody Turn Us 'Round.' "

Certainly, the Selma situation was not resolved by all this. Nor was the voting rights act clear of all opposition. But there is no denying that Selma, and particularly the march to Montgomery, had a decisive impact. Not only did they facilitate the passage of the Voting Rights Act, but they also expressed a changing strategy in the nonviolent movement. There was more force to it now, more emphasis upon political coercion and effective coalition politics.

The Voting Rights Act of 1965 passed the United States Senate only two months after the Selma to Montgomery March. House passage followed in early August, and Johnson signed it into law on August 6 with words of praise. He was correct in describing it as a landmark law, for the Voting Rights Act was strong in substance. The new law covered all states where literacy tests and other screening devices had been used to limit the franchise as of November 1, 1964, and it applied also to states in which fewer than half of the voting-age population was registered by that date or where fewer than half voted in the 1964 presidential election. The act also prohibited poll taxes in local and state elections and provided for federal registrars with the authority to enforce equity in registration and even to register voters themselves.

Virtually all of the mainstream civil rights leaders lauded the passage of the Voting Rights Act. This success, however, was not nearly enough to endear King or SCLC to the increasingly separatist militants who saw the Selma campaign and its aftermath in extremely negative terms. Some, like John Lewis and Julian Bond, were among the moderate critics who focused

170

largely on King's compromising strategy. Many others were quite outspoken in calling the Selma campaign outright capitulation. Eldridge Cleaver wrote in *Soul on Ice* that:

> much of the anger Negroes felt toward Martin Luther King during the Battle of Selma stemmed from the fact that he denied history a great moment, never to be recaptured, when he turned tail on the Edmund Pettus Bridge and refused to all those whites behind him what they had traveled thousands of miles to receive. . . the violence and brutality of the system. . . ruthlessly exposed. . . . As it turned out the March on Montgomery was a show of somewhat dim luster, stage-managed by the Establishment.[11]

Closer to the truth is the conclusion that the Selma campaign and Voting Rights Act furthered a trend toward more assertiveness in the nonviolent movement. David Garrow has expressed this transition in terms of modification of strategy. Of the tactics in Selma he wrote "This shift from *nonviolent persuasion* (he italicized this) to a more aggressive *nonviolent coercion* was based upon a very shrewd and wholly accurate understanding of the dynamics of protest and of what would most aid the movement in its attempt to secure the enactment of a new federal voting rights act."[12] Garrow's point is valid in regard to the strategic dimensions of the protest, but it is important to keep other aspects in view. King had assumed before the Selma campaign began that a voting rights act would be passed and was already looking beyond its enactment to more fundamental social and economic reforms. Nor did he lose sight of the "beloved community" ideal, although he was becoming more pragmatic about prospects for realizing it in the foreseeable future.

That was indeed a point of crucial meaning to King. Still convinced in 1965 that a "transformed and regenerated human society" was the only basis for durable reform, he also recognized more clearly by then that his seemingly eschatological language was stirring more expectations than could historically be realized in the short term.[13] This presented a dilemma, but within it King saw the germination of seeds of a solution. He and the overwhelming majority of his SCLC associates were fundamentally separated from those who were turning to militancy or who, from the beginning, were motivated by secular revolutionary views.[14]

Thus, King's shift to nonviolent coercion, while certainly real, was not unqualified. In *Where Do We Go From Here?*, published after the Selma campaign, he admitted that "We (blacks) must frankly acknowledge that in past years our creativity and imagination were not employed in learning how to develop power."[15] It appeared to King after Selma that the black movement had to face this deficiency and exploit "areas of untapped power" in its quest for social and economic progress. Sophisticated methods and increased understanding, however, would be necessary concomitants of this new power.

Simply to increase the number of black voters or to put pressure on white politicians to make changes favoring blacks, would not be enough. Rather, blacks would have to develop with their own political representatives more authentic relationships, based on confidence and trust. "We shall have to create leaders who embody virtues we can respect, who have moral and ethical principles we can applaud with an enthusiasm that enables us to rally support for them." With that kind of morally strong and reciprocally beneficial relationship, black politicians could enter into the "smoke-filled rooms where party debating and bargaining proceed."[16] That is, blacks through a more effective kind of political leverage, could attain the ability to enter into the *de facto* process of political creativity. This was quite different from coercion of the type used in Birmingham or Selma. Both strategies would characterize King's movement after 1965.

The thrust of the post-Selma policies of SCLC was, then, directed toward what King called "the accumulation of power." This included many specific content factors, many of them internal, such as reducing the degree of disunity within the black movement. Criticisms of blacks by other blacks was, in itself, potentially good. But King was not pleased by black leaders who failed to recognize the genuine progress that had been made but, rather, were always criticizing those who seemed to be accommodating when in fact they were confronting the segregated system effectively. "Too often," he wrote, "a genuine achievement has been falsely condemned as spurious and useless, and a victory has been turned into a disheartening defeat for the less informed." It was time for black leaders and their followers to learn the difference.[17]

Organizing for the New Stage

Martin King was not truly an organizational man. To him, organizations were less important than compelling ideas and good leadership. Moreover, he saw the black organizations of the middle sixties, including his own, as frail. They were weak primarily because of "their disunity and petty competition."[18] And they had a tendency to lose touch with the common people who were ultimately the essence of the movement. King recalled a lesson learned years before from a story of two men who were flying into Atlanta for a conference with a civil rights leader. At the airport when they attempted to talk with the leader, a porter sweeping the floor came over and began to converse with him about something that was troubling his life. After about fifteen minutes, the interviewers were growing quite impatient and one of them said angrily, "I am just too busy for this kind of nonsense. I haven't come a thousand miles to sit and wait while he talks to a porter." The other one was bothered by this and replied "When the day comes that he stops having time to talk to a porter, on that day I will not have the time to come one mile to see him."[19]

What King was primarily interested in after Selma was achieving the kind of organizational program that had the requisite influence to effect change without losing its spontaneity or grassroots orientation. That was one very basic reason, albeit comparatively neglected by scholars of the civil rights movement, for his rejection of the "black power" militants. They appeared to King to lack depth or perspective. In their enthusiasm for confronting the system they forgot that "a fighting spirit that is insufficiently organized can become useless and even hazardous."[20] Such undisciplined zeal was one of the major dangers of the movement.

Another was complacency. Most civil rights leaders recognized that the many barriers to full freedom not dealt with by the Civil Rights Act or Voting Rights Act would be more difficult to demolish than those confronted in the past and that people would probably approach them with less commitment. University of Alabama sociologist Harold Nelson wrote in the *Crisis* in late 1965 that violence would likely abate after these landmark laws but that further change would come less easily. That was an interesting observation in view of the fact that many people had been hurt or killed in the struggle to that point. Nelson's point was that a different kind of sacrifice would be necessary. Civil rights advocates would have to be "much more involved with covert discrimination—*de facto* discrimination—a form not embodied in sheriffs, police dogs and cattle prods, one much more widely supported than was its forerunner."[21]

SCLC leaders fully concurred in this estimation. In March 1965, King wrote in "Let Justice Roll Down," the fifth in his series of articles in the *Nation*, that future progress would depend upon more sophisticated strategies. While the gains of the past were in themselves significant, the cardinal lesson learned from them was the value of a "massive coalition of white and Negro forces" in bringing about those changes. "The larger transformation of our political and economic structure, "he argued, would require more of the "cool, intelligent selection" reflected by blacks' use of the vote in 1964. That King was also linking the black struggle to global issues of social politics can be seen in his argument that the Negro's cause in America was inspired by "the ferment of revolutionary change by the backward and dispossessed peoples of the world."[22]

What this meant to him and to the Southern Christian Leadership Conference was not that they should strive for socialism or to overthrow the traditional American system, but rather to transform it and infuse it with a sense of equity. Many people, though, were already criticizing the black movement precisely in those terms. For example, in 1965 Senator James Eastland of

174

Mississippi charged that the black movement was communist-inspired and harmful to American stability.[23] As he often stressed, however, King was not drawing his ideas from Marxism or seeking to bring about anti-bourgeois alliances. He had in mind the development of a poor white-black coalition "in the privacy of the polling booth," rather than in class struggle confrontations.[24]

There was some disagreement within the SCLC leadership about what precise moves to make in 1965. In early April, just after the Selma to Montgomery march, the board of directors met in Baltimore for their spring planning session. A number of things were troubling them, not the least of which was the violence that attended the Selma crisis. Particularly stunning was the murder of a white Detroit housewife and mother of five, Mrs. Viola Liuzzo, by white men who fired upon her car as she was hauling marchers back to Selma from Montgomery at the end of the trek. The Baltimore meeting was held just days after that tragedy, and its effects still reverberated in the minds of the directors. Mrs. Liuzzo's husband had appeared on national television asking for a boycott of Alabama goods, and King was thinking along the same lines.

Debate was unusually sharp in the Baltimore board meeting. Several members wanted to concentrate on a massive voter registration drive in 120 counties from Virginia to Louisiana and Mississippi. King agreed with the proposal but preferred to concentrate his own efforts on a boycott of Alabama goods and investment projects. He wanted to leave the administration of the voter registration project to Hosea Williams while he pursued the boycott and, interestingly, an exploratory outreach into the northern states. King was planning a series of appearances in northern cities that became known during the summer as a People-To-People tour.[25] Pressure from Al Raby of Chicago led King to begin an operation there under James Bevel and a staff that included Jesse Jackson, who would head within a few months an Operation Breadbasket program in the city.

The proposed boycott of Alabama businesses was problematical and illustrative of the complexity of the "new phase" strategy. Economic issues could not be defined strictly by race, nor could the effects of such broad selective buying tactics be shielded from blacks. If Alabama businesses were hurt, this would necessarily affect all of the population. Consequently, several board members vigorously opposed the boycott, but they yielded to King's insistence. The plan was far-reaching: 1) To urge that businesses suspend plant expansion into the state and the federal government to step up enforcement of Title VI of the 1964 Civil Rights Act; 2) To ask private institutions like churches and labor unions to examine their investment portfolios to determine whether prospective contractors and businesses were discriminatory; to urge the federal government to withdraw tax money deposited in Alabama banks; and 3) To boycott specific businesses and products on the grounds of discriminatory practices.[26]

The proposal was a bold one, but as it turned out not a very successful one. The boycott or "economic withdrawal," did not have much impact on Alabama. About 144 businesses and groups did agree to cooperate, but there were notable exceptions. The Hammermill Paper Company of Pennsylvania, despite SCLC efforts to get its administrators to comply with the boycott, went ahead with its $125 million plant construction in Selma.[27] Still, the principle of a boycott remained basic to several of SCLC's activities and was, as King saw it, one of the underrated aspects of the campaigns in Birmingham and other southern cities. The dramatic features of the larger campaigns had obscured the effectiveness of selective buying as lever in negotiations.[28]

King's outreach to the North began tenuously. For SCLC to attempt to apply its southern strategies in northern industrial cities was, Wyatt Walker once put it, "a whole new ballgame." A different cultural ethos existed in the North, and the conditions of blacks were unlike those of Selma or Birmingham. The political and industrial power structures of cities like Chicago, New York, and Detroit might not be moved by the strategies that desegregated much of the South.

Nonetheless, King was convinced that there was an inextricable linkage between the regions. For one thing, the tacit acquiescence of northern blacks and whites toward the inequities in the South suggested a failure of collective effort. SCLC had unwittingly confronted national dimensions of segregation in Albany and Birmingham, but after Selma it was becoming apparent that only a thoroughgoing revision of racial relations across the entire nation could take the black movement beyond statutory reforms. However unwise or unrealistic it seemed to some, King considered it imperative to broaden the geo-political boundaries of the nonviolent movement. Until 1965, SCLC's operations had been confined to the South and led almost entirely by blacks, albeit backed by white liberal financial supporters like Levison and certain philanthropic foundations. This could not remain the same if the civil rights movement were to progress beyond desegregation of public facilities and the right to vote.

In essence, the nonviolent movement and its allies had achieved by 1965 three cardinal gains. First, it had raised hopes among southern blacks and to some degree blacks in other parts of the country. The psychology of black Americans was fundamentally altered, not simply in the sense of increased expectations, but also pride and confidence in themselves as people. That was probably the most important result of the first decade of the southern movement. Secondly, blacks had mustered unprecedented political leverage in gaining desegregation of facilities and polling booths. That too was quite basic. Without the vote, blacks remained largely isolated individuals whose only real hope for mobility and freedom was unusual success in their careers. With the vote, they were a strategic force that could affect the outcome of local and even national elections.

In the third place, the movement by 1965 had done what only a few Americans would have considered possible as late as 1960. It had directed the conscience of the nation to the glaring evils of segregation and racial discrimination. That it did not thereby eliminate them is clear enough, but it did give a realistic ring to what King said in 1962. "We feel that we are the conscience of

America. We are its troubled soul. We will insist that right be done because both God's will and the heritage of our nation speak our echoing demands."[29] That King spoke of social ills as "evils" rather than simply social problems or aberrations was the key to much of his success and the appeal of SCLC.

More than is realized, the Civil Rights Act and Voting Rights Act were helpful to northern blacks. So were the consciousness-raising features of the southern movement. Pride was lacking in the North, too, and there is no way to estimate quantitatively how much impact SCLC and other southern organizations had on blacks in northern and western communities. But the situation there was quite different from the South, and blacks were less closely tied to churches. Moreover, cynicism and hopelessness in urban ghettos fed on deep streams of changelessness. Many of the ghetto dwellers of the sixties were living in conditions unchanged since Harlem and the Flats of Chicago sank into the ennui and deprivation that followed their early, more glorious days. And beyond that, many of the black activists of the North and West had acquired an educational level and practical experience that made them more inclined to respond to notions of black power and ethnic pride than to images of being led out of Egypt or reaching the Promised Land.

It was with difficulty, therefore, the SCLC ventured into northern urban centers with its nonviolent message and strategy. Three weeks after the Baltimore board meeting, King made several speeches in the North, hoping to engender support and to survey the social landscape. On April 21, 1965 he addressed the New York City Bar Association, telling the attorneys that their profession had been vital to previous gains in civil rights and would continue to be an essential component of the struggle for equality. King cited needs in the areas of education, housing, and jobs as priorities of the future, and reminded the presumably conservative audience that previous accomplishments had been made nonviolently. Nonviolence would be the approach for the future.[30] Appealing to their best instincts, the SCLC leader recalled famous attorneys like Oliver Wendell Holmes, Clarence Darrow, and the contemporary Thurgood Marshall who had

178

contributed to justice. With some difficulty, he also explained why he had at times broken laws in his quest for black liberation. King spoke of unjust laws and the need to oppose them "openly and nonviolently." As for the future, "with this faith we will transform the jangling discords of our country into a beautiful symphony of brotherhood."[31]

In other urban centers King echoed the same message, emphasizing the plight of the poor and the imperative of further reforms. At the same time, he became more aware of the tensions between his nonviolent approach and that of the black militants. The "jangling discords" were apparent all around in 1965, and talk of brotherhood seemed to many people to be visionary. In addition, American involvement in the Vietnam War was becoming extensive, causing King to speak out against it and thus alienating him from the President. Since Johnson was the black movement's strongest ally in high political position, this was no small matter.

During this period of adjustment, King and SCLC were preparing organizationally for a nationally-focused "second phase" of the nonviolent movement. Thus far the gains had cost Americans very little economically. In the "first phase," as King called it, a decade of nonviolent campaigns had achieved certain non-economic advances as the United States went through "a struggle to treat the Negro with a degree of decency, not equality."[32] But the emergent "second phase" would entail genuine sacrifice for the "full realization of equality." The Selma campaign marked the critical juncture in this evolution of the movement, since there "The paths of Negro-white unity that had been converging, crossed. . . and like a giant X began to diverge. Up to Selma there had been unity to eliminate barbaric conduct." But after Selma and the shift of emphasis to economic and social issues, "unity had to be based on fulfillment of equality, and in the absence of agreement the paths began inexorably to move apart."[33]

More was involved in this divergence of the races than economic interests. Full equality would require closer personal relationships, cooperative endeavors in communities, and a host of other demands not so readily supportable on the basis of previous coalitional patterns. Therefore, SCLC decided to undertake programs designed to facilitate better racial relations and opportunities for cooperative community development, as well as programs more specifically economic in orientation. In a very real sense, the civil rights movement was over and being supplanted by a more demanding community-building effort. "Jobs are harder and costlier to create," wrote King, "than voting rolls."[34]

The Southern Christian Leadership Conference enjoyed considerable organizational momentum in this early post-Selma period, although support from white liberals was slackening. Its annual budget reached, then surpassed, the $1 million mark, and new programs were added.[35] Andrew Young remained in the executive director's post and attempted to move with the times as he spearheaded several of the new outreach subdivisions of SCLC. Young was professional in his approach and tried to refine the workings of SCLC national headquarters and build more effective connections with the SCLC affiliates. In both endeavors he was bolstered by a very capable staff.

In order to facilitate dealings with the federal government, SCLC had opened its Washington Bureau in early 1964 under the direction of future Congressman Walter E. Fauntroy. A young Baptist minister and a native of Washington, Fauntroy was a graduate of Virginia Union University (1955) and Yale Divinity School (1958). Fauntroy, pastor of the New Bethel Baptist Church, was extremely active in the black movement. In 1963 he helped organize the March on Washington and assisted with the campaign in Selma in 1965.

The Washington Bureau had two major purposes: 1) to interpret SCLC and its concerns to the federal government; and 2) to interpret federal programs to black Americans in general and SCLC affiliates in particular.[36] In 1964 as Fauntroy and his organization were busy lobbying for the Civil Rights Act, they worked with the Leadership Conference on Civil Rights, a group made up of some fifty leaders from labor unions, churches, civic organizations and social and fraternal organizations. Fauntroy was deeply involved with a 'strategy team' in the House to support passage of the Civil Rights Act. Its counterpart in the Senate included, among others, Hubert H. Humphrey.

By 1965 the Washington Bureau was, in Fauntroy's words, a veritable "beehive of activity."[37] It promoted a Get-Out-The-Vote Tour of five northern cities during the 1964 presidential election campaign and brought King to major urban centers like Chicago, Detroit, Cleveland, and Baltimore to drum up voter interest. After that, the Washington Bureau concentrated on the Voting Rights Act of 1965, while simultaneously seeking federal support for the Selma campaign. Fauntroy was pivotal in the Congressional visit to Selma and traveled to Alabama to work with the march to Montgomery. Fittingly, Walter Fauntroy was present on August 6, 1965 for the signing of the Voting Rights Act. The Washington Bureau continued to be important in the later sixties and beyond with its involvements in Congressional lobbying, education, the SCOPE program, and other interests of SCLC.

While the Washington Bureau had distinctive relevance to issues of the middle sixties, the affiliate structure of SCLC linked the national organization to its grassroots support. The affiliates were also the key to SCLC's ability to be simultaneously an organization and a movement, as King saw it. In August 1965 at the annual convention in Birmingham, he spoke pridefully of the achievements of the affiliates and their director, C. T. Vivian. The network of affiliates had always been loosely organized, but nonetheless responsive to the campaigns initiated by the Atlanta officers. Furthermore, they took the initiative in numerous local projects, thus providing a depth of penetration never acquired by SNCC or CORE in the South. Mutual reinforcement was the basic value of the affiliates. Often they were churches, and that added to their capacity to organize local activities. In 1965 SCLC was still adding affiliates, which also served as a source of income to the organization.[38]

Two SCLC programs operative in 1965 had a direct bearing on cooperation between blacks and whites, although in quite different ways. Both were innovative, and although not the resounding successes SCLC hoped for, they were indicative of the trends of the period and SCLC's capacity to deal with them. The first of these was Dialogue, headed by Harry G. Boyte, a dedicated supporter of the nonviolent movement, who had suffered physical harm and had his life endangered by gunfire in St. Augustine. A veteran of reform campaigns, Boyte was a white who was regarded as a true believer in human brotherhood. Working with Mew Soong Li and Rachael DuBois, Boyte gave form and ideological substance to the Dialogue Program. A native of South Carolina, he was by temperament and experience a man of the common people, having worked for eighteen years with the American Red Cross. After July 1963 he was a special assistant to King, and in 1964 began to lead Dialogue.

Boyte was convinced that poverty was morally intolerable in a land of plenty. In his view, poverty went hand in hand with cultural deprivation and thus reinforced biases, illiteracy, and self-denigration. He doubted that white initiative alone could help the black very much. Blacks themselves had to provide the "organizational power base to mount the thrust necessary for this societal challenge."[39] At the same time he worked to bring the poor and culturally deprived of all races together in a communicative and functional 'dialogue' with each other and more advantaged people for the twin purposes of social progress and reconciliation. Few programs of any organization had as much fundamental interest in human betterment as SCLC's Dialogue.

The Dialogue Program was future-oriented in some of its concerns. Boyte, for example, was one of the early critics of the effects of automation and cybernetics. He recognized that rapidly moving technological changes were leaving behind many people whose education could not keep up with technical innovations, a concern shared by King. Ahead of its time, Dialogue was interested in redirection of education to prepare workers for job opportunities of the future.[40]

Communication and reconciliation were the main substance of Dialogue. Its leaders initiated programs among poor whites designed both to help them and to forge ties with blacks in order

182

to create "a coalition of these forces so that through joint organized effort the causes can be attacked constructively, transcending all racial forces."[41] Dialogue also sponsored Group Conversation sessions in which participants could express their frustrations and hopes in an atmosphere of mutual respect and interaction. Sociologist Margaret Mead was so impressed when she witnessed one of these sessions that she wrote "After seeing Group Conversation demonstrated, I consider it a real social invention for bringing people together in an atmosphere of friendly understanding. It should be diffused throughout the country."[42]

Central to Dialogue's outreach was Dr. Rachael Davis DuBois, an organizer and writer. She and Dr. Mew-soong Li and SCLC program director Randolph Blackwell, along with Harry Boyte, Janet Boyte, and Betty Harris, developed the early programs in group interaction and planned for further expansion. In addition to Group Conversation, DuBois helped institute several Dialogue Round Tables which brought together clergymen, educators, and civic leaders for in-depth discussions of human relations. The Dialogue Department also led workshops and other direct efforts to reach across racial and social barriers. Though weakened by the waning civil rights movement after 1966, Dialogue was a forerunner of several later SCLC anti-poverty and human community programs.

The other major outreach program of 1965 was the Summer Community Organization and Political Education Project or SCOPE. Inaugurated at a retreat in mid-June at Morris Brown College in Atlanta, SCOPE was intended to be both informational and inspirational. Some 900 volunteers participated in the orientation retreat, more than four times the number who founded SNCC in 1960. Over 500 of the SCOPE volunteers were northern whites. Bayard Rustin and King were among the principal speakers at the conference, and they apparently prompted considerable enthusiasm for the new program.

The three leading goals of the SCOPE project were community organization, voter registration, and political education. King told the young volunteers that SCLC's strength had always been "in the large numbers of grassroots people mobilized to fight discrimination and segregation." Now the task was to carry the work a step further by training people to continue the work after the students left. What they would accomplish during the summer would have lasting results, because people of all ages and races—some of them illiterate, poor, and isolated—would "know that the rest of America cares about them and is watching the South." In addition, the sight of their sons and daughters "working together with white youngsters from the North will give [them] faith in the future."[43] It is of more than minimal relevance that King made this address several weeks after he supposedly shifted from a persuasive to a coercive brand of nonviolence.

SCOPE found its early efforts difficult. But under Hosea Williams and many others, it did achieve some notable successes. Beneficial to the effort was the extensive support of SNCC's Alabama staff. There was none of the usual SNCC-SCLC tension in this project because SNCC in this kind of setting found more assets than liabilities in connecting itself with King's drawing power.[44] By November 1965 Williams could report that SCOPE had functioned well in six southern states incorporating 125 black belt counties and fourteen Congressional districts.[45]

SCLC secured 1,200 workers for the project, including 150 paid SCLC staff members. The Political Education classes reached over one million people, and over 660,000 were involved in the community organization programs. More than rhetoric was involved. In Americus and Crawfordville, Georgia, and in Allendale, South Carolina, Plymouth, North Carolina, and several other places, Williams' efforts publicly demonstrated the need for the Federal Registrars established by the 1964 Civil Rights Act. Since SCOPE involved a large number of white people, it had a symbolic and practical significance beyond such statistics. As Williams viewed it, "the movement embarked upon a true 'Grand Alliance' for the first time."[46]

As these programs grew and older ones like Operation Breadbasket were expanded, SCLC enlarged its office staff to 71 and its field staff to more than 300. Increased financial resources brought the annual budget to $1,576,000 for fiscal 1965, more than doubling the 1963–64 outlays. SCLC was at its highest level of organizational activity, still benefitting from the public exposure of the major campaigns of 1963 to 1965.[47] Although it was taking $130,000 per year to raise its operating money, and another $450,000 to run the organization, SCLC was putting the bulk of its resources into direct-action and educational enterprises. About $60,000 was used to aid affiliates in their local activities. As executive director, Andrew Young had ambitious plans to both expand the scope of SCLC programs and to upgrade their quality. Some $20,000 was spent with his encouragement for printing equipment to handle the greater demand for promotional and educational materials.

If the programmatic thrust of SCLC reached a new plateau in 1965, so did its self-perception. At the organization's ninth annual convention in Birmingham in August, there was much reflection on the previous decade and some very revealing analyses of the political status of the organization. The theme of the gathering was "Human Rights—Basic Issues—the Grand Alliance." Though somewhat awkward, that concept was quite appropriate for the occasion. Nineteen-sixty-five was the tenth anniversary of the Montgomery bus boycott, and Rosa Parks was present for a special ceremony in her honor. Fred Shuttlesworth, then secretary of SCLC, made the opening remarks, taking the opportunity to remind the audience that it was in Birmingham that SCLC field leaders had "developed their fitness and proved their ability by arousing a community to positive nonviolent action."[48]

Conventions were, and still are, highlights of SCLC's activities. Always the planning committee seeks to develop a theme reflective of current trends and inspirational to the delegates. And the Birmingham convention of 1965 was especially instructive as a measure of the organization's capacity to engage its past and experiment with new concepts. Most of what was said during the three-day convention was oriented to the decade of struggle just completed but at the same time reflective of confidence that there was a future for the leadership conference in the black movement. When Rosa Parks was honored at the annual banquet, Mrs. Constance Baker Motley said to her, "Rosa Parks, we honor you tonight because yours is the kind of courage and determination and nonviolent spirit we all need for the future. Your name will be remembered as long as freedom is abroad in the land."

Andrew Young delivered the keynote address, which he entitled "An Experiment in Power." Young expressed pride in the achievements of SCLC, but more significantly, he shared his thoughts about the implications of the measure of power gained by the desegregation and enfranchisement drives of the previous decade. Blacks, he observed, were not a rich people or an unusually brilliant people or a morally superior people, "But somehow, God has chosen us as His people, and called His children from the far corners of the world, the diverse nationalities of our nation, and the myriad religious expressions of our time to gather around us in a glorious procession to a land of freedom and justice."[49]

The Voting Rights Act, Young recognized, had produced a new opportunity to reform the political structure of the United States. But this would require effective organization. He wanted to avoid an irreversible attachment of SCLC to a particular political grouping. "The Goldwater forces ran us out of the Republican Party, but this means that it is even more imperative that we not be considered captives of the Democratic Party."[50] What Young had in mind was an independent organization working closely with the Democratic Party but capable of functioning independently and "switching whenever the opportunity affords it."

Young's basic theme was that American blacks now had the legal bases of exercising power. Theirs would be a "coalition of classes" that represented not only all geographical regions, but all strata of society as well. It was truly an experiment in power that would require the highest values, best organizational skills, and the highest degree of political insight Negroes could muster. He stressed several specific points, the most basic of which were self-help, effective use of voting rights, and the need to deal with the problems of America's cities. He also criticized deepening U.S. involvement in Vietnam and Central America. Young dissociated SCLC from the peace movement as such. Although he opposed the Vietnam War, Young saw the peace movement as less clear in its moral and political bases. He would not identify SCLC in any direct way with it.

In his presidential address on the same day, King also looked to the future as he spoke of the different challenges ahead. "With all the struggle and all the achievements, the plant of freedom has grown only a bud and not yet a flower. Negroes in 1965 are freer, but they are not free. Negroes in 1965 have more dignity and self-respect than they have known in their history, but they are still far from equal."[51] He was thinking specifically about economic conditions of blacks, many of whom were "strait-jacketed in society as its most unskilled, most underpaid strata." King was increasingly conscious of a point Harry Boyte had made about such jobs being not only menial and low-paying, but likely to be less relevant to the future economic system of the United States.

Urban Riots and the Post-Selma Agenda

While SCLC met in Birmingham, blacks were venting their frustrations on the streets of Watts in Los Angeles. This harbinger of years of violent eruptions in urban ghettos would soon draw King and SCLC into political confrontations much more divisive than anticipated in the speeches on the convention platforms. As noted, King feared that the Harlem riots of 1964 were only the prelude to more, but the reality of seeing the numerous outbursts of 1965 stunned him and strained his sense of relevance.

The ghetto riots spread over the following three years to more than 300 American cities, causing billions of dollars in damage and numerous deaths and injuries. Urban riots were not new, to be sure. In the first decade of the 20th century, there were six major upheavals in places like Springfield, Illinois. The NAACP, in fact, came into existence in 1909 largely because of such

Chronological Table No. 3: Broadening of SCLC'S Outreach Programs in Education and Nonviolence 1962–1966

	1962	1964	1966
Executive Directors:	Wyatt Tee Walker (1960–1964)	Andrew J. Young (1964–1972)	
	Albany Campaign 1961–1962	*Birmingham Campaign* 1963	*St. Augustine Campaign* 1964	*Selma Campaign* 1965	*Chicago Campaign* 1966
		MARCH ON WASHINGTON (August 1963)	1964 *CIVIL RIGHTS ACT*	1965 *VOTING RIGHTS ACT*

Education
CEP (CITIZENSHIP EDUCATION PROGRAM)
(Septima Clark, Dorothy Cotton, Andrew Young)

Dorchester Center in Georgia
Training of adult leaders
Basic literacy
Voter registration/education

SCOPE (Summer Community Organization and Political Education Project 1965 (Hosea Williams *et al.*)

Organizational Network
Atlanta National Headquarters/local chapters, affiliates, New York Office

Washington Bureau (Walter Fauntroy) 1964
Enlargement of Affiliate system (C.T. Vivian)

Relations with federal government interpretation of programs
Links to local churches, groups
Fundraising/campaigns

Relations Between Races and Classes
Nonviolent, multi-racial policies of SCLC and other civil rights ogranizations

DIALOGUE (Harry G. Boyte. Mew Soong Li, Rachel DuBois) 1964

Group discussions
Sharing of hopes, fears
Uplifting poor
Communication/reconciliation

Economic Advancement
Transit and pro-job campaigns

OPREATION BREADBASKET (Fred C. Bennette) 1962

Uplifting black family income, housing, health care
Pressuring businesses for equal opportunities

problems in the cities. They continued during and after World War I. East St. Louis erupted in 1917, the year of the Russian revolution and American entry into the European war. Forty-eight people died in that rioting and hundreds were hurt. The same year Houston, Texas was marred by urban violence which left seventeen dead.

After the war, dozens of other cities exploded, among them Chicago in 1919, where twenty-three whites and fifteen blacks died and more than 500 were injured. A few months later Tulsa was torn by racial battles, and by 1919 the "Red Summer" riots marred Washington, Knoxville, Omaha and many more. John Hope Franklin explained this widespread violence in terms of disillusionment among blacks caused by the gap between hopes that fighting in defense of the nation would lead to post-war improvements in the status of blacks. When the war ended, blacks who had "imbibed freely of the democratic doctrine that had been expounded so generally during the war," found themselves in competition with white veterans for jobs.[52] For years American cities witnessed periodic outbursts of racially-related violence.

The relative quiet of the cities from 1940 to the early sixties was due in large measure to the influence of organizations like the National Urban League and the NAACP. Nonviolent direct-action groups like CORE and later SCLC also had ameliorative effects. But the truth is that the legal gains of blacks from 1954 to 1965 hardly touched chronically poor urban blacks. Many of them lived in debilitating poverty with few, if any, outlets. Bayard Rustin has pointed out a related factor that weakened the tenuous urban peace. For the first time, Rustin argues, a large number of young blacks entered well-paid professions and they, along with their energies and resources, left the ghettos. "With their departure," he says convincingly, "a stabilizing element was removed from the structure of ghetto life, and this loss affected the black community's political fabric, the condition of its housing, its potentiality for organizing to demand improved city services, and of course, the already spiraling crime rate."[53]

In short, ghetto life was becoming even worse by the middle

sixties, especially in contrast to the improved conditions of more fortunate blacks. The escalation of the Vietnam War also was a factor since it weakened confidence in the federal government and drew large numbers of blacks into the high-casualty conflict. In fairness, it should be noted that the Johnson administration was trying to alleviate some of the cities' problems, including the horrid conditions in Watts. The newly established Economic Opportunity Act (EOA) in 1964 created the Office of Economic Opportunity (OEO), and through it some $70 million was sent to Los Angeles and channeled into the Economic and Youth Opportunities Agency. But this was too little, too late. About thirty percent of working-age blacks in the region were unemployed and housing was usually delapidated and dangerous, if it was available at all.

The August 1965 Watts riots were triggered by the arrest of two black youths on August 11 for alleged speeding and intoxication. What might have been a minor incident, however, led to a major riot as a crowd of young blacks gathered around the arrest scene. A skirmish ensued, and before long Watts was in utter chaos. For several days, blacks shouted "Burn, Baby, Burn!" as they sought to destroy the physical symbols of their plight.[54] Over 1,000 people were hurt in the foray and thirty-four died. Over $40 million damage was done to buildings and their contents.

King rushed to Los Angeles from a post-Birmingham convention trip to a religious conference in Puerto Rico. He was appalled by what he saw in Watts as he arrived by car with Bayard Rustin and Andrew Young on August 17. King countered the rioters' slogan with "Build, Baby, Build!" and "Organize, Baby, Organize!" To him, it appeared that the riotous approach was suicidal. Visibly moved by the carnage he said, "Let me say first of all that I deplore the events that have occurred in Los Angeles these last few tragic days. I believe and have said on many occasions that violence is not the answer to social conflict whether it is engaged in by white people in Alabama or Negroes in Los Angeles."[55] Yet King from this point on was convinced of the absolute necessity for the United

States to make a concerted effort to heal the urban rifts, not simply by counseling nonviolence but by specific, massive corrective programs.

King pledged that he and SCLC would seek to minister to the blacks who had been innocent of the violence in Watts and, insofar as was possible, to those hurt by the rioting. Furthermore, he said about the rioters, "Our Christian effort must be to redeem them and to leave no stone unturned, despite their guilt, to help them find a useful place in building a good society in which they can share as equals." King also said he had come to Los Angeles to confer with various segments of the white community who had helped blacks and who must also, like millions of blacks, be hurt and dismayed. Fourthly, King said that he would work with local leaders in Los Angeles to propose programs to help eliminate some of the causes of the eruption.[56]

There was a larger context that also concerned King. Since the July SCLC rally in Petersburg, Virginia, where he criticized the escalation of American involvement in Vietnam, he had become more convinced of the folly of the conflict. In Birmingham just days before his visit to Watts he again spoke out against Johnson's policy in Vietnam and urged the delegates to condemn the conflict. While there was much reluctance in SCLC to do so, the convention did pass a resolution questioning the conflict on the grounds that "The war in Vietnam is a serious challenge to our concept of brotherhood, as is indeed any war," and out of respect for King, the resolution continued, "We recognize that Dr. King is one of the world's foremost moral leaders. . . We commend him for courageously expressing these concerns and encourage him to continue his forthright moral leadership."[57]

Basically, King's controversial stand on the Vietnam conflict harmonized with his perennial views on war. Since at least the summer of 1959 when he told an Italian journalist that nonviolence was relevant not only to local small group situations, but to relations among nations as well, King had linked his philosophy to foreign policy. But the Vietnam war tremendously influenced his thinking in this area. To him, the war, the urban riots, and prospects for further progress in human relations were all intertwined. The forces that produced the war and the riots were essentially destructive, he felt, but they could be channeled into creative activity with beneficent results for all of America and even the world. This was the essence of his interrelated rejection of the war and support of urban reform.

Unfortunately for King's image and the vigor of SCLC's efforts after 1965, his stance was not popular either among moderate blacks or the white majority. His opposition to the war and his related promotion of urban reform did increase his stature in the eyes of SNCC activitists, since they agreed with him but felt compelled to restrain their feelings in the interest of avoiding even worse relations with the government.[58] While SNCC admired King for his forthright criticisms, in general he was largely isolated at that juncture because of his position.

The Johnson administration was also lost as an unqualified ally. The first rift occurred on August 6, 1965 when King pressed the President for additional reforms in the economic area. He asked Johnson for a commitment to eliminate poverty among blacks in northern cities and to support home rule for Washington, D. C. The President rejected both. "That day," wrote Jim Bishop, "King lost whatever rapport he had with Johnson."[59]

Actually King's call for a negotiated settlement in Vietnam and his strong emphasis upon the war as a drain on the country's social programs was more decisive in causing the rift between SCLC and the Johnson administration. "Is Vietnam to become a 'civil rights' issue?" queried the editors of *U.S. News and World Report*. Certainly to King it was, for he was convinced that the expense of the war "was taking away from the poor" necessary funds for improvement and calling into question the moral integrity of American foreign policy. In September 1965, King spoke with UN Ambassador Arthur Goldberg about the war and urged negotiations and admission of communist China to the United Nations. Senator Thomas J. Dodd of Connecticut, a respected Democrat, questioned King's credentials in this area, saying that the SCLC president had "absolutely no competence to speak about complex matters of foreign policy." King countered with "I would not be living up to the responsibility given me with the Nobel Peace Prize if I did not bring all the influence I could as a minister of the Gospel in behalf of world peace." The *Christian Century*, one of a few journals always faithful to King, defended his stance in a way that is worth recalling.

His [King's] right to advocate a negotiated peace in Vietnam and the admission of Red China to the United Nations is about as solidly grounded as a human right can be. He is a human being who knows that his life, that of his loved ones and the lives of all men are directly imperiled by the escalating war in Vietnam. He says No to that war. . . . King is the world-renowned leader of a particular form of social protest. . . . If his way is right anywhere, it is right everywhere. He cannot condemn violence in one set of human relations without condemning it in all.[60]

The damage was irreparable. Johnson would never again fully support King's movement. Nor would King have as much rapport with the NAACP or other cautious organizations who feared the negative repercussions of this interjection of foreign policy issues. It was not clear whether King would continue his outspoken criticisms, but FBI surveillance was again increased, not only of King, but of Levison and others related to SCLC.[61]

Obviously, the black movement's proverbial transition from "protest to politics" was painful. Circumstances militated against a smooth evolution into an era of sophisticated give and take among whites and blacks in the interest of progress. Rather, the seemingly dramatic shift of King's views brought him into conflict with the federal government, with more moderate civil rights leaders, and, for quite different reasons, with black militants. Actually King was in part the victim of too much media exposure which had given the impression before 1965 that he was more limited in his expectations than was actually the case. In 1966 he stated to the SCLC convention that "Negroes can no longer afford the luxury of abiding by the traditional gradualism of the respectable modifiers of the status quo." Ironically, that was precisely what he was in the minds of millions of Americans. Was he changing his course?

SCLC's venture into the North was also problematical. It caused further erosion of support by moderates and brought King and his associates into direct competition with the Black Power movement. King hoped that his nonviolent strategy would work in northern cities, and he certainly believed that its philosophical underpinnings were applicable there. That Chicago was chosen as the test case, however, complicated the effort. If Chicago could be moved to provide better jobs and housing, this would likely bring progress in many other cities. But the strong presence of Black Power advocates and the strength of the political machine run by Mayor Richard Daley were more formidable obstacles than those in Birmingham or Selma.

The Chicago campaign grew out of contacts between local reformers and SCLC leaders, and a series of visits by King in 1965 culminating in his People-to-People tour of July 24 to 26.[62] The Chicago effort was a joint venture undertaken in cooperation with the Coordinating Council of Community Organizations (COCO) established and led by the Reverend Albert A. Raby. The initial target was Benjamin C. Willis, the public school superintendent. Willis had raised the ire of local blacks and whites by his presumably inadequate approach to desegregation and was just beginning a new four-year term. At 63, Willis was scheduled to retire in two years, but many people did not want to wait.

This was not the best kind of issue with which to initiate a major campaign. Nor was it at all clear that the methods used in the South could effectively deal with city politics and urban militancy. In short, the Chicago campaign was as risky as any undertaken earlier. Even the *Christian Century* suggested that King was fighting "the wrong battle in the right war." The thirty or so speaking engagements King made in the early weeks, at a time when he was again nearly exhausted, hardly made a dent in sophisticated, cosmopolitan Chicago. The effort ran the risk, as *Christian Century* editors put it, of being "just another State Street parade—or a passing irritant."[63]

That King and SCLC had much more in view was indicated by

the fact that the SCLC president moved into a Chicago slum in early 1966 and prepared for another "long, hot summer" different from the 1965 riotous upheaval. At the University of Chicago on January 27 he reflected on the causes of the deterioration of the black family described in the Moynihan Report (1965)* as a cause of urban unrest and injected some qualifications and some sobering implications for the Chicago campaign:

> When you deprive a man of a job, you deprive him of his manhood, deprive him of the authority of fatherhood. Place him in a situation which controls his political life and denies his children an adequate education and health services while forcing his wife to live on welfare in a delapidated dwelling and you have a systematic pattern, humiliation which is as immoral as slavery and a lot more crippling than southern segregation.

SCLC planners projected an eighteen-month campaign, but at the end of the first month little had happened. Downtown merchants feared violence, but it did not come. The view that King always incited uprisings wherever he went, however, persisted, and Daley took steps to deprive SCLC of an occasion to cause trouble. His government announced slum clearances and other gestures of good intentions in regard to the city's housing problems. King was not needed in Chicago. That was the implicit, and sometimes explicit, message Daley was giving. The Mayor had enough supporters within the black movement, moreover, to keep him always one step ahead of SCLC planners.

On February 23, SCLC joined the West Side Federation and COCO in seizing a slum tenement on North Kenmore. It was a move of questionable legality, but those who did it felt that they

---

* The formal title of the report was *The Negro Family: the Case for National Action.* It was issued a few months before the Watts riots of August 1965 by Daniel Patrick Moynihan, Assistant Secretary of Labor. Its intentions were good, but in some respects it may have compounded the problems. The gist of its findings was that at the heart of the deterioration of Negro society was the "deterioration of the Negro family." The report pointed to the matrifocal structure, the deprivation, the lack of role models, and related problems. Some have criticized the research methodology of the report as unscientific. See Jones, *Prejudice and Racism*, pp. 48–49.

were morally justified. Immediately they placed the tenement under "trusteeship" and began to clean it up. Ironically, the owner was an old, sick man almost as poor as the tenants.[64] To many people, the seizure of the property was tantamount to an act of revolution, and certainly it hurt chances of winning supporters among Chicago's white community.

During this time King and his family tried to find a few quiet times together, and he still held his associate pastorate at Ebenezer. King also joined a group known as Clergy and Laymen Concerned about Vietnam, which brought him into contact with a number of prominent opponents of the war. In March another article in the *Nation* series appeared under the title "The Last Steep Ascent," in which King clearly underscored his new emphases. "Slums with hundreds of thousands of living units are not eradicated as easily as lunch counters or buses are integrated. Jobs are harder to create than voting rolls."[65] That same month King traveled to Europe with Harry Belafonte to raise money for the Chicago campaign. Large crowds turned out in several European cities to see them and to support the Chicago effort.[66] King was still hopeful that SCLC's first northern campaign would succeed and open the door to a transformation of urban life.

You cannot separate peace and freedom, they are inextricably related.
                                                    Coretta Scott King

7

The Last Steep Ascent
1966–1968

When King returned from his European fund-raising tour in early April 1966, he brought with him more than $100,000 for the Chicago campaign. He also evinced more determination to speak out on the Vietnam War, which he saw as a major cause of cutbacks in anti-poverty programs. King shared his feelings with the SCLC board in Miami in mid-April, telling the directors pointedly that the issues of poverty and peace were connected. The war was draining national resources, he said, and keeping the public's mind distracted from important social needs. Some board members had serious reservations about publicly linking the two matters, but King did get a vote of approval for his anti-war policy. This was certainly more of a concession to him than a strong consensus on the wisdom of opposing the war.[1]

There was more agreement in Miami on enlarging SCLC's overall outreach, in keeping with the organization's more vigorous emphasis upon economic and social issues. Andrew Young reported on intensified public relations activities, especially a greatly augmented program of printing and dissemination of the SCLC message. An improved Newsletter, educational materials, and political campaign support for black candidates and sympathetic whites were among many specific publication projects already in progress.[2] Young by now seemed confidently in charge of the executive director's office and dreamed of bigger and better things for SCLC.

However, the black movement at this time was beginning to polarize visibly, causing King and his associates no small amount of worry. The rising stars in SNCC and several other organizations were more militant, rather cynical toward nonviolence, and far from integrationist in their objectives. Some of them were promoting a version of "black power" that was anti-white in thrust, although the Black Power movement was too complex to categorize this way. What bothered King most was that Black Power advocates seemed to be aggravating racism by appearing racist themselves. "One unfortunate thing about Black Power is that it gives priority to race precisely at a time when the impact of automation and other forces have made the economic question fundamental for blacks and whites alike." It would be better, King thought, to adopt a slogan such as "Power for Poor People" rather than "Black Power."[3]

Anyone with half an eye could see that King and SCLC were bothered by some features of the Black Power movement, especially its militant language that denied the efficacy of love and had little regard for the theological foundations of human brotherhood. Yet, King did not attack these new young militants personally. He understood their predicament. What he proferred was another kind of power that would not only strengthen the black community but redeem all people. "Nonviolence is power, but it is the right and good use of power. Constructively, it can save the white man as well as the Negro."[4] Coercion and militancy could not win. It would take genuine cooperation among all races. If the movement were to go beyond mere legislative victories, the "aroused conscience of white America" was an indispensable ally. "Ten percent of the population," King concluded, "cannot by tensions alone induce 90 percent to change a way of life."[5]

Those who have concluded that "the real Martin Luther King" was an incipient radical, bent more on a coercive strategy than a fulfillment of his social theology articulated from the fifties through 1963, distort the truth about him and the SCLC movement after Selma. After 1965 a greater, not lesser, emphasis was placed on the importance of a moral consensus cutting across

198

racial and class lines. There were many barriers, of course, some of which King wrote and spoke extensively about between 1965 and 1967. Furthermore, he had his own doubts about the willingness of white Americans to commit themselves to full equality for all and about the dedication of blacks to a nonviolent approach to healing national rifts and bringing about a better society. But this did not mean that he became a disillusioned extremist, a communist sympathizer, or an outmoded idealist. Despite deliberate efforts by some critics to present him in such a light, King continued to believe in his dream which, as he saw it, was derived from the will of God and the principles of the American democratic tradition.

Chicago did not move very much as a result of the SCLC campaign there, and that certainly caused some adjustments in SCLC's strategy. Also, experiences in Chicago and in Mississippi during the Chicago campaign brought King into a headon collision with the black militants led by Stokely Carmichael. Out of all this would come a vigorous effort by SCLC to demonstrate that nonviolence would work anywhere, not just in Bull Connor's Birmingham or Jim Clark's Selma. And from King came a passionate plea to America to shift its priorities in the direction of peace and justice and away from the war in Vietnam and the backlash that snowballed after Selma.

Confronting Black Power

But while SCLC busied itself with visions of new beachheads in both North and South, Chicago remained on dead center. On May 26, King announced that a march would be made on city hall in late June and warned that Chicago could have a "long hot summer of peaceful demonstration."[6] On the same day city officials announced that a large government loan had been promised by the Housing and Urban Development Department under Robert Weaver. Hundreds of dwellings would be improved with these funds as slums were cleared and new units constructed. Things seemed to be improving when violence in the Cicero section added fuel to the smoldering racial tensions in the city.

SCLC was hoping to channel agitated emotions into an effective nonviolent march, but before it materialized, news of the shooting of James Meredith in Mississippi upstaged the event. After desegregating the University of Mississippi, Meredith had graduated in 1963 and had gone on to graduate studies in Nigeria and later at Columbia University. Now in the summer of 1966 he was back in Mississippi leading a march to test the effects of the civil rights laws of 1964 and 1965. On June 6, he was shotgunned by a group of whites and was taken to a hospital in Memphis, Tennessee. The next day, several black activists rushed to Memphis, among them King, the new SNCC chairman and Black Power spokesman Stokely Carmichael, and CORE's Floyd McKissick. Despite their differences, these men hoped to carry on Meredith's march.[7] King hoped, too, that their cooperative venture might smooth some of their disagreements.

If anything, the Mississippi March made matters worse. Despite the fact that Roy Wilkins, Whitney Young, and with some reluctance, Floyd McKissick supported a manifesto calling for a nonviolent "silent suffering army" march, Carmichael took every opportunity to espouse Black Power and to exploit King and SCLC. It was enough to discourage King and to drive John Lewis out of SNCC.[8] King warned that Black Power militancy was unrealistic in a nation where blacks represented only 10% of the population (although Black Power advocates themselves took a global perspective, which changed the demographics). At a deeper level he worried about the morality of the approach.[9] Thus, as Carmichael insisted "I'm not going to beg the white man for anything I deserve," King argued for a realistic facing of the facts. "We have neither the resources nor the techniques to win." SNCC, some in CORE, the Deacons for Defense, and a few others felt differently.

Carmichael had little faith in nonviolence, and his presence in SNCC was transforming that organization into a militant body. Young and articulate, Carmichael did have a strong appeal to many blacks, especially the young. He had begun in 1965 to use the Black Power slogan during a campaign in Lowndes County Alabama and by 1966 it was his watchword. There was no room in his version of black power for the things King articulated. "We had only the old language of love and suffering," said Carmichael. "And in most places—that is, from the liberals and middle class—we got back the old language of patience and progress. The civil rights leaders were saying to the country, 'Look, you guys are supposed to be nice guys, and we are only going to do what we are supposed to do. Why do you beat us up?'[10] To the young SNCC leader, nonviolence seemed as self-defeating as militancy did to King. "Those of us who advocate Black Power," he said, "are quite clear in our own minds that a 'non-violent' approach to civil rights is an approach that black people cannot afford and a luxury white people do not deserve."[11] He called for black self-defense and readjustment of the economic foundations of the country to help black people gain control of their lives.[12]

Armed with this kind of militant rhetoric, Carmichael and his followers "stole the show," as *Newsweek* put it.[13] The three-week march through Mississippi took the growing crowd across two hundred miles of hot country-side and through countless small towns. Blacks were encouraged to register, and in some areas hundreds were added to voting ledgers. Generally, the march was peaceful, except for internal quarreling, but not always. Harrassment was not infrequent. And at Philadelphia, Mississippi—where the three civil rights workers were murdered two years earlier—the marchers were attacked. At that time King requested federal protection and promised a return march at a later date. Another frightening incident occurred in Canton, where police attacked the marchers' camp with tear gas and clubs.

For King, who was simultaneously trying to keep in touch with the Chicago campaign, it was an unusual and trying experience. The old fear that he might stir up a maelstrom and then leave the local people alone to face the consequences was voiced from time to time. And some of the militants actually called for blacks to seize power in areas where they were predominant. King was presented by some as an obstacle to further progress, allied as he was with the "white establishment.'' One close observer of King's career, and generally a very friendly one, caught the essence of the dilemma he faced:

> The character of this march was different from any King had led in the past. For the first time demonstrators were questioning the effectiveness of passive resistance. Carmichael had originally urged that this be an all-black march, saying, ''We don't need any more white phonies and liberals invading our movement.'' The marchers sang ''We Shall Overcome,'' but when they got to the words ''black and white together,'' many remained silent. Others changed the lyrics further to ''We shall overrun.''[14]

It was not easy for even the King charisma to keep the march on a nonviolent course, not so much this time because of volatile emotions in a crowded urban ghetto but rather because of a worse enemy. . . disillusionment. The dream was on trial as never before. Had it reached an impregnable wall in, of all places, Grenada Mississippi? And a wall not primarily of white racism, but of black power militancy and waning faith in nonviolence?

As the march progressed, it seemed that Carmichael and SNCC had taken control. Meredith, now recovered sufficiently, joined the marchers during the last few days. Again, the press focused more on that than upon the presence of King. But it was not so much the upstaging as the onslaught on nonviolence that moved King to strike back with words and emotions. On many occasions he countered Carmichael and McKissick's reliance on the Black Power and Freedom Now slogans. At one point Carmichael looked pointedly at King and said ''Power is the only thing respected in this world, and we must get it at any cost. Martin, you know as well as I do that practically every ethnic group in America has done just this. The Jews, the Irish, the Italians did it, why can't we?'' The embattled SCLC president disagreed. ''That is just the point, he retorted. 'No one has ever heard the Jews publicly chant a slogan of Jewish power, but they have power. Through group identity, determination and creative endeavor, they have gained it. The same thing is true of the Irish and Italians. . . . That is exactly what we must do. We must use every constructive means to amass economic and political power.' But this must come through a program, not merely through a slogan."[15]

True to his promise, King led about 300 nonviolent marchers back to Philadelphia, Mississippi on June 24. There they knelt and prayed at the court house steps, as a large crowd of whites gathered and Sheriff Lawrence Rainey (who had held the three young civil rights workers just before their death in 1964) made spiteful remarks. "I believe the murderers are somewhere around me at this moment," whispered King. "You're damn right," said Rainey as he overheard. "They're right behind you." King was able to joke later about not wanting to close his eyes as he prayed, and recalled that Abernathy said he had prayed with his open, too.[16]

When the march finally terminated in late June, SCLC aides of King were determined, as Bernard Lee recounted later, to "keep Stokely off Dr. King's coattails." For his part, King was more determined than ever to stand up for nonviolence. "I've decided," he said, "that I'm going to do battle for my philosophy. You ought to believe in something in life, believe that thing so fervently that you will stand up with it till the end of your days. I can't make myself believe that God wants me to hate. I'm tired of violence. . . And I'm not going to let my oppressor dictate to what method I must use. . . We have a power. . . a power that cannot be found in bullets and guns."[17] And in his book *Where Do We Go From Here: Chaos or Community?* he opted for community. "In a multiracial society no group can make it alone. It is a myth to believe that the Irish, the Italians, and the Jews—the groups that Black Power advocates cite as justification for their views—rose to power through separation. It is true that they stuck together. But their group unity was always enlarged by joining in alliances with other groups."[18]

Carmichael admitted to King that he exploited him by using the march to vocalize his Black Power concept in order to force King to take a stand. King replied with a smile, "That's all right, I've been used before. One more time won't hurt."[19] It did hurt, but it also made King take a stand, a stand firmly in favor of nonviolent community. A man ought to believe something in this life, and Martin King did. He was ready to go back to Chicago to demonstrate that nonviolence would work.

Some have seen King's participation in the Meredith march as a tactical error. Perhaps it was, but at the time there seemed to be little choice. Oates argues that it was "a terrible blunder. He had undertaken it to unify the civil rights movement and confront white Mississippi under the banners of nonviolence. Instead, the march had unleashed a combustible slogan that embarrassed and bewildered him and that fragmented the movement, perhaps irreparably."[20]

Actually, Carmichael would have found some other forum to proclaim his black power perspective if King had not participated in the Meredith march. And his presence at least had the effect of countering the militant position with the nonviolent message, and perhaps more significantly, it moved King to articulate more completely his own perspective on black power. He wrote extensively about it in *Where Do We Go From Here?* published the following year. The book was the closest thing to an intellectual autobiography King had done since *Stride Toward Freedom* in 1958. And his reasoning on black power in the 1967 book is impressive. King did not reject the notion of power. "There is nothing essentially wrong with power," he reflected. "The problem is that in America power is unequally distributed. This has led Negro Americans in the past to seek their goals through love and moral suasion devoid of power and white Americans to seek their goals through power devoid of love and conscience. . . . It is precisely this collision of immoral power with powerless morality which constitutes the major crisis of our times."[21]

Andrew Young was also stimulated to respond to Black Power theory. To him more than to King, it seemed fairly close to what SCLC was trying to do. Much of the problem was semantics and emphasis. Carmichael, Young thought, was basically trying to take the place of Malcolm X after his 1965 assassination. "He's trying to project a militant image, push Negro protest as far as he can, carrying white liberals along with him as far as they will go.

204

Then he may edge back a little. Actually, SNCC's position on Black Power isn't too far from ours except in style and semantics."[22]

Young was only partially correct. While it is true that SNCC in this period talked of violence as a means of self-defense, Carmichael at times presented a different perspective. He spoke candidly of what he considered "racist assumptions of white superiority" and argued that the white power structure was maintained by force.[23] His strongly worded rhetoric often alarmed white people and many black moderates. Carmichael was linked in the minds of many officials with communism and its front organizations.[24] Even within SNCC he was regarded by some as a damaging leader, and his tenure as chairman was short-lived.

On the other hand Carmichael's background and education had given him a more sophisticated view of Black Power than that of some militant self-defense organizations like the Black Panthers. A native of Trinidad, Carmichael graduated from Howard University. During his college years he worked with CORE in the 1964 voter registration drive in Lowndes County. The following year he was instrumental in the creation of the Lowndes County Freedom Organization and moved away from both major political parties. The organization chose a black panther as its symbol, a fact that led some to identify it with the Black Panther Party, though inaccurately. Carmichael assumed an independent stance and began articulating the Black Power position that caught the eye of the press so widely in 1966 as he became head of SNCC and the most visible leader of the Meredith March.

Carmichael understood Black Power in political and economic terms. In the fall of 1966 he published an article in *The Massachusetts Review* under the title, "Toward Black Liberation." In it he presented the essence of his comprehension of Black Power, noting at the outset that "Negroes are defined by two forces, their blackness and their powerlessness." Pursuing the implications of this, he described America as a country with two communities, one that was white and controlled the power structure, and the other that was black and "excluded from participation in power decisions that shaped the society," and thus dependent upon the white majority.

If there was any possibility of rectifying this situation, Carmichael believed, it would have to come from a new approach by blacks, different from that of Randolph or King's SCLC. Carmichael believed that the traditional gradualist approach was too limited to be effective in the 1960's and beyond. What was needed, he felt, was for blacks to take advantage of their strategic position caused, ironically enough, by segregation. As 10% of the population, black Americans could unite and put to use "the full voting potential" of their numbers. That would allow blacks to swing elections and influence political and economic decisions. Black leaders would thus cease to be "vote delivers" for white politicians and become more effective organizers of "black power." He noted that in several key cities, including Philadelphia, Washington, and Newark, blacks comprised a high percentage of the local population and, in fact, were a majority in the nation's capital. But could northern ghettos be organized for action? To Carmichael it was a necessity.

> Without the power to control their lives and their communities, without effective political institutions through which to relate to the total society, these communities will exist in a constant state of insurrection. This is a choice that the country will have to make.[25]

Carmichael eventually made his choice to leave the United States. But in the summer of 1966 he was voicing what he thought of as an alternative to the nonviolent movement as understood by King. As we saw, King did not criticize Carmichael or the other militants at a personal level. He had respect for their concerns, and they had respect for him as a person and a leader while disagreeing with his methods. Still, their differences were more than results of temperament or differing views of strategy. King saw the militants as being oriented more to Frantz Fanon's *Wretched of the Earth* logic than to Gandhi or the Judaeo-Christian value structure.[26] Fanon predicted that the non-white people of the world would eventually rise up and throw off the yoke of colonialism and white dominance. An important work, Fanon's book did influence a number of black militants, including many in SNCC. Especially vulnerable were the newer SNCC members who had not been part of the southern civil rights movement and thus not as immediately exposed to connections between Gandhian and Christian principles and black activism.[27]

In any case it became quite obvious during the Mississippi March that there were fundamental differences between King and the Carmichael approach, and this rift would become more intense over the following months. When the Mississippi March ended on June 26 and Carmichael called upon blacks at a rally in Jackson to build a power base "so strong that we will bring whites to their knees every time they mess with us," King was all the more determined to effect a nonviolent victory in Chicago. . . and beyond.[28] Andrew Young was convinced that "We have got to deliver results—nonviolent results in a Northern city—to protect the nonviolent movement." Both the Black Power challenge and the dissipating public momentum demanded it.[29]

Inevitably the Chicago effort fell short of these expectations. It was not to have the success of Birmingham. While the campaign did have momentum as July began, the work had to be more slowly done than in the case of the big southern campaigns. Jesse Jackson observed that SCLC anticipated a three to five year effort there, but the press demanded a three to five month campaign.[30] In hopes of mounting a rapidly enlarging assault on legally sanctioned segregation and inadequate housing and jobs, SCLC went through with its delayed march. Anticipating a crowd of over 100,000 a Freedom Sunday rally was held at Soldier Field on July 10, and King was there with a blistering speech on the need to work and to hold to nonviolent methods. He was insistent, very insistent, that blacks would have to dedicate themselves and perhaps go to jail.

This day we must decide to fill up the jails of Chicago, if necessary, in order to end slums. This day we must decide that our votes will determine who will be the next mayor of Chicago. We must make it clear that we will purge Chicago of every politician, whether he be Negro or white, who feels that he owns the Negro vote.[31]

Then, in the sweltering heat, the SCLC president led about 5,000 of the 40,000 who showed up for the rally, to city hall. There he posted on the door eight demands on slum clearance, welfare reforms, school desegregation, and various economic issues directly affecting blacks and the poor.[32] Reminiscent of the Ninety-Five Theses nailed by Protestant reformer Martin Luther, whose name King bore, the act had a certain symbolic significance. But Daley was not even in town, and when black leaders did meet with him the following day, he was polite but made no real concessions. Daley seemed to King to be a man without bigotry, but one who did not grasp "the depth and dimension of the problem." The mayor, in turn, expressed doubt that the blacks of Chicago would fill the jails or that King would break any law. After all, he was pledged to nonviolence, Daley mused.[33]

Violence did come that week. On the West Side on July 12, a group of children turned on a fire hydrant for relief from the 90-plus temperature, and when police came to shut it off, a riot ensued. Gangs hit the streets, and as he tried to restore calm, King found himself in a situation not unlike Albany. Several people were injured and looting was rampant.[34] In the wake of the rioting, Daley blamed anarchists, communists, and SCLC for the upheaval, but ameliorated his criticism of King's organization and agreed to a five-point program of limited ghetto improvement. Spray nozzles would be installed on selected fire hydrants to allow the children some relief. Swimming pools and playgrounds would be constructed, and operated on an integrated basis. Furthermore, a citizens' council would investigate the police department and seek to improve its relations with private citizens.

Important as they were, these concessions did not touch the substantive economic demands, and the tension continued in the windy city. Other regional cities, including Cleveland, also exploded that same summer with racially-related rioting. Chicago officials urged King to leave, arguing that his presence was actually contributing to violence, but he decided to see the campaign through. And as he did, he met some of his most discouraging opposition. During one of the outbursts of violence in early August, King was hit by a brick or rock as he marched in a nonviolent demonstration. He was stunned by the viciousness of the opponents. "I've been in many demonstrations across the South," he said publicly, "but I can say that I have never seen, even in Mississippi and Alabama, mobs as hostile and as hate-filled as I've seen in Chicago."[35] To make matters worse, American Nazi Party leader George Lincoln Rockwell brought his modern day stormtroopers to town to preach their racist doctrines and try to intimidate the SCLC leaders.

At that point King took a respite from the turmoil in Chicago to attend SCLC's annual convention in Jackson, Mississippi. Ironically, he found a much friendlier audience in a southern state known for its strict segregationism. He obviously had Chicago and racial tension very much on his mind. "There is a restlessness and urgency about the Negro's mood and his needs, which at once demands militant and aggressive leadership, coupled with mature and stable patterns of organization and strategy for change," he told the SCLC delegates on August 10. The theme of the convention was "Human Rights, the Continuing Struggle," and certainly it matched the 1966 atmosphere.

A week later the Chicago campaign came to a controversial end. The climax, or more precisely anti-climax, came with the much publicized march to the racially tense Cicero section of town, where violent confrontations had already claimed a number of lives. Everyone knew that such a demonstration in Cicero would trigger possibly serious trouble, and diplomatic efforts were made to head it off. But a ten-hour meeting of officials, clergymen, union leaders, and others, on August 17 failed to convince the militant black leaders, who proceeded with their potentially dangerous plans. King believed that the negotiations of August 17 had produced an acceptable plan, and that if its terms were carried out, much progress could be made in Chicago. But the militants labeled it a "sellout" and were determined to march on Cicero in early September.

By some measures, the August 17 agreements had real teeth. The city had already committed itself to a $500 million slum clearance project and several other gestures of conciliation. Promises were made to crack down on real estate brokers who made discriminatory sales, to enforce housing regulations, and to have the Chicago Real Estate Board withdraw a law suit before the state supreme court to contest the validity of state occupancy laws. But this was not an official summit and Daley was not even present. The prospect of a Cicero march, however, caused Daley to act with some dispatch as he made public appeals for order.

On Sunday, August 21, King announced that on the following Sunday he would help lead a march to Cicero, a community in southwest Chicago that had not witnessed a new black family since 1951 and which had once been headquarters for Al Capone and other classic gangsters. Cook County Sheriff Richard Oglivie warned that if the march occurred the National Guard would be called up and the affair would be "suicidal." Young kept up his pressure to force the issue. Daley, disturbed by the prospect of an upheaval and eyeing the November elections, called another meeting, this time more of a true summit. It was held at the Palmer House on Friday, August 26, two days before the slated Cicero march.

At the Chicago Summit were seventy-nine representatives, including King and his aides, Daley, Archbishop John P. Cody, and Ross Beatty, head of the Chicago Board of Real Estate, as well as business, banking, and civic leaders. Several important pledges were made by the city representatives, including a promise that open occupancy would be fully endorsed if applicable to owners as well as brokers. Furthermore, it was agreed that the Chicago Housing Authority would begin placing families, without regard to race, in the best possible housing. Bankers would agree to lend money for housing on a nondiscriminatory basis. The Roman Catholic Archdiocese and the

Church Federation of Greater Chicago, the Chicago Board of Rabbis and other religious organizations would also use their influence to secure fair and adequate housing for all.

King was delighted as it seemed that a victory had been pulled from the jaws of defeat. To the militants and many of the ghetto residents, it was less satisfactory, perhaps another "sellout" designed for public relations more than blacks who needed fundamental reforms. To them it was still tokenism that would hardly change their standard of living. Once again, writers suggested, King was emulating Martin Luther. Having moved the masses by his "Ninety-Five Theses" he appeared to some to have now rejected the "peasants' demands" and sided with the establishment in putting down their revolt.[36] Actually, this is not a very apt comparison. Luther in the sixteenth century had never endorsed social revolution as King had with his nonviolent strategy. Nor was King calling, as Luther did in the 1520's, for the crushing of the "murdering, thieving, rabble horde of peasants" but rather, seeking tangible concessions for the Chicago leadership to weaken the militants and begin the process of improvement in Chicago's housing. One must remember that for Martin King, ends and means were inextricably bound to a common moral base.

Those who had some stake, or at least faith, in the nonviolent movement rallied to King's support. *Christian Century* proclaimed that the SCLC president was "Still King" and elevated him above his detractors.[37] Jesse Jackson viewed Chicago in perspective and saw what SCLC and others did there as contributory to later solid gains like improved housing laws. Mayor Daley hailed the summit agreements as a "great day for Chicago." And across the nation opinions divided along now quite familiar lines. Even in the Congress, there was a growing mood of disenchantment with civil rights demonstrations and black demands. King and SCLC were hit from two directions: by those who thought the black movement was going too far and needed to slow down, and by those of a more militant posture who believed that nonviolence had burned itself out and was no longer relevant, if it ever had been.

The militants were through with the Cicero march on September 4, but it was ineffective to say the least. Only about 200 marchers made the trek, protected by more than 3,000 state and local officers. Even with the massive police force present, violence was rampant. Bottles, rocks, and abusive words showered the marchers, who were forced to retreat to Lawndale. It was a microcosmic symbol of the Chicago campaign as a whole, some surmised.

Follow-up reports indicated that the Summit Agreements were not kept. Nor did the Daley machine follow through with a civil rights thrust. Daley was re-elected a few months later with 73% of the vote. Possibly 80 to 85% of Chicago's blacks voted for him.[38] Yet, Daley, beginning his fourth term in the Windy City, pledged to preserve law and order rather than the Summit Agreements. Ironically, both the nonviolent movement and the militants waned in the aftermath of Cicero. CCCO fell apart after Al Raby resigned in 1967, and SNCC and CORE found their audiences declining.

The work in Chicago after that fell largely to the Reverend Jesse Jackson and his Breadbasket Operation. Within a few short years Jackson would become the principal leader of Chicago's 1.5 million blacks and form the organization known as PUSH (People United to Save Humanity).[39] Only twenty-five years old in 1966, Jackson was just beginning his impressive rise to national stature as the Chicago campaign ended in that year.

Opposing the War in Vietnam

After Chicago King gave more of his time to criticizing the deepening conflict in Vietnam. Americanization of the war had grown to a gargantuan scope by then, renewing many of the concerns he had expressed since 1965. King's first round of overt criticism of the conflict had elicited negative responses by both friends and foes alike. And the Johnson administration was repulsed as well. The renewed emphasis upon the war by King and some of his aides in 1966 and 1967 brought even more hostile response adding to the sense of alienation they experienced and driving deeper wedges between the nonviolent movement and the federal government.

King's criticisms of the war were grounded in his theology of nonviolence but shaped by the increasing economic and human cost of American involvement. When he first spoke out publicly on the issue at the Petersburg, Virginia rally and the SCLC convention in the summer of 1965, he focused chiefly on the contradiction between American democratic and moral values and the damage done both to Vietnam and international stability. King was convinced that military conflict anywhere in a world of superpowers and nuclear arsenals was too dangerous to go unopposed. "It is worthless to talk about integrating if there is no world to integrate in. The war in Vietnam must be stopped." To that end King approached UN Ambassador Arthur Goldberg, offered his personal services in mediation, and spoke out openly against the war on the CBS program Face the Nation.[40]

Steadily the issues surrounding the Vietnam problem developed into a complex set of specific concerns that comprised King's public stand against it. Particularly disillusioning to King was the growing evidence that President Johnson's obsession with the war was wrecking social programs. "The promises of the Great Society," King insisted, "have been shot down on the battlefields of Vietnam." It was taking about $332,000, the *Washington Post* estimated, to kill one Vietcong troop. "It challenges the imagination," wrote King, "to contemplate what lives we could transform if we were to cease killing."[41] By 1967 the war was costing about $16 billion *per annum*, far more than all the social programs supported by the federal government in one year and about half the total spent on some 500 Great Society programs between 1965 and 1970.

Such arguments meant little to Johnson at that point. In view of the mounting costs of both domestic and military activities, he felt compelled to cut the former. As 1967 began, the President had decided on a more restricted federal budget. An $8.1 billion deficit was staring him in the face as he told Congress "I have weighed the alternatives and made the hard choices."[42] Perhaps the country *could* fight poverty and the Vietcong simultaneously, but Johnson doubted that it would. The Great Society would have to wait. That struck King as a distortion of legitimate priorities.

Venturing into foreign policy had already proven detrimental to King's image, but as social programs floundered and destruction increased in Asia, he felt driven to crusade against both that particular war and the militaristic tendencies in American foreign policy. He blasted the war both for its destructiveness and its moral contradictions. And in a well-publicized and controversial speech at Riverside Church in New York on April 4, 1967, he argued that the Vietnam War was violating the very essence of American society and human compassion. He spoke of American bombs wiping out villages, killing trees and animals, maiming children and ravaging the countryside of a backward pre-industrial country. As many prominent members of an organization called Clergy and Laymen Concerned about Vietnam looked on, the SCLC President let it all out: the frustration over declining support, the rising toll of the dead on both sides, the widening gulf between himself and Johnson, and one could surmise, some of his own feelings of helplessness in the face of international war.

Some of King's closest supporters stuck by him in this period of isolation. Coretta wrote later that "I was very glad when Martin was able to take a strong position on the question of peace, because I felt that he had something important to contribute."[43] His father, who had been reluctant to endorse the anti-war crusade, was moved by King's impassioned oratory in favor of a negotiated peace and a major modification of American policy in Asia. And, as we have seen, since the spring of 1966 the SCLC board was on record against the war. "Our men and equipment," SCLC's directors affirmed, "are revealed to be serving a regime so despised by its own people that in the midst of the conflict they are seeking its overthrow." Furthermore, "the confused war has played havoc with our domestic destinies by narrowing various domestic welfare programs, making the poor—white and Negro—bear the heaviest burdens both at the front and at home."[44]

214

Press reaction to King's stand, especially his Riverside Church speech, was generally hostile. Even some of the stalwart sympathizers with the civil rights movement like the *Washington Post* and the *New York Times* were harshly critical. The *Post* accused King of fabrication and misleading rhetoric. The *New York Times* referred to his "simplistic political judgment" and said that King was jumping in "over his head." That was painful for King since it came from a paper he had long admired and could generally count on for objective coverage. Also *Newsweek* was strongly opposed to King's position. In May, Emmet John Hughes wrote in a critical editorial about the "curse of confusion" in the movement. As Hughes saw it, King "achieves perhaps the greatest irony in his fancy that the civil rights movement can be strengthened by enlisting the moral passions excited by Vietnam. On the contrary, the equation can only confuse."[45]

At times blacks were no more sympathetic. U. S. Information Agency Director, Carl T. Rowan, who generally defended King in his running battle with the FBI and viewed the files of King's personal life as mostly "barnyard gossip," blasted him for his Vietnam war stance. In the September 1967 edition of *Reader's Digest*, Rowan criticized King's "one-sided broadside about a matter on which he obviously had an abundance of indignation and a shortage of information." Echoing Johnson administration views, Rowan reviewed the list of King's critics like black leaders Roy Wilkins and Senator Edward Brooke. He suggested that King had played into the hands of Kremlin propagandists and, while recognizing King's positive contributions in the past, stated that the SCLC president had jeopardized "by his ill-advised pronouncements of Vietnam, the movement he so ably served."[46]

It is true that Wilkins, Brooke, and indeed Rustin, among others, thought King's position was unwise. A week after the Riverside speech, Wilkins openly criticized King at a board meeting of the NAACP, and Rustin expressed dissatisfaction with this *de facto* linking of civil rights and peace movements. But there was a difference between their misgivings and the attitude of outright critics and the Johnson administration. Their point was one of strategic wisdom, not content as such. The FBI intensified its investigations of King and deliberately sought to weaken his influence, even more so when it thought he might be considering running for President, on a peace ticket.[47] Wilkins, Rustin, and other associates of King who raised questions in 1967 were apparently thinking largely of the effects a civil rights-peace linkage would have on their reform efforts. But perhaps Benjamin Mays had the soundest perspective when he argued that history would show whether King was right or not.

King was not deterred, although he was troubled by the unexpected scope of the opposition to his peace efforts. In mid-April he participated in the Spring Mobilization for Peace rally in New York, and SCLC deepened its connections with anti-war protest efforts across the country. King, though, could not sign the manifesto proffered by the Spring Mobilization in 1967, although he did sympathize with its anti-war sentiments. He displayed a mixture of sentiments in this troubled year when he appeared to be departing from his previous positions.

The real significance of all this was lost at the time. In the minds of many, King's criticism of the war linked him with pacificism and the rising radicalism of the late sixties. David Halberstam, who traveled with King in 1967 to Cleveland and other cities, caught the changing mood of the man *Time* had named its Man of the Year a few years earlier. According to Halberstam, King was the one who was changing, not the movement leaders generally. He was now more of a "radical critic of society," even something of a "nonviolent Malcolm X."[48] It was not so much that Wilkins or Rustin or Young was changing and abandoning King, but he was leaving them behind. King, to Halberstam, was a "frustrating man" difficult to categorize. At once he appeared radical and conservative, internationalistic yet very American. It was not a critical article, as such, but an effort to understand Martin King in his last year.

Only a few people understood what King was saying about Vietnam. In truth, it was not the Vietnam War as such that concerned him primarily. Nor was he willingly giving support to

Hanoi or Moscow. His fundamental concern was that violence, both at home and abroad, was mushrooming. It was an illusion, he felt, to think that bombs and chemicals could solve the problems of Vietnam, or for that matter, protect the world against the expansion of communism. People had to work hard for and love peace for its own sake and come to realize that the best defense against communism was identical with the best defense against social disorder.[49]

Reinhold Niebuhr was one of a comparative few intellectual leaders who wrestled seriously with King's position and gave it the benefit of the doubt. As much as any American Niebuhr had struggled with questions of war and peace. Over the years, as we have emphasized, he was known for his realistic theology. But he saw in King's views much that was positive. Niebuhr understood that King, like himself, had rejected outright pacifism. Pacifism and nonviolence were not synonyms. Nonviolence is the active pursuit of peace, in fact a love for peace that causes one to work for it. "I think, as a rather dedicated antipacifist," wrote Niebuhr, "that Dr. King's conception of the nonviolent resistance to evil is a real contribution to our civil, moral, and political life."[50]

As a contribution to SCLC's history, King's stand can best be seen in his composite view of the Vietnam war situation. He was concerned about the war's impact on the Vietnamese people themselves, as well as upon Americans of all races. Furthermore, the war was sending the wrong message to the world, both in terms of American ideals and the appropriate approach to combatting communism. Too, he felt that as a Nobel Peace Prize winner, and especially as a minister of the Christian Gospel, he was compelled to stand with Christ, not some government or military agency. Above all, the Vietnam War in King's view denied the fundamental human reality that God's purposes were global and historical. Community under Christ affected all.[51] "The Vietnamese are our brothers, the Russians are our brothers, the Chinese are our brothers, and one day we've got to sit down together at the table of brotherhood."[52]

"The Kingdom of God May Yet Reign":
Roots of the Poor People's Campaign

King's position on Vietnam was clearly an outgrowth of his nonviolent philosophy, not an aberration from it. Unfortunately for his stature as a black leader, that point was lost to many people, black and white. Increasingly, King had become an overt critic of American society, and he admitted as much to Halberstam. But he refused to become a separatist. It was a significant dilemma, as King was pulled in two directions. "For years," he said, "I labored with the idea of reforming the institutions of the South, a little change here, a little change there. Now I feel quite differently. I think you've got to have a reconstruction of the entire society, a revolution of values." When Halberstam suggested that he was sounding more and more like Malcolm X, King replied sharply that he was not a separatist. "We are all on this particular land together at the same time, and we have to work it out together."[53]

But how, and around what kind of rallying banner? Those were the elusive questions for King and SCLC in 1967. Opposing Vietnam would not accomplish it, and besides, King could not endorse some of the radical planks of the peace movement. He was losing support among moderate blacks. The answer seemed to lie in creating a vast coalition of people who saw poverty as the supreme social evil in the world and who would use it as a touchstone for a renewed movement. It would be more of a human dignity movement than one of civil rights. SCLC had already laid the groundwork with its promotion of economic opportunities in such programs as Operation Breadbasket. If Breadbasket could be enlarged to a national scale, it might add momentum to a large-scale anti-poverty program.

At SCLC's Tenth Anniversary Convention at Ebenezer Baptist Church in August 1967, economic opportunity was the central concern. Under the theme "Where Do We Go From Here?" the delegates reminisced about the movement since Montgomery. After all it was an anniversary convention. But they also voted to extend Operation Breadbasket and to continue encouraging blacks to register to vote. Several major

218

businesses, including General Motors, the Kellogg Company, and Del Monte, were targeted for pressure to hire blacks. Breadbasket leaders would also ask large companies to deposit more money in black-owned banks in ghetto areas and to employ black service companies. Business leaders would be asked to provide transportation and other conveniences so as to accentuate the human dimensions of work. As Jesse Jackson put it, "We want them to understand the Negro's dilemma and suffering. We want them to think of profits in terms of flesh and blood, not only dimes and dollars."[54] Changing minds and attitudes was the basic thrust of the convention. When Sidney Poitier delivered the keynote address he referred to King as "truly a new man in an old world."[55] In keeping with the "Where Do We Go From Here?" theme, he said "to change the world we must first change men."

In his presidential report, King was unusually hopeful, considering the circumstances of 1967. He said it was "a great time to be alive," and spoke of "doors of opportunity" that were gradually "being opened to those at the bottom of society." He revealed no inner confusion or despair, but he did underscore the uncertainty of the moment. "Every crisis has both its dangers and its opportunities. In a dark confused world, the kingdom of God may yet reign in the hearts of men."[56]

Already King had a plan for the next big move of SCLC, the purpose of which was to revive the nonviolent strategy and at the same time dramatize the needs of the poor and the benefits of helping them. SCLC would launch a national campaign culminating with a march to Washington and a large-scale sit-in, or more precisely, camp-in demonstration at government offices in the nation's capital. This Poor People's Campaign would tie together Puerto Ricans, Mexican-Americans, Indians, blacks, and whites in a nonviolent army to get Congress to implement something like Randolph's Freedom Budget proposal of 1966.[57] Government agencies, hospitals, Congress. . . all of Washington, would feel the impact of this Birmingham-style demonstration. But this time it would be at the heart of national government.

It was the best of times and the worst of times for such an undertaking. National economic problems, the Vietnam War, and flagging enthusiasm for reform militated against success. In Congress there was little confidence that the country could sustain both foreign war and anti-poverty efforts. The administration, likewise, was in no mood for troubling the political waters with new social commitments. Said HUD secretary Robert Weaver, "We have gone about as far as we can go."

On the other hand, the Kerner Report* in February 1968 did underscore the need for basic reforms in behalf of the poor, and the anti-Vietnam War movement was gaining strength and respectability. Soon Senator Eugene McCarthy and Robert Kennedy would launch their presidential bids, and both were opposed to the war. Opinion polls of the period showed that in appeal to the public, King and his nonviolent philosophy still far outstripped the militant blacks.[58] President Johnson still favored social and economic reforms despite the war and his alienation from King. In any case, for Martin Luther King and the Southern Christian Leadership Conference, time was a critical factor.

King was probably at his low point early in 1968. "Dr. King's faith was draining," said Andrew Young.[59] Numerous suggestions that he was failing hurt him, as did the militancy of blacks including some in his own circles. On February 4, just two months before his assassination in Memphis, he preached a strange sermon at Ebenezer Baptist in which he talked about

* The 600-page Kerner Commission report (National Advisory Commission on Civil Disorders) was published in February 1968. In it, two societies were seen emerging in the U.S., one disadvantaged, the other privileged. It contained a lengthy section on the historical development of blacks in the United States and emphasis upon the violence in urban ghettos and the rise of Black Power. "Black Power rhetoric and ideology actually express a lack of power," the commission reported. Violence erupted because of a sense of declining influence and hopelessness. It chided government agencies for their failures to head off the ghetto riots by preventive reforms. In Part III, the Commission recommended sweeping new policies, including short-term and longer-range reforms. Community development was especially emphasized. "Only if all the institutions of the community—those outside the government as well as those inside the structure—are implicated in the problems of the ghetto, can the alienation and distrust of disadvantaged citizens be overcome." (pp. 234, 294–99)

220

death, including his own. Pensively anticipating his own funeral, King said that on that fateful day he wanted someone to say "Martin Luther King, Jr. tried to give his life serving others. I'd like somebody to say that day that Martin Luther King, Jr. tried to love somebody. . . . I want you to be able to say that day that I did try to feed the hungry. I want you to be able to say that day that I did try in my life to clothe the naked. . . . And I want you to say that I tried to love and serve humanity." King wanted to be remembered as a "drum major" for justice, for peace, and for righteousness.

But there was little time for such heavy ponderings. On February 12, two events of pivotal significance for King and SCLC occurred. In Memphis Local 1733 of the American Federation of State, County, and Municipal Employees went on strike. Eleven days earlier two blacks employed by the city as garbage collectors were crushed to death when the automatic compressor mechanism was accidentally set off. It was a painful catalyst in a situation that was hardly bearable for many Memphis sanitation workers. In New York garbage workers went on strike at the same time, further incensing local Memphis workers. When Memphis Mayor Henry Loeb demanded that all workers go back to their jobs or be fired, it caused an impasse that would draw King and his aides to Memphis at a time when the Poor People's March on Washington was taking shape.

The other event of February 12 that concerns us here is the planning session in which the SCLC staff decided on the details of the Poor People's Campaign. There had been opposition in a board meeting in New York in January, but King's view prevailed and now on Lincoln's birthday, it was set in motion. SCLC and its associates would seek a $12 billion "economic bill of rights" to help the poor. This would involve guaranteed employment at decent wages, enforcement of school integration, fair housing laws and programs, and direct aid to those who needed it most. The demands were framed rather generally to avoid legislative obscurantism and the danger of another failure. The scope of demonstrations on the West coast and in Washington would depend upon the response of Congress.[60]

The basic plan called for the convergence of people from five rural areas and ten cities in the Appalachian region, the Deep South, the East and Midwest. One of the models was the work of Marian Wright Edelman, who had made pioneering efforts among the poor in Mississippi. She had attempted to make poor people aware of existing programs of assistance so they could take advantage of them. That was one of the central goals of the Poor People's Campaign of 1968. Perhaps the tensions that produced rioting could be defused by knowledge of available aid, while at the same time promoting further reforms. Cadres from Chicago's Lawndale ghetto, Mississippi, West Virginia, and elsewhere, numbering about 3,000 would march on the nation's capital to dramatize the campaign and pressure Washington officials.[61]

These marchers would live in an improvised town (Resurrection City) and make daily marches and visits to officials' offices over a three-month period beginning on April 20. King came up with the idea of accompanying this with a mule train that would travel from Mississippi to Washington to further accentuate the needs of poor people. He traveled widely marshalling the nonviolent cadres for the campaign. By early March he was planning also to enlist other minorities like Puerto Ricans, Indians, and Mexicans, as well as poor Appalachian whites. It was an imaginative and creative project worthy of several others SCLC had led.

But King would not live to see it. His decision to go to Memphis to assist the striking sanitation workers would cost him his life. For as King journeyed to Memphis so did James Earl Ray, a habitual lawbreaker capable of firing bullets into the body of another human being. King knew the risks, as his comments and speeches clearly indicate. But somehow to this preacher of *satyagraha* and *agape* it was an imperative of his overall commitment to enter the Memphis struggle regardless of the dangers. As he would say the night before his death:

Well, I don't know what will happen now. We've got some difficult days ahead. But it doesn't matter with me now. Because I've been to the mountain-top. And I don't mind. Like anybody, I would like to live a long life. Longevity has its place. But I'm not concerned about that now. I just want to do God's will.

And He's allowed me to go to the mountain. And I've looked over. And I've seen the promised Land. I may not get there with you. But I want you to know tonight that we, as a people, will get to the promised land. And I'm happy tonight. I'm not worried about anything. I'm not fearing any man. Mine eyes have seen the glory of the coming of the Lord.[62]

At age thirty-nine, King was a weary but hopeful man. He had rarely seen a restful day for fifteen years. He had been stabbed, hit with rocks and bricks, and arrested. He had been praised, honored, loved; and he had been hated. His message and example had aroused black people as no individual before him had. It is ironic that his presence in Memphis was something of a digression from his Poor People's Campaign. He went there in March and again in early April amidst widespread traveling to engender interest in that campaign. The problems in Memphis were immense. An injunction barred a planned march. Police protection was inadequate. The FBI was less than supportive to say the least, and some have believed it knew of the assassination plan. But as he was shot down on the balcony of the Lorraine Motel on April 4, 1968, and his life slipped rapidly away despite feverish medical efforts. King died a free man who was thinking of Biblical truths and a moving spiritual he had always loved, "Precious Lord, Take My Hand." Musician Ben Branch would play the song not at the planned rally, but King's funeral.

PART 3

THE DREAM AND CONTEMPORARY AMERICA

8

Tragedy and Transition, 1968–1969

The death of Martin Luther King not only deprived the Southern Christian Leadership Conference of its seminal leader, but also severely damaged its inner confidence and sense of direction. This did not go unnoticed by the press. A *Newsweek* article entitled "SCLC on the Couch" reported in December 1968 the disarray in SCLC leadership ranks reflected in an unusual meeting at Paschal's Motor Hotel a few days earlier. At Andrew Young's suggestion these men shared their personal feelings in the presence of trained psychological counselors for two days. "And there in raging, wrangling, name-calling, finger-pointing group therapy, fifteen top hands of Martin Luther King's Southern Christian Leadership Conference tried to work out their own tensions—and SCLC's future—by exorcising the ghost among them. 'We've never buried Dr. King,' said one of them going in, 'and we won't be able to do anything until we do.' "[1]

The Reverend Dr. Ralph David Abernathy, whose friendship and labor with King have been interwoven in these pages, succeeded King as president. For almost a decade, from 1968 to 1977, he doggedly tried to keep SCLC moving forward without its founding president. Abernathy's problems were legion, since King's death inevitably led to the enshrinement of his memory and dulled the sharp edge of his original message.

Soon, plans were made for a suitable memorial to King, and the family-sanctioned Martin Luther King, Jr. Memorial Center was the result. Although only incipient in 1968, the King Center would evolve into a complex institution dedicated to keeping the nonviolent dream alive and engaging national and world problems. Eventually it would be called the Martin Luther King, Jr.

Center for Nonviolent Social Change and would serve as an archival center as well as a training-educational institute with modern facilities and a well-trained staff. Bernita (Mrs. Fred C.) Bennette, a close friend of the King family and a leader of the organization, viewed its emergence as a natural outgrowth of the nonviolent movement. "Whenever Dr. King's death had occurred," she said, "something like this Center would have emerged to carry on his work and its world-wide vision."[2]

Coretta King, the driving force behind the King Center project, had a dream of her own. She anticipated that the nation would invest $20 million to build the Center and support its programs. Despite her husband's death, Mrs. King was determined to carry on the nonviolent tradition and she helped develop plans for a library, a suitable entombment for her husband, and myriad social and recreational, as well as educational and direct-action institutes. Dr. Julius S. Scott, Jr., who became executive director, and Coretta King affirmed that the Center would not be a "momument of brick and mortar" but a vital organism devoted to keeping the Dream alive and functional.[3] The Center would be an autonomous entity with its own special role in perpetuating nonviolence.[4] That it would rival SCLC, her slain husband's major instrument for reform, was not intended. However, during Abernathy's presidency, the King Center did in some ways compete with SCLC, particularly in funding.

Another problem Abernathy faced was the inherent difficulty of succeeding a person as charismatic and historically significant as Dr. King. Any of King's associates would have encountered some of the same kinds of problems Abernathy faced after 1968. But they fell particularly hard on Abernathy, whose style was quite different from King's. Like King, Abernathy was a Baptist minister and a long-term civil rights activist. He and his wife Juanita, as we have seen, worked closely with the Kings from Montgomery onward. Abernathy was with King at the fateful moment of his assassination in Memphis and he cradled the dying SCLC president on the motel balcony and stayed with him to the end. Furthermore, he was King's legally chosen successor as president. But he was not the intellectual or literary figure King was, and his style was more that of the fervent preacher and organizer than the eloquent orator of nonviolent ideology. His nine-year presidency would be difficult for him personally, but it is to his credit that he wanted to do what King would have done had he lived beyond 1968. Abernathy contributed to SCLC several distinctive elements never fully explored because virtually all historical accounts of the SCLC movement end with King's death.

The first challenge to Abernathy and indeed to the entire nonviolent movement was the ordeal of King's assassination, the funeral, and the immediate demands of transition. King was young, a fact which made his sudden death all the more difficult to bear. Despite the trauma and grief, the King family went through the experience with admirable dignity and humility. King was a Christian minister, and the strength of his family's faith saw them through. Close friends and public displays of sympathy also helped. King's body lay in state at Spelman College and at the Ebenezer Baptist Church during the five days before the April 9 funeral. Thousands came to pay their respects to the slain hero of the nonviolent movement. President Johnson declared Sunday April 7 a national day of mourning and made this statement:

> No word of mine can fill the void of the eloquent voice that has been stilled. But this I do believe deeply. The dream of Dr. Martin Luther King has not died with him. Men who are white, men who are black, must and will now join together as never in the past to let all the forces of divisiveness know that America shall not be ruled by the bullet, but only by the ballot of free and just men.

The short but highly symbolic funeral at Ebenezer seemed to be in line with what King's family and friends believed he would have wanted. Around the country there were many memorial services that drew prominent leaders as well as masses of people who simply cared for Martin King. One such service was held at Morehouse College where King had studied as a youth, but the main funeral service was at his home church. A wagon drawn by two mules pulled his casket through Atlanta as a kind of parable, his associates felt, of his identification with the poor and more specifically with the campaign planned in their behalf.

Public response was warm and supportive. King's father was deeply impressed by the city's massive display of concern.

> The outpouring of sympathy was the greatest the city of Atlanta had ever witnessed. Atlanta was magnificent! The eyes of the world were on the city, and it was at its best. . . Atlanta had only a few hours to prepare for the multitude that thronged the city—a multitude of humanity, the influential such as Governor Nelson Rockefeller, the Vice President of the United States Hubert Humphrey, governors, mayors, senators, congressmen, high officials of every major organization of goodwill in the world; and the nameless poor, those valiant men and women who had marched with M.L. from Montgomery to Memphis.[5]

A sense of continuity was crucial at that moment. Martin's voice had been silenced, Daddy King realized, but that people still believed in what he stood for brought comfort. The work must continue, this bereaved father felt, both for the King children and all the followers of the nonviolent movement.

Coretta was also lifted up by the expressions of support, especially indications that many wanted to go on with the movement. In Memphis she told a gathering at City Hall that she sensed the mood of support and charged them:

> And those of you who believe in what Martin Luther King, Jr. stood for, I would challenge you today to see that his spirit never dies and that we will go forward from this experience, which to me represents the Crucifixion, on toward the resurrection and the redemption of the spirit.[6]

"Here was a man," said Benjamin Mays at King's funeral, "who believed with all of his might that the pursuit of violence at any time is ethically and morally wrong; that God and the moral weight of the universe are against it; that violence is self-defeating; and that only love and forgiveness can break the vicious circle of revenge." Not all blacks, however, responded with the sobriety of those who understood King best and agreed with him. "Dr. Martin Luther King was the last prince of nonviolence," said Floyd McKissick. "Nonviolence is a dead philosophy, and it was not the black people that killed it. It was the white people that killed nonviolence, and white racists at that." Blacks spoke of white people's having "declared war" on them. Many of them took King's death as the ultimate denigration of nonviolence and turned to looting and rioting in the aftermath of his assassination.

This new outburst of black frustration was a mixture of genuine disappointment over King's tragic end and an excuse to vent anger of a more diffuse nature. Some one hundred cities witnessed looting and burning. The destruction in Washington alone ran into the millions of dollars as people took radios, television sets, clothing, and whatever else they could grab from damaged buildings. "It was no tribute to King's memory," wrote the editors of *Christianity Today*, "that violence, looting, and arson became the widespread Negro response to the Memphis murder."[7] In their view the murder of King had already reinforced Ho Chi Minh's announced view that the United States was a nation of violence, racism, and special privilege. It behooved all Americans to take a sane approach to the Memphis tragedy, urged this religious journal.

As Abernathy assumed the leadership of the troubled SCLC, he too decried the violence. The new president knew as well as anyone that the movement could be further disrupted by outbreaks of destruction and he pushed ahead as quickly as possible with the Poor People's March on Washington and continued the nonviolent transformation begun under King.[8] SCLC's partner in many projects and campaigns, the NAACP, took a similar stance. "The riots that erupted in 100 cities across the country in the wake of Dr. King's assassination dishonor the memory of a great and good man," wrote its editors. NAACP viewed King as a martyr to the cause of freedom and quality and urged a more pacific and creative response to his death.[9]

It was during the Selma campaign more than two years before his death that King had first broached the topic of Abernathy's succeeding him as head of SCLC. According to Abernathy's recollections, King at that time said, "Ralph, nobody, living, dead or unborn knows me better than you do, knows my philosophy better than you do or has the stability to hold the staff together like you can." A few weeks later King expressed these views to the board of directors and Abernathy came to be considered King's heir-apparent.[10] Then Abernathy was named vice-president-at-large, in addition to being treasurer and financial secretary. In 1968 Abernathy was only slightly older than King, and the Memphis assassination unexpectedly thrust him into the national limelight.

Ralph David Abernathy was born in 1926 in Linden, Alabama, the grandson of slaves and the tenth of twelve children in a farming family. His father, Willie L. Abernathy, was the successful owner of a 500-acre farm in Marengo county. Ralph was close to his family, particularly to his mother, and grew up with a strong sense of purpose. After serving overseas in World War II he earned a B.S. degree from Alabama State College in 1950 and subsequently enrolled at Atlanta University for graduate study in sociology. But his Christian calling led him into the ministry, and he began preaching. After some earlier experience, he became pastor in 1952 of the historic First Baptist Church in Montgomery. It was there that he came to know the Kings, and he and his wife Juanita became two of their closest friends and associates in the work of the Montgomery Improvement Association.

When SCLC was founded in 1957 Abernathy served as its treasurer and financial secretary and in 1961 moved to Atlanta as pastor of West Hunter Street Baptist Church where he was closer to the nerve center of the organization. By then he had received an honorary LL.D. degree in 1960 from Allen University in South Carolina. Abernathy continued his work with SCLC and was pivotal in a number of its campaigns. Despite severe nagging health problems, he remained energetic and good tempered, having a natural affinity to the Christian nonviolence of King.

The sudden, jolting manner in which the SCLC presidency fell on Abernathy's shoulders left him rather stunned, but he assumed the task with a mixture of humility and bold commitment.

Only eleven hours after King's death Abernathy publicly committed himself to the SCLC presidency on the morning of April 5, 1968. He was tired from lack of sleep and saddened by his rapidly changing world as he said:

> The assassination of Martin Luther King, Jr. has placed upon my shoulders the task—No, make that the 'awesome task' of directing the organization which he established, which has given—what do we say here—hope? So much hope to the black people—to the oppressed people of this nation. Even after fifteen years of sharing the struggle with Dr. King, I tremble as I move forward to accept this responsibility. No man can fill Dr. King's shoes.[11]

Most of the intimate circle of SCLC leaders and supporters accepted Abernathy, but there were detractors and over the next few months even major rivals contending for his position. But King had named Abernathy successor, a place he had earned by fifteen years' association with King and the nonviolent movement. As early as 1958, in *Stride Toward Freedom*, King had described Abernathy as "my closest associate and most trusted friend. We prayed together and made important decisions together. His ready good humor lightened many tense moments. Whenever I went out of town I always left him in charge of the important business of the association, knowing that it was in safe hands."[12] Now Abernathy had the entire organization of SCLC to care for. His mentor was at rest in a tomb that bore the inscription:

> Free at Last. Free at Last.
> Thank God Almighty,
> I'm Free at Last.

By his own admission, Abernathy was not prepared to become president of SCLC. "I had no preparation," he says, "because I did not have any idea I would live one day without Martin Luther King, Jr."[13] He and King had been so close for fifteen years, that he expected any assassination move to hit him as well, probably in a motel bombing. But as it turned out, not only was King cut down while Abernathy was spared, but the new

SCLC leader had the sad task of picking a casket and a suit for his slain friend and making the short-range plans for dealing with his body in Memphis. Mrs. King was awaiting her 8:25 P.M. flight to Memphis, when Dora MacDonald rushed to the Atlanta airport to tell her her husband was dead. With that she turned around quickly and went back home to tend to the bewildered and frightened children.[14] Abernathy and the close circle of friends in Memphis thus went through the first night with only each other and a sense of hope to comfort them.

Abernathy was clearly the person to succeed King as the revised SCLC constitution indicated, but he needed the overt support of Andrew Young, Jesse Jackson, Hosea Williams, Bernard Lee, and the others immediately around him in Memphis. Outspoken Hosea Williams unequivocally gave his. At a very late night staff meeting Williams told Abernathy: "Mr. President! I loved King, but King is now dead. He will never return. I want you to know, we have a leader, and that leader is you. I pledge allegiance to you."[15] Young and the others followed suit in giving the stunned and troubled Abernathy their loyalty, and Jesse Jackson headed for Chicago to help organize a group to participate in the funeral services.[16]

Even in the midst of the tragedy, with the funeral still several days away, Abernathy and the other SCLC leaders decided that it was imperative to carry through with the planned march in Memphis early the next week. It had to be demonstrated that there could be a nonviolent march in Memphis despite the death of King and stories of government involvement in the assassination. It was risky, but the conclusion was that it was a necessary move.[17] Mrs. King concurred. She came to Memphis on Friday, April 5 to fly back with King's body on a plane provided by Senator Robert Kennedy. Then on Monday, feeling that it was what her husband would have wanted, she returned to Memphis as Abernathy and others had urged her to do. Accompanying Mrs. King were her three oldest children and close friends Harry Belafonte and Justine Smadback.

Against all odds, there was a peaceful march in Memphis on Monday, April 8, 1968 just one day before Martin Luther King,

Jr.'s funeral services in Atlanta. "It was successful," Abernathy said much later, in what was really quite an understatement.[18] Senator Kennedy appeared, although somewhat apprehensive about the dangers. At City Hall in the troubled southwestern Tennessee city, several speeches honored the slain leader. Coretta got up enough stamina from the inspiration of her husband's dream to speak to the huge throng. "How many men must die," she asked soberly, "before we can really have a free and true and peaceful society?"[19] It was more than a rhetorical question. Within nine weeks Senator Kennedy would be shot to death in California.

It is significant that the death of King caused virtually all of his close followers to rededicate themselves to the work he had begun. Mrs. King wrote later that since his work was not finished she had to carry on with it, and furthermore, that others should do the same. It is apparent that Abernathy had the same inner motivation. But for him it was a particularly hard task. King was a close friend as well as a leader to whom he gave a unique kind of loyalty. On Sunday before returning to Memphis, his sermon was "A Short Letter" to his slain friend, expressing like the Apostle John in his Second Epistle, his longing to join him. Even though a huge crowd turned out to support him, Abernathy had to go through a lonely period of soul searching. There was no 'Ralph David Abernathy' to play the role for him that he had for King, he recalls. Many people who knew him felt that Abernathy never quite clarified his own identity, but he did take time to meditate and arrived at the comforting conviction that no one could ever fill King's shoes and that he, Ralph Abernathy, had some "sandals of his own to wear." He felt that God was helping him to believe in his own distinctive place in continuing SCLC's work.[20]

The new SCLC president pledged to stay on the nonviolent course and to continue several important projects already underway. For a while, the shock of King's death engendered something of a revival of national interest in the problems of blacks and probably helped in the final passage of the 1968 Civil Rights Act on April 10. The Senate had passed the bill by a vote of 71 to 20 on March 11, and now the House followed suit just a week after King's assassination. This belated version of the aborted 1966 bill was passed in the House by a vote of 229 to 195, not a comfortable margin but enough to get it through. Johnson signed it into law the next day. The law's most important feature was Title VIII on fair housing practices. By its terms most categories of housing could no longer be discriminatory, and even vacant lots were covered. Thus blacks could not be kept from building homes in suburbs.[21] The act contained other protective provisions for blacks, Indians, and others.

Furthermore, the Johnson administration implemented several urban renewal projects and job and educational programs to help blacks and others caught in the eddy of urban deterioration. The Department of Housing and Urban Development (HUD) under its black leader, Robert C. Weaver, was deeply involved over the following months in various pilot programs for housing development and other forms of improvement in many cities. Johnson asked the Congress for $500 million for cleaning up cities and an additional $17 million for rent assistance to the needy. All this was on top of Johnson's approximately $2 billion educational assistance program.[22] Despite Vietnam, Johnson hoped to keep the Great Society going.

Notwithstanding these massive urban and poverty-related programs, Abernathy and SCLC decided to carry through with the Poor People's Campaign King was planning at the time of his death. In fact King's assassination seems to have made some of his aides, including Abernathy, all the more determined to go on with the project. Bernard Lafayette, a young Washington coordinator for the march declared almost immediately that the planned campaign would continue. "The march is going on," he said. "If ever there was a March, this one will be held."[23] Abernathy said much the same thing.

Respect for what King had begun was certainly one of the reasons for the decision to go ahead with the planned march on Washington connected with the Poor People's Campaign. But there were other reasons as well. For one thing, the projected Great Society urban and economic reforms would not necessarily help the hard-core poor, and Abernathy had a natural inclination to identify with the needy, despite his middle class life style. He wanted to carry the effort through successfully out of his growing personal concern for it. Also, he was conscious of the need to establish his own leadership credentials. Quite often, he had to contend in the early days of his presidency with suggestions in the press and elsewhere of his inability to measure up to King. Frequently Abernathy found himself asserting that he was the leader and that he also had a dream, suggesting that he was aware people were questioning his leadership.

Abernathy was also conscious of the problems SCLC, even under Martin King, had experienced because of the Black Power advocates. Although the militants would soon experience a dramatic decline in their own appeal and inner coherence, this could not clearly be seen in 1968. The new president could not accept the idea that SCLC and its nonviolent approach had been supplanted by those advocating violence. To Abernathy that would be letting King down and giving up on more than a decade of human investment in his dream.

Poor People's March on Washington

The temporary 'city' that was planned for the Washington march would be the campsite for campaign cadres from around the nation, but more significantly, it would serve as a symbol of the needs of millions of poor Americans. On April 29 a "Committee of 100" visited Congressional leaders and executive offices in Washington to describe the plight of the poor and to ask for help in resolving this chronic condition that plagued millions of Americans of all races.

The appeal was timely since the nation was in fact becoming more conscious of urban problems and poverty by 1968. *Time* was preparing a major article on poverty for publication on May 17 which described pockets of perennial poverty in the deep South and Appalachian region.[24] Other journals and newspapers were making similar efforts. Presidential candidates also discussed these issues in the spring of 1968. Johnson's March 31 announcement that he would not seek another term, opened the field for Humphrey, Robert Kennedy and others who were strongly inclined to view urban problems and poverty as campaign issues.

On May 2 after memorial services for King in Memphis, the great trek of the "Freedom Train" for Washington began. Participants came from all regions of the United States: from Memphis; from Marks, Mississippi by mule train; by bus and on foot from Edwards, Mississippi in the Southern Caravan; from New England in the Northeast Caravan; from Milwaukee in the Midwest Caravan; and from the West beginning at Los Angeles and San Francisco. About 3,000 were to come to Washington in this first leg of the campaign and build a shanty town of plywood A-frames near the Lincoln Memorial. The Marks and Memphis contingents were to arrive first and begin laying out the city.[25]

Under James Bevel's direction, the first group reached Washington on May 12, as officials prepared for possible trouble. Mayor Walter E. Washington said that he was convinced the march would be nonviolent but that officials and police were ready in case any provocateurs were among the participants. Several dignitaries participated in the first few days of the Washington campaign, among them Coretta King, and the wives of Harry Belafonte and Senator Joseph Clark. One interesting gesture in the first few days was the placing of a huge Mother's Day card at the steps of the Congressional Club, whose officials had recently refused to meet with a group of welfare mothers.[26]

Resurrection City was built rapidly of canvas and plywood on a 150-acre plot in the West Potomac Park area near the famous Reflecting Pool. Architect John Wiebensen of the University of Maryland guided the construction of dwellings, churches, and even a 'city hall' placed along two 'streets' [20-foot lanes] running the length of the tree-lined makeshift city. Local churches provided housing and food while the town took shape. Out of such modest material there emerged what Abernathy described a few weeks later as an "unbelievably dramatic demonstration of poverty in the shadow of America's mightiest monuments and government buildings." To Abernathy, Resur-

238

rection City was a microcosm of America, with all the problems of poverty and the beauties of human dignity.[27]

That it was also vulnerable to politics, personal ambitions, and some measure of obscurantism became obvious over the six weeks of its existence. Money for completing the three 1,000-person communities of Resurrection City was not easy to get, and at first it appeared that shelter and food would last only about one week. But Abernathy, Bernard Lafayette, Anthony Henry, Andrew Young, and many more worked diligently to raise the funds and secure supplies. The City managed to survive until forcefully dismantled by police raids on June 24.

The ghetto realism was actually too graphic. Although most of the citizens of Resurrection City were orderly and nonviolent, a significant number of drug-addicts, drunks, and troublemakers showed up and had to be held in check. The City's second 'mayor,' the Reverend Jesse Jackson, managed to get many of the disruptive elements under control with his frank and hardhitting rhetoric. "Now, let's get something straight, "Jackson told them, "I'm a preacher but I can talk that talk and walk that walk just like you can. There ain't going to be no takeover of this camp. I have been named mayor of this city. I'm moving in today. I'm going to run things and can tell you now that all this 'down home' and 'on the block' hell raising is over. We are on the Lord's business and every living one of you is going to get in line."

If Jackson was useful in quelling the rowdiness of the city, he was somewhat less helpful to Abernathy's efforts at keeping the black movement unified around his SCLC presidency. Jackson was named mayor after James Bevel's too obvious anti-war stance caused some public relations problems. But the press tended to view Jackson, only 26 years old, as a challenge to Abernathy. He seemed to be stealing the show. He led several unauthorized marches. Abernathy, in fact, came from his temporary residence at the Pitts Motel to demote Jackson back to 'city manager' and an SCLC attorney said Abernathy was only joking in the first place about making the young Chicago Breadbasket leader 'mayor.' SCLC stalwarts like Hosea Williams saw Jackson as trying to take over, a fact that was particularly disturbing in view of the fact that Jackson had previously argued against the Washington effort.[28]

At times Abernathy was quite dramatic in articulating the message of the poor to the nation and the Congress. He sounded like a veritable Moses as he spoke of "plaguing Pharaoh until he lets our people go." Abernathy urged citizens to pressure their Congressional representatives to meet the plight of the poor with substantial aid and job opportunities. Without specifying the groups he had in mind, the SCLC president warned that there were violent elements waiting to capitalize on the black movement if the Poor People's Campaign failed. "This may be the last nonviolent march in the history of this country," he said.[29] It was essential for Congress and businesses to act soon.

The climax came on Solidarity Day, June 19, or "Juneteenth"as it was called. Although it was not nearly the rousing demonstration that the 1963 March on Washington had been, the rally did draw 50,000 people to the nation's capital for speeches and gestures of unity. Some 700 buses carried the groups from places like Detroit, Watts, Kansas City, and Laredo. They gathered like a human sea around the Washington Monument, but this time the mood was less hopeful, less forward looking than five years before when King cried "I have a dream." Twenty-six speeches, including a 75-minute talk by Abernathy, went forth over the amplification system, and the crowd gradually dwindled to less than 10,000.[30]

Abernathy tried his best to keep the focus clear and to identify himself with King's cause. Some felt he went too far in this direction as he said "I don't care what they do to me. If I must join Robert Francis Kennedy* and Martin Luther King, I still will not bow. . . . I shall be free—someday." Abernathy's main thrust, though, was in the direction of the poverty issue. His Solidarity Day speech appealed to Congress and all Americans to "Let no child go hungry. . . . Let no man be without a job. . . . Let no citizen be denied an adequate income. . . ." He

* Robert Kennedy was shot in Los Angeles on June 5, and died the following day.

240

echoed King's misgivings about the war in Asia. "The promise of a Great Society was burned to ashes by the napalm in Vietnam and we watched the Johnson administration perform as the unwitting midwife of the sick society." He pledged to see the fight through and not bow down "to a racist Congress" or to "an administration that refuses to administer the blessings of this nation to the poor."[31]

Coretta King spoke, too. She recalled the 1963 march and moved the audience with words of appreciation for their presence which she said reflected their deep love for what her late husband had stood for. Mrs. King read a telegram from Mrs. Robert Kennedy, widow of the young Senator who just thirteen days before had been added to the growing list of slain leaders, after his important presidential primary victory in California. Mrs. Kennedy's message said that "the finest memorial to Dr. King would be the implementation by the government of the programs that Dr. King and Senator Kennedy believed in."

Other speakers, notably Roy Wilkins and Walter Reuther, emphasized the need for economic justice. It was not enough for the government to provide welfare support. The generic roots of poverty, they said, had to be removed through effective programs of job training, equal employment opportunities, and improved housing. Both Wilkins and Reuther noted that blacks were especially in need of corrective governmental action because racial discrimination had deprived them of opportunities to advance in the economic system. Even while they spoke, however, Washington officials were making legal maneuvers to close Resurrection City at the end of its six-week license on the grounds that it was becoming a slum and attracting disorderly people. Rectifying conditions that produced slums and antisocial behavior was precisely what Wilkins and the other speakers were calling for.

A few days later the Resurrection City effort came to a stunning and violent end. Heavy rains turned the city into a muddy quagmire, but this physical inconvenience was minimal compared to the police raid of June 23–24. A small army of about 1,000 policemen surrounded the plywood town and arrested 343 'citizens'. The crackdown was triggered by a sit-in at the Department of Agriculture doorway. Tear gas was used the night of the 23rd and during the rioting that followed the forced closing of the poor people's town. There were few incidents during the arresting process in the afternoon of the 24th, but in its wake many angry blacks began hurling various kinds of objects at store windows and police.[32]

This was hardly a glorious ending for Resurrection City, but neither was it a total loss. Jackson was no longer directly connected with the project, so that the weight of the apparent failure fell chiefly on Abernathy. But he could still assert a few weeks later that Resurrection City, USA "is an undying symbol of poverty and the lasting determination of poor people to escape their misery." Whether it could be more than a symbol was not clear, but Abernathy continued to emphasize the poverty issue throughout his presidential tenure.

Ralph Abernathy spent twenty days in jail after his arrest on June 24, fasting in behalf of the poor. Press coverage of Resurrection City's abrupt termination was largely negative. *Newsweek* described it as the "end of the Dream" and quoted Andrew Young as saying that the affair had gotten out of hand and "whoever ran us out did us a great favor." From his cell Abernathy averred that the Poor People's Campaign was not over. During the following weeks SCLC's newspaper *Soul Force* literally filled its columns with articles and editorials on poverty, peace, and rights of Indians, blacks and other minorities.

There was little time for lamenting the problems of Resurrection City. National political conventions lay just ahead, and SCLC had to plan its own national convention. Abernathy had needed a victory in Washington, and when it seemingly eluded him he determined all the more to push the poverty issue and its ramifications during the presidential election campaign of 1968. The cool, if not sometimes hostile, attitude of Congress did not augur well for dramatic legislative victories in the near future. Nor did the death of Robert Kennedy in early June or the big pre-convention lead held by Richard Nixon in early July seem to hold forth much hope for a strongly pro-black presidential candidate. Democrat Hubert Humphrey was near a first ballot nomination total by then, but his association with Johnson's increasingly unpopular Vietnam policy presented some problems among blacks as well as white liberals despite his excellent record on civil rights.

As we have seen, SCLC had linked the peace and social reform issues well before King's death and this continued under Abernathy. Opposition to the war, however, had outstripped civil and economic rights as a priority and had become so diffuse as to produce a kaleidoscopic array of radical forces by the summer of 1968. At the same time, the administration was witnessing a growing opposition to some of the Great Society's pivotal programs including the Office of Economic Opportunity. Johnson's people made little effort to resist.

Abernathy and SCLC made appeals to both major parties before and during their 1968 conventions. On July 31 the SCLC president appeared before the Republican Party Platform Committee in racially troubled Miami and urged the GOP leadership to write strong anti-poverty planks. He expressed alarm over the fact that he had heard that the platform was already determined and was "a document of vague generalities."[33] That would not be sufficient, said Abernathy, to elicit black support or to prevent possible recurrence of the kind of trauma Miami was experiencing. "I am here," he declared, "both as Dr. Martin Luther King, Jr.'s successor as President of the Southern Christian Leadership Conference and on behalf of the poor people of America." In an effort to move the committee by practical considerations, Abernathy alerted them to the fact that the next stage of the Poor People's Campaign would be largely political and that blacks would be "very active" in all levels of the fall elections. He then briefly summarized the proposals he represented: first, that both parties endorse the findings of the President's Advisory Committee on Civil Disorders (Kerner Commission) and; second, that both parties support the demands of the Poor People's Campaign.[34]

The Republican convention nominated Richard Nixon and

Spiro Agnew, and the platform adopted did express concern for poverty and civil rights. "We must attack the root causes of poverty," it said, "and eradicate racism, hatred, and violence." In a long section on the urban crisis, the platform also committed the party to helping the poor acquire adequate housing, transportation, and jobs.[35] Interestingly, while Abernathy was in Miami, Governor Claude Kirk asked him to help placate some of the insurgents in a new outburst in the Liberty City section. Abernathy agreed and made a visit to talk with some of the riot leaders.

SCLC held its own convention in mid-August just before the Democratic National Convention in Chicago. There had been some doubt that an SCLC convention in 1968 was possible anywhere and some very serious misgivings about holding it in the city where King had been killed in April. But by July 20, it was determined that SCLC would meet in Memphis as a symbol of its continuance and its faith in the possible peaceful resolution of local Memphis problems and the black movement as a whole.

The theme for the Eleventh Annual Convention of the Southern Christian Leadership Conference was "New Life for Poor People." It was the first convention since King's assassination and the last before the new political approaches were attempted. In that sense it marked an important juncture in the history of the organization. Slated for participation was the typical array of highly visible black leaders but this time police security was heavy and Memphis nervously anticipated possible violence. The expected 2,000 delegates did not materialize and pre-convention estimates ranged steadily downward to a few hundred. The actual number of delegates and guests was about 1,200. The fact that SCLC was there at all, however, was more significant than numbers in 1968.[36]

There were elements of continuity and change in the Memphis Convention. Abernathy was unanimously elected president, thus officially making him King's successor. With the convention vote all speculation that Young or Jackson or some other black leader might head the SCLC at that point ended. Young accompanied Abernathy to Memphis and consistently maintained his posture of endorsing the new SCLC president. Abernathy still had rivals, notably the Reverend Jesse Jackson, but for the moment Abernathy was a symbol of continuity in the nonviolent movement.

Nonviolence was reaffirmed as the strategy of SCLC, although another group of young blacks known as the Invaders put in a dramatic appearance at the convention and expressed their opposition to Abernathy and Young. The Invaders ordered Young out of town because of his allegedly insulting insinuations that the militant youth had indirectly contributed to King's assassination. Abernathy, board chairman Joseph E. Lowery, Young, and several more SCLC representatives declared their adherence to nonviolence. Echoing King, Abernathy said, "Nonviolence is the most potent weapon available to an oppressed people." Lowery stated flatly, "We reject violence." "There has been a dialogue on integration," Young affirmed, "and we have taken our stand for nonviolence."[37] The presence of Mrs. King, who was now on the SCLC board of directors, further underscored the prevailing consensus. In behalf of her late husband she accepted the Rosa Parks Award for his service to black Americans.

An interesting modification of SCLC strategy was implied by Abernathy in his presidential address. While reaffirming nonviolence as SCLC's method and goal, he said that the organization would no longer serve as a device for controlling riotous behavior by other blacks. He recalled at some length the recent experience in Miami, especially Governor Kirk's appeal for assistance in the Liberty City riots. Abernathy told the convention delegates that he had agreed to help the Governor but that in the future he would not be available when leaders "got in trouble."[38] This was one of several hints in Abernathy's very long speech that SCLC was assuming a more militant, or at least non-parental, role in civil rights activism. "There are too many Uncle Toms and 'Nervous Nellies' in the organization," and it appeared to him that it was time for a new vigor.

Basically this was not a new departure. We saw SCLC's image change with the heightened militancy of the sixties and its more precise focus on socio-economic issues. Some increased militancy was strategically inevitable, but the resolutions passed by the Memphis convention were consistent with SCLC's previous approach. They called for seeking social justice through peaceful means and on a biracial basis. They called for ending the Vietnam War and reordering the priorities of the nation. In behalf of blacks in several southern states, they asked the Democratic Party not to seat the regular delegations. Abernathy promised to appear in Chicago with a symbolic mule train to accentuate the plight of the poor. This plan was later dropped in view of the nature of the Chicago convention.

What is most significant historically is that the nonviolent movement survived King's death and was seeking better ways to articulate its message in an era essentially different from that of the early and middle sixties. Abernathy was plagued by internal dissension in SCLC ranks and the heavy burden of forging a new perception of the nonviolent dream. He preferred 'vision' to 'dream' and attempted to assert his own leadership, without fully succeeding. The organization as a whole shared many of his problems and would face declining financial support and confidence over the first few years of his presidency. The Memphis convention confirmed SCLC's transition to its new position. With the King Center occupying an increasing amount of Mrs. King's time and resources, and with national economic and political problems becoming more complex, little that SCLC might do after 1968 would be easy. It was the organization's most trying time since Albany.

The Democrats held their convention in Chicago two weeks later and nominated Hubert H. Humphrey and Edmund Muskie. The peace candidate Eugene McCarthy and other challengers fell to the Vice-President's political drive. The convention itself was one of the strangest in American history, marked by an almost military-camp atmosphere. Some 700 civilians and 83 police were injured in the riotous battles outside the Amphitheater. The war loomed large to the young and not-so-young radicals who disrupted the usual carnival atmosphere of such gatherings. It rivaled the August Soviet-Czechoslovak crisis in media appeal. The country's shift of mood to a 'law and order' mentality was furthered along by the Chicago spectacle. Nixon and Agnew would make the law and order issue work for them in the campaign that followed.

Blacks were visible at the Chicago convention, notably because of several delegation seating challenges and the appearance of young Julian Bond as a candidate. Bond headed the interracial Georgia group that challenged Governor Lester Maddox's nearly all-white delegation and won at least a partial victory. The Credentials Committee decided to split the Georgia delegation and seat half of the insurgent delegation. There were other quarrels and ill-fated compromises over delegations from Mississippi, Alabama, and even Texas in this "battle of Chicago." Julian Bond, a Georgia state legislator, put himself forth as a vice presidential candidate although constitutionally he was too young, at twenty-eight, to hold the office.

The Democrats, nevertheless, managed to complete their convention. Their platform called for peace in Vietnam and an extensive program of relief for the poor. Great Society theory came through clearly in the section on 'Opportunity for All.' "We of the Democratic Party believe that a nation wealthy beyond the dreams of most of mankind—a nation with a twentieth of the world's population, possessing half the world's manufactured goods—has the capacity and the duty to assure to all its citizens the opportunity to enjoy the full measure of the blessings of American life."[39]

The net result of all the internal and public turmoil at the Chicago Convention was a division of the Democrats that gave the Republicans a significant advantage in the election. Nixon started the fall presidential race with a sixteen point lead, and would win in November by a narrow popular vote margin of half a million, but a more decisive electoral vote of 302 to Humphrey's 191. Humphrey carried only Texas in the South. While losing Illinois and the Midwest and the Farwest to Nixon, he did carry Minnesota and Michigan. Strong third-party candidate George Wallace carried five southern states with forty-five electoral votes.

Nixon's victory in November brought to an end a decade of Democratic presidential leadership under Kennedy and Johnson. It did not necessarily spell trouble for blacks, but many doubted that Nixon's civil rights policies or economic proposals would match the liberal approach of the previous administrations. Nixon knew that he suffered from a bad image among blacks and always felt it was an unfair estimation. By his own confession, Nixon was "politically unbeholden" to various pressure groups and thus freer to act in a disinterested and practical way on matters such as race relations. The President-elect opposed the extremism that was rampant in 1968 and set himself to the task of enforcing already achieved legal gains.[40] Even before his inauguration Nixon called six black leaders to meet with him to discuss civil rights and racial problems. Abernathy was included in the group, as were *Ebony* and *Jet* publisher John Johnson, Negro Elks leader Hobson Reynolds, National Baptist Convention vice-president Sandy Ray, National Newspaper Publisher's Association president John Murphy, and Dr. Nathan Wright, chairman of the Black Power Conference. Nixon promised them that he would "do more for the underprivileged and more for the Negro than any President has ever done."[41]

In his inaugural address on January 20, 1969, the new President spoke of the need for peace in the world and at home. He called upon the nation to quit its internecine fighting and turn to reasonable discourse. "We cannot learn from one another until we stop shouting at one another—until we speak quietly enough so that our words can be heard as well as our voices." He promised that government would listen and that "those who have been left out, we will try to bring in. Those left behind, we will help to catch up. This means black and white together, as one nation, not two. The laws have caught up with our conscience. What remains is to give life to what is in the law. . ."[42]

President Nixon did not find it simple to effect a civil rights policy. In his own mind he felt that his record was good. But at the same time he recalled vividly the negative results among blacks in his losing 1960 campaign against Kennedy and never felt confident that blacks would ever give him credit for what he had done and felt. Nor would opponents of civil rights reform give him respect for his efforts to "strike a moderate balance." He wrote in his later reflections, "I could deliver the Sermon on the Mount and the NAACP would criticize the rhetoric. And the diehard segregationists would criticize it on the grounds that I was being motivated solely by public pressure rather than conscience."[43] Furthermore, Nixon had incurred political debts during his 1968 bid for the presidency, notably to arch conservative Strom Thurmond of South Carolina. Thus he found it difficult to deliver on his most significant campaign promise to blacks, namely, to promote black business enterprise in the United States.

In February 1969 Nixon met with NAACP director Roy Wilkins at the White House. Somehow he convinced Wilkins of his sincerity in wanting to improve his image among blacks by taking actions that would demonstrate his commitment to civil rights. Still the problem persisted. Under pressure from Thurmond and Clarke Reed of Mississippi, Nixon dropped or cut short several of his civil rights efforts including promotion of black businesses and cutting off school funds to enforce integration. John Mitchell, Nixon's former law partner and campaign manager and now Attorney General, favored a voluntary desegregation policy and this had considerable impact on Nixon's administration.[44]

Nixon did make some moves that furthered the cause of civil rights during the first few months of his presidency in 1969. Three hospitals in Mississippi were given 30 days after April 7, 1969 to comply with laws on race or face cutoff of federal funds under the authority of the 1964 Civil Rights Act. Similar warnings were issued to hospitals in Alabama, Mississippi, South Carolina, and Texas. The Justice Department filed job discrimination suits against the Cannon Mills Company. A few schools also received HEW warnings about desegregation, although that office gave a rather optimistic report of overall compliance with the law.[45]

None of this convinced black leaders that the Nixon administration would be forceful on civil rights, and it did not begin to meet the rising demands of many militants in the spring and summer of 1969. Some of these expressions seemed quite outrageous as practical proposals. James Forman, for example, interrupted the services of the Riverside Church in New York on May 4, 1969 to present his *Black Manifesto* which called for $500 million in reparations to be paid by Christians and Jews to redress the effects of slavery and discrimination. Though Forman did have some creative plans for using the money, there was no possibility that the nation's churches and synagogues would pay such a penalty.[46]

Abernathy and SCLC took a different approach but were no less insistent upon action. As winter yielded to spring in 1969, Abernathy seemed to be more confident of his personal role and of SCLC's potential as a national black organization. Perhaps the therapy session at Paschal's late in 1968 had released some of the tensions of the first few months. In any case it gave him a chance to express openly his inner conflicts over succeeding Martin Luther King. As April 4, 1969 approached, Abernathy was calling for more extensive nonviolent direct action. In an article honoring King, he spoke out in *Soul Force* on the first anniversary of his colleague's death:

> I urge you to join me, the Southern Christian Leadership Conference, and many national, regional, and local organizations of the rich and poor, young and old, in a new movement to save America. This movement begins on April 4th, one year after the assassination of Dr. Martin Luther King, Jr. On this day, all over the nation, there are commemorative services, vigils and marches. But it would be a disservice to Dr. King and to poor people if we were to let it go at that. Dr. King stood for action, and I mean to honor him meaningfully by having nationwide action that will continue past April 4.[47]

What Abernathy had in mind was a variety of demonstrations including boycotts, school walkouts, work stoppages, peace demonstrations, and rent strikes. April 4, he hoped, would be the signal for many thousands of blacks to make their demands felt by refusing to work, go to school, etc. These demonstrations on Good Friday were to mark the beginning of "Chapter Two of the Poor People's Campaign." Abernathy journeyed to Memphis to lead a march of 20,000 to officially begin the new phase of the anti-poverty campaign. Senator Edward Kennedy appeared with the SCLC president for the rally and march.

These 'Days of Commemoration' activities spanned the period from April 4–12, 1969. Altogether about fifty cities had vigils, marches, or other commemorative observances, and in a few instances there were significant strikes. In the national media the most visible of these activities was the SCLC Memphis rally led by Abernathy. He spearheaded a march from City Hall to the Lorraine Motel where King was gunned down one year before. On that same balcony, Abernathy stood with Massachusetts Senator Edward Kennedy, who rejected special security arrangements, and said, "If there are risks, we will take them." At City Hall Abernathy introduced the young brother of slain John and Robert as "the next President of the United States." That brought cheers from the crowd, which had a friendly disposition toward the Kennedy family because of its stand on civil and human rights. The Senator spoke briefly to the marchers, saying, "Let us resolve once more as we honor the memory of Dr. King all over America, that yesterday's grief and today's crises will be tomorrow's opportunity."[48]

Many other local and national luminaries added their words of respect for King and his movement. Nixon sent a message to Mrs. King in which he expressed his sadness at King's death in 1968 and his hope that the future would bring greater justice in the United States. It was delivered personally by HEW Secretary Robert Finch. In Atlanta, Coretta King placed a cross of red and white flowers at her husband's tomb in a simple ceremony. She took the occasion to remind the world of King's message of peace, love and justice.

In Selma, Alabama, 2,000 people reenacted the historic march of 1965. Singing and marching as they had done four years earlier, they crossed the Edmund Pettus Bridge. Only this time the police waited in silence as the symbolic drama was played out. SCLC field director Hosea Williams failed to show up, and

251

after a three-hour wait a local black minister, the Reverend Louis L. Anderson, led the mile-and-a-half mule-train march. There were also several more commemorations across the South. In Charleston, South Carolina, a strike by hospital workers was underway, and in North Carolina a Hyde County student strike to protest a local desegregation plan.

In northern cities, too, the anniversary of King's death witnessed a variety of public services. In Washington, car headlights were turned on in honor of the occasion, and SCLC's Reverend Walter Fauntroy spoke at an ecumenical service at Greater New Hope Baptist Church where he said, "They have killed our dreamer. The question is what shall become of the dream? Despite councils of despair, despite hatred and violence, we shall overcome if we are united. What they could not stop with a bullet will be realized."[49] In New York, Governor Nelson Rockefeller and the National Urban League's director Whitney Young issued statements of support of King's cause. Richmond, Louisville, New Orleans, and dozens of other towns and cities paused to remember and reflect on the meaning of King's life and movement. On the West Coast Andrew Young told an audience of 1,500 at the University of California at Los Angeles that the dream was still alive, and nearby at the Federal Building a day-long vigil began.[50]

One of the most publicized outgrowths of this period of commemoration was a hospital strike in Charleston, South Carolina. On Thursday, March 30, a dozen employees of the South Carolina Medical College Hospital had struck under the leadership of a black local union leader, Mary Moultrie. The principal issue was low pay. Hospital workers were typically receiving $1.30 an hour, or about $52.00 per week. Furthermore, the black workers felt that they were being discriminated against in terms of treatment, promotion, fringe benefits, and job classification. SCLC entered the strike effort and helped to organize blacks and poor whites in a common cause of reform. Abernathy's organization worked closely with the local labor union 1199 in organizing the community. It was a difficult challenge but one that demonstrated the capacity of SCLC to work in a labor crisis. Abernathy and his wife Juanita took it very seriously and led several marches there. Carl Farris, Jesse Jackson, Septima Clark, and many more SCLC people participated.

SCLC had been involved in labor disputes before. King had marched with striking workers in the middle sixties, and his final undertaking was in behalf of the striking sanitation workers in Memphis, who carried signs saying "I am a Man." But the Charleston strike gave the SCLC leadership a sense of having reached an historical juncture. Young, who continued as chief executive officer of SCLC under Abernathy, wrote in June 1969 that the Charleston strike meant a tangible beginning of the effort to alter the economic order in the United States.

> Montgomery ignited the contemporary human rights movement. Birmingham defeated the social evil of legal segregation. Selma touched off a political revolution. And now, in Charleston, with a conscious coalition of labor and civil rights, we are starting the movement for reform of the economic order, by organizing to raise the income and power level of the working poor.[51]

Not everyone would agree with this estimation of the importance of the Charleston strike. Its importance for the nation was minimal, but in the prespective of SCLC's growing support of labor coalitions, it provided at least a symbol of progress.

The strike lasted 113 days and ended with an impressive victory in July 1969. By SCLC's calculations, pay increases and other benefits that resulted from the long ordeal amounted to about $12 million annually. Walter Fauntroy hailed it as a "blessing to the poor of the nation, a tribute to the leadership of Dr. Ralph David Abernathy."[52] It also suggested to Fauntroy a paradigm for future SCLC activities. SCLC should become more deeply and effectively involved in labor problems and forge coalitions where possible with labor groups compatible with the nonviolent movement.

"Where do we go from here?" King queried in 1967. He had asked this generic question in the middle sixties amid black militancy and white backlash and declining interest in civil rights. Now SCLC had to ask it in an era without Martin Luther King, Jr. as its guiding light. White America was beset by growing and complex problems. Economic decline was hurting the middle class now, and worse conditions lay ahead. Many people, black and white, still adhered to the dream of a peaceful and just society. But was it feasible? Not only blacks, but also Hispanic Americans, native Indians, women, and a host of other groups that had suffered one kind of injustice or another were beginning as never before to articulate their own needs. There was less confidence by the end of the decade that the nation was economically and spiritually capable of resolving its problems. To casual observers and serious social analysts alike, the civil rights era was over for all practical purposes. That was perhaps the greatest problem facing SCLC by 1969. King seems to have anticipated this situation and one wonders how he would have dealt with it. But at the very minimum, we can assume that King would have felt that if the movement indeed were finished, it had not succeeded in realizing the essence of his dream. The "Promised Land" he spoke of just before his death had not yet been reached in America or elsewhere in the world.

But while blacks have become participants in American society, we must not forget that they have not achieved full integration into our social and economic systems.

Bayard Rustin

9

Abernathy and the Second Stage 1969–1973

A certain rhythm of organizational activity was being established in SCLC during the second year after King's death, much of it determined by his ongoing influence. In January, SCLC participated with the King Center in observing King's birthday. In April, the anniversary of his assassination was marked by ceremonies and the initiation of a new campaign. During the summer, SCLC leaders busied themselves with preparations for the annual convention, which was somehow even more important now that King was gone. The fall often brought local and national elections, and that, of course, was always of interest to SCLC.

King's picture surrounded by the SCLC seal still hung, as it does today, near the entrance of the national headquarters in the little changed Masonic lodge building which had housed SCLC since its early days. Inside, newspaper clippings and other memorabilia reminded SCLC personnel, and above all Abernathy, of the ubiquitous presence of the founding president. But it remained to be seen whether his legacy could be translated into a continuing "second stage" movement as he had defined it in the last major presentation he made to his staff in a meeting at Frogmore, South Carolina in November 1967. There he reviewed the history of the movement from its earliest days to the "second stage" when black-white collaboration was decreasing and resistance growing. It was necessary, King had insisted, that a "new course" be defined, one that would attack ghetto poverty and other ills with "new tactics which do not count on government good will, but instead serve to compel unwilling authorities to yield to the mandates of justice."[1]

The initial thrusts in that direction had not gone well. But SCLC was in better condition to try to renew the movement than were the other leading activist organizations of the sixties. CORE was in decline after its phenomenal heyday, and SNCC was falling apart by the time Stokely Carmichael resigned in July 1969. SCLC faced serious problems, too, but was sustained by the intimate connection with King and the fact that a number of its central figures stayed with the organization during the time of transition into the post-King era. Furthermore, the looseness of the SCLC structure, which at times had made its operations difficult, now proved to be a disguised blessing. The fact that the national staff was more limited and funds were short did not mean that SCLC ceased to function in the many local communities where it had affiliates.[2]

Above all, the concept of the "dream" still had potency. To it, Abernathy and company rallied, largely in terms of the language of the pre-Selma period, but qualified by the urgency and increased militancy of the King of the late sixties. SCLC leaders had little confidence in the view so often proffered by the press and some scholars that King was an incipient revolutionary in his last months. They would not have concurred with the notion that the late King developed a "view of man and society (that was) light years different from what it had been a decade or more earlier."[3] It was the comprehensive thrust of King's career and personality that SCLC projected as its legacy from him. They knew that he had always been more "revolutionary" in some respects than the press had recognized. It was revolutionary to defy segregationism in the deep South with a nonviolent message and certainly it was a radical departure from the norm of American political culture to talk of the day when descendants of both slaves and slave-owners could be brothers.[4]

This was a crucial factor in SCLC's history after 1969. King's movement had appealed to many kinds of people—older blacks with strong religious beliefs, young people with newly found ambitions, clergymen with responsibilities for the complex ministries of local churches, politicians, and myriad others. What people saw in him depended upon their own experience and intellectual or spiritual bearings. If SCLC had opted for one particular dimension which, after all, was contextual rather than indigenous to its history, the results would have been disastrous for the organization. At the same time, it was precisely this deeper rootage that permitted SCLC to continue long after SNCC, for example, had scattered.

The Post-King Challenge: The Politics of Poverty

Three possibilities presented themselves most clearly to black leaders by 1969: 1) to work through organizations like NAACP, SCLC, or the National Urban League in carrying on the post-civil rights movement until a greater measure of equality was achieved; 2) to perpetuate the memory of King and cultivate broader public awareness of the meaning and relevance of nonviolence; and 3) to work through the political process by means of a coalition to extend social and economic opportunities to blacks, the poor of all races, labor, and possibly other social elements. Significantly, the concept of "black leader" was radically changing, and this in turn affected the viability of all of these strategies. By the end of the sixties, the desegregation movement, the Voting Rights Act, and the experience of activism had produced large numbers of better-educated, more confident black Americans who were finding more outlets in their careers and personal lives and had less need for the traditional "black leader" who spearheaded contacts with the white majority community. Some even resented the idea that they required such a spokesman to represent their interests which, in many cases, were not identical with the interests of the leader or his organization.

Thus, SCLC inevitably found it difficult to approach what King had termed the "second stage." Like a number of other

257

organizations, it opted for a combination of the three strategies most visibly present in 1969. When the period of mourning ended, Ralph Abernathy was already talking about organizational programs, cultivating nonviolent theory further, and developing an early version of the rainbow coalition. But he had to nurture his own leadership style and find the practical bases for developing a post-King coalition that could meaningfully be tied to the "prophetic power" emphasis of the King years.[5]

Within SCLC leadership circles, there was much reflection on what it all meant. This was exactly what was needed, serious analysis of the events of the previous decade in the light of current challenges. The lessons of the movement could be put into perspective and to Abernathy, the prime consideration was SCLC's place in the spectrum of American politics, especially its relation to other approaches to reform. As he saw it, SCLC had to avoid both absorption into the political system and any tendencies toward resentment and violence. "Once it [SCLC] becomes part of the system, it will become ineffective as so many of our organizations are today. And if it leads people down the path of destruction and violence, it will also become an ineffective force because it will also be destroyed."[6] The best route, Abernathy thought, was for SCLC to continue the emphasis upon fighting poverty. This was King's main concern at the time of his death, Abernathy fondly recalled, and it seemed like a necessary and viable part of any continuing SCLC operation.[7]

Another SCLC official who pondered the meaning of the nonviolent movement and tried to gauge the opportunities still there for SCLC was Andrew Young. As he looked back on Birmingham and the other major campaigns he saw things not noticed during the crises. For one thing, nonviolence was much more complex and inclusive than its adherents had time or historical perspective to realize at the time of the campaigns.

We often talk about nonviolence like four proverbial blind men attempting to describe an elephant. We talk about that part that we've been most involved with, and very few of us really struggle to get a full sense of the whole nonviolent movement and what it meant. . . I continue to see the significance of things that we did unconsciously, and I now understand how important that was.[8]

One thing Young saw more clearly from the vantage point of the early seventies was that the Birmingham campaign had succeeded ultimately because of the "creative tension" that accompanied the negotiating process. That appeared to the SCLC executive director to have been lost in great measure after the high tide of the movement was reached in 1964 and 1965 and had largely dissipated by the early seventies. Many blacks seemed more interested in quarreling among themselves, and with whites, than in negotiating for progress. Young knew that if it could not be recovered, there was little likelihood that even the best of intentions would lead to further progress in the movement.[9]

Of equal importance to the continuance of an effective Southern Christian Leadership Conference was focus. King's organization had never done well without symbolic targets like Bull Connor, Jim Clark, and visibly discriminatory practices to oppose. But who was responsible for poverty? One might better ask *what* was responsible for it, quite apart from persons. King himself had implicitly recognized that fact years earlier when he pointed out that "Jobs are harder to create than voting rolls." In a capitalist economy jobs are generated by production and profits. It could be argued, and often was, that better job opportunities and higher wages for blacks depended upon a healthy growing economy more than upon anything specifically concerned with civil rights.[10]

On the other hand, there is no doubt that being black was a disadvantage in the economic practices of the late sixties and early seventies, despite federal legislation guaranteeing the civil rights of all Americans.[11] Inadequate education was often a liability, especially as the economy entered the high-technology age. Moreover, what has often been described as "white backlash" operated against blacks when they applied for jobs or attempted to advance up the organizational ladders of

259

businesses.* Add to that the widespread deficiencies of housing, medical care, and basic comforts—all of which take large sums to correct—and the picture appears even bleaker.

The Nixon administration became the symbolic target of black anti-poverty rhetoric, not because black leaders believed that he caused poverty, but rather because he did not seem to view it as an appropriate sphere of federal endeavor. Nixon's approach was philosophically identical with Eisenhower's in the fifties: enforcing the law and reconditioning public attitudes were the best strategies of government in bringing about change. "I believed," Nixon wrote later, "that with the right approach we could persuade people in the South and elsewhere not just to obey the law because it was the law, but gradually to bring them to an understanding and acceptance of the wisdom and humanity that lay behind it." In the interest of preserving unity, the President felt, "the federal government should be an instrument of persuasion rather than an engine of coercion."[12]

In the late fifties when black leaders had received the same response from Eisenhower, they seized the initiative themselves and gradually compelled the federal government to bring its power to bear on civil rights. At the end of the sixties, beginning with Johnson's shift of emphasis and continuing into Nixon's first term, history seemed to be repeating itself. As early as the spring of 1969 several black organizational spokesmen were criticizing Nixon for not pressing forward on civil rights and some were raising questions about the sincerity of his concern for the poor. Wilkins of the NAACP said in June that Nixon had made civil rights a "tertiary consideration in apparent deference to Dixie pressures spearheaded by Senator Strom Thurmond of South Carolina."[13]

* The sixties had brought progress in some spheres. The nonwhite portion of the work force in the United States (90% of them black) rose from 4% to 7% in the professional and technical fields, from 5% to 8% in clerical jobs, and from 5% to 7% in blue-collar jobs. But unemployment was 16% in this group, compared to less than 5% among whites. Blacks were much more heavily concentrated in the lower-paying jobs. Only 11% of blacks were in professional. managerial, or technical jobs compared to over 25% for whites.

This time, however, it was not possible to confront the government or the general public with clear-cut issues of justice. White backlash reinforced by the view that blacks had gained all that the American system could appropriately guarantee, was a more formidable force than the morally questionable patterns of segregation and overt discrimination. Nor was it possible to use demonstrations effectively because the connections between poverty and denial of rights were not clear.

Abernathy, though, was convinced that a reordering of national priorities was both possible and potentially efficacious. The place to begin was the federal government, but his efforts to accomplish something substantial in that area ran into serious difficulties just a few weeks after Nixon's inauguration. Abernathy was unable to move Nixon with his appeals, and the gulf between the two men widened. The SCLC president approached the administration very critically and in terms that questioned its sensitivity to poor people. This incensed Nixon and others in his administration without greatly troubling them about the prospect of SCLC's being able to muster any significant political leverage against them.

Abernathy's problems with Nixon began as early as May 1969 during the Charleston hospital strike. Beginning on May 12 Abernathy led the Poor People's Campaign's multi-racial Committee of One Hundred in five days of intensive lobbying and demonstrating at federal agencies in Washington. On May 13 they managed to get an audience with Nixon, officials of the Urban Affairs Council, and members of the cabinet, including Patrick Moynihan. Although the committee had asked Nixon to meet with all of them, the President agreed to consult with a smaller group in the Cabinet Room at the White House, while the others waited in the Indian Treaty Room at the Executive Office Building.

As it turned out, last-minute preparations and crowded conditions caused Abernathy to arrive late and he had to push his way through the corps of reporters to deliver his prepared statement. Nixon was negatively impressed, not only by Abernathy's tardiness but also the style and content of his speech. The SCLC president candidly criticized the administration for budget-cutting and other ostensible signs of not caring about blacks, Mexican-Americans, Indians, and Puerto Ricans. Abernathy also mentioned joblessness among minorities, hunger, the slow pace of school desegregation, and the Charleston strike.[14]

Already convinced that Abernathy was less a leader than King, Nixon was further alienated by the blistering critique. Abernathy, wrote Nixon, "was either unprepared or unwilling, or both, to have serious discussion."[15] In the President's view, Abernathy's statement was simply a catalogue of demands lacking real substance for negotiation.

After the conference, Abernathy made negative comments to the press, calling the audience with Nixon "the most disappointing and fruitless meeting so far in Washington."[16] Clearly bothered by the tone of the meeting, he felt that Nixon and his aides "did not have time for the poor." Nixon had argued that his administration was doing what it could for the poor in view of other obligations, but Abernathy felt that by reordering priorities the government could do considerably more about a serious problem affecting millions of blacks and whites across the nation.

Although much of the reaction to Abernathy's statement and his subsequent criticism of the conference was negative or only midly favorable, some voices were raised in his behalf. The editors of the *Washington Post* criticized Nixon for not meeting the seventy poor people's representatives waiting in the Indian Treaty Room, among them several American Indians. The President might also have done much good, they argued, by offering mediation in the Charleston strike. These "extra efforts" could have made the symbolic meeting with the poor people's representatives a source of encouragement for progress. In short, Nixon had missed an opportunity to establish a good relationship with them and defuse political tensions.[17]

On some issues Nixon and the delegation had passed in the dark. Abernathy had made a meaningful point, and Nixon's people did miss an opportunity to take a strong public stand on poverty without serious political risk. On the other hand, the Committee of One Hundred did not realize that Nixon was already taking a hard look at welfare and other aid to the poor and was considering ways to expand such programs. Ironically, the Nixon aid programs that materialized over the following months exceeded those of Johnson's Great Society, although they did not deal strongly with the causes of poverty or preserve certain social programs deemed vital by the black leaders.

The two months following the White House conference found Abernathy and SCLC busily engaged in numerous labor disputes. On May 17, Abernathy traveled to southern California to support a grape workers strike led by the United Farm Workers Organizing Committee. Composed mostly of Mexican-Americans, but including some blacks, this organization had sought for over three years to gain official union status and to secure better wages and working conditions. The march and rally it held at Calexico drew some national figures like Senator Edward Kennedy. Abernathy was there to expand SCLC's connections with labor. His basic idea was to link blacks with poor and marginal workers of various ethnic and racial composition in a functional political coalition. Other SCLC personnel were involved in local boycotts and strikes, as well as union organizing.[18]

This kind of activity demonstrated SCLC's shift away from its traditional direct-action techniques to a type presumably more consistent with the times. It signalled a reordering of the coalitional basis of the black movement, at least as understood by a number of SCLC leaders. White liberals as a societal grouping would be less important than ethnic groups and workers who shared common interests with blacks. Operating on the not entirely accurate assumption that the federal government would not act in the interests of the poor and working class unless forced to do so by their combined political pressure, these groups hoped to forge enough strength both to effect specific gains in their jobs and to modify federal policy.

There was a broader purpose, however. Abernathy wanted to accomplish in the sphere of public policy toward poverty what the great campaigns of the King years had in the area of integration. He knew that there was a certain amount of momentum favoring fair hiring and advancement practices, and that poverty had become a national issue. White backlash notwithstanding, it was conceivable to Abernathy that the conscience of the nation could again be sensitized to a pressing national issue, as it had been in Birmingham and Selma.[19]

Some of the means SCLC used to heighten public consciousness of poverty were effective in dramatizing the plight of the poor, but were less realistic politically. One effort that illustrated the inherent problems involved in using demonstrations to confront systemic economic inequities was the SCLC-sponsored rally at Cape Kennedy in the summer of 1969. On July 16, the nation and the world watched in awe as the Apollo 11 spacecraft lifted off to carry man to the moon for the first time. The project had cost about $24 billion to implement. And as the moment of man's first steps on the lunar surface neared, Hosea Williams was leading a mule train to Cape Kennedy to dramatize the poverty of millions in a country that could afford such huge sums to explore space. Only a small portion of that money, SCLC argued, could help malnurished children, poverty-stricken mothers, and unemployed fathers.[20] The "giant step for mankind" that Neil Armstrong took on July 20 sharply contrasted with the failure of the United States to make a bold move to rectify chronic poverty.

Abernathy and Williams were right, of course. Even four or five billion dollars wisely deployed in the war against poverty might have done wonders. But the demonstration at Cape Kennedy lacked the political realism of previous campaigns. In Selma, Sheriff Clark was a *de facto* representative of a system that discriminated against blacks. The space program was not. Indeed, the lunar flight was much more than the fulfillment of Kennedy's dream of beating the Russians to the moon. NASA and the federal government, as well as private businesses, dreamed of tremendous economic profits from space that would help all people regardless of race. And the money already spent had stimulated business since it was used to secure equipment and services for the lunar program.

SCLC leaders knew this. Their purpose was to underscore a need and to challenge national priorities. But success was limited by the fact that there was no tangible relationship between the causes of widespread poverty and the specific activities of the space program. Several of SCLC's leaders, including Williams, were conscious of their dilemma and wrestling with practical options for augmenting the kind of public drama used at Cape Kennedy with concrete steps to alter national spending policies.

If the demonstration seemed to some to be histrionic, it did not lack substance. Budget priorities affected human life, and that was one area where both history and disposition had made SCLC strong in the past. And in that spirit, its leaders pursued strategies for effecting change when the twelfth annual convention met in Charleston three weeks later under the provocative theme: "America's Dilemma: Billions for the Moon, Pennies for the Poor." Attendance was unusually good, as approximately 1,000 delegates assembled in the city where the hospital strike had recently occurred. It was an important conference psychologically, for it demonstrated that SCLC had an organizational life after King. Enthusiasm was high, and speakers were bold in their criticisms of current policies.

Even so, SCLC's national leaders recognized that it would be impossible to engage in the kinds of campaigns that propelled the movement in the previous decade. In a closed session with the board on August 13, executive director Andrew Young outlined a new course he had in mind. A year earlier Abernathy had announced that SCLC would no longer play a major role in maintaining order among demonstrators. Now in 1969, Young said that SCLC would put much less emphasis upon direct-action marches and demonstrations. The primary focus in the future would be three areas: 1) voter registration and education, 2) political activities, and 3) organizing labor coalitions. He did not say that SCLC would no longer organize protest marches, but that they would be largely sustained at local levels. Where necessary and possible, SCLC's national office would provide financial assistance. But its typical role would be to give advice, counsel, and moral support. Each local campaign "must be prepared to depend on its own power, generated in the local situation and capable of achieving specific gains for those people."[21]

Young explained that this modified strategy was necessitated by the realities of the political situation. It could not be otherwise at a time when blacks "have no friends in power" in the present administration and when, furthermore, the nation will not listen. "There can be no general dramatizing of the problem in hopes that the nation will respond. They won't. They may promise, they may play games, but there will be no concessions granted; they will have to be taken." Young hailed the success of the Charleston hospital strike and the electoral results in Greene County, Alabama where blacks had gained political control on July 29. Such specific, local, tangible results would be the new goal.[22]

This sounded very much like nonviolent coercion written in specific language. "There will be no concessions granted; they will have to be taken." Actually, that had always been the case in the sense that the signal accomplishments like the civil rights and voting rights legislation had been the result of effective interaction of nonviolent pressure, public sentiment, and Congressional action, always accompanied by inner tensions and considerable debate. But the difference between those earlier situations and the one faced in 1969 and beyond was that national input, both from the federal government and public opinion, would be much less potent.

Ironically, the Nixon administration was at that moment moving toward a massive enlargement of poverty-relief. On August 8, the President had announced in a national television address that he was seeking sweeping revisions of the welfare system and large increases in aid to the poor, including food stamps. Nixon wanted an initial outlay of $1 billion for such aid, rising to $5 billion within a few years. Surprising many people, he also called for improved welfare procedures, a revenue

266

sharing plan to help meet the costs, a job training and placement program, and a restructuring of the OEO along more innovative lines. In defiance of his image among blacks, Nixon criticized government for doing too little to relieve poverty.[23] His proposals were actually higher in some key areas than the Poor People's Campaign leaders, including Abernathy, had requested.[24]

But it was too soon to tell whether these programs would truly alleviate poverty, or whether they would even be enacted by Congress. For the moment, then, Nixon's announcement did not deter a continuing emphasis in SCLC upon fighting poverty, not just by immediate relief measures, but through comprehensive public programs to remove the underlying causes of chronic poverty. Since that was only a remote possibility, SCLC people were thinking along lines of a large-scale fund-raising effort to help the poor with advice, information, and other forms of support. The keynote speaker at the Charleston convention, SCLC's west coast director Thomas E. Kilgore, made that concept the heart of his address. Widely known as a critic of the Vietnam War, Kilgore linked the issues of peace and anti-poverty measures, calling for a "new peaceful, nonviolent mobilization of students against the war" and a network of offices to aid the poor.[25] He believed that SCLC could initiate a campaign to raise at least 1.2 million from churches to establish centers in twelve cities, including Washington and Baltimore, to help the indigent and victims of discrimination. It was possible, he speculated, that as much as $15 million could be raised this way.[26] Kilgore also wanted SCLC to offer its services to draft-evaders and peace movement organizers.

What makes Kilgore's proposals and SCLC's reaction to them more than interesting is that they came just four months after another black activist, former SNCC chairman James Forman, made a strange appeal that reverberated across the country that year. On May 4, Forman had interrupted the morning worship services at the prestigious Riverside Church in New York to present what was called the Black Manifesto which had been formulated by the National Black Economic Conference in

Detroit in late April. In effect, the Manifesto called for $500 million in reparations from American churches and synagogues to assist blacks economically. To Forman, this was the minimum owed by white Americans for the detrimental effects of slavery and discrimination over the centuries. The money would be used to establish a land bank, publishing houses, various kinds of training centers, and several more devices for improving the job qualifications and economic welfare of blacks.[27]

This was not the kind of thing Kilgore or the Abernathy administration had in mind, but they did agree in principle with Forman. The gist was that it would take large sums of money to make solid improvements, and that churches had moral obligations to help those in need. In an article in the *Christian Century* in August 1969, the SCLC president criticized Forman's technique but supported his message. As a minister, Abernathy could hardly appreciate an interruption of a worship service, but he referred to Forman as a "prophet" and compared his intrusion to the voice of prophets who called ancient Israel to a sense of justice. Too many churches, suggested Abernathy, were resting casually on false assumptions about poverty and racism and neglecting their responsibilities to the poor. "Are we not much like the rich young ruler when we admit to having gathered our stores in huge ecclesiastical barns only to find that this day the soul of our denomination is required of us?" Were American Christians and Jews ready to listen to God as he spoke, as the SCLC president saw it, through this unexpected way?[28]

Abernathy was now frequently referring to "soul power" linked to "labor power," using the Charleston strike as his model. "This is an effective combination that worked in Charleston and will work for us elsewhere in the months ahead." He had been jailed in Charleston and virtually thrown out of his cell when he tried to use his incarceration for leverage, as he and King had done many times earlier. The jailing was a symbol to Abernathy of his commitment to follow King wherever the road led. And the Charleston strike could be duplicated, he believed, in other cities.[29] In fact, the Charleston convention was adjourned and then resumed in Chicago where SCLC joined about sixty other organizations, including Jesse Jackson's Operation Breadbasket, in the Black Coalition. The objective was to get more jobs for blacks in the urban renewal project underway in Chicago.[30]

Meanwhile, Nixon's welfare reform proposals languished. In the Senate they died in the Finance Committee, closing the door to passage in that session of Congress. Preoccupied with the complexities of the Vietnam struggle, the administration said little about anti-poverty measures as 1970 began. And in this setting, Abernathy prepared a six-point program which he described as SCLC's "New Thrust in Politics."

Abernathy outlined his ideas to the Board of Directors in Birmingham in April 1970. The focus was upon six issues with broad implications: 1) land reform, 2) economic development, 3) equal administration of justice, 4) localized control of public schools, 5) citizenship education for all ages, and 6) voter registration. Land reform was a comparatively new emphasis for SCLC but an important one in several parts of the country. The gist of Abernathy's proposal was to make use of thousands of acres currently neglected. What he envisioned for SCLC was a campaign to garner the required capital to secure the land and put people to work on it. SCLC would also, he hoped, assist blacks in acquiring the requisite skills in farming and marketing to make it pay.[31]

Echoing King, Abernathy spoke of other possibilities for cooperative work and ownership, hinting at a structural reordering of the American economy along lines of a mixed private and collective control of capital resources having features of capitalism and socialism, but different from either. "What needs to be established with the available investment capital, however, is not an industry or enterprise that cavorts itself in the usual manner by leeching off the poor for the benefit of the rich, but one that shares all with everyone."[32] This "capitalism with a conscience" approach had not made much headway under King, and despite Abernathy's expectations, there were even more obstacles to it in the early seventies. Disillusionment with the

Great Society had already spread widely, and conservatism was looking in quite a different direction, toward more freedom for economic activity and far fewer social commitments by business and government.

If SCLC's projections seemed far-fetched, they were not out of line with what other black spokesmen were saying as the seventies dawned. Black leaders were universally conscious of a "second stage" of the movement. Millions of blacks had apparently lost confidence or interest, or both, in federal aid in the old sense. It was not welfare, but tangible progress that they wanted. They referred rather frequently to the "post-civil rights era" and spoke of a sophisticated process of black input into the economy and society. "Blacks are not so interested now in marching from Selma to Montgomery," declared Georgia State Senator Julian Bond, "as in doing something in Selma."[33] The movement was not dead, insisted Urban League director Vernon Jordon, it was just changing. Blacks were not concerned anymore about where to sit on the bus. They wanted to drive the bus, or sit on the bus company's board of directors. Blacks, said Jordon, must have more decision-making power. Black power "will remain just a shout and a cry unless it is channeled into constructive efforts to bring about black political power and to influence the established institutions of American society."[34]

The War Against Repression

The political atmosphere was inauspicious for undertakings such as SCLC projected. Anti-poverty and anti-war sentiment were real enough, but they were divisive. In late 1969 and early 1970 Nixon and Henry Kissinger were pursuing a "Vietnamization" policy to extricate the United States from the conflict while preparing the South Vietnamese to carry on the battle. Massive amounts of military aid were channeled to South Vietnam, and Nixon appealed to the "silent majority" to support U.S. initiatives and counter the critics of the war and liberal politicians. There were large-scale anti-war demonstrations in October and November 1969, but Nixon was steadily gaining popular support. Counter-rallies were held to support the Pres-

270

ident's policies. "We've got those liberal bastards on the run now," he proclaimed, "and we're going to keep them on the run."[35]

A disastrous turn of events in the spring of 1970 nearly turned the tables. But again, there was polarization. As the administration gambled on extending the war into Cambodia in an effort to force serious negotiations and weaken the communist position, students protested more vigorously. This led to numerous confrontations between students and authorities, sometimes with tragic results. At Kent State University in early May 1970, four students were killed and ten others wounded as the National Guard opened fire on the war protesters. Ten days later at Jackson State University in Mississippi, police killed two black youths and wounded a dozen more. The nation was stunned, and battle lines were drawn between Washington officials and a growing segment of the country's young people.

The spillover from Kent State and Jackson State affected SCLC directly and deeply. In Augusta, Georgia on May 12, several blacks were killed in rioting. Till then, the march had been largely peaceful, but anti-war sentiment fused with racial tensions to produce an uprising that triggered SCLC's major demonstration of 1970 and the formal beginning of its political campaigns for that year. SCLC's basic plans for "Politics '70" were already in place, and now the Augusta crisis provided the spring board. Like so many other conflagrations of the early seventies, the Augusta upheaval began spontaneously and spread rapidly. After a peaceful march in the downtown area, some black youths burned a Georgia flag they had ripped down from a government building. Tempers flared, and with stunning rapidity, fighting and looting spread across the city. Police killed six young blacks and wounded twenty more. Governor Lester Maddox ordered the National Guard to the beleaguered city.[36] And as the troops moved into Augusta, rioting broke out in Sandersville, Atlanta, and other cities.

Blacks began to organize for defense and protest. Some of the groups were overtly militant, which seemed to strengthen the "law and order" approach proffered by the Nixon administration and now increasingly attractive to what he had called "the silent majority." Abernathy's organization, while rejecting the violent methods, displayed a quite determined opposition to the events in Augusta and to the growing conservative reaction. SCLC's policy was a deliberate rebuttal to Nixon's 1970 Southern Strategy. SCLC announced a March Against Repression to protest the new wave of urban violence and the political indifference that presumably had contributed to it.

Nixon's Southern Strategy was apparently influenced by Kevin Phillips' book, *The Emerging Republican Majority*, which assumed that a majority of Americans were weary of liberalism and were looking for a new conservative consensus resting in the Sunbelt from California to Florida. It would skirt around blacks for the most part, as well as northeastern liberals, and unite the white labor force, moderates, and conservatives in a majority movement. Ben J. Wattenberg's *The Real Majority* also had considerable impact on the strategy of the Nixon camp. Written, interestingly, by a former Johnson and Humphrey speech writer, this work pointed to the common political interests of the "mostly unyoung, unblack, and unpoor" who were disturbed by violence, student disorders, and increasing crime and sexual promiscuity.[37]

It was precisely the young, the black, and the poor, that SCLC's "Politics '70" effort hoped to reach. The administration's strategy thus added to the momentum of the March Against Repression. On May 17, SCLC announced its general plans for a nonviolent counteroffensive and pledged to "speak to the South, to the nation, and to the world with the trampling of thousands of feet and the voices of local, state, and national leaders." Again, the specific precipitating issue was augmented by other concerns, not the least of which was extension of the Voting Rights Act and the granting of the franchise to 18-year-olds as the pending bill provided.* Also, SCLC linked the march

---

* President Nixon opposed this method for establishing the 18-year-old voting age, preferring a constitutional amendment. But he signed into law on June 22, 1970 a five-year extension of the Voting Rights Act, while protesting the rider giving 18-year-old youth the vote. The new form of the Act banned literacy tests till 1975 and added States

to protests against "national climate of fear and repression which had been created by a national administration in pursuit of a racist political 'Southern Strategy' and a militaristic foreign policy." It also decried the "shoot to kill mentality of the Lester Maddoxes of this country."[38]

Abernathy hoped to make the March Against Repression as broadly representative as the Selma to Montgomery March of 1965. That did not happen, but the march did become a significant trek that eventually drew thousands to the final rally. Despite pleas by Governor Maddox to cancel the march, a group of black leaders headed by SCLC's vice president Hosea Williams and Richard Lyles, an assistant regional director of the National Urban League, met to complete their plans. The march would originate in Perry and proceed northward to Atlanta. Representatives from across the state, especially those areas like Perry and Augusta and Sandersville which had recently been rocked by violence, would form a 'Liberty Train' and would culminate in Atlanta with a rally and presentation of grievances to the Governor.

With shouts of "Soul Power" and "I am Somebody," the band of 300 marchers left the small town of Perry, Georgia on May 19. At the head of the march was a mule-drawn coffin symbolizing the recent violence. As they left, Williams told the marchers in a sweltering meeting hall that "Our actions will determine whether America lives as a democracy, or whether H. Rap Brown is right—that you must burn it down and hope to build a new nation."[39]

Other people were intensely concerned about the renewed violence, as was indicated by several supportive gestures across the nation that week. Columbia University cancelled classes on May 19 in memory of the slain youth, and a group of high school students in New York asked for a day of mourning. Nor was the federal government unconcerned about the crisis.[40] Attorney

---

and political subdivisions that had a test or device as of the 1968 Presidential elections. It also relaxed residence requirements of voting in national elections. On July 5, 1971, Amendment XXVI to the United States Constitution confirmed the 18-year voting age minimum.

General John Mitchell asked law enforcement officials to "keep their cool" and named an investigative team to determine whether federal laws had been violated. But this was not enough to satisfy the march leaders.

On Saturday, May 23, the 110-mile March Against Repression ended in Atlanta with a huge rally of 10,000 people. Mrs. King addressed the crowd, criticizing federal policy and public apathy. Abernathy took the occasion to indicate the "ten most unwanted politicians in America" and called upon those with fresh ideas to "turn this country upside down and right side up." He also blasted the Vietnam War and a misguided economy "geared to war instead of building schools and hospitals."[41]

Over the following months Abernathy's language became increasingly critical as he described the "repression in the United States." At the annual convention in Atlanta in August, which stressed the theme of representative government, he announced that SCLC would probably lead a large demonstration in Washington in early 1971.[42] In this frame of mind SCLC carried out its "Politics '70" campaign throughout the summer and fall. Insufficient time and personnel to do the necessary research and campaigning marred the effort from start to finish. The coalition did not develop to the degree hoped for as the various groups tended to favor their own candidates rather than those people who supported specific coalitional goals. Blacks often felt that electing black candidates was essential since the persistence of segregation and discrimination required black leaders to counter it. SCLC gave particular attention to Andrew Young's effort to gain the Fifth District Congressional seat in Atlanta.

Young's campaign proved to be one of the most important aspects of "Politics '70." He was defeated by white Republican Fletcher Thompson, but Young and his aides engineered an exemplary campaign that appealed for a "coalition of good will" that could "prove the existence of a New South, a South that might be willing to elect a black Congressman,"[43] That was a meritorious objective, and although the campaign did not succeed it was highly educational to Young, who would run again in

1972 and become the first black elected to the Congress from the South since Reconstruction.

Blacks did well in the November 1970 elections. Of the 370 candidates who sought public office, 110 were elected. According to SCLC calculations, this brought the total of black elected officials in the South to 665, compared to just over 70 before the 1965 Voting Rights Act. Since thirty-five were incumbents, the net gain was seventy-five.[44] Black sheriffs were elected in three additional Alabama counties, and in Greene County a black was elected probate judge.

In the Congress blacks now held thirteen seats, with Republican Senator Edward Brooke of Massachusetts heading the list in prestige.* The net gain for blacks in Congress was three but much larger gains were made in local governments. The Voting Rights Act was clearly changing the patterns of American politics. In 1971 the thirteen black Congressmen formed the Black Caucus to coordinate their strategies and perhaps increase their impact.[45]

A few weeks later, SCLC was delighted by the nomination of its Washington Bureau director Walter Fauntroy for the renewed congressional seat in Washington. In January 1971 Fauntroy began to seek the post in a complicated race against numerous rival candidates. Fauntroy's candidacy was doubly significant. The District of Columbia had not had a seat in Congress in the twentieth century, so that the re-establishment of Congressional representation marked a step toward 'home rule' for Washington, although it would be a non-voting seat. In the second place, Fauntroy was a seasoned SCLC organizer and would presumably be a valuable asset in Washington.

The 1971 off-year elections and the larger 1972 campaign were

* In addition to Brooke this included Ronald V. Dellums of California; George W. Collins and Ralph H. Metcalfe of Chicago; Parren J. Mitchell of Baltimore; Charles Rangel of New York City; Charles C. Diggs of Detroit; Louis Stokes of Cleveland; Robert N. C. Nix of Philadelphia; John Conyers, Jr. of Detroit; Augustus F. Hawkins of Los Angeles; Shirley Chisholm of Brooklyn; and William L. Clay of St. Louis. For a sketch of each see "Black Lawmakers in Congress," *Ebony*, v. 26, no. 4 (February 1971), pp. 115–22.

already on the minds of SCLC leaders, and "Politics '72" was soon organized. In May 1971 Fauntroy handily defeated his rivals in Washington as he ran on a "black and white together" platform, despite the fact that Washington's population was 70% black.[46] Fauntroy's bi-racial coalitional appeal seemed to confirm the viability of what SCLC had been saying since 1969. In any case SCLC hailed his victory as historic and prepared for an all-out effort to make further gains and to defeat Nixon in 1972.[47]

The importance of SCLC's political campaigning in this period is difficult to exaggerate. Like other black organizations, the leadership conference founded by Martin King was learning the art of politics. SCLC leaders quickly grasped the significance of the huge increase in potential voters (approximately eleven million) with the lowering of the voting age to eighteen years. SCLC calculated that there was a good chance they could be moved to support "advocates of justice" if approached with the right appeals. They began to collect demographic data and to calculate possibilities based on analysis of age, groups, income levels, and percentages of blacks in local areas. In the South alone there were over 160 counties where blacks comprised 35 to 49% of the population, a potentially decisive factor in elections. There was additional strength in northern and western areas where blacks could combine their vote with other minorities and ideological groupings.[48]

So much of this was theoretical, however, that there was little certainty that such a coalition could be effected or that an agenda with broad appeal could be defined. In the words of Bayard Rustin, "A successful liberal political alliance is enormously difficult to build and, once pieced together, even more difficult to maintain, given the inevitable tensions, rivalries, and antagonisms of the various partners."[49] While it is obvious that SCLC, like many black spokesmen of the early seventies, was learning the strategies of political organization, the issues that were central to its stance were centripetal in their effects. Racial tensions were still very strong in 1971, and they were aggravated by the beginnings of an economic slowdown that made social programs more costly. SCLC's war against oppression was derived from concepts deeply embedded in its historical consciousness, but to transpose them into political specifics was divisive. What had given the civil rights campaigns their efficacy was a sense of movement, whereas the essence of coalitional politics was interest-group collaboration.

SCLC and the Radical Left

Abernathy and his aides made an attempt to synthesize the "Politics '72" campaign with the appeal of a vital movement to rid the country of racism, chronic poverty, and militarism. At times, this caused them to support people who were quite controversial, among them Angela Davis. Beginning in February 1971 Abernathy hailed her as a champion of freedom, a young woman who learned early in life the necessity of struggle, "struggle for survival, for her people, for justice."[50] This was only a few months after the FBI had arrested her for possible involvement in a 1970 shootout at Marin County Courthouse in California which left Judge Harold Haley and three others dead. This was not the first time she had been in trouble with authorities. In 1969 Davis was dismissed from her faculty position at UCLA because of her connections with the Communist Party of the United States. Governor Ronald Reagan and the Board of Regents decided not to renew her contract for 1970, although the Department of Philosophy in which she taught was pleased with her work.

In view of her communist philosophy, it seemed strange that SCLC was defending Angela Davis, and certainly Soviet-influenced countries exploited her case. In East Germany, Cuba, the Soviet Union and elsewhere, she was taken as a symbol of martyrdom by a "repressive capitalist system."[51] But she was black, and she was an outspoken supporter of racial liberation. Furthermore, Abernathy was convinced that in the public mind she was already convicted without a trial. He linked his demands for her exoneration to the "liberation of twenty-five million black people and forty million poor people" in the United States.[52] The truth is that the American system of justice worked, and she was eventually acquitted and a federal court ordered her reinstatement at UCLA.

Less troublesome ideologically was SCLC's support of the Wilmington Ten, which included a young black minister Ben Chavis, along with eight black teenagers and a white mother. In January and February 1971 Wilmington, North Carolina was in turmoil. The Gregory Congregational Church under white pastor Gene Templeton opened its doors to rallies, and the Klan responded with a campaign of terrorism. A black youth, 17-year-old Steve Mitchell, was killed by police, though no charges were ever placed. With violence raging, city officials imposed a curfew and the National Guard was called in for assistance. Wilmington was the site of vigilante law and racial tensions for months. Several black activists, including Rev. Chavis, were arrested and charged with various counts of inciting and destroying property. Though some of the charges were dropped, the Wilmington Ten were imprisoned and continued to be an issue for several years. Collectively, they faced a possible 282 years in jail. SCLC came forth overtly in their defense.

In March 1971 SCLC joined with the National Welfare Rights Organization in a welfare campaign in Nevada, where they protested against the termination of welfare recepients and reductions in benefits. In this case, a victory was scored when a federal district court ruled that the Nevada State Welfare Department had violated the families' rights. All over the country, SCLC national officers, state presidents, and hundreds of local leaders engaged in a variety of specific campaigns.

SCLC also carried its "war against repression" theme to Washington and New York to protest the continuing Vietnam conflict. In late April the nation's capital was the scene of the largest anti-war demonstration in American history. Rivaling in scope the 1963 March on Washington, this rally drew 175,000 mostly young people. Sponsored by the National Peace Action Coalition, it was the seventh mass anti-war rally in Washington since 1965 and the best organized. Ten United States Senators and twenty-nine members of the House endorsed the rally, and prominent leaders from around the nation participated. Veterans

Against the War were there, casting away their medals and calling upon the government to end the conflict.

Coretta King, one of the principal speakers, echoed her late husband's criticism of the war as she said somberly, "We gather here today again to raise the question of an inhumane and insane war being waged by the United States Government in Southeast Asia. . . destroying children, women, villages, churches. . . the life and culture of the Vietnamese people. . . . And then we are destroying our own society. . . . This war is clearly an enemy of poor and black people. The war is an enemy of the American people." Mrs. King continued with biting criticism of the domestic impact of the war, especially in distracting from vital human issues and giving the extreme right a rationalization. "The insane character of our government's actions in Southeast Asia is consistent with the repressive domestic policy that we witness here at home."[53]

Some in the crowd were more radical than Coretta King. Here was another case of the confluence of the radical left with peace and social reform advocates in the United States. Signs bearing the names of Leon Trotsky, Mao Tse-tung, and other symbols of communism could be seen.[54] But the basic point of reference was significantly different. Mrs. King appealed to good will and good sense. In his address in Washington on April 24 Abernathy called the war a "racist war" pure and simple. He alluded to the disproportionate level of casualties among blacks and referred to the conflict as a blight against the poor and needy of the nation. After calling upon the government to stop poverty, war, capital punishment, and a host of other "social evils," he urged young people to organize politically. "So get it together. Peace and power to the people."[55]

For months, SCLC continued its value-charged political campaigning, sometimes sounding quite radical, at other times clearly reflecting its roots in nonviolent church-related southern reformism. Essentially, the organization did not depart from its historical role, although its rhetoric was more hostile toward apparent injustices in American society and foreign policy.

SCLC did not become a political organization, but remained an advocacy coalition.

Some journals continued to support the organization, discounting SCLC language in the light of the intensity of feelings engendered by the Vietnam war and racial backlash. In May 1971 *Christian Century* argued that SCLC was "being faithful to its function" in launching its campaign against repression and war. "What is distinctive about SCLC's work," its editors said, "is its singleminded attack on the systems that oppress the poor: war, corporate greed, the uneven administration of justice, and the general lack of understanding of welfare rights."[56] They argued that the emphases of the organization under Abernathy were consistent with what King had pursued, and judged that what SCLC was doing, despite the political character of many of its programs in 1971, was essentially rejecting the purely political approach of a third party. The sit-ins, marches, demonstrations and other overt direct-action techniques were still being used despite the criticisms by many who regarded them as romantic. Perhaps there was a veiled challenge in the final comments of the editorial. "The SCLC directors wisely concluded that if they altered their style too drastically, they would have nothing distinctive to add to the fight for the deliverance of the poor and black. They opted to do what they can do best, leaving it to other groups to take the 'political' route to liberation. In other words, the peculiarly 'Christian' SCLC has decided to continue using peculiarly 'Christian' methods in its courageous advocacy of the 'least of these,' the poor."[57]

Did SCLC alter its style too drastically to retain a distinctive voice in the black movement? Most of the evidence strongly suggests that it did not. Much of what SCLC officers and field workers did in their "war" against oppression was generically similar to what they had done in the past. James Orange, R. B. Cottonreader, Dorothy Cotton and other SCLC workers active in the "Politics '70" and the "Politics '72" campaigns visited college campuses and southern communities to enlist new voters and volunteers. Despite small budgets and limited personnel, they managed to help hundreds of voters register and did so while continuing to teach the importance of nonviolent means to change. In the early seventies, SCLC's literature carried stories of people like Fannie Lou Hamer, a black woman who helped other black candidates and liberal white office-seekers while running her own race for the Mississippi state legislature.[58]

SCLC tried with considerable success to maintain its connections with grassroots support. As one scholar has graphically put it, SNCC workers "scattered like seeds in the wind, after their radicalism could no longer find fertile ground in the southern struggle," while SCLC in a functional sense remained deliberately linked to its ideological roots.[59] Even while he scathed publicly what he saw as a repressive America, Abernathy continued to tell blacks that "if you will organize and fight, if you will use your vote and march on the ballot boxes across the country, then the forces of justice and peace will take over this nation."[60]

"We have a plan now," stated Congressman Fauntroy at the 1971 SCLC convention. "That plan is to master the arithmetic of power politics."[61] Blacks were now in a strategic position to affect the outcome of elections and in that way to achieve their goals nonviolently. Fauntroy at the same time saw the necessity for interracial cooperation. "Now be under no illusion, we cannot do it all by our black selves alone. If we are in fact to reorder the disordered priorities of this nation, we must weld a viable vote—those "forces of good will" that Dr. King talked about—black and white, young and old, affluent and poor." Fauntroy criticized the polarization of blacks and whites and other elements in American society. It was time realistically to face the tasks still unfinished in the movement, without artificial barriers between age groups, races, parties, or "city and suburb."[62]

It is obvious, then, that within the leadership of the Southern Christian Leadership Conference in 1971 there were people fundamentally dedicated to staying on the course defined by the organization's history and King's nonviolent approach. There is no doubt that the organization was changing, as all life does with time. Fauntroy is illustrative of this. As a Congressman he could never again be to the organization what he had been in the past. But this is not to say that he would be less influential upon it or the black movement. Indeed, he was moving into larger areas of service, as soon would Dorothy Cotton, Leon Hall, Andrew Young, Stoney Cooks, and many more who had been drawn to the magnetic attraction of the King movement. SCLC was not so much "coming apart" as it was going out into the new environment it had helped to create. It had never been a tightly-knit organization. King had held it together for thirteen years. In the early seventies its bond was memories of King's life and courage, the challenge of trying to implement the dreams the people who surrounded him inevitably internalized, and perhaps above all, the conviction that somehow blacks were still the "conscience, the troubled soul, of America."

Until America is Redeemed

Any sensible analysis of SCLC, then, reveals that the organization had not been radicalized. It rejected draft-dodging, class struggle, and black separatism. But one must keep in mind the broader impact of the forces impacting upon it in the early seventies. Nonviolence, after all, was a strategy, even if those who were in the King tradition viewed it as a great deal more. It had to work as a strategic device if the larger spiritual implications were to be realized. Abernathy and his organization opted for a pressure approach, in conjunction with labor, welfare organizations, advocacy groups, and the like. Yet, they also kept up the moral imperative emphasis. As the elections approached in 1972, the leadership conference prepared for a "Resurrection City II" to be built in Miami, where the national political conventions were slated to meet. While intended as a successor to its 1968 precedent in Washington, it would be quite different. SCLC's new executive director, Stoney Cooks, would make detailed arrangements with local police for guidelines and security.[63] The major activity would be the distribution of literature promoting the new "Poor People's Platform" prepared by SCLC and other organizations.

"SCLC is still on the case," Abernathy told the board of

directors just a few weeks before the Miami demonstrations. "Our ranks are thinned and our resources low, but we are in a struggle for justice and we are going to continue that struggle until America is redeemed."[64] One can only speculate on how the SCLC directors felt as they heard King's successor react to the many criticisms of SCLC being made by journalists that spring. Roy Reed had written earlier that SCLC was changing its tactics by focusing on a large number of small campaigns and diversified activities. People were saying, Reed noted, "that the organization is coming apart."[65]

Abernathy could not accept that judgment, although he was visibly disturbed by it. He summarized several personal activities and organizational projects, pointing to successes such as the election of the first black councilman in the history of Grenada, Mississippi. SCLC had helped in that campaign. Also he and his wife Juanita had traveled to Scandinavia, eastern Europe, and Ireland in late 1971 and early 1972, bearing "another witness to the oppression and repression of people" as they spoke out against South African apartheid and American discrimination. "Along the highways and byways of the rural South, SCLC had continued its traditional quest for justice, and in the larger world context had kept its faith intact."[66] SCLC now had to do something "to wake up America so that [it] can make the right decisions in November." While millions of blacks and poor whites were better off than before, far too many still remained outside the mainstream benefits of American democracy.[67]

SCLC did demonstrate in Miami in 1972, but with little to show for it. Richard Nixon easily won re-election in November, and as he began his second term he told the Congress that "Only by holding the line on federal spending will we be able to reduce the inflation rate further in 1973."[68] Countering this to some degree was the overall success of black candidates in 1972. Some six hundred new black officials were elected in the South, bringing the total to just over 2,000. Twenty-two additional blacks were added to the 199 already serving in state legislatures prior to 1972.[69] This propelled the movement of black Americans more deeply into the political process.

For SCLC, the most important victory by a black in 1972 was Andrew Young's election to Congress from Atlanta. Young's network supporters put together an impressive election day turn-out, despite heavy rains, and he carried the district with a sizable white vote in his behalf. Abernathy hailed Young's success as an historic breakthrough.[70] It was. Young was the first black Congressman elected in the South since Reconstruction, as well as one of the most experienced and dedicated nonviolent activists ever to sit in Congress. His election, along with that of Texas State Senator Barbara Jordan, added to the variety of black leadership in Congress and brought the number of Afro-Americans in the House to fifteen. Edward Brooke was easily re-elected as well, so that there was still one black Senator. This was still far short of the fifty-five needed to give blacks proportional representation in Congress, but encouraging nonetheless.

The strong reformist coalition SCLC hoped for, however, did not materialize. Youth, workers, and ethnics did not vote as a bloc or follow through with a unified drive for economic reform. Indeed, SCLC continued to lose financial support as the old liberal coalition waned further. The eighteen months that followed the 1972 elections proved to be the most trying period in SCLC's history since King's death. Problems seething beneath the surface began to burst into view, bringing Abernathy to his most painful experience in his sixteen years of affiliation with the nonviolent movement.

Still, hope was alive, qualified by a keener sense of political realities. Dovetailing racial and economic issues had always been problematical, and many in SCLC remembered King's realism on this point. They also recalled that he had concluded late in his life that "A true revolution of values will soon look uneasily on the glaring contrast of poverty and wealth."[71] No doubt, there were many Americans who did feel uncomfortable by that contrast and who could be moved to act on their convictions.

For myself, I continue to look toward a day when we shall have one world and one people, when far will not be far and long will not be long, when we live together, neither black nor white, but one.

Reverend Martin Luther King, Sr.

10

Search for New Directions 1973–1977

Explanations of the crisis that SCLC faced in the middle seventies are varied, ranging from the view that King's successors were unable without him to propel the organization forward, to the more general conclusion that there simply was no movement after King. The scenario of a great historical figure's being followed by lesser lieutenants unable to carry on without him was repeated countless times in the press and most of the scholarly accounts of the problem. Actually, scholars for the most part neglected the post-1968 developments, choosing to focus on King and the high tide of civil rights activism.

But it is essential to recall that King's associates were hardly passive. Many of them had significant responsibilities and injected ideas of their own into the movement. Furthermore, several were strong personalities who disagreed at times on strategy but were held in check by their common devotion to King and the movement. A certain amount of rivalry, even jealousy, was inevitable after King's assassination. Should SCLC remain a direct-action, demonstrating organization as it had been in the old days? Certainly Hosea Williams felt that it should and criticized what he saw as a tendency to rely on government grants, or to cut back on the activist role of the national offices.[1] Or was the proper path for SCLC to become a public educator, providing seminars and workshops on nonviolence such as the organization had done with regard to citizenship education in the sixties? Others, like Ralph Abernathy, were bent on continuing the activism in the form of a broad coalition of interests which could stimulate the conscience of the nation while making tangible progress on a number of economic issues.

Underlying all of its problems was SCLC's difficulty in keeping up with the history it had helped to shape. Journalist and Jesse Jackson biographer Barbara A. Reynolds has concluded that "Abernathy became the prey of progress as the movement forked. One branch moved forward building political and economic beachheads on the inroads established in the sixties. The other lumbered in place. . . SCLC arrived at this juncture by not arriving. As history zigzagged tumultuously forward, SCLC stood still, dazzled by its string of victories, all belonging to the past."[2]

This hints at the peculiar dilemma of SCLC. As an organization it was an extension of the King movement and naturally gloried in that. It was difficult for Abernathy, as it would have been for anyone, to exploit that legacy in changed circumstances. That is, the King legacy tended to be elevated to the point that it completely overshadowed anything SCLC attempted to do after 1968. However, SCLC did not simply stand still under the aura of its past successes. The Poor People's Campaign and its later derivatives had substance in publicizing some of the major problems of the poor and prodding the nation to tackle them. Abernathy was far from just drifting in confusion after 1968. Nor could people like Stoney Cooks, James Orange, board chairman Joseph Lowery, or R. B. Cottonreader and others be accurately described as being so past-oriented that they had no sense of historical process. Such an oversimplication completely misses both the reality of SCLC in the seventies and the nature of its problems.

What was happening can best be described as fragmentation. This did not always—or even usually—mean internal quarreling or power struggles, although there was a considerable amount of

286

that kind of tension. Dissatisfied with certain internal policies and some specific actions, Hosea Williams departed, for all practical purposes, in 1971 to head his own SCLC in the Atlanta-DeKalb area. To the chagrin of Mrs. King, other board members, and several active staff members, Williams set up the Atlanta chapter and began to publish "The People's Crusader" and to hold regular rallies and demonstrations.[3] Williams was, and is, a strong personality with candid features. He had been a pivotal front-line fighter in many campaigns and wanted to continue that approach. Abernathy eventually recognized the Atlanta chapter, but one can readily see his concern with the dangers of too much diffusion of the organization as he told a crowd of Williams' followers "I am granting this charter to the people, not to Hosea Williams. This must be a people's organization and not one individual's. I know your great abilities; I know your great works. You have earned the charter; you deserve it."[4] Williams never truly left SCLC in this period, but he was an essentially independent entity.

About the same time a more decisive break came between SCLC national leaders and the Reverend Jesse Jackson. Jackson's effort to assume a major leadership role in SCLC had marked the entire period since King's death but had been dormant for some time when it erupted again in late 1971. The occasion was some alleged mishandling of funds in the Black Expo in Chicago. This Black and Minorities Business and Cultural Exposition, as it is officially known, began in 1969 and grew by 1971 to a huge, complicated affair that drew over half a million people. These crowds milled through the massive Chicago International Amphitheater to admire black art, crafts, talent, and business output. The Expo was sponsored by Operation Breadbasket, the economic arm of SCLC, and proceeds went to further the work of Breadbasket and the parent organization.[5] In 1971 there was a potential income of over $500,000 from gate receipts based on an estimated attendance of 700,000 including children. But there were some discrepancies between income figures given by Jackson's people in Chicago and SCLC's in Atlanta. One fourth of the proceeds were to be channeled to the national leadership in Atlanta, where there was the belief that far more than $500,000 must have been collected from tickets and paid entertainment.

But the problem ran deeper. SCLC officials did not charge Jackson with taking any money; it was more a matter of not keeping up with attendance figures and receipts accurately and the fact that thousands were apparently admitted free.[6] Even more significant was the fact that Jackson, on his own, had organized the Expo as a non-profit corporation separate from Breadbasket and thus also from SCLC. This occurred on September 14, 1971 in secret legal moves in Chicago just a few months after Abernathy in April had ordered Jackson to move the Breadbasket offices to Atlanta. In essence, it was a break with the SCLC national leadership at a point when Jackson apparently had concluded that he needed a separate base of power. Jackson began to assert himself more vigorously in Chicago politics and economic direct-action within the context of his own growing personal following.[7]

By December the rift was open. Abernathy and an eleven-member executive committee met on December 3 and suspended Jackson with pay for sixty days from his post as head of Operation Breadbasket. In explaining the move to the press, Joseph Lowery stated publicly that it was due to Jackson's "repeated violations of organizational discipline as an employed staff member of SCLC."[8] Jackson, of course, defended himself and pledged that although his title was gone, he would continue meeting his responsibilities in helping the poor. In his comments on the dismissal, Abernathy was quick to point out that the SCLC leadership was not charging Jackson with "fiscal dishonesty" but rather was dissatisfied with certain of his actions connected with Black Expo '71.

Had Jesse Jackson been so inclined, he might have made this the kind of rift the press played it for, but he took another route. Within a few days, he formally created his own organization known as People United to Save Humanity (PUSH). PUSH was opened on December 18, 1971 in South Chicago in the Metropolitan Theater, a cold, drafty building symbolizing the fact that "there was no room in the inn" for the infant organization.[9] Jackson had resigned from his national directorship of Operation Breadbasket on December 11 and turned over all of its assets, including the profits from Black Expo. "We ain't taking no money," he declared. "We don't own nothing. . . . I love the organization I grew up with, but I need air. I got to grow." The SCLC board rejected his resignation, but with growing support in Chicago, Jackson moved ahead with the implementation of his PUSH operation.[10] In many respects, the fifteen-point program of PUSH was similar to SCLC's, but with more emphasis upon attacking the inequities of corporate America. Its fifteenth point epitomized the whole spirit of the Jackson organization: Push for black excellence.

Jackson's departure was not in itself the major cause of SCLC's increasing difficulties, and in fact it may have simplified some of the problems since Jackson's absence reduced an immediate challenge to Abernathy's leadership. More influential was the fact that many capable young men and women who had worked with SCLC in the sixties were now moving into other areas of service. Like Jackson, they too wanted room to develop. More than the public knows, young SCLC workers assumed leadership positions in government, business, and human rights service by 1972. A number of them were ambitious and anxious to use their experience and legal rights, but SCLC offered to them only horizontal growth. At that juncture there was more challenge in an elective office or a business or profession. This is not to say that they were disillusioned with SCLC. Apparently, most retained a sense of being in the "SCLC family," but their specific efforts would now be channeled in other directions. Many would continue to associate with the organization, deliver speeches at rallies and conventions and otherwise maintain contact for years after their departure, but history was moving them away from activities in SCLC.

Their exodus had more than minimal impact on SCLC, although this was offset to some degree by the continuance for a while of experienced people like Stoney Cooks and white public relations expert Thomas Offenburger. But Cooks and Offenburger also left SCLC to work with Andrew Young's campaign and then his organizations after 1972. As financial problems increased, the SCLC board cut back the operation to essentially the Atlanta national office and affiliates with less extensive operations in formerly pivital regional centers. The Washington chapter was greatly reduced, whereas it had once been the nerve center of the East Coast operations. Other offices were also reduced, and some SCLC staff resigned in opposition to the reduction of scope.[11]

On top of all this, finances were now running at a deficit. The general atmosphere of the economy and society was a contributing factor. Another cause of the malaise was a five-year Internal Revenue Service probe of SCLC growing out of the Poor People's Campaign of 1968. The IRS learned of SCLC's using some money which had been placed by SCLC attorney Chauncey Eskridge in a Washington bank for the Poor People's Campaign, to meet needs in the general budget. This apparently hurt SCLC's ability to raise funds, at a time when confusion over the relationship between the King Center and SCLC was already weakening the fund-raising effort.[12] Finally, in 1973, the courts found no deliberate misuse of funds by SCLC, but the effects were already felt in the critical period of 1972–1973.

Whether this was a deliberate government effort to weaken SCLC is debatable, but it is clear that SCLC had been the target of federal attacks before. Also, as the Watergate break in of June 17, 1972 led to a national scandal in 1973, it became apparent that the IRS had been used on numerous occasions to gain information on, and to undermine several organizations viewed as leftist. This included some of SCLC's operations and former associate organizations like SNCC.[13] Scholars are pursuing these questions currently, and a more complete picture will eventually emerge. At present, it is clear that SCLC's fund-raising capability was lessened by the IRS probe.

Nor was the SCLC leadership question fully resolved after Jackson's departure. Abernathy still had to contend with criticisms that hurt him and moved him to test the depth of his support. From the streets came rumors that he was not viewed as being closely attached to the poor, despite his emphasis upon fighting poverty. King had come off better in that regard, and his financial sacrifices were often contrasted with Abernathy's comfortable life style. The truth is that neither was poor, and Abernathy had given of his means over the years just as King had. Yet Abernathy never quite acquired the same public image as a friend of the poor that King had enjoyed.

Furthermore, Abernathy had never entirely freed himself to be his own man, despite his disclaimers of any intention simply to be another King. At the same time, he repeatedly underscored his own leadership position, to the degree that some analysts have taken this as a sign of insecurity.[14] Actually, Abernathy was widely respected, even loved, by friends and associates. He was viewed as a man of compassion who cared about his parishioners and about the sufferings of others.[15] His work in the movement was respected. As King's closest friend and most constant companion in the campaigns of the fifties and sixties, Abernathy had earned an important place in the history of black liberation. But somehow the qualities that made him ideal for that kind of role, were not viewed by everyone as the ones needed by the chief executive of SCLC.[16]

Particularly discouraging to Abernathy was the middle class blacks' apparent indifference to the ongoing operations of SCLC. As a minister he naturally saw parallels between them and figures in the Bible who were helped by God and then did not use that help as a springboard for service to others. In the final analysis, it was probably this feeling more than press criticisms or backlash from white people that prompted him to resign. Consciously or not, his decision was a test of his support. After weighing his options, as well as "much prayer and countless hours of thought and meditation," Abernathy tendered his resignation to board chairman Lowery on July 6, 1973. In a carefully prepared letter, Abernathy explained to the board why he was taking this step. Those who have argued that Abernathy was simply grand-standing to elicit a display of support are underestimating the depths of Abernathy's concerns at that juncture.

As he resigned from the presidency, Abernathy made it clear that he was not quitting SCLC. In the future, he pointed out, he would continue his efforts at reform, but would also give more time to his pastorate at West Hunter Street Baptist Church. He reaffirmed his faith in massive nonviolence as "the only effective weapon poor people have in our struggle during these critical days." Then he singled out three principal reasons for his resignation: 1) the failure of black people who then "occupied improved positions because of our struggle" to support SCLC financially; 2) SCLC's inability to employ the necessary staff to carry on "a live and vibrant program;" and 3) his own increased responsibilities at West Hunter Street Baptist Church where an "expansion and rebuilding program was in progress."[17]

A few days later, Abernathy explained his resignation to a rather stunned press corps. Basically in terms of the letter sent to Lowery, the SCLC president commented on his decision. Recalling the "seventeen long and difficult years" he had spent with the organization, he reviewed a few highlights of the movement since Montgomery. Mostly he cited victories, but he also alluded to some of the difficult times, including thirty-six arrests, attacks on his home and person, and other obstacles. Then he called upon the nation to help the struggling SCLC organization:

> I feel very strongly that if the people of this nation want the non-partisan, prophetic, free voice of SCLC to cry out in this wilderness, then the people themselves must make it possible so that the hands of the organization and its leaders will not be tied and controlled by the power structure.[18]

A little later as he stood near the tomb of the slain SCLC leader, Abernathy also had some words for Martin King, his late friend and mentor. "I did what you asked. I tried to keep the team together. I hope you can find it in your heart to forgive me for resigning this day. I'll see you in the morning."[19]

Abernathy was quite correct about the need for a genuine display of support by a broader range of people. SCLC still had potential as a critical non-partisan voice in the United States.

292

But for this to materialize SCLC had to live with its viable options and bridge some of those partisan barriers that he drew into the discussion. For the dream to be vital it had to recover its essential community-building thrust despite the barriers of resurgent racism and social conservatism. At that moment at least, SCLC had not found a way to accomplish that. There were more people willing and able to raise funds and supply leadership than was realized, but they had to be drawn more fully into the movement. Partisan, separatist and nationalist attitudes would only aggravate SCLC's problems and defer the realization of that kind of cooperation. Middle class blacks as a whole were not indifferent to the problems of their racial brothers who had not fared as well. Nor were whites totally turned off to further progress in areas of race relations and poverty. Far more than the nation as a whole realized, the black movement at that juncture was in trouble, and basically because the bases of linkage among people of all races were so inadequately articulated. If what SCLC had stood for for seventeen years had moral validity and political viability, there were reasons enough to pursue its continuance. In a peculiar way, that issue lay upon SCLC, its black supporters, and the general population of the United States.

For about a month Abernathy's resignation was publicized in the press and debated by black leaders. There were several who either wanted to succeed to the SCLC presidency or who were suggested as possibilities. Mrs. King, not surprisingly, was named, but her deepening involvement with the King Center and her disinclination to get into racial leadership politics ruled her out. Nor was Walter Fauntroy desirous of moving back from his Congressional role. There was also Wyatt Tee Walker to consider, as well as Jesse Jackson, who had considerable support among board members and a substantial popular following.[20] But Jackson also had opponents, and he already had a growing organization to lead.

Abernathy's resignation was to go into effect after the Sixteenth Annual Convention scheduled in mid-August in Indianapolis. The board of directors and Joseph Lowery, in the mean-

293

time, began to look for a successor. A national committee was formed to spearhead the search, although discussions of various prospects were already underway.[21] There was some problem with each of the possible successors, and considerable disagreement on what to do. For his part, Abernathy had begun to sound like a candidate himself. During a rally in his honor in Chicago on July 21 he again criticized the black middle class for its failure to support SCLC, eliciting the ire of some present, including former SCLC fund-raiser Edwin Berry of the Chicago Urban League who believed that Abernathy had failed to carry out a truly professional fund-raising program.[22]

Abernathy would not endorse any individual for his post, and the board was split on a replacement. Thus, there developed a plan to retain Abernathy—a prospect he was open to—while attempting a reorganization of SCLC to relieve him of some of his work load and to rejuvenate various programs. To that end a committee prepared a blueprint for the establishment of five regional offices covering all areas of the country, and each headed by a vice-president and a director, in order to redistribute the work. Additionally, a fund-raising drive utilizing professional advice and local leadership would be implemented to meet immediate deficits and to augment certain outreach programs.[23] As Lowery told the press during the Indianapolis convention, the board's approach was to try to solve the problems Abernathy cited in his letter rather than accept his resignation.[24]

No doubt, there were some who felt that the board should have accepted Abernathy's proffered resignation and gone on with new leadership. The general uncertainty, however, that anyone else could have succeeded without further internecine struggles at a time when SCLC could ill afford them became the driving force behind Abernathy's retention as president. This was strongly felt by staff members and some board members who opposed the other candidates. During the Indianapolis convention, Abernathy's supporters continued their pressure in his behalf as they had done since July. They won over Abernathy's critics, and he was clearly ready to accept a draft.[25]

When news came that the board had rejected the resignation

and Abernathy had agreed to stay if the convention wanted him, a long, exhuberant demonstration broke out, rivaling the most energetic floor demonstrations at the national political conventions. As one writer put it, events in Indianapolis "ran close to script." This interpretation continues: Abernathy had resigned—though not sincerely—and he had gotten the display of support he so direly needed.[26] The statement made by Lowery that although there were other capable people who could lead SCLC, Abernathy "at this moment in history is the man for the job" dispelled any expectations of a change in command.[27] Now Abernathy could say that he had a mandate not only "from Martin and God, but also from black America."[28]

In all likelihood Abernathy would have quit if the board had been more unified on his resignation or if a candidate with broader appeal had come forth. If Abernathy was seeking reassurance personally, there was more involved in his resignation. He was troubled about the condition of SCLC and the black movement in general. In a real sense, his move ended the SCLC-Jesse Jackson controversy as far as the presidency was concerned, and paved the way for gradual reconciliation between the parent organization and PUSH.

Interestingly, Abernathy's near resignation coincided with the worsening of the Watergate scandal which by the summer of 1973 had implicated President Nixon in a coverup of the breakin at the Democratic National Headquarters, and much more. As Nixon aides revealed the intricate details to the special investigative committee, an iceberg of political corruption was displayed to the nation. Nixon continued to maintain his innocence in the face of overwhelming evidence to the contrary and would not resign until the summer of 1974 when impeachment appeared likely. In September 1973, *Christian Century* contrasted Abernathy's offer to resign with Nixon's insistence on staying in office. "Abernathy agreed to step down if the people did not want him; Nixon not only insisted on staying in office, but also accused his enemies of keeping the 'relatively unimportant' issue of Watergate before the country to sabotage his noble plans for world peace and domestic tranquility."[29]

One might expect that from a journal which had always supported SCLC's position and often criticized Nixon's policies, but the comparison was not meaningless. What bothered some Abernathy critics, and friends who liked and respected him personally but questioned his leadership, was that he did not carry through and actually step aside for someone else. He had always been extremely effective as a support person and could likely continue for years in such a role. This was impractical at the moment since the alternatives to Abernathy were problematical and, furthermore, Joseph Lowery and the board were enlarging their role. From a political point of view Abernathy would be a better man to work with than any available successor.

Abernathy, no doubt, was easier for the public and the media to stereotype than Vivian, Young, or Walker. His continuance as president would perpetuate many of the criticisms levelled at him since 1973. Yet he was encouraged by the display of support and was apparently uplifted somewhat in his determination to carry on King's work. And that is precisely the way he viewed his position. With all the complexities of the situation, many of which he would never resolve, Abernathy was as sincere as anyone in SCLC in pursuing his understanding of justice. His position was derivative rather than generic, as King's had been. But whatever his problems, or SCLC's, he would preside over the organization at the time of the United States Bicentennial celebrations during the Ford administration and to the eve of Jimmy Carter's presidency in early 1977.

Abernathy's resignation and other evidence of disarray in black leadership organizations prompted more commentaries in the press about the slackening movement. The New York Times, for example, ran a lengthy five part series on black Americans since 1963, focusing primarily on progress and shortcomings. The fourth article in the series examined the status of the leading civil rights organizations in the seventies. While crediting the activist organizations with some gains over the previous decade, the article argued that only the NAACP had retained its identity. The others, including SCLC, had suffered decline as blacks shifted their interests to smaller, more specific groups like the National Welfare Rights Organization, PUSH, and the Movement for Economic Justice. The article also noted that there was less black-white cooperation or sense of movement. SCLC was described as broken and disorganized.[30]

SCLC at The Bicentennial: The Struggle for Revival

True, SCLC was not as well organized as it had been in its heyday, but was hardly broken. To its board of directors and officers it was clear, however, that the organization could not stand still long. It had to exploit its remaining support and somehow learn from its adversities. More than a few times in the past SCLC had turned difficulties into opportunities. Albany had led to Birmingham, the tragedy in Memphis to the Poor People's Campaign. In late 1973 it was essential for SCLC to try to turn leadership disputes, financial troubles, and haziness of focus into a confident but measured effort in the areas of its expertise. There was no point in SCLC's competing with PUSH, or Abernathy's feeling compelled to be an extension of Martin Luther King. Above all, SCLC's leaders needed to avoid a scatter gun strategy with little potential for tangible progress.

The starting point would have to be a revitalization of the loose network of affiliates. When the Reverend Fred D. Taylor became SCLC's national director of chapters and affiliates in 1973, he knew that the odds were against an immediate revival of the affiliate structure. Although SCLC could claim approximately 200 affiliated groups, a realistic appraisal would indicate that less than half that number were active. The Washington Bureau no longer functioned, and the District of Columbia chapter had a very low profile despite commendable efforts by Henry Silva and others.[31] The Chicago chapter ran into problems trying to compete with PUSH, and for all practical purposes was in decline. Furthermore, without the impetus of coordinated major campaigns, many local chapters and affiliates had fallen into desuetude since 1968, some even earlier.

But Taylor was not particularly impressed by mere numbers. In his view, the issues that SCLC had tried to resolve were still not settled, and thus the organization had a mandate from its history to try to revitalize its operations.[32] Well-liked and respected in SCLC circles and beyond, Taylor related well to his fellow ministers. Able to articulate social issues intelligently, Taylor also appealed to deep thinkers and his easy-going personality made people of various levels of education comfortable in his presence. By 1973 he had four years experience with SCLC, having joined the staff as research assistant on chapters and affiliates in 1969. He then worked as office manager and consultant on a number of projects during the period when T. Y. Rogers and Calvin Morris directed affiliate operations.[33] Taylor knew what he wanted to accomplish, and during the critical period of 1973 and 1974, began to see some signs of improvement.

It is interesting to see the kinds of things SCLC chapters were doing at this time. Because of their geographical locations, some of them had never been in the center of the dramatic civil rights campaigns and consequently their leaders had always had an uphill struggle to elicit enthusiastic involvement. But as the middle seventies brought about changes in the nature of the black movement, some affiliates which had previously been less visible now excelled in innovative efforts. In Louisville, Kentucky, Reverend Charles Kirby led his chapter in the direction of providing free food to needy families and individuals and thereby won recognition.[34] Other chapters as far away as California engaged in similar community projects, helping to alleviate the suffering of the indigent, the elderly, and shut-in.[35] This was hardly noticed by the media, but it did indicate that SCLC was continuing to provide services in local communities. Other involvements by local chapters included legal aid, counseling on welfare problems, assistance in voter registration, and support in cases of racial discrimination in jobs. Several chapters also participated in community programs for youth, including summer recreation, child-care for working mothers, and intern programs that gave young people productive work.[36]

Still, it took several years for the affiliate network to return to a sustained level of growth. There was less money for assistance from the national headquarters, so that many of these undertakings were financed by local giving and fund-raising projects. Area churches underwrote various projects, and community leaders appealed for donations. The fact that SCLC was still committed to voter registration and political gains by blacks and progressive candidates caused political frictions that at times militated against fund-raising. The Southern Christian Leadership Conference was not included in United Way or other cooperative community giving programs, and thus its finances were strictly voluntary.[37]

"Looseness still haunted us," Taylor said. For years, SCLC did not have a formal membership because of King's determination not to rival the NAACP and other organizations. It had always operated without a high degree of centralization. But the new circumstances of the seventies necessitated organizational tightening if SCLC were to focus its energies effectively. This could not be accomplished immediately or simply by a decision of the leaders in Atlanta. It would take cooperation with the leaders of the strongest state organizations, Alabama, Florida, and Virginia, as well as with pivotal local chapters like Los Angeles, Philadelphia, Louisville, Cleveland, Detroit, and Indianapolis. Key individuals remained fundamentally important, among them John Nettles of Alabama, Curtis Harris, Henry Silva, and Terry Wingate in the Virginia and District of Columbia regions, and R. N. Goodin in Florida. C. K. Steele's work in Tallahassee had been seminal and the Florida program was carried on by him in his later years and by younger leaders who had been inspired by him.

As SCLC reflected on its history in the middle seventies, it tended to underscore three major accomplishments and a fourth area of concern that bridged the past and the present. It had 1) led in the dismantling of the segregationist system in the South; 2) spearheaded the mass movement to win the right to vote for blacks in 1965; and 3) put poverty on the national agenda by the Poor People's Campaign of 1968 and derivative activities of 1969 and beyond.[38] The fourth SCLC contribution was, as the conference's literature emphasized, providing a "voice of conscience" in behalf of world peace and justice. Repeatedly, the SCLC nonviolent ethos was linked to the common people, especially the poor. Among the various black organizations, SCLC viewed itself as still poised at the forefront of reform for those who otherwise had little voice in politics or economics.[39]

There were both strengths and weaknesses in this approach. The truth is that all of the major civil rights organizations had shifted their primary focus to economic and social problems. This was central to PUSH and the National Urban League, as well as the NAACP. But SCLC saw itself as the organization most dedicated to helping the poor and unorganized masses, the "voice of the voiceless," the advocate of all those who had no power to confront the biases of American society. Thus virtually anything with a hint of injustice was of concern to SCLC: barriers to voting, police brutality, educational segregation, discrimination in the military, misguided foreign policy, and more. For draft evaders, SCLC sponsored a National Amnesty Program in cooperation with the Congressional Black Caucus.[40] These countless concerns, as important as they were, were not in themselves a program.

The Bicentennial celebrations of 1974 to 1976 seemed to offer an opportunity to at least talk of renewal. The Bicentennial Administration, in fact, announced that the goal of the countless observances across the country was "To forge a new national commitment, a new spirit of '76, a spirit which revitalizes the ideals for which the Revolution was fought; a spirit which will unite the nation in purpose and dedication to the advancement of human welfare as it moves into its third century."[41]

Actually, the Bicentennial celebrations were played out against a background of political scandal at home and stunning reversal in Vietnam. In August 1974 Nixon lost the opportunity to preside over the nation at its 200th anniversary, when he resigned to ward off impeachment. Vice President Gerald Ford assumed the Presidency, promising to end the "long nightmare" of Watergate and to set the country on a course of "binding up the wounds" and dealing with pressing economic problems.[42] Within months, however, the Vietnamization policy failed, and the United States began its last phase of withdrawal from the war that had preoccupied the country since 1964. The long ordeal was over, but it was hardly a happy ending. South Vietnamese forces would eventually crumble before the advancing communist armies as many desperate South Vietnamese tried to escape with the Americans.[43] President Ford did not find it easy to dispel the notion that the United States had suffered a serious setback that would diminish its role in the world.

If the country as a whole was experiencing a mixture of pride and embarrassment in the middle seventies, the same could be said for virtually all advocacy groups. SCLC was hoping to see some solid evidence of renewal in 1974, only to find that the organization had not yet reached the bottom of its decline. In line with the Bicentennial commemorations, Philadelphia was chosen as the site of the seventeenth annual convention. In the city where the Declaration of Independence had been signed two centuries before, SCLC met under the theme of "Moving Forward. . .New Directions to Redeem the Soul of America."[44] Two thousand people were expected to attend, twice the number of recent conferences, but only a few hundred showed up. A planned march to Independence Hall where Abernathy was to present a "Black Declaration of Independence" had to be cancelled.

Press accounts dwelt on the failure of SCLC to stimulate interest, contrasting Abernathy's pre-convention evaluations with the disappointing turn out. The SCLC president had described his organization as "the largest and most vibrant organization working at the grassroots level to bring about justice for all."[45] But the attendance was so small that the awards dinner planned for the main ballroom at the Sheraton was moved to a small black church where only about 300 appeared to see Frank Wills, the security guard who discovered the Watergate breakin, honored. The workshops and speaking sessions were also poorly attended, and the mood of discouragement was heavy.

Abernathy told the press that the basic cause of the small showing was the same one that plagued all civil rights efforts at

301

the time, namely complacency. Blacks had slackened their efforts, and whites were not supportive of further progress. Some blacks had become discouraged about lack of gains and in some cases were fearful of losing what they had attained. "But they ought not to forget the bridge Martin crossed. . . . Black America owes it to Martin to keep his dream alive."[46]

Abernathy was not the only one bothered by the poor attendance at the convention and the apathy of blacks toward the movement. Comedian Dick Gregory blasted the apparent despair of the delegates. "Look at you, SCLC, tired and broke after Dick Nixon, and with few friends in the White House. . . . But there are still some concerned people left. It means we've got to tighten up and move ahead."[47] Discouragement was deep, but a number of SCLC leaders resisted the temptation to quit, and in fact were talking of revival. At that point SCLC's decline levelled off. No one was quite certain, however, just how to "tighten up and move ahead," as Gregory had challenged them to do.

It is essential to see that SCLC's remaining optimism was grounded in a particular perception of what King had done and what he had left undone. Although by then several searching biographies of King had exposed the complete man, flaws and all, virtually all of them had failed to underscore the aspect of King's career that was most important to his followers during his life and to those who continued to promote his movement after his death. In the final analysis, it was not King's successes in desegregation or voting rights that accounts for his impact, but rather his faith. To put it another way, it was the strength of an idea that demarcated King from other leaders and which was the main impetus for the continuance of SCLC. Among recent writers, Elizabeth Hardwick has probably grasped this as well as anyone. King, she notes, had developed a very basic belief in the interconnectedness of religion, politics, and justice and had voiced more than simply a clever, homiletic appeal for brotherhood. He had said, in effect, that without the mandate of a higher morality, that is, without God, "all our efforts turn to ashes and our sunrises to darkest nights."[48]

In that light, King's death had not only ended a dramatic public career, but it had threatened perhaps the best hope for black liberation and the creation of a matrix within which it could work on a permanent basis. Hardwick was not sure whether King's assassination meant an end or a new beginning. "Perhaps what was celebrated in Atlanta," she wrote in reference to the eulogies to King, "was an end, not a beginning—the waning of the slow, sweet dream of Salvation, through Christ, for the Negro masses."[49]

Certainly there is a thin line the scholar must tread between a virtual deification of the King legacy and a critical understanding of it in relation to SCLC. But to avoid it because of the risks is to do an injustice to the historical record. Much has been made of the radicalization of King's later thought and his growing discouragement with the prospects for realization of his dream. Not enough has been said about the fact that he remained a hero to many who continued in the black movement, or about the almost mystical way King transcended his own disillusionment as he spoke in April 1968 of having made it "to the mountain top" but not into the "promised land." His friends remembered and took it seriously. In his last public words, King had tried to reinvigorate hopes that the process would be completed because it was God's will. To discount this as emotionalism from a man who sensed his death was near, is unconvincing as a serious effort to understand the movement.[50]

The meaning of this for SCLC's history in the 1970s was that some of its leaders believed that without merely looking to the past it was still possible to exploit what King had accomplished. Understandably, Abernathy had personal reasons to be preoccupied with the past, but he evinced an awareness that the most important issue was what would be done in the future.[51] Board chairman Lowery, among others, was convinced that this demanded a new approach to leadership. There was no point in looking for another extraordinary individual comparable to King, Lowery argued. He or she simply did not exist. The movement had to have more collective and cooperative leadership.[52]

In two important respects SCLC was showing signs of institutional life that defied the judgment of outside observers, and some within its own company, that it had died. First SCLC leaders were seeing more clearly that past accomplishments could not sustain the organization, for the very nature of the changes it had helped bring about militated against continuance of a concerted movement-organizational front based on charismatic leadership and driven by the fervor of evangelical social reformism. Black leadership by the middle seventies was too complex and specialized, as well as too deeply rooted in local power structures, to be brought together again in the style of the great nonviolent campaigns of the past. The effort to "keep the team together" had occupied Abernathy from 1968 to 1973. From 1974 onward that was clearly impossible. The nucleus of the team was scattered, and the concept of an inner circle of charismatic ministerial leadership had less relevance to the *de facto* experience of black Americans. Yet, the largely unchallenged conclusion that SCLC had attempted from 1966 onward to take on too much in its efforts to become a national organization and "become swallowed up among other national movements" ignores the qualifying fact that some SCLC leaders were looking anew at that southern base and wrestling with the challenge of revitalizing it.[53]

Another sign of continuing vitality was SCLC's reevaluation of standards by which to measure success. This was one thing SNCC, in contrast, was unable to do. That SCLC did revise its criteria for success enabled it to continue to operate. Previously, quantitative measures were the yardstick of progress: numbers of people in a demonstration, specific concessions by a local government, or tangible guarantees established by law. Not only were such standards applied by outside observers, but they conditioned black leaders as well. When measureable gains appeared to reach their limits, some blacks despaired of any future relevance for the movement. James Bevel, for example, stated after the 1965 Voting Rights Act that there was no more civil rights movement because "President Johnson signed it out of existence.''[54] By this logic all subsequent efforts would be rather anti-climactical and predictably weak.

The image of a faltering SCLC organization, unable to survive without King, yet trying belatedly to become an effective structure after a decade of charismatic leadership, is intricately tied to this line of reasoning. No doubt, this view is partially correct. A sense of failure dogged several SCLC leaders, especially as they confronted problems that could not be rectified primarily by laws. They were often frustrated by minimal results from their efforts and further strained by serious differences of view. Judged by the same standards used to evaluate the earlier campaigns, the best of the post-1968 SCLC undertakings appeared empty.

Recent studies have rarely departed from this increasingly orthodox approach. ''The Poor People's Campaign was a failure,'' wrote Nick and Mary Kotz in their work on George Wiley and the National Welfare Rights Organization. ''The mass of poor people mired down in the mud of 'Resurrection City' on the Mall in Washington inspired only negative feelings.''[55] Other writers include virtually all of SCLC's post-King efforts in the losing category. The departure of Jesse Jackson, insisted Adam Fairclough, ''rendered SCLC's attempts to mount ambitious national projects increasingly futile, and critics complained that the conference engaged in an endless round of rallies and marches that produced little more than angry rhetoric.'' Blacks were disillusioned with the American political system, continues Fairclough, and ''faith in the ability of nonviolent direct action to bring about change had all but evaporated.''[56]

While it is true that disillusionment was widespread in the 1970s, it is not accurate to conclude that confidence in nonviolence had almost totally disappeared or that blacks turned away *en masse* from the political process. A more accurate picture is one of adjustment and revision. Far more blacks were registered voters by 1974 than at any point in the past. In Alabama, for example, registered blacks comprised only 13.7% of those eligible in 1960, whereas a decade later this had climbed to 64%. In 1960 Mississippi had a scant 5.2% registration rate among blacks, but by 1970 some 68%. Other states in the South showed a similar trend.[57] The increase in numbers of black elected officials was even more impressive, as VEP reports indicate:

Black Elected Officials in the South, 1966 and 1974

State	1966[58]	1974[59]
Alabama	7	149
Arkansas	—	150
Florida	3	73
Georgia	6	137
Louisiana	7	149
Mississippi	1	191
North Carolina	6	159
South Carolina	7	116
Tennessee	16	87
Texas	7	124
Virginia	6	63

Several SCLC leaders and former officials joined the ranks of black public officials. In addition to Fauntroy and Young in the Congress, Hosea Williams, Septima Clark, John Lewis of SNCC and SCLC, and others gained offices in local and state government. As a whole, the organization continued to put much into political campaigning and voter registration. In 1974, Hosea Williams' Atlanta chapter actively campaigned against George Wallace in his bid for re-election as Alabama's governor. Wallace had been paralyzed by bullet wounds in an attempted assassination during his race for the 1972 Democratic Presidential nomination, but he was ready by 1974 to campaign for another term as state leader. Although Wallace won handily, the SCLC effort was indicative of continuing participation in the political process.[60] In numerous other contests between 1974 and the national elections of 1976, SCLC campaigned actively.

There were other indications of SCLC's involvement in politics. Executive director Bernard Lee, who had succeeded Stoney Cooks, was in regular contact with many welfare, political, and economic programs such as the Pushout Projects of the Southern Regional Council.[61] SCLC also kept extensive files of Civil Rights Commission reports, government agency programs, and interest group campaigns, and continued to work

306

with individuals who confronted problems because of race.[62] In relative terms, this kind of activity, of necessity, occupied more of SCLC's time than in the past.

In such circumstances, the activities of SCLC took on a more businesslike quality, and the necessity to measure progress in terms of piecemeal changes came into much sharper focus.[63] It is best to see this not as a sharp turn, but a gradual bend in SCLC's strategy. The organization's leaders had never fully adopted the evaluative criteria of the public media.[64] Theirs had always been a more sophisticated awareness of contextual progress than was realized by outside observers. The case of the Poor People's Campaign is illustrative. In evaluating this program SCLC officials saw more than the mud, the crimes, and the anti-climactic quality of the destruction of the tent city in Washington. While Abernathy's glowing descriptions were not echoed very widely, there were several key figures who saw the experience in positive terms. Some who were overtly critical of it from the inside were never very enthusiastic about the campaign. Among those who supported it, including Andrew Young and Stoney Cooks, there were limited expectations. They knew that the demonstration would not immediately or completely turn the country around in its thinking on poverty, but it could raise public consciousness and pressure government agencies.[65]

To the extent that it nudged the government to provide food stamps and other relief measures, the Poor People's Campaign could be considered successful.[66] The implication of the Kotz' analysis is that blacks did not think this way. But they did. Coretta King and the King Center in Atlanta operated in the same vein, seeing progress as contextual and incremental rather than dramatic and final.[67] Such undertakings as the Poor People's Campaign and voter education by their very nature were ongoing process activities, as important because of blacks' involvement in decision-making as their specific short-term results.[68] It is true that the NWRO was disillusioned by the meager results and turned back more vigorously to its own organizational approach.[69] But SCLC was fundamentally different from, and broader in scope than, NWRO.

While this approach was indicative of creative thinking within SCLC, it was also problematical. In a sense, SCLC conceded that the dream of "beloved community" that was basic to King's 1963 speech and to his entire career was more elusive than past rhetoric implied. Blacks and whites seemed sharply divided and often hostile. Violence was widespread during the Bicentennial period, and federal policy remained conservative under Gerald Ford. Many blacks were disappointed that Ford did not seem to be altering the Nixon social and economic policies.[70] Abernathy continued his forthright criticism of American society, especially when he spoke out in defense of blacks confronting problems with law enforcement and juridical officials.

And there were several widely publicized instances of confrontation that provided occasions for angry comments. In Pensacola, Florida in late 1974, five black men were drowned in the waters of Santa Rosa Sound. The boat of the experienced fishermen was discovered floating aimlessly and still containing their life jackets. Reportedly they had quarreled with a local white shopowner, and some people believed they had been murdered. SCLC appealed to Georgia Governor Jimmy Carter for an investigation, and the Justice Department looked into the matter but withdrew pending further evidence.[71] For weeks in the spring of 1975, Pensacola witnessed rioting, violence, and hostile verbal exchanges. Police and other officials were charged with racist remarks and indifference to black safety. Abernathy spoke out critically.

At the same time, the controversial case of Joan Little, a young black woman charged with murdering a sixty-year-old white jailer in Washington, North Carolina elicited involvement by women's rights groups, civil rights organizations, and hundreds of individual demonstrators. Miss Little, at 22, was beginning a prison term for burglary when she was held in the small North Carolina town. During the night of August 27, 1974, she stabbed the jailer repeatedly with an ice pick and escaped. SCLC's North Carolina state director Golden Frinks then

308

helped her turn herself over to authorities. She did not deny killing the guard, but argued that he had attempted to rape her and that she had acted in self-defense. The prosecution charged her with luring him into the cell to kill him.[72]

Hundreds of demonstrators surrounded the courthouse as the fiery trial of Joan Little went on for weeks. Abernathy called it the "most publicized form of repression against our people" that he had seen of late and asked for a nation-wide expression of opposition to the prosecution. He promised to build "Resurrection City III" in protest to the charges against Little. The trial's coincidence with many other cases of violence and charges of police brutality across the nation heightened its intensity.[73] That Little was young, a woman, and black made her case important to a wide range of advocacy groups. Finally, after the long trial, she was acquitted of the murder charges by a jury of six blacks and six whites after less than ninety minutes of deliberations.[74] She was then moved to the North Carolina Correction Center in Raleigh to complete her burglary sentence.

Other cases drew SCLC participation. In Washington, D. C., SCLC demonstrated in behalf of black school superintendent Barbara A. Sizemore when she was removed from her post for alleged failures in her duties and an attitude of insubordination. Again there was a heated confrontation with criticisms and counter charges, arguments and claims of racial prejudice.[75] This time, the decision went against the black woman and she was dismissed from her post after a five-month battle.[76]

No SCLC involvement in public issues was more controversial than its stand on amnesty for Vietnam draft resisters and deserters. Naturally, this was an emotional question which touched the feelings of the families of the dead and wounded in a profound way and engendered no small amount of anger among people who felt that the draft dodgers and deserters had betrayed their obligations as American citizens. SCLC's position, which was by no means unique, was that just as Ford had pardoned Nixon to get the "nightmare of Watergate" behind us, these young men should be pardoned in order to get the war out of the way once and for all and "introduce a measure of compassion and justice into the tragic record of our experience in Vietnam.'' SCLC's position was based on the premise that the war was wrong in the first place, and thus to punish resisters would be tantamount to ''compounding the injustices of this tragic episode in American history.''[77] The conference's amnesty proposal covered all draft resisters, deserters, persons convicted by courts-martial for military offenses not punishable under civilian law, veterans with dishonorable discharges, and civil protesters against the war. SCLC rejected the idea of alternative service as a form of punishment.[78]

The amnesty question was too torrid to be settled easily or quickly, and it was still moot when Jimmy Carter became President in 1977. There was much to be said for some form of amnesty, but it is understandable that families that had suffered directly from the war would strongly resent a general unconditional amnesty. SCLC argued that imprisonment or alternative service would work a special hardship on black families. The organization's interest in the issue was heightened by the fact that one of its young staff members, Robert Johnson was sentenced to imprisonment and five years' hard labor for his resistance to the draft. Abernathy, Tyrone Brooks, Young, and the Black Caucus worked in Johnson's behalf, and the young black was eventually released from most of his sentence. Abernathy called this a ''profound victory for SCLC'' and stated that the amnesty campaign had ''forced President Ford and the racist military machine'' to free Johnson outright.[79]

Such talk of racism as a continuing problem in American institutions was not easily received by the public. Surely it could not be accurate. But Abernathy was only one of many black spokespersons who saw it as a very real problem. Several SCLC affiliate directors and field workers reported a growing racial backlash and felt that they should keep the issue before the public lest it slip into oblivion without being rectified.[80] SCLC's offices stayed busy with specific cases of black workers, military personnel, black women jeopardized doubly by being both black and female and many more who felt that racial discrimination was hurting them. Those who doubted that this could be

310

happening in the middle seventies would have been surprised by the volume of cases SCLC, the NAACP and other organizations dealt with at that time.[81]

The King National Holiday

Not unrelated to this was one of the most basic undertakings of SCLC and the King Center. Since 1969 SCLC had observed Martin Luther King's January 15 birthday as a holiday and often joined with the King Center and other organizations in marking mid-January with various memorials. New programs were announced in January, and SCLC proceeded as if the King holiday were already in place. Actually, many years of battling for it lay ahead. Although King had already been recognized by many nations as an historic hero, the United States in the seventies still did not honor him with a holiday. SCLC argued that such was a necessity in view of his influence upon blacks, his contributions to the liberation of all races, and the fact that no black person had ever been so honored. To SCLC, as to the King Center, this special honor would be supremely fitting.

The legislative battle for the King holiday began as early as April 8, 1968, just four days after King's assassination in Memphis, when Congressman John Conyers introduced a bill in the House to designate January 15 as a national holiday. But there was little support, and the proposal did not reach the floor for debate. Conyers persisted in his efforts for many years, and Senator Edward Brooke of Massachusetts pushed for it in the Senate, but with the same negative results. As time passed after 1968 and the public awareness of King waned, it seemed that the issue might die quietly. That it did not was due to the inner core of people around Mrs. King and in Congress, state and local officials, entertainers like young Stevie Wonder, and a host of King's followers, including Abernathy, who actually carried some three million signatures to Congress in a mule caravan in 1971. SCLC would not wait "for Congress to act." Waiting there was, however, as Congressional opponents pointed out the economic cost of another holiday. They were numerous enough

311

in both houses to defer passage of a King holiday bill until well after the Abernathy presidency. Proponents argued that the perpetual inspiration it would be to black youth, as well as its value in reminding the nation of the historic nonviolent movement and ongoing dreams of a better society would more than offset the dollar cost.[82]

Not all of the arguments against the bills were economic. As the holiday campaign was intensifying in 1975, the Senate Select Committee known as the Church Committee (for Senator Frank Church who headed it) held hearings on domestic intelligence operations against King and SCLC. Major newspapers carried stories of the unfolding exposé of wiretapping, FBI surveillance of King's personal life and the bureau's efforts to destroy his reputation, along with other aspects of the FBI's investigative process. Certainly, as David Garrow has shown, King was not simply a "reassuring reformer" cultivating good relations with white America, but rather a very basic reformer.[83] But the mid-seventies investigations of FBI tactics against him raised questions about whether King was the noble visionary he was often taken to be, or a radical who undermined the American system.[84] To some observers the investigations indicted the FBI more than King, but the process of raising again the questions of communist influence and personal misbehavior provided opponents with additional arguments for rejecting the proposed holiday.

This was a crucial question, not a peripheral debate, for SCLC. More was involved than adoration, or condemnation, of Martin King. In all this, King appeared to his supporters as the superlative prophetic voice in American history, and to his most severe detractors as one who harbored radicals and undermined American capitalism. But between the extremes there was much valuable discussion about the meaning of his life and the nonviolent message to the world. Even if the legislators focused on other matters in their own debate, the public heard a more intense articulation of the significance of black liberation in America. Support became increasingly multi-racial and encompassed not only black entertainers such as Bill Cosby, Harry

Belafonte, Stevie Wonder, and Diana Ross, but many white politicians like Senators Ted Kennedy and Birch Bayh and several more. By drawing up statements, lobbying in the halls of Congress, and making symbolic demonstrations, the King Center, SCLC, PUSH, and other organizations that urged passage of the bills said more about nonviolence than at any time since 1968, and quite possibly acquired clearer perspective.

In some ways, the infancy of nonviolence in American political culture ended in the middle seventies. No longer was it exploratory and hesitant, but was becoming more sophisticated and bold. The violent deaths of John and Robert Kennedy, Martin King, blacks and whites in urban riots, more than fifty thousand American youngsters in Vietnam, and millions of naive perceptions of longevity in a relatively secure American populace, all served to make nonviolence more appealing to the intellect, even if not quite believable. Somehow, King did make it credible. That he died violently did not merely elicit panegyrics from those who wanted to elevate him above his imperfections. It demonstrated that he believed in what he was saying. While so many political leaders and their constituents in both hemispheres watched with almost fatalistic dismay the burgeoning MAD (mutual assured destruction) logic of nuclear deterrence, King had tried to offer an alternative. Unconvincing to many people because of its nonspecific and moral nature, King's message nonetheless did express what millions of people wanted to be true and workable. Undoubtedly, King injected into the seemingly realistic and sophisticated analyses of weapons experts and diplomatic traditionalism an affirmation of God's presence in history. Nonviolence could no longer be readily separated from world affairs.

What of other implications of nonviolence? Could SCLC, or any organization during the Bicentennial period offer tangible, believable specifics on how to make it work in politics, the economy, education, or personal living? It had exposed the fallacies of legally-enforced segregation. Perhaps it could also provide some guidelines on how to engage in business dealings or neighborhood crime prevention. It might even be possible to link it to national defense, as Gandhi had attempted to do three decades earlier. A number of organizations like the King Center were indeed exploring those kinds of possibilities. And SCLC made some creative moves in that direction during the last few years of the Abernathy period, several of which rivalled in quality such undertakings as Dialogue in the sixties.

One particularly interesting effort worth mentioning here was SCLC's discussion of the notion of a "nonviolent economy," A National Task Force on the Black Economic Agenda headed by Dr. Virgil A. Wood prepared a lengthy report for the 1975 convention in Anniston, Alabama. It was a well-structured position paper that was the basis of one of SCLC's best workshops since King's death. Dr. Vivian Henderson, President of Clark College in Atlanta, and Dr. Edward B. Irons of Atlanta University, Chairman of the Black Caucus of American Economists, led a special session on the topic. The paper was based on reports by the U.S. Civil Rights Commission, articles and books by economists, and excerpts from the writings of King and Gandhi. It stressed the urgency of the economic condition of many blacks and poor people of other races, but was hopeful in tone. "Just as nonviolence exposed the ugliness of racial injustice, we must now find ways to expose and heal the sickness of poverty, not just its symptoms, but its basic causes."[85]

There was nothing in the report to confirm the popular belief that blacks wanted more welfare. On the contrary, it emphasized the opposite. Nor did it hint at separatism, nationalism, or hostility toward whites. Rather, it invited "broad participation by persons from all over America, as part of the Bicentennial awakening, to new opportunities to show how great our Nation and its people can be."[86] The fundamental need was to get people involved. "We will have to repent in this generation," said this paper, "not merely for hateful words and actions of the bad people, but for the appalling silence of good people. Human progress never rolls in on the wheels of inevitability, it comes through the tireless efforts of men and women willing to be co-workers with God, and without this hard work, time itself becomes an ally of the forces of stagnation."[87]

No one could define exactly what a nonviolent economy would be, but as a point of reference the report took a section of King's *Where Do We Go From Here: Chaos or Community?* in which he called for a mixing of individualism and collectivism to achieve a "just society." The purpose of such an economy, the report said, was not to bring about proletarian socialism, but to eliminate poverty and gross inequities.[88] Its realization would "make partners of the oppressed and the former oppressors" while forging some real answers. It would also presumably work to the benefit of all by reducing crime, welfare dependency, and the gap between black and white family income. The spirit of the paper and the workshop was similar to the outlook of a *Time Magazine* report that summer which concluded that "Much of the demand for greater equality is really a protest against the injustices that a capitalist society could perfectly well remedy— while remaining capitalist. The greatest need is to improve the lot of the poor, and for that purpose nothing can replace a resumption of non-inflationary growth."[89]

In some respects the dream of human brotherhood was being refined, taking into account American tradition and economic realities. To some neoconservative thinkers of the period, this was merely re-hashed idealism that failed to discern the dangers of socialistic tendencies and welfare state dependency. This was not the way SCLC viewed it. However liberal or idealistic it seemed, the synthesis of faith and justice was essential. Only in that way could the nonviolent liberation movement begun in Montgomery in 1955 be completed. Indeed, the twentieth anniversary celebration honoring Rosa Parks in Montgomery in December 1975 caused a number of black leaders to reflect on what had been accomplished during the two decades since the bus boycott and, to commit themselves to more effort.

During the three-day commemorative conference Andrew Young said "I am a Congressman because of the suffering of black people here."[90] Several others voiced identical feelings of indebtedness to the movement that began in Montgomery. Coretta King, King's father, Congressman John Conyers, among others, stressed the historic and personal impact it had.

Rosa Parks urged them "Don't stop. Keep on keeping on." Psychologically, the conference was a turning-point for several of the participants.[91]

By then, SCLC had reached the nadir of its decline and was beginning, almost imperceptibly, to regain some confidence. By many pragmatic measures the organization should have closed its doors. That it did not was due to a great degree to the fact that people who had benefitted from its labors retained a personal sense of obligation to continue.[92] But above all, SCLC continued because it met a distinct need within the black community. Those who were deeply attached to churches and the tradition of specifically Christian nonviolence felt that SCLC was indispensable. This did not mean they did not respect the NAACP or other organizations promoting justice in the United States. Yet, SCLC provided for them a synthesis of faith and reform not embodied as fully in these other groups. If SCLC had ceased to operate, in all likelihood something like it would have been created to replace it. This cannot be understood simply from documents or news clippings. It is best discerned from participation in SCLC conventions, conversations with staff and field leaders, and intimate awareness of the music, sermons, and position papers of the conference. Music is particularly meaningful in this regard.[93]

Moreover, SCLC shared with the King Center the distinctive of combining idealism and practicality. It spoke openly of pursuing a "dream," and although this sounded unrealistic to many, it was crucial to SCLC's identity. It is not unusual to hear a speaker at an SCLC convention ask the audience to "Say Amen! Let the Church say Amen! Let the whole Church say Amen!" There is no separation of church and state in the traditional American sense in the socio-political theory of the Southern Christian Leadership Conference. Issues of poverty, equality, racial brotherhood, and peace are inseparably related to morality and the kingdom of God concept. This is true of much of the larger black community as well. As one recent writer has observed, "When white fundamentalists entered the political arena in the late 1970s they were breaking new ground.

316

But in the black church, religion and political struggle have long been fused. Distinguishing the two is inconceivable.''[94] For many blacks historically, the church has been the only institution they have controlled, and thus it was a natural forum for reformism and self-expression. But it also gave expression to values and ideas inseparable from the cause of freedom.

Thus, SCLC found strength in its nature as a faith-motivated organization. To be sure, it was unable to bring about any highly influential campaigns in the Bicentennial period, but it did participate in a number of local drives in which the theme of American renewal was accentuated. In April 1976, for example, SCLC national program director Golden Frinks led a march through Halifax, North Carolina where a Bicentennial celebration marked the 200th anniversary of the Halifax Resolves that set the thirteen colonies on course toward freedom. While Governor James Holshouser expressed the hope that the celebrations would weaken the nation's critics, Frinks and SCLC protested the ''gentle treatment'' of a white woman who had not long before killed a black man in nearby Scotland Neck. They called for a new set of Halifax Resolves against discrimination, inequality, and bigotry.[95]

The Continental Walk for Disarmament and Social Justice was SCLC's largest Bicentennial involvement, although it was a cooperative venture of several organizations, notably peace advocates. Structured to begin from several starting points and enlist participation by thousands of people, the march would proceed across more than thirty states and converge on Washington.[96] SCLC organized the Southern Walk which began in New Orleans on April 4, the anniversary of King's death. There Bernard Lee spoke of the possibility that violence might again erupt if nonviolent strategies did not succeed in improving the social atmosphere.[97]

The Continental Walk became a major affair as people from feeder routes sustained the cross-country trek. Not surprisingly, the marchers met resistance. In Mississippi group leaders complained of opposition.[98] Affiliate director Fred Taylor protested when Alabama officials refused to allow the marchers access to city streets for their march in Birmingham in late July. Several were arrested. When they were released the next day, they held a celebration rally and resumed the march. For six months, the walk continued and in mid-October culminated with an anti-weapons demonstration at the Pentagon that brought more arrests.[99]

End of the Abernathy Administration

Actually by then the nation was more interested in the forthcoming presidential election which pitted Democrat Jimmy Carter against incumbent Gerald Ford. A Baptist and a moderate populist, Carter was forging ahead of Ford as he appealed to those who wanted to reduce big government and to those who saw Carter as a sincere advocate of social justice. Blacks overwhelmingly favored Carter. His election in November gratified those blacks who felt that his administration would reverse the policies of Nixon and Ford.[100]

Jimmy Carter's election had some significant effects on SCLC. Since blacks helped elect him, Carter appeared to be indebted to them, and SCLC soon expressed that notion. In his campaigning Carter had endorsed the principle of affirmative action in helping blacks secure better jobs and education and had otherwise promised considerable support for minorities. He also was pledged to bringing more blacks into government, and in December 1976 he made a gesture in that direction as he asked Andrew Young to leave Congress and represent the United States in the United Nations.[101] Young's acceptance triggered a series of events that produced a change of leadership at SCLC national headquarters. As Young vacated his 5th Congressional District seat in Atlanta, about a dozen aspirants began to seek the office, among them Ralph David Abernathy.

In early January 1977 Abernathy announced his decision, offering the voters his record in civil rights. "To this post I will bring the totality of my experiences acquired during the last twenty-five years of my professional life in the struggle for peace, justice, and economic prosperity."[102] He had glowing words for the potential of Atlanta, describing it as "the world's

Chronological Table No. 4: Principal Campaigns and Programs of the Abernathy Period 1968–1977

1968	1970	1972	1974	1976	1978
Assassination of Dr. King (April 4, 1968)	*Richard Nixon* (President 1969–1974)		*Gerald Ford* (President 1974–1976)	*United States Bicentennial*	*Jimmy Carter* (President 1977–1981)
Ralph Abernathy succeeds King POOR PEOPLE'S MARCH/RESURRECTION CITY Washington 1968	*Politics '70*	*Politics '72*		United States Bicentennial	
		Walter Fauntroy elected to the House 1971	Andrew Young elected to the House 1972	Andrew Young named UN Ambassador 1977	
	KING HOLIDAY EFFORTS 1969 on ward		Abernathy resigns but re-elected 1973	Abernathy runs for Congress and resigns SCLC presidency/Lowery: acting president	
	Poverty Demonstration at Cape Kennedy 1969		Support of various labor strikes, welfare reform campaigns	CONTINENTAL WALK FOR SOCIAL JUSTICE 1976	
	CHARLESTON HOSPITAL STRIKE 1969	MARCH AGAINST REPRESSION 1970	extended into several areas		
		Anti-war Demonstration in Washington 1971			
			Pressure on political conventions/candidates to support anti-poverty measures		
			RESURRECTION CITY II 1972		

next greatest international city." He promised to help Maynard Jackson, the city's first black mayor, to raise funds for carrying out public programs and pledged himself to assisting the ill-housed, elderly, and jobless. He promised to promote industry in the city and to cultivate its international appeal.[103]

For about a month Abernathy tried to campaign while serving as SCLC president and continuing to pastor at West Hunter Street Baptist Church. This proved to be too much for him and in mid-February he announced his resignation as SCLC president. With that, board chairman Joseph E. Lowery stepped in as acting president while a search committee looked for a permanent full-time replacement. It was not clear at that time whether Lowery would consider becoming the president, but Abernathy supporters argue that it was understood that Abernathy would have the privilege of returning to his SCLC post if he lost the Congressional race.[104]

In any case, it was the end of Abernathy's nine-year executive leadership of SCLC. His re-election at the nineteenth annual convention in Biloxi, Mississippi the previous summer proved to be the last time he would be chosen to head the organization he had worked with for two decades. By the time of the Twentieth Anniversary Convention in 1977, SCLC would have a new president. As Abernathy was campaigning for the 5th Congressional District seat, Lowery and the board were already moving to implement changes that they hoped would strengthen SCLC and its system of affiliates.

Abernathy's Congressional campaign did not go well. Julian Bond and other prominent local blacks endorsed John Lewis, the former SNCC leader and director of the Voter Education Project. Lewis, in his mid-thirties, was a strong candidate who was not plagued, as Abernathy was, by the view that he was moving outside his field of expertise. In late February Young also endorsed Lewis. Abernathy was angered and hurt and said publicly that Young had promised not to endorse any candidate.[105] When the first round of voting in the special election was over on March 5, a young white attorney, Wyche Fowler, Jr., led the field with Lewis a close second. Abernathy was fourth,

320

with less than 5% of the vote. Blacks supported Lewis, who also received extensive white support. In April, Fowler defeated Lewis in the run-off.

If Abernathy's presidency was over, SCLC's problems were not. Those who tended to blame Abernathy for the organization's difficulties soon learned that there were other causes. Abernathy was disappointed by all this, but he took it philosophically and remained available for work in SCLC. His name and personality still had much appeal, and somewhat ironically, his image as a statesman seemed to increase once he was out of office. Abernathy had been through as much strain and suffering as virtually anyone in the black movement. He had been King's closest aide and had been handed the most trying challenge of his life—to succeed King in an era when King himself would have faced negative odds. On balance, the record shows that Ralph David Abernathy helped keep SCLC and its dream alive despite his own and the organization's problems.

"Now, a decade later, the challenge to each of us is not merely to admire Dr. King, but to follow him still."

Jesse Jackson

11

I Remember Martin: Lowery and Agendas for Renewal 1977–1980

The quartet of SCLC leaders who emerged in 1977 were as different in personality and style as background. Acting president Dr. Joseph Echols Lowery was elected president at the Twentieth Anniversary Convention in Atlanta in August, becoming the third chief executive of SCLC. A well-educated Methodist pastor, Lowery continued the tradition of ministerial leadership of SCLC, bringing considerable experience into the office. Capable of appearing on one day smartly dressed in a vested suit and the next in denim jeans and jacket for a march or rally, Lowery presented an interesting combination of sophistication and common man identity.

Rebounding from his defeat in the Congressional election, Abernathy was named president-emeritus, a life-time honor designed to recognize his previous contributions and to link him to SCLC's future. While there were those who viewed this as a means to smooth over friction, Abernathy acted quickly to underscore the unity of SCLC's leaders. He placed Lowery's name in nomination at the Atlanta convention to "disappoint the forces of evil, those who want to see us divided." Likewise, Hosea Williams, who had agreed to take a high post in the Lowery administration, seconded the nomination. "In the name

323

of unity," said Williams, "and as one of the true custodians of the legacy of Martin Luther King, I'd like to second the motion."[1] With these gestures of unity and disclaimers to the press that there were ideological divisions within SCLC, Lowery was unanimously elected to succeed Ralph Abernathy.[2]

Reverend Williams was named executive director, a post from which he hoped to reinvigorate the direct-action role of SCLC. Closely linked to the great campaigns that toppled the segregation of the deep South, Williams was still a strong advocate of marching, demonstrating, and other overt techniques. He felt that SCLC had stepped back from that policy in the seventies and needed to revive the image it had in the sixties.[3] Williams was involved in a number of activities in his Atlanta chapter, his chemical business, and politics, but he managed to keep all of them going while holding the director's post at SCLC.[4]

The fourth principal officer after the 1977 reshuffling was Congressman Walter E. Fauntroy. As a member of the House and a pastor, Fauntroy was pulled in several directions, but his devotion to SCLC was strong. Replacing Lowery as chairman of the board, the vigorous Fauntroy brought the complex experience of his two decades with SCLC to the position, as well as his valuable ties to the Congress. With an easy smile and a hard-hitting pulpit style, Fauntroy too embodied the ministerial leadership tradition, but with an additional dimension of an increasingly important role in the House of Representatives.

To be sure there were differences of view, particularly on strategy, among these SCLC leaders and indeed across the conference. But that had always been true. More important were the things that held the organization together—nonviolence, Christian values, and advocacy for the needy, as well as common hopes for the future. If the press focused on their differences and the absence of a Martin Luther King figure, the SCLC leaders themselves knew better than their critics that their most decisive challenge was to keep alive the dream that King epitomized.[5]

In some ways the largest challenges fell on Joseph Lowery. His involvements in civil rights activism had been extensive, but more local and regional than that of the others. As a Methodist, he did not have quite the degree of flexibility and mobility enjoyed by King, Abernathy, and others as Baptists. He needed the consent of his bishops, for example, to assume major positions, whereas in the Baptist structure, congregational support was sufficient. By 1977 Lowery had been a United Methodist pastor for many years and in several states, among them Alabama, Georgia, and Tennessee. From 1952 to 1961 he pastored the Warren Street Methodist Church in Mobile, where he was involved in several local desegregation drives. From Mobile he drove to the meetings out of which SCLC emerged in the late fifties.[6]

In 1961 Lowery moved to Nashville to serve as promotional director and administrative assistant to Bishop Charles F. Golden, episcopal director of the Nashville-Birmingham Area of the Central (Black) Jurisdiction.[7] Lowery was also on the governing board of the United Methodist Publishing House, a job he held until 1972. In that capacity he promoted fair hiring practices that helped give the Nashville-based publisher an excellent record of interracial hiring. All the while, he served on SCLC's directing board and promoted its programs and fundraising efforts. In 1966 he called for the breakup of racial subdivisions in his denomination and contributed to the 1968 reforms that envisaged over a period of time the jurisdictional desegregation of the Methodist Church.[8]

Upon King's recommendation Lowery became the chairman of SCLC's board of directors in 1967, and for months wrestled with King's request that he move to Atlanta to become an executive officer at national headquarters. The pastorate was Lowery's "first love," he recalls, and he decided to stay with it. But events of 1968 changed his plans. King's assassination in April coincided with the reform of Methodist jurisdictional structure which Lowery had worked on for several years. Bishop Golden asked him to head a special Commission on Religion and Race which the denomination had established to oversee these matters and promote a more inclusive policy. If he was not interested in that, Golden told Lowery, he would like to see him move to Atlanta to pastor the Central United Methodist Church.[9]

Two months after King's death Lowery took the pastorate at Central and over the following decade chaired the SCLC board in Atlanta. This put him at the nerve center of the national organization during the Abernathy years and gave him opportunities to work more closely with its routine operations. The Central United Methodist Church supported his larger role in SCLC, and the congregation itself grew to over 1,600 and was deeply involved in a variety of programs such as low-cost housing for the poor and a host of other social ministries. Mrs. Evelyn Lowery established herself as a leader in her own right, especially working with women, young people, and family support programs.

The Campaign for Rejuvenation 1977–1979

As we have seen, the strains of the middle seventies left their scars on SCLC, so that Lowery's election to the presidency in 1977 was not without its problems. He brought into the national office a new style of administration. Furthermore his staff was severely limited. Only three or four people carried the routine load and some of them were trainees funded by CETA. The organization's income barely topped $100,000 and SCLC had debts of almost $20,000.[10] It was imperative to raise more funds, tighten organizational structure, and above all to engender a new sense of movement. In that regard, Lowery could build upon a number of Abernathy's efforts, but certain adjustments had to be made for changing conditions. The tasks Lowery and his associates undertook were larger and longer-lived than they anticipated, but so were the results. At a time when it seemed that civil and human rights advocacy organizations would surely decline further, the leadership conference King and Abernathy had led began to show signs of new growth. That the press was slow to recognize this did not prevent many within the black community from seeing that Abernathy had been right all along. There was still sufficient reason for the nonviolent movement to continue.

326

Lowery's election coincided with the early months of Jimmy Carter's presidency, and the new SCLC chief quickly seized upon the Carter record for leverage. Lowery's verbal jabs at Carter elicited enthusiastic response at the Atlanta convention and helped dispel the notion that he might be too conservative. "We've got a claim on you," he cried out apostrophically to President Carter. Noting that blacks had helped put the former Georgia governor in the White House, the SCLC president argued that the Carter administration was already backing away from many of its campaign promises, especially in the area of fighting poverty. "We might have to pull on our marchin' shoes," he said. "We're going to telephone you, Mr. Carter, we're going to telegraph you, and if (they) don't reach you, the tramp, tramp, tramp of our feet will reach you." Repeatedly the new SCLC president shouted with rising voice "We've got a claim on the White House. We're not going to lose by default." He reminded the President that George Washington Carver of Tuskegee had made the peanut a precious commodity so that, in effect, a black man had provided the means by which the Carter family had become wealthy.[11]

Actually, Lowery had not given up on Carter. It was not the President's sincerity or good intentions that he questioned, but his will to close the gap between campaign commitments and actual delivery.[12] In general Carter appeared to be on the right track. But it had been a long time since the White House had actively pursued the kinds of objectives SCLC sought, and the Carter administration had the potential for reversing the increasing *laissez-faire* mentality of the Nixon and Ford years. Four months before the Atlanta convention Lowery and other board members had met with the President to discuss a wide range of issues and Lowery had taken the occasion to urge a concerted federal effort to eliminate poverty and provide job opportunities on a more equitable basis. As of August, little had been accomplished. Thus, Lowery could challenge federal policy and, at the same time, establish himself more clearly as an outspoken leader of the nonviolent movement.

It is obvious that president Lowery and his colleagues, as well as sympathizers outside the organization, wanted to see SCLC become more active and effective. As John Lewis poignantly observed, SCLC had to get off dead center so that it would not be "primarily a paper organization that might limp along for a thousand years on the image of Dr. King and never accomplish anything meaningful." The structure needed to be modernized, said Lewis, mirroring a growing consensus of the later Abernathy and early Lowery periods. Lewis believed that SCLC "still had a significant role to play," but to realize it would not be easy.[13]

The Renewal Program

Lewis was correct. It would take a gargantuan effort to get SCLC moving forcefully in the environment of the late seventies. Exposing shortcomings in federal policy had political potential, since SCLC had always sought to move the conscience of presidents and spur them to action. But this was not enough for a renewed movement. SCLC's structure would have to be overhauled, and its base of resources enlarged. The initial task would be to revitalize the image of SCLC among blacks, but in the long run something like the interracial consensus of the sixties would have to be restored. Above all, SCLC needed to reassert its nonviolent approach as a viable force in the new socio-political setting of the post-Watergate period.

Little time was lost. In the fall of 1977 Lowery and his staff worked on a unified statement of goals and a structural reorganization plan. At a retreat at Camp Calvin in December, the renewal program was presented and hammered into shape. The communications department would be enlarged and given the task of cultivating a more positve image of SCLC as an active, vibrant organization. Through a national *SCLC Magazine*, the "Martin Luther King Speaks" tape series, printed promotional materials and other media advertisements, SCLC's visibility would be heightened.[14]

As Wyatt Walker had done in the early sixties and Andrew Young later in the decade, Lowery's people sought to stimulate a sense of new motion. What was missing was a high tide of fervor in the broader community, so that in some respects the challenges of 1977 were greater than those of earlier years. But, Lowery insisted, SCLC was still needed because "the nonviolent philosophy which underscores the efficacy of love in human relationships in ours to proclaim. Its ours to stamp on the hearts and minds of the American dream."[15] The new SCLC chief dwelt in his remarks upon what he called the "outness" of blacks. Still excluded from many of the economic benefits of American citizenship, he emphasized, blacks had a long way to go. Continued political progress would be needed, but Lowery also cited the necessity for realizing "our values and goals beyond the political process."[16]

Objective evidence has confirmed the accuracy of what Dr. Lowery was saying. Progress for black Americans was uneven, though substantial. Indeed, SCLC was insisting that much had been gained by the nonviolent movement of the past. The view that progress had *not* been made was already becoming part of the orthodox rhetoric of the extremist wing of the new conservatism of the late seventies in order to discredit King and others who had led the nonviolent campaigns in the South. Their perspective, as opposed to SCLC's, was that the activist leaders of the sixties had misled blacks and whites alike, making the former more dependent upon welfare programs and the federal government.[17] Lowery's point was that the movement was not yet complete, just as King and Abernathy had maintained. It is quite significant that Lowery held to the same premise of nonviolence that had motivated the King movement all along.

In truth, the economic aspect was the most glaringly troublesome. Blacks had acquired the vote, higher median educational levels, and important inroads into a larger range of jobs and professions. But during the seventies, their composite economic gains were eroding. From the late fifties through the early seventies, black Americans rose economically faster than whites. While virtually all workers of both races made economic gains in that period, blacks' income increased enough to catch up partially with whites. But as the seventies progressed, blacks lost ground, leaving them at about the same relative levels of personal income they had in the 1950s. Black family income stood in the seventies at only about 50–60% of white family income, depending on the type of families compared.[18] For female-headed black families the gap was much larger. In addition, unemployment, inadequate housing, and deficient job training were much higher in many sectors of the black population. The recession of 1973 to 1975 triggered by the energy crisis and inflation left its marks on America's blacks just as it did on the aggregate economy. But the result for many blacks was not simply stagnation, but decline.[19]

Thus, the Lowery administration did have a substantive issue for the movement, and it was only one of several problems that were either incompletely resolved or worsening in 1977. If SCLC could find a way to reach the blacks who had risen above poverty, the government, and the general public with this message, there was a real possibility for a vigorous new resurgence. On the other hand, higher taxes and uncontrolled inflation were working in another direction, toward fiscal restraint and cutbacks in social programs.

But SCLC's first task was to put its own house in better order. As part of the strategy for renewal, its leaders decided to tighten organizational control and promote growth in its chapters and affiliates. The administrative committee would meet more frequently and more input would be expected from its members. Each board member was encouraged to help organize local groups linked to SCLC and to raise $1,000 annually for the budget. For fiscal 1978 that budget was set at $439,000 and personnel would be limited to a cost-efficient number. Each officer would be expected to deliver results so that a balance could be struck between numbers and programs.

The national officers would now consist of the president, six vice-presidents, an executive director (with supporting staff), a secretary, a treasurer, a chaplain, and a general counselor. Enlarging the affiliate structure was a cardinal feature of the plan. Lowery discovered that there were some local affiliates that were passing unnoticed in Atlanta and surrounding areas.

There was also evidence that people in many communities across the nation wanted to organize and to affiliate with SCLC. Not only did SCLC try to revamp programs in places like Washington, where there had been pivotal chapters in the past, but also to develop new ones. Along with this quantitative increase, a more centralized administration was established, on the logic that local campaigns were important but could be preempted in emergency situations by directives from the Atlanta headquarters.[20]

Individual membership was also viewed quite differently at this point. In its early days, SCLC had opted not to be a membership organization, although there were periods when such was attempted. Now, some of the reasons for rejecting the membership approach no longer applied. There was no cause in the late seventies to be as concerned about competition with the NAACP, and there was less pressure on individuals who might fear, as they did in the sixties, being listed as members of an organization under surveillance by the FBI and other federal agencies.[21] It was valuable in the new era to cultivate a sense of belonging, as well as to create a network to recognize distinctive service and thus encourage more participation. And by early 1978 Fred Taylor had begun a concerted membership drive. His office greatly increased the number and frequency of mailings to churches, clubs, and associations, as well as individuals who might lend support to help organize an SCLC affiliate.[22]

To increase efficiency the affiliate structure and its fund-raising procedures were revamped. With the primary focus on the Southeast, a network of six regional chapters—including a new one for Kansas, Oklahoma, and Texas—was set up. These would be the focal point of state chapters. In turn the state organizations would be the contact line with local affiliates. Fund solicitation would be limited to the particular state in which a chapter was chartered in order to prevent duplication. The national SCLC treasurer now headed a standing committee which prepared the national budget for approval by the board.[23]

Fund-raising goals were high. In addition to the basic budget of $439,000—most of it for salaries and office functions (although

Lowery himself was not paid)—more would be needed for campaigns and special activities. It was estimated that approximately $560,000 would be needed for the following year, with a sizable portion of it ($300,000) to be raised from federal agencies. SCLC had never relied on federal funds, but the changing times were reflected in the forthright challenge put forth in 1977 to local, state, and national officers to seek financial resources from HEW, HUD, the Department of Labor, and other federal agencies.[24] An additional $150,000 was expected from a direct mail campaign and the balance from the *SCLC Magazine* and funds raised directly by board members and from the sale of membership cards.

As important as these organizational reforms were, even more crucial was perspective. What was it all about? Did it have relevance to contemporary life? Those were questions answered in a distinctive way by SCLC and its friends. They wrestled with the historical legacy and meaning of Martin Luther King, Jr. and the nonviolent movement. And in doing so they challenged the views of those who had, in their minds, closed the civil rights era. As Jesse Jackson noted in a speech in 1977, history has a tendency to "castrate the images of prophets." In Jackson's view, there was a real danger of losing the meaning of the nonviolent work of King in a maelstrom of analysis and investigation. The PUSH leader was convinced that what many people remembered about King was "only a homogenized shadow of the essence of the man and his work."[25] Jackson would not accept at face value the character-demeaning reports by the FBI or the emerging view that King was radical or subversive. "Don't believe the historians—remember, instead, what was really happening." This was an important point, since the history of the internal workings and relationships of the movement was not recorded very completely by journalists or scholars. Nor could it be, since much of it was not written. It had to be observed and lived.

Lowery was thinking along the same lines as he began his presidency. In numerous speeches and sermons, as well as a poem entitled "I Remember Martin," Lowery praised the first

SCLC president and claimed an ongoing relevance for his socio-political ideas and moral principles. King, he argued, was a prophet who embodied the basic spirit of the reformist black clergy. Both in word and deed, King had shown the proper course for America and the world to take, insisted Lowery.

According to Lowery the Christian mandate was to preach a holistic deliverance affecting "every phase and facet" of man's experience. No ivory tower exclusiveness was acceptable for theology, he said. Lowery argued both in terms of a universal imperative of love uniting all people and a practical religious experience that promoted freedom as well as morality, equality as well as salvation. He noted the contradictions between the love King had taught and the hatred that had killed him. "God is in all men," said Lowery. No person can hate, oppress, mutilate, or otherwise harm another without doing those things to God.[26] "I remember Martin," he wrote, "because his dream was in essence the dream of a nation that had forgotten. . . and more than that it was in truth the dream of a Creator who had not forgotten and who made 'of one blood all nations of men to dwell upon the face of the earth.' "[27]

Lowery was also impressed with the increasing interconnectedness of various nations of the world. In his view provincialism and chauvinism were counterproductive. The world was increasingly a community requiring cooperation and peaceful relations. Tremendous strides in communication, transportation, and common economic concerns had broken down many of the barriers that separated nations, yet there were still numerous obstacles to peace and brotherhood. They could not be separated, Lowery argued, from the contextual meaning of religion. "There is no way we can separate our relationship with our fellow man from our relationship with God. It is in the context of the Christian faith that the redemptive love of Christ is made efficacious in the relationship between black and white, rich and poor, East and West, North and South, little and big."[28]

Lowery's view of social deviance was also contextual. Crime, poverty, and estrangement were related causally. "One cannot talk about crime in the streets," he said, "without talking about crime in the suites."[29] Just as Jean Valjean was trapped by a system in Victor Hugo's *Les Misèrables*, Lowery argued, many poor people were propelled toward a life of crime by the dire circumstances of survival economics. Lowery wanted to broaden the American perspective on social deviance to include the underlying causes and a commitment to rectify them.[30]

As far as the black movement was concerned the new SCLC president felt that renewal was both necessary and possible. He recognized that the civil rights movement had not done enough for the masses. Nor had the election of many more black politicians brought much improvement to millions living in poverty. This fact had caused many blacks at the grassroots level to lose confidence in black leaders. It was time, Lowery believed, for SCLC to "rekindle that confidence and speak to the total community."[31] He specifically wanted to continue the economic uplift emphasis of the late King and Abernathy years. He knew that this would not be easy. "You've got no symbol to fight any more—except for tokenism," Lowery noted. A white bank president might be pictured in a newspaper with a black teller, and everyone appear happy and satisfied, but "the truth is that the median income of blacks is less than 55% of the median income of whites. And that's even less than what it was several years ago."[32]

James Lawson also challenged SCLC at this juncture of renewal to see the picture clearly and to anticipate the realities of any serious effort to look to a meaningful role in the future. He noted in late 1977 that no one person could hope to speak exhaustively on the meaning of the nonviolent movement. "What movement are we talking about?" he asked. Was it specifically the King movement, SCLC, or something broader? Lawson speculated that "Perhaps the most important thing that has happened in America as a consequence of the King movement is that America now has a conscience."[33] He said two other things about the general impact of the King movement. It had brought racism into the clear light of public awareness and showed, Lawson said, "that somewhere along the line the question of race, racism, and segregation either must be finally settled or it will finally settle America.''

Among black Americans, noted the SNCC founder, the King movement had stirred awareness and produced a new style of leadership. The new leader was service oriented, willing to organize the masses and to identify with the majority rather than the elite ten percent. In many areas of public and private life, Lawson noted, essentially nonviolent pursuits in education, business, and personal relations were underway. But, he went on, there were reasons to be discouraged. ''I think we have to say that, for us, the nonviolent movement is scattered and highly demoralized.'' That had to be faced and dealt with. To ignore it was dangerous and non-productive.[34] Lawson sensed the dichotomy between typical political involvement and dealing with the painful experiences of the masses. Having moved to Los Angeles in 1974 Lawson had engaged in numerous political campaigns while serving as pastor of a large church. He confessed his feeling that such involvements, while valuable, did not meet the everyday needs of millions of people. It looked like a losing battle. ''No matter how many we pick up, the economic order throws down ten more for every one we pick up.''

Lawson saw the movement as having become too divided and competitive since King's death. Many black leaders had tried to use the press, radio, and television to propagandize in behalf of reform. This had accomplished little. What was needed, said Lawson, was to do the kinds of things that would bring the press to the movement, not the other way around. ''Let's realize that nonviolent, direct action is not irrelevant. . . Let's get a focus of action, and put our attention there. And then see what happens.''[35]

The program adopted by SCLC at the end of 1977 was, in fact, action-oriented. The Camp Calvin session outlined sixteen issues for emphasis by SCLC. The hope was that they would elicit more interest among blacks as well as in the Congress and state and local legislatures. Significantly, six of them were economic in nature: jobs, housing and community grants, tax evasion, hunger, problems of the working poor, and renewal of Operation

Breadbasket. Breadbasket had been one of SCLC's all-time most successful programs. Although hurt by Jackson's departure, it still had viability, and Lowery wanted to renew it. It would be pivotal in a number of the economic issues and provided a sub-organizational vehicle for keeping up the pressure on the economic front. Its high visibility in several cities gave it an inherent structural and policy relevance that could be exploited. Lowery wanted it to remain essentially the same in its objectives and procedures. It would seek to generate jobs and income for blacks by pressuring businesses and local governments to hire them, invest in their businesses, and otherwise elevate the black economic community.[36]

A second group of projected issues concerned the foreign policy of the United States as it affected race relations in the United States and the world. Militarism was condemned as wasteful and dangerous. Investments in, and trade with, South Africa was singled out for criticism. South African *apartheid* had become a world issue by the late 1970s and was affecting that country's athletic teams, world commerce, and overall image in a negative way. Still United States companies were trading with South Africa and SCLC continued to criticize that commerce. When the Atlanta-based Southern Company was contracted to buy 7.7 million tons of low-sulfur coal for its subsidiary Gulf Power Company, Lowery spoke out against it and wired President Carter and UN Ambassador Young to halt the sale. Lowery called the contract a "ghastly contradiction of current efforts to end human oppression" and noted that although the coal was low in sulfur, it "contains the highest levels of human shame."[37]

South African *apartheid* was a major issue for SCLC and, as it turned out, a long-lived one. Since King's time, as we have seen, SCLC had considered foreign policy as one of its legitimate concerns and had been faulted for exceeding its proper bounds. But South Africa as an issue had much potential and would become one of SCLC's principal emphases into the 1980's. Indeed, it would symbolize SCLC's announced quest for a worldwide justice which the United States as a super-power was in a distinctive position to promote. Along with it came an

SCLC drive against militarism and nuclear weapons and for promotion of more even-handedness in the Middle East and Africa.

The third cluster of issues could be summarized under the rubric of domestic racial justice. The report singled out racism, equal opportunity, crime and the administration of justice (including police brutality), young people and student movements, welfare reform, and a Freedom Plan for the nation. To highlight these and other problems, SCLC planned to launch a nonviolent campaign in 1978.

The fourth category was related to the third, but was more specifically concerned with opportunities for advancement: education, testing, compensatory affirmative action, and equal opportunity. These were in jeopardy by 1978 as the *Alan Bakke Case* appeared to be bringing a major set-back to the affirmative action policy of recent years. The *Bakke case* raised the thorny problem of "reverse discrimination" and alarmed black and other minority advocates as nothing had in recent years. Charles Lawrence, III, in the *Saturday Review* said that "it may be the most important constitutional case since the 1954 *Brown* decision outlawed segregated schooling.[38] The implications for Affirmative Action were tremendous. Bakke, a civil engineer, had applied in 1973 and 1974 for admission to the medical school of the University of California at Davis and had been rejected. He brought suit when he learned that about sixteen disadvantaged minority applicants had been admitted by special procedures despite low MCAP scores, and after extended court proceedings his case went to the Supreme Court.[39] On June 28, 1978, the nation's highest court decided in favor of Bakke.

The *Bakke case* underscored the fact that Affirmative Action was by no means an absolute. Ramsey Clark called the decision "psychologically, legally, socially, and morally devastating."[40] SCLC, like many other groups concerned with minorities, was disturbed and set out to prevent further erosion. It is true that U. S. Solicitor General Wade H. McCree, Jr. had appeared in the Bakke proceedings and affirmed the federal government's support of the reduced requirements for admitting the minority students, but the Carter administration seemed to be moving toward supporting Bakke's reverse discrimination position during the summer of 1977 and thus contributed to no small degree of concern among black leaders. Of significance to many was the fact that there was only one physician of any race for every 4,248 blacks (as compared to one for every 649 in the general population). Racial quotas for admission to medical and other professional schools thus appeared as more than a legal question, but one of survivability and provision of basic necessary services and opportunities for advancement. That they were not viewed that way across the nation was increasingly clear.

If the *Bakke case* was a setback, more challenging was the inward turning of American social philosophy. In some ways, this was paradoxical. Americans had displayed a greater ability to live together in integrated circumstances, yet there was an increase in racism and even violence in some sectors. And as the tenth anniversary of the Kerner Commission Report approached, there was no small amount of reflecting on the progress, or lack of it in some respects, of blacks since the late sixties. Significant figures, including President Carter, were calling for completion of the tasks begun earlier. But taxpayers were beginning to rebel against heavy burdens on their earnings and were turning increasingly to a more conservative view of government that echoed nineteenth century liberal *laissez-faire* perspectives. Aggravating public fears were many economic forecasts in 1978 that conditions would worsen. It was expected that purchase of durable goods would decline, with negative reverberations in industries such as home building, steel production, and automobile manufacture.[41] With the overall economy slipping drastically, the mentality of "making it" for oneself became a more compelling mind-set. Programs, however meritorious, sounded to many people like unbearable expense. If the Great Society of the sixties was dead, how could a just society be realized in a time of fiscal conservatism? That dilemma moved some Americans to develop a cynical view of social reformers that branded them as "liberals" and "dreamers" with only a method and no substance. It dragged downward the best instincts of people who wanted to help but who were convinced

338

that leaders of the past, black and white, had misled them into thinking that money and programs could solve problems, when in truth they only saddled the nation more heavily with weighty financial burdens.

SCLC's position was that a democratic nation founded on Judaeo-Christian moral principles could not afford to have its priorities confused by the sheer weight of social and economic uncertainty. The relative silence of the seventies had to be broken and the nation reminded that millions of people, and certainly not all of them black, remained hopeless and in economic distress. As the Civil Rights Commission reported in mid-February 1978 in a 129-page statement, progress had indeed been made over the previous decade, but it cited "high unemployment and poverty rates among minority groups and women, and the inadequacy of programs to deal with the problems of low-income urban residents." Echoing this, John Herbers wrote in the *New York Times* a few days later that "The division between white and black Americans still exists and the prospects of healing the rift may be more dismal today than they were ten years ago."[42] If Hubert Humphrey's death in January 1978 symbolized the passing of a generation of moderate liberal reformers, it did not mark the arrival of a new era when racial and economic tensions were resolved.

"Nipped in the bud!" That's the way Lowery described the hopes of many blacks in his address in May 1978 to the NAACP-sponsored National Leadership Conference in Chicago. He had been re-reading the Kerner Commission Report, too. He told the Chicago gathering that he had dusted off his copy of the thick paperback and had been thinking about its implications. The SCLC president recalled the "dark and dismal future" it had predicted in 1968 and noted that the median income of blacks in 1978 was about the same as it had been then. "Thank God," Lowery said, "that some blacks have climbed higher on the income ladder. But for the most part, each time we climb another rung on Jacob's ladder, old Esau saws the bottom of the ladder off, and we keep standing on the bottom."[43] As for preferential treatment, Lowery averred that sometimes it is appropriate. It was consistent, he argued, with Judaeo-Christian ethics when used to correct injustices and inequalities. Color should be regarded when it has been, and is, a barrier to rightful advancement. Special regard for historical and moral inequities ought to be given, he said.

Lowery was aware, too, of the importance of emphasizing the special role of blacks in the historical struggle for justice. Integration was not, he said, the "movement of all things black to all things white, but the therapeutic, corrective movement of all things wrong to all things right." Like James Cone and Albert Cleage, Jr. of the black liberation theology movement, Lowery spoke of blackness in an ontological sense. "God has chosen blackness, as he chose the Hebrew children in Biblical days, to be that vessel through which he pours out justice and liberty for all His people."

Lowery's orientation, however, owed more to King's version of Beloved Community than to the Black Theology movement. The latter identified Christianity, and indeed Christ himself, with black liberation. Lowery's perspective was much broader. In "I Remember Martin" he showed admiration for King's "understanding of the theological implications of the struggle and his devotion to the moral imperatives of the feat."[44] To Lowery the central compelling force was still the linkage of justice, peace, and morality that King had articulated. SCLC would "continue to fulfill the dream."

> The dream must be translated into sustained effort to bring about the systematic change needed to commit the nation to full employment; to put an end to repressive criminal justice systems; to bring peace with justice to all the world; to usher in the day of brotherhood and end the long night of wrong.[45]

But how could SCLC continue to fulfill the dream and effect that systematic change necessary to commit the nation to such problematical goals as full employment and judicial reform? Economic problems, growing fear and hostility toward the Soviet Union, and tremendous backlash against the Great Society concept were all working in opposite directions from what

340

Lowery envisaged. Blacks as well as whites were difficult to enlist in movement affairs. A different generation of youth was on the scene by 1978, as Lerone Bennett observed in an incisive article that summer. Blacks born since 1948, noted Bennett, were of a different mold from those who had spearheaded the civil rights movement of the fifties and sixties. They had not felt the pains of segregation, and many of them had seen racist signs only in history books. Now black youth were attuned to popular music, clothing styles, and habits of mind far removed from those of a Rosa Parks or Fred Shuttlesworth in their youth. "The New Generation is freer on the inside," Bennett said with some concern, but it has "a new and different and profoundly ambiguous orientation to the roots and archetypes of the Black experience."[46]

Ambiguity was perhaps a more appropriate word than indifference, for both blacks and whites. Changes effected in the sixties had by 1978 brought blacks and whites together without the old restrictions. They had become fellow workers, friends in some cases, and most importantly, participants in the common American socio-economic mainstream. If this was a hint of partial realization of King's dream of brotherhood, it also complicated dealing with unrelenting problems like poverty.

Lack of motivation, then, was one of the obstacles to renewal of SCLC. There were ample reasons for the organization to continue, but they would have to be defined in terms relevant to the new situation. Phase Two logic, or emphasis upon the economic dimension of the black experience would of necessity be the central focus. Here, a second barrier came into view, only to be blurred by the first. Not all blacks or even a majority were poor. Those who were well off, or affluent, could not always see their situation in the light of a 'prophetic' mission of the black race any more than rich white people could view themselves in relation to their own poor.

Marching Again in the South

But there was little time to ponder these attitudinal problems. As Lawson had suggested, it was a time for action, and the year following the Camp Calvin retreat found SCLC busily seeking to implement its rebuilding program. Dr. Lowery met several times with Jimmy Carter upon the President's request and once with the Black Forum. He also traveled widely to rejuvenate local chapters and try to revitalize grassroots support. Other SCLC officials followed a similar pattern. National executive director Hosea Williams and his special assistant Tyrone Brooks were involved in a number of undertakings designed to enlarge SCLC's impact on American society. Brooks had been communications director from 1973 to 1977 and now directed field operations. Named 'Young Man of the Year' by the U. S. Jaycees and 'Outstanding Young Man of the Year' jointly, Brooks was a talented vigorous activist who believed deeply in reaching out to people in need exactly where they were, on the streets, in jail, on small farms, or wherever. He was involved in several major cases pursued by SCLC, including the Pensacola deaths, Operation Military, and defense of the Wilmington Ten.[47]

Many others in SCLC were engaging in local and regional campaigns. It was symbolic of the renewed vigor that SCLC leaders spent the first hours of 1978 negotiating a settlement of a strike against Atlanta's Piccadilly Cafeteria which had begun on December 29. Others were involved in a march in Palatka in Putnam County, Florida in behalf of black students and job opportunities. An incident of corporal punishment of a seventeen-year-old black student at Palatka High School triggered the march, but it broadened into a larger effort to secure jobs, educational opportunities, and a human relations board in the town. It was a small demonstration of about sixty marchers, but Fred Taylor and Tyrone Brooks were there for SCLC.

A more extensive campaign was led by SCLC in Gadsden, Alabama in the wake of the January 20, 1978 death of a black youth, Collis Madden, Jr., who was shot some fifteen times by police after he was caught reportedly driving under the influence of alcohol. Several black organizations and public officials took the matter very seriously, and SCLC decided to hold demonstrations in Gadsden on the tenth anniversary of Dr. King's death on April 4, 1978. The theme was "The Right To Live," as about 3,000 people participated in the memorial march from the site of Madden's death to the county courthouse. There they demanded the dismissal of the officers who had shot him, as well as reforms in local government and businesses.[48] SCLC stayed in Gadsden after April 4.

Meanwhile in late March, President Carter sent to Congress a proposal to establish means to ease a number of urban problems. It included steps to coordinate and simplify existing federal programs and to add several to assist the hardest pressed areas. Carter also encouraged neighborhood voluntarism to help the unemployed and poverty-stricken.[49] Also included were several projected additions to the cultural and social life of cities, such as parks, social and community centers, art exhibits, and immediate relief for the very poor. Some 14% of the planned $8.3 billion would go to state and local relief along lines of President Ford's Anti-Recession Revenue Sharing Program. The bulk of the funds, though, were earmarked for businesses, in order to stimulate economic growth and trickle down benefits for the masses. That made the Carter plan vulnerable to the criticism that it was neither new nor comprehensive, but the same old story of making labor and cities dependent upon big business.[50] On the more positive side, the proposal did call for increased funding for the Comprehensive Employment Training Act (CETA) program established in 1973 to assist the hard-core unemployed. With black youth unemployment topping 49% in 1978, that much at least was welcome news in several cities.[51]

The basic problem of the Carter proposals was the high cost. With the economy declining, there was little hope that they could be fully implemented. Furthermore, they would likely have little effect on unemployment. Some felt that passage of the Humphrey-Hawkins Full Employment and Balanced Growth Bill, which Carter had finally endorsed in early 1978, was a necessary accompaniment to the urban aid plan. Sponsored by the late Hubert Humphrey and black California Congressman Augustus (Gus) Hawkins, the bill aimed at a 4% interim unemployment rate by placing full employment above balanced growth and requiring the President to plan for it. SCLC, along with a number of other black organizations, strongly supported the Humphrey-Hawkins Bill and argued that its passage would be the best way to honor the late Senator.[52]

When SCLC met for its annual convention in Birmingham in August, that bill and the *Bakke decision* were very much on the minds of the delegates. In step with current concerns, the theme of the meeting was "Economic Justice—Basic to the Dream," and a host of speakers addressed matters such as jobs and poverty relief. SCLC brought in Eleanor Holmes Norton of the Equal Employment Opportunity Commission, as well as President Carter's special assistant Martha Mitchell, and Curtis McClinton, Director of Special Projects for the Economic Development Administration. The Carter administration had already affirmed its continuing commitment to "an aggressive affirmative action program," but the delegates were troubled by the ambiguity of the case and were not altogether convinced that the administration meant what it said.[53]

If black leaders were troubled by uncertainty in the summer of 1978, the realities of the next few months were even more discouraging. In October, President Carter signed into law the Humphrey-Hawkins Act, hailing Humphrey as a "great and compassionate American who dreamed of the day when everyone who wanted a job could find a job," and he commended the 95th Congress for the bill and for extending CETA. Then Congressman Gus Hawkins interjected a realistic note as he said soberly that "I'm quite sure that none of us is so naive as to believe that this is the end."[54] Hawkins was right. The last quarter of 1978 brought more gloomy forecasts and a deficit estimate of almost $40 billion. With that came a growing grassroots antipathy to government spending that affected the November elections, confirming what *Newsweek* had referred to as "a revolution of falling expectations about what government can or ought to do."[55]

Taxpayers were rebelling against more taxes, and after the November 1978 elections, the new 96th Congress was deeply affected by the influx of moderate to conservative freshman legislators who believed that cutting the federal budget was an absolute prerequisite to economic recovery. Many of the older members were also convinced that fiscal belt-tightening was necessary to halt the spiraling inflation and growing federal deficit. A poll by *U.S. News and World Report* indicated that all of the new House members wanted budget cuts, largely outside the area of defense, anticipating the policies of the later Reagan administration. Over 23% were quite willing to cut social programs.[56]

In the meantime, President Carter was preparing a budget message to Congress for fiscal 1980. The press was quick to publicize the fact that the budget would seek to trim the deficit to $29 billion, partly by cutting into many of the same programs Carter had previously supported. This ominous sign disturbed Lowery, and in early December he issued a statement to the press charging the President with a "systematic retreat from his commitment to sustain the fight against unemployment and provide better services for the poor of this country."[57] Lowery insisted that Carter's administration was forcing the poor to bear the greatest burden of the budget balancing effort. Despite some energetic efforts, the President was unable to give an explanation that would satisfy Lowery or the other leaders like Jordan and Hooks who also called Carter to task.

SCLC then prepared a demonstration against Carter's budget-cutting, to coincide with the President's visit to Atlanta in January 1979 to participate in ceremonies marking King's fiftieth birthday. It was more than a token visit since Carter had just sent a proposal to Congress to make King's birthday a national holiday and was slated to receive the Martin Luther King, Jr. Nonviolent Peace Award. When the Carters arrived in Atlanta on January 14 for the ceremonies at Ebenezer Baptist Church, a large crowd of SCLC-led demonstrators were readying themselves for a different kind of greeting: a poor people's march protesting the new austerity program that they felt would undermine anti-poverty efforts.

Inside the church where King and his father had pastored, Carter spoke at length about King's contributions to American life and world peace. He also spoke critically of South African *apartheid* and hailed Young's bold stand for justice in the world as UN Ambassador for the United States. To the delight of many in the audience, the President announced his strong support for the King birthday holiday, saying "We must never forget his dream." When he was handed the Nonviolent Peace Award, Carter seemed genuinely pleased. "I come here grateful, and I accept this award not as an honor that I have earned, but as an affirmation that I share the tremendous progress left to be made." Carter believed that such progress could be made only through cooperative efforts around the nation and the world.[58] King's father added to the President's joy by describing him as "the greatest president in the world" and endorsed him for re-election.

Outside, the atmosphere was quite different. About 150 Iranian students gathered to protest U.S. support of the ousted Shah whose regime was rapidly collapsing. Soon the Shi'ite extremist known as the Ayatollah Khomeini would return to Teheran and topple the stop-gap government that succeeded Shad Pahlevi. Others in the crowd were shouting for jobs.[59] In Central Park, SCLC assembled about 1,000 marchers for a trek along Auburn Avenue behind a huge banner inscribed with "SCLC: Poor People's Message to Jimmy Carter." At the front was Lowery, flanked by Abernathy, Reverend Ivory Simmons of South Carolina, and Julian Bond. Bond had been critical of Carter's 'band-aid' approach to fighting poverty. Several more organizational representatives were there, including NAACP local president John Evans, Reverend Ted Clark of the National Association of Minority Economic Involvement, and SCLC executive director Hosea Williams. When the demonstrators reached the police barricades, Lowery read a statement urging Carter to "Fulfill your campaign promise to aid the economically disadvantaged and heed your own call to the nation to solve the problems that still face those Martin Luther King, Jr. always championed: the poor and the oppressed."[60]

Carter was bothered by the demonstration, but his face was set now toward the tighter budget. A week later he presented his budget message, which, in his own words, was 'lean and austere.' CETA would see its public service jobs shrink from 625,000 in 1979 to 467,000 by the end of 1980. There would also be cuts in public works projects, free lunch programs, and loans for rehabilitation of poor neighborhoods.[61]

If there was a lesson in the experience in Atlanta it was surely that a 'poor people's message' as such had little bearing on national economic policy. Whether Carter's 1980 budget would help or hurt the poor depended upon how it affected the economy overall. Actually, the budget marked the end of an era. Since 1964, outlays for defense had been declining in percentage, as they had in all the major industrial states except the Soviet Union, and expenditures for human resources and social services had been increasing, from 29% in 1964 to 53% in 1980.[62] That defense consumed 23% of the total budget in 1980 was a reflection of wrong priorities to advocates of greater expenditures for social services, but Britain, France and West Germany and many other states hit hard by world economic problems were after 1979 holding the line of modestly increasing defense while limiting or decreasing their expenditures for welfare and other social items. In that sense the United States was part of a common global trend. With Soviet intervention in Africa and soon in Afghanistan (December 1979), came an even greater determination to increase NATO military strength in reaction to the new threat. Talk of enlarging jobs programs, welfare, and social services was not very influential anywhere in the Atlantic world as the seventies ended.

If the Atlanta demonstration against the new budget did not change it, no one in SCLC was surprised. Everyone knew that the federal budgeting process was too complex to permit reorientation on the basis of demonstrations. But Lowery and his associates in the march saw the act as symbolic and Carter as the focal point of a challenge to the priorities of the nation. The blacks who walked in the march were, furthermore, themselves symbolic of millions more who were in worse condition than the nation as a whole. That is what it was all about, an effort to accentuate the fact that seemingly logical decisions in allocating national funds affected the lives of common people, many of them already in dire need, now facing further decline. As the King Center honored Carter for his contributions to peace, SCLC was saying that what Martin King had done during his life was to identify with the poor and oppressed.

This was not the last time SCLC called into question national priorities in 1979. Just two weeks after the march in Atlanta, SCLC organized a conference in San Francisco to discuss the implications of the Jonestown, Guyana tragedy of late 1978. There, Congressman Leo J. Ryan, along with members of a delegation sent to investigate the cultic community of Jim (James Warren) Jones, was shot and killed on November 18 by terrorists at the Port Kaituma air strip.[63] At the same time, 913 people, many of them black, died in one of the most shocking spectacles of mass suicide and murder ever recorded. Men, women, and children clung together in death as they followed the fanatical People's Temple leader in forcing cyanide down the throats of babies and then poisoning themselves. Jones had apparently convinced them that Ryan's investigation was the prelude to a destructive attack upon their commune and that everyone should die voluntarily and with dignity.

If there was dignity in the orgy of death at Jonestown it was difficult for anyone to see. It was an unabated tragedy, and in its wake came official investigations to determine why it happened and whether there was any improperity in government dealings with the commune. SCLC's conference in San Francisco in February was also concerned with the systemic factors that caused people to turn to this kind of escapism. Lowery had gone to Jonestown shortly after the suicides, in December 1978, to see the site of the tragedy. With him were Dr. Harry B. Gibson, Ombudsman of the Board of Global Ministries of the United Methodist Church, and Dr. Nelson H. Smith of Birmingham, a past president of the National Progressive Baptist Convention and then SCLC chaplain. "I have never heard anything like it," said Lowery after listening to a taperecording made just before the mass suicides, "and I hope I never hear anything like it again."[64]

At the San Francisco conference about 200 clergymen and interested observers, some of whom knew members of the Jonestown commune, wrestled with the meaning of the suicides. Lowery expressed the feeling that Jonestown was a manifestation of disillusionment. He took it as an object lesson that the nation should become more sensitive to people's needs so that they would not be lured into "Promised land" illusions that could end in such nightmares as the one in Guyana had. Lowery doubted that the suicides were all "voluntary," since he had seen bullet wounds and injections on some of the bodies that were photographed. He also wondered whether the federal government had done all it could have in advising and aiding the communards.

Dr. Kelly Miller Smith, a perennial NAACP and SCLC leader and one of the principal organizers of the conference, put Jonestown in the perspective of problems blacks faced. "Wherever black life is disrespected, Jonestown is there, the bush is burning and God is speaking. . . . Jonestown is the blatant racism of southern Africa. . . Jonestown is a national budget which disregards that which will sustain and prolong the lives of blacks and other poor while increasing the capacity of the nation to take away human life through deadly warfare."[65]

The House of Representatives was also interested in the implications and causes of the Jonestown suicides and appointed a committee to investigate. In May 1979 its report reached some of the same conclusions the black religious leaders had in February. The report criticized the State Department's handling of the crisis and the breakdown of communications with the American Embassy in Guyana. Although the long report did recognize the difficulties involved in dealing with such a situation, it recommended better procedures of investigating such groups and suggested detailed studies of cultic activities.[66]

This issue, seemingly peripheral to a history of SCLC, was in fact quite germane to both the condition and message of the organization. It illustrated the wide gap between what many blacks were saying about national priorities and foreign policy and the policies of the national government. Correctly or not,

SCLC was convinced, as were many other black organizations, that the issues and national policy were all interconnected. Poverty, alienation, violence, and disillusionment with the mainstream society were viewed as inseparable. Despite the rising tide of conservative rhethoric, many blacks believed the United States needed to re-direct, not just modify its national priorities.

Because of the uncertainties of the end of the decade a number of black spokesmen and civil rights advocates feared that not only was progress slowing, but was actually being reversed. Lerone Bennett told a gathering in Philadelphia in March 1979 that black Americans were facing their "most severe crisis since the Civil War." About the same time, Civil Rights Commission research writer Larry Riedman said that "many of us who have worked for the cause of civil rights have voiced a fear akin to panic that the growing social and political restiveness of the American public imperils the civil rights gains of the past few decades."[67]

SCLC's efforts at rejuvenation, therefore, were undertaken in less than auspicious circumstances. Answers for the country's economic problems were elusive, giving rise to a resurgence of American nationalism, fiscal conservatism, opposition to anything suggestive of unearned welfare, and heightened concern about the neo-imperialism of communist countries. The pendulum was swinging to leaders like Ronald Reagan and his supply-side economic advisers.

Black elected officials were at best only cautiously hopeful. An *Ebony* poll of 4,500 of them in 1979 revealed that more than 60% did not believe that the dreams of the fifties and sixties had been fulfilled. They expressed doubts about many aspects of black progress. Some 30% said that they believed that it would take another 100 years to achieve full equality of the races in the United States, and 23% said that it would never be achieved.[68] A quarter century had passed since the *Brown* case of 1954, and while most overt barriers to advancement had been removed, the Civil Rights Commission reported that many lingering inequities marred the social landscape. The possibility of a permanent underclass of hopelessly poor people loomed large.[69]

"I am sorry to look into the 1980's," wrote Benjamin Hooks, "and see such a bleak future for civil rights." The NAACP director saw only limited progress in the seventies and dim prospects for the new decade. "The 1980's will, no doubt, perpetuate the racial superstitions that track Blacks and Whites in segregated schools, and divide neighborhoods according to class and race." Yet there could be changes, Hooks surmised, if blacks counted on effort, not self-pity or anger, or even protest, and if whites were willing to cooperate and squarely face their own responsibilities.

To win racial justice, we need an educated and aware people—the involvement of freedom fighters from all walks of life. We need our young people and our senior citizens. We need our White people working with Black and Brown people. We need Christians and Jews. We need laborers and professionals to rekindle a spirit of "can" and "will." [70]

"Let modern dictatorship not serve as an alibi for our conscience. We have failed to fight for right, for justice, for goodness; as a result we must fight against wrong, against injustice, against evil."

Abraham J. Herschel

12

Fighting Back in the Eighties

On balance, the discouragement felt by virtually all the leaders of civil rights organizations at the end of the seventies was not entirely justified. Much progress had been made, both in terms of specific advancement of blacks and other minorities, and public attitudes. And even the sense of decline had its positive side. "Civil rights advocates *can* turn this crisis into opportunity," wrote Larry Riedman, "*can* turn this reaction into reform and progress, but we will have to modify or abandon some of our most familiar characterizations of our fellow citizens, our adversaries, and our way of work."[1]

As part of the Civil Rights Commission's mid-Atlantic office, Riedman knew much about the "changing climate" of the civil rights movement, but he felt that its leaders should avoid reeling back in fear and pessimism since this would not only deny the positive attitudinal changes already achieved but also weigh heavily on all specific efforts to move ahead.[2] At best, however, the movement faced some very serious difficulties.

An important aspect of the new climate of civil rights advocacy was a kind of leveling of public opinion on treatment of blacks and other distinct social categories. Polls showed that slightly more than half the population (52%) believed in 1979 that minorities were treated equally or better than whites and some 39% thought that blacks received "too much" special consideration by employers.[3] Affirmative action—especially forms that mandated quotas—was under attack, as were busing for racial integration, many job training and welfare programs, and virtually all social entitlements requiring large government expenditures. Anti-liberal sentiment was one of the decisive factors in the new mood, but cost and tough questions about the efficacy of government aid were also crucial. From many corners came data suggesting that welfare had actually harmed its recipients and should be entirely revamped or abandoned.[4]

A number of black scholars, especially economists and social scientists, added their own distinctive criticisms. This was not as new as it seemed to some journalists, but neither was it trivial. Both the scope and intensity were larger than in the past, and the arguments were more candid. To some of them, racial discrimination was an overworked issue, especially by leaders of activists organizations like SCLC and PUSH. "For years now," wrote black economist Walter E. Williams of George Mason University, " 'Black leaders' have been pretending that all the problems of black people can be attributed to white racism."[5] Williams saw this as an error and suggested that a better approach would be to encourage more self-reliance and capital development, along lines of the Reagan administration's emphases after 1981.

Not all black leaders were making white racism their point of departure, and in some ways such arguments distorted their real views. Nor did most of them see as the answer to blacks' problems a larger intervention by government, except where government had a natural role in protecting rights and forcefully setting an example of equitable treatment. On the contrary, they were often intensely concerned about reducing welfare dependency. But the other image was projected, and they had to contend with it.

Some detractors were less generous than the scholarly critics and were blasting the black leadership of the civil rights movement as misled and misleading. "Someday," wrote Richard Viguerie in his manifesto announcing that the "new right" was ready to lead the country, "an American black is going to become a great leader of his people by pointing out that those

354

blacks they thought were kings had no clothes on all this time.'' One wonders who would be included in such a list, and what value there would be in disparaging their achievements, but Viguerie did say that "most" black leaders since the fifties had "led blacks down a path of slavery, deceit, and poverty."[6]

More disturbing still was the resurgence of racist organizations. From 1975 to 1980, an intense propaganda blitz by the Ku Klux Klan that emphasized the nonviolent and Christian nature of the various klan groups brought impressive gains. Membership grew in that period from about 5,500 to over 10,000. And that was only the hard core. Another 75,000 to 100,000 received its white supremacist literature or contributed financially to more than a dozen klan subsidiaries or branches. The membership was also younger on the average, indicating that the Klan had made new inroads.[7] It is true that some Klan organizations were more symbolic than actively violent, but events demonstrated that neither traditional racism nor racial violence was dead. SCLC had a number of significant confrontations with both, as did many Jews and other blacks.

Countering the 'Assault on Black life'

SCLC was not alone in describing the collective impact of these trends as an "assault" on black life. But the leadership conference was one of the most vigorous proponents of that view. In its convention themes of 1979 and the early eighties, in its local campaigns and agendas of the period, and its criticisms of federal policies SCLC continually warned against the possibility that past gains could be lost and that violence was still a reality in race relations. Moral commitment was flagging, SCLC officials argued, and the place to begin a rejuvenation was precisely in that sphere. "Racism is still a problem," Lowery told a Methodist ethnic leadership seminar in New York in late 1979, "because we have not dealt with it from the moral perspective." Repeatedly, he and other SCLC spokesmen tried to re-establish the close linkage between conscience and public action that had been the dynamic of the nonviolent movement for decades.

Naturally, there were some disagreements on this spiritual dimension of the movement. The King tradition had never claimed that white racism was the universal cause of blacks' difficulties or that political actions were all that was needed to correct them.[8] On the other hand, King had often called government to task for its failure to lead adequately in matters of social justice, and SCLC's tradition had incorporated the same strategy. Thus, a complicated pattern emerged by the late seventies. Like the general public, SCLC was critical of governmental policy, but for different reasons. To separate the moral appeal for decisive government and public involvement in "fulfilling the nonviolent dream" from seemingly partisan politics was more difficult than ever before in the movement's history. To cut through rhetoric and political labeling with community-building faith was the largest challenge SCLC or any other advocacy group faced as the new decade began.

The last year of the seventies set the stage for the specific efforts of SCLC to move ahead in this direction. In the spring of 1979 the board of directors met in Washington to plan strategies and to try to resolve an internal dispute over the recent dismissal of executive director Hosea Williams. While there, Lowery spoke before the Senate Judiciary Committee in behalf of the King holiday bill. He told the committee that it was imperative to honor King this way because of his importance to blacks and to the nation as a whole. King, said Lowery, had given "all Americans—white, black, red, and brown—a new sense of worth and dignity." Adequate recognition would include more than an observance of his birthday each year. It would also demand, said the SCLC president, efforts to realize his "woefully unfulfilled" vision of society by getting on with the task of fighting poverty and other problems that had concerned him most. Simply to commemorate his birthday without trying to pursue those substantive issues would be, Lowery averred, "a Pyrrhic victory."[9]

Neither the holiday nor an anti-poverty program had much chance of passage in Congress in 1979. The economic arguments against a special day for King were even more compelling than before, and critics were again raising questions about King's personal life, presumably hidden in the sealed FBI spy tapes, as well as the political affiliation of some of his associates. As for any kind of massive anti-poverty funding, the odds were even more remote. In the board meeting, Lowery spoke of the virtual "betrayal of the poor" at the federal level and chided President Carter for failing to "pursue justice for blacks and poor at home" with the same vigor he brought to getting a peaceful resolution of differences between Israel and Egypt.

At the same meeting, the internal rift reached a new level of intensity. For several weeks, Lowery and members of the board of directors had been critical of Hosea Williams' outside involvements and urged him to give more time to his job as executive director. Finally he was dismissed, and the board upheld the decision during its Washington meeting, despite fervent displays of support for Williams by a number of his friends and associates.[10] Williams was hurt and angered, and some of his close aides, notably Tyrone Brooks, rallied to him. By mid-April tensions ran high, and an incident at SCLC national headquarters attracted media attention, as Brooks and Robert Johnson refused to leave the building when its doors were locked and security guards posted. When Williams arrived on the scene he charged that this "destroys every ounce of nonviolence that Dr. Martin Luther King stood for."[11] Lester Hankerson also protested locking the "poor people's doors," and bitter feelings and words marred relations among people who still shared much common ground, but, for the moment at least, were openly at odds.

These differences were real enough and the affair did engender ill-will and some embarrassment. In the long run, however, it did not have the disastrous results some people expected. The Lowery administration made some adjustments in personnel, and Williams and Brooks continued to be active in the nonviolent movement. Williams had his own organization to run, as well as various business involvements, church activities, and serving in the Georgia state legislature. He retained a strong sense of identity with King and expressed the view that his dismissal was inappropriate since King himself had made him "field-general in the sixties."[12] King's vision of justice was deeply instilled in Williams' thinking. "That dream never died. . . never died. You see Martin gave us hope. . . The dream will never die." As for SCLC, Williams felt that it had lost or modified some of its traditional emphases. In his view, it had to remain true to what it did best. SCLC could never outdo the Urban League or the NAACP in their special areas of expertise, but SCLC could, and must "be what Martin intended for us to be. Otherwise we might as well dissolve."[13]

Tyrone Brooks also became a state legislator and remained active in nonviolence as head of the Martin Luther King, Jr. Movement. More of a fellowship than an organization as such, it favored: helping the poor, educating children in the traditions of nonviolence, anti-racist education, among others. Brooks was especially concerned about making sure children knew, and were equipped to build upon, the nonviolent tradition. And as time passed he assimilated the 1979 crisis into his pluralistic perspective on black unity. There were always differences among black reform leaders—no less in the sixties than in 1979. Rather than perpetuate serious disagreements, however, Brooks felt that "We need to talk about how we can come together, to develop a deeper commitment and strategies for the 1980's and 1990's and into the year 2000, to talk about fulfilling the dream of Martin Luther King."[14]

These were not easy times for anyone involved with SCLC or who still loved the memories of previous attachments to it. There were some—among them pivotal leaders of the campaigns of the sixties—who wondered whether the rift was actually a signal that SCLC had outlived its time. Howell Raines recorded the emotional turmoil of Dorothy Cotton as she viewed the crisis.

Suddenly, tears splashed down Dorothy Cotton's smooth brown cheeks as she spoke of the power struggle raging within the Southern Christian Leadership Conference. It's a disservice to SCLC and to Martin Luther King, Jr.'s memory to let happen what's happening now. . . If SCLC's purpose has been served, somebody ought to be big enough to let it go, let it die.[15]

These were difficult words for Cotton, who had worked for some twenty years with SCLC, and in fact she had not given up on the organization. But her last few years in Atlanta were spent working at the King Center, and from there she moved to a position in a major university. After 1979 she could be seen occasionally at SCLC conventions, including its Silver Anniversary celebration in Birmingham in 1982.

SCLC did not quit. Before April ended, Hosea Williams was replaced by veteran activist C. T. Vivian, who, as we have seen, was one of the many young people attracted to SCLC in the freedom ride period and who previously had held offices in the organization. Lowery welcomed Vivian with the comment that "He brings a wealth of experience and fresh vigor to this position." Vivian expressed his own delight at being back and said that SCLC "probably has more to say in this period than in the last ten years."[16] Coming from Vivian that was a particularly meaningful comment. He knew the realities of the nonviolent movement and was toughminded enough to avoid naive optimism.

Vivian cited as his top priority bringing in people with expertise and consulting with the community for programmatic input. As for direct-action, he said that protests would be used selectively where "necessary and meaningful."[17] In many ways Vivian was the epitome of the metamorphosis of the freedom-riding youth of the sixties. Once vice-president of the Nashville Christian Leadership Conference and one of the organizers of the freedom rides into Jackson, Mississippi, he had also served as director of affiliates and was instrumental in putting together the campaigns in Danville, St. Augustine, Birmingham, Albany, and Selma. Furthermore, Vivian had been a member of the SCLC board of directors and a special adviser on African affairs and had once led the Chicago chapter. Although intended as an interim executive director, Vivian took on his new role with the vigor of a permanent officer.

Other addenda were made to the SCLC staff at this time. A former SNCC organizer, Reverend Thomas Brown, became administrative assistant to the president, a newly established position that continued to have importance well into the next decade. Brown was pastor of the Ebenezer Baptist Church in Indianapolis and had taught religion at Bishop College in Dallas, Texas. He, too, had spearheaded reform campaigns and was a veteran of the voter registration drives of the early sixties in North Carolina, Texas, and Alabama.[18]

Vivian and Brown were joined in the reshuffling by Reverend Albert T. Sampson, another former King associate, and young Rick Dunn, a journalist who had graduated from Henry W. Grady School of Journalism at the University of Georgia. Sampson became national program director, a position for which he was particularly well-suited because of his background in promoting education, housing, and economic opportunities for blacks and poor. He had been involved in the Lester Maddox-Pickrick Restaurant case and in 1968 had brought the first group to Resurrection City in Washington. The younger Dunn had missed the movement of the sixties, but was eager to be a part of the contemporary movement and reflected the style of the newer black activists who appreciated the past but wanted to see tangible progress in the present.[19]

Another new member of the SCLC team was Reverend Albert E. Love, who was eventually given the title of director of voter registration and administration. A strongly built athlete and former Air Force officer, Love drew metaphors from his athletic experience. He compared SCLC to a team which had "peaked too soon" but still had capability for victory, and he closely linked his Christian faith with social activism. If the specialities of other organizations like the NAACP and the Urban League were distinctively theirs, SCLC had its own 'lane' to follow. To him, that SCLC distinctive was to carry out the liberating ministry to the poor and oppressed with which Christ himself had identified: "The spirit of the Lord is upon me because he has anointed me to preach good news to the poor. . . to proclaim release to the captives and recovering of sight to the blind, to set at liberty those who are oppressed." Love totally rejected the view that the slower pace of change in the movement was an indictment of its relevance. If SCLC remained faithful to its tasks, said Love, the desired results would come eventually. "We are barely weaned," he said of SCLC. "We are just twenty-five years old."[20]

Others who had been with SCLC for years remained on the Lowery staff: Claudette Matthews, Elaine Tomlin, Hattie Brooks, Fred Taylor, Lester Hankerson—until his retirement from active work—R. B. Cottonreader, and experienced field workers like Frederick Moore who had generally remained outside the national limelight. Newer ones like Bernice Alexander, Peggy Perry, Elaine Day, Eddie Mathes, and many more became part of a national office staff that numbered about twenty by the early eighties. In addition, the network of affiliates and chapters continued to grow.

Soon, Reverend E. Randel T. Osburn re-joined the Atlanta-based national staff. Coming from Cleveland, Osburn had been almost totally immersed in direct-action as long as he could remember. A native of Alabama and a first cousin of Martin Luther King, Jr., Osburn had long been associated with SCLC. His background in the sit-ins and anti-war protest gave him rare experience in nonviolent confrontation, and he was the youngest person to be chosen project director by King. In all this and later work in Louisville and Cleveland, he came to know the joys and pains of the movement. Over the years he was jailed more than sixty times and beaten to the point of requiring hospitalization more than twenty times. He was also extremely active in anti-war protest, political election campaigns of hundreds of black and pro-civil rights candidates, and travel to several countries to promote peace. Osburn also established an organization for providing housing to low and moderate income families. And with all this, he worked in education and youth development, establishing, among other things, the Martin Luther King Youth Foundation. At first an SCLC vice-president and special aide to Lowery in the early eighties, Osburn eventually became director of chapters and affiliates.[21]

With this new team taking shape, SCLC moved beyond rebuilding to enlargement of operations. Fighting poverty and discrimination remained its central concern, but with the increase of racial violence in many parts of the country, it also stepped up its counteroffensive against racist propaganda and crime. Thus, for SCLC 1979 was a year of economic campaigns, anti-Klan programs, and attempts to define an agenda to counter the apparent mood of indifference. In the spring, Lowery and others traveled to the Jeanerette area of Louisiana to support poverty-stricken sugar cane workers. Conditions there were so bad that the CBS *Sixty Minutes* had done a special exposé, and SCLC followed with its own surveillance and protests.[22] In another economic campaign in the South that same spring, SCLC joined hands with a number of families in Harris Neck, Georgia who were attempting to regain land lost during World War II when it was claimed as an emergency air base. In addition, SCLC continued to speak out in behalf of the hundreds of black farmers who were losing land at alarming rates.[23]

But it was violence that triggered SCLC's most vigorous public protest campaigns of 1979 and the early eighties. In May 1979, SCLC officials went to Decatur, Alabama to lead a commemorative demonstration in behalf of Tommy Lee Hines, a twenty-five-year-old retarded black man arrested in 1978 on a rape charge. R. B. Cottonreader was sent to Decatur to initiate the protest, and a tent city reminiscent of Resurrection City was erected and named "Justice City."[24] The Ku Klux Klan came, too, and held counter-demonstrations. The result was extensive violence that injured many and killed several, including two Klan members. There was also an attack on Mrs. Evelyn Lowery as she drove along the march route into downtown Decatur.

When Joseph Lowery heard that there was a plot to kill him in Decatur, it was decided that Evelyn would not march that day but ride along slowly behind the marchers as they made their trek into the little Alabama town which stretched out along one main street. As they rounded a bend near the downtown business district, hooded Klansmen pushed through the crowd toward the marchers. Shots rang out and pandemonium broke loose. Two black marchers, Larry Lee Smith and Bernice Brown, suffered head wounds, and police fire apparently struck one klansman in the chest, and another was hit in the leg. Lowery was spirited to safety by aides.

As the march came to a halt, the cars behind it could not move. Sitting in the second car behind the demonstrators, Mrs. Lowery realized that she was sandwiched in and the assailants knew the Lowery car. Bullets ripped into the vehicle, one of them striking the visor near her head, and she instinctively dropped to the floor. Broken windshield glass was all over her as she waited for what seemed an eternity, not daring to move. She had no way of knowing what happened to her husband, but feared he had been shot. She could hear police officers, she recalls, addressing the individuals by name and telling them not to shoot. After some minutes Mrs. Lowery managed to get the car moving again, and darted away. From there she went to a church where, after more moments of distress, her husband arrived. Both were safe, but more than ever aware that racial hostility was not simply a problem of the past and that public service in civil rights could still bring life-threatening dangers.[25] Relieved that his wife was all right, Lowery saw in the ordeal a providential escape and seemed to be steeled in his resolve to go on with the task in Alabama.[26]

From this disturbing incident came an SCLC-led "March Against Fear and Injustice" which drew support from, among others, the Congressional Black Caucus. On June 9, about 3,000 people participated in the march in Decatur, this time better controlled by the presence of heavily-armed state troopers. But Klan leader Bill Wilkinson was there with his followers marching in defiance of the demonstration. SCLC's literature explained that the purpose of the march was to counter "the rising level of racism that threatens to deny the basic rights of life, liberty, and justice to all black Americans."[27] Again, the old familiar cries of "outside agitation" were levelled at SCLC for its intervention in the Hines case.

But there was a deeper meaning to the protest. For more than a century, one of the Klan's major sources of strength was fear. Steadily over the years blacks had learned that intimidation was the key to the Klan's hold on their minds and were beginning to counter it at its roots. Klan propaganda was now rebutted by means of information, protests, and appeals to public officials to vigorously enforce the laws. What happened in Decatur was the prelude to a much larger effort by several organizations, including SCLC, to counter the physical and psychological effects of violence and threatened violence.

Before the end of summer, there were other such incidents, including one in Birmingham where a young black woman, Bonita Carter, was shot and killed by police who assumed that she was aiding a robber as he held up a store. A citizens' review committee concluded that she was actually a victim of the black man who committed the robbery and forced her to drive the intended get-away car. She had complied, they determined, in order to save her life.[28] In alliance with chapter head Abraham Woods, SCLC came into the city in July 1979 to demand the dismissal of the police officer who shot her, and a revamping of the mostly white police department.[29] Field director R. B. Cottonreader warned that "Alabama is in the forefront of an increase of violence towards blacks and the resurgence of the Ku Klux Klan throughout the South. But the people of Birmingham should make a choice as to which image they would prefer to have—blacks would nonviolently fight a return to the racist ways of days gone by."[30]

The march that ensued in Birmingham on July 20 was almost as large as the Decatur demonstration, as some 2,500 people, including the mayor, marched. If it was small compared to the massive 1963 outpouring in the same city, it echoed the economic coercion approach of the earlier campaign. "We'll stop the cash registers from ringing," proclaimed Lowery, "and pretty soon you'll hear the Chamber of Commerce singing 'the Klan and Sands (the white police officer) will have to go.' "[31] Sands, as it turned out, was merely reassigned, but the following months did bring some notable changes in Birmingham. In November a black, Richard Arrington, was elected mayor. More blacks were added to the police force, and in some respects black participation in public life improved.

In August, SCLC met in Norfolk, Virginia for its twenty-second annual convention, where much emphasis was placed upon fighting violence with reason and information. C. T. Vivian declared that there would be no truly new South until the Klan was stopped.[32] After several sessions on the problem of violence, SCLC held a special workshop on the issue at the end of the convention, with about fifty people from eighteen states participating. It was an analytical, rational discussion, focusing on the historical roots, psychological and sociological dimensions of violence, as well as methods to combat it. An Anti-Klan Network was developed out of earlier precedents, and SCLC agreed to provide coordination and to disseminate current information to participating organizations and individuals. C. T. Vivian, who was deeply interested in countering the Klan, would soon step down from his interim directorship at SCLC and give full time to the anti-Klan movement.[33] SCLC itself continued to stress the anti-violence theme throughout the year and into the eighties.

By mid-1979 yet another sobering confirmation of the persistence of violence was coming into view in Atlanta, SCLC's home base, as a series of kidnappings and child murders began to plague the city. By the end of the year it was becoming apparent that they were probably not isolated, unrelated crimes. By 1980 a dozen black children had been ravaged, and Atlantans formed a Coalition to Save Our Children which worked with authorities and other concerned citizens to halt the murders and assist the families who had suffered losses.[34] Many groups tried to help, including SCLC and its subsidiaries. If there were doubts in some minds that SCLC's warnings of the dangers of violence were realistic, the tragedy in Atlanta certainly demonstrated the urgency of public safety and cooperation to achieve it.

The missing and murdered children in Atlanta grew in numbers in 1980 and 1981, and the chilling ordeal attracted national and world attention. Outside experts joined Atlanta authorities in the search for the killer or killers, and no one could be sure whether some crazed individual was perpetrating the crimes or a group venting its racist or subversive beliefs. In any case there were many impressive efforts to resolve the crisis and prevent further suffering. Within SCLC several people tried to learn from the tragedy. Albert Love saw in it a challenge to do more to save children, not only physically, but socially and spiritually as well. He wrote about the urgency of teaching children to survive, both in body and mind.[35] President Lowery spoke out in favor of interracial cooperation in dealing with the ordeal. "No, we will not as blacks against blacks, nor blacks against whites, be tricked into turning on each other. We shall turn *to* each other in common effort to rid our community of this murderous presence which threatens all—and then go on to build the kind of community that stands in adamant opposition to violence, injustice, and hatred."[36]

One of the groups most directly involved in trying to ameliorate the Atlanta crisis was a new organization within SCLC's ranks known as SCLC/WOMEN, founded in late 1979 by Evelyn Lowery. During the long months of the crisis, the organization reached out to the families of victims by raising money in their behalf, attempting to bring comfort to the bereaved, and supporting measures to protect children. Along with other organizations and the city government, SCLC/WOMEN helped plan safe summer programs for children and to undergird the families with as much support as possible. As early as December 1979, just two months after its founding, SCLC/WOMEN provided a Christmas party for Atlanta children and on Valentine's Day a "We Care Fellowship" for the families of victimized children to try to give some measure of encouragement.[37]

The stand taken by advocates of nonviolence during the Atlanta ordeal was not unimportant. Coming from responsible public officials, the King Center, SCLC/WOMEN, and many more sources, it injected voices of sanity into a volatile and distressing situation. Moreover, the many discussions and public projects to help the children and their families engendered a dialogue that led to broader considerations of the problems of violence, child abuse, family problems, and law enforcement.

Elsewhere in the nation, there were many other eruptions of violence during the decade's last year, including a bloody confrontation in Greensboro, North Carolina in early November. For months Greensboro had been torn by racial hostility, especially after the Ku Klux Klan in July showed the classic film *Birth of a Nation*, long considered a racist movie. Tempers were at high pitch by the time of the November 3 anti-Klan rally. With television cameras rolling, a fastmoving and violent sequence of events began, leaving five people dead from gunshots.[38] When authorities prosecuted some of the anti-Klan rally participants, SCLC joined with SOC (Southern Organizing Committee for Economic and Social Justice) in calling upon state prosecutors to drop all of the charges against them.

In that same city in early 1980 an interesting spectacle of another sort transpired. In conjunction with the Inter-Religious Foundation for Community Organizations (IFCO), SCLC participated in a commemorative rally in Greensboro, marking the twentieth anniversary of the sit-in of 1960. Now middle-aged, the four black men who had refused to move from the Woolworth's lunchcounter returned to Greensboro for the occasion. Governor James Hunt activated National Guard Troops to head off any recurrence of violence.[39]

As 1980 progressed the question of violence became even more pressing to SCLC, as well as to other advocacy organizations. Black leaders spoke openly of an "assault on black life" and saw it as a composite of increased resistance to reform, racial hostilities, certain trends in foreign policy, and public ignorance of what was going on in concentrated areas of poverty.[40] Some of the lethargy was shaken in May as Miami exploded in a sixties-style ghetto riot. For months the Florida resort city had smoldered while the courts prosecuted the case of four white police officers who had beaten to death a black insurance man. When the decision of the all-white jury to acquit the officers was publicized, the resultant upheaval left three dead and twenty-eight others hospitalized on May 17. After three additional days of rioting in Liberty City, sixteen more had died and over 400 had been hurt. Major papers and journals took note of the violence in Miami, as well as in several other cities like Boston, Wichita, and Wrightsville. "The ghettos are in worse shape economically," wrote *Newsweek*, than in the hottest of those bygone long hot summers.[41] And David Tatel frankly stated in the *Washington Post* that:

Unless we are prepared to deal with this fundamental fact, and to demand that our institutions ensure equal opportunity and equal justice in all aspects of American life, Miami will not be the last urban riot we will have read about in this decade.[42]

Mayor Maurice Ferre invited Andrew Young, along with Joseph Lowery, Jesse Jackson, and Benjamin Hooks into Miami to view the effects. They met with Attorney General Civiletti, who was heading a federal investigation into the killing of Arthur McDuffie, the black businessman whose death had sparked the crisis. But there was little anyone could do except marvel at the damage and the hostile signs saying "Pay Back!"

That same month the little town of Wrightsville, Georgia was the scene of yet another violent confrontation. On May 19, while Miami was torn by rioting, SCLC's Fred Taylor was attacked and beaten by a white mob on the steps of the Johnson County Courthouse in Wrightsville. Sheriff's deputies seized Taylor and spirited him to a nearby county and told him to stay out of the town. For fifteen years Wrightsville had been periodically troubled by racial tensions, and for the most part had been left behind in the civil rights movement. Although the population was 45% black, there were no black officials, and since 1966 hundreds of complaints had been lodged by blacks against discrimination on school buses, hiring practices, public facilities, and against rough handling by police. Some gestures of conciliation had been made by business leaders, but in early 1980 clashes between young blacks and whites triggered a resurgence of hostility in April and May. SCLC led marches in April and again in May and June, and the KKK appeared and sparred with demonstrators. Both the federal Justice Department and the

Georgia Governor's Office were involved, hoping to get whites and blacks to sit down and work out a compromise.

By early June an Assistant U. S. Attorney General announced the convening of a special grand jury in Savannah to investigate civil rights violations in Wrightsville, as SCLC continued to carry signs urging people to "Right the Wrongs in Wrightsville," and sponsored voter registration drives. On June 7, the leadership conference led a "March for Justice, Jobs, and Dignity" in the community and drew about 600 demonstrators.[43]

The story goes on, but enough has been said to underscore the reasons for the "survival" themes of SCLC and some other organizations as they planned their agendas for the nineteen-eighties. Along with the Atlanta child killings, and the distressing turn of events in international affairs in late 1979 as the Soviet Union invaded Afghanistan and the Ayatollah Khomeini's followers seized the American embassy in Teheran and took 52 Americans hostage, these numerous manifestations of violence came down hard on many blacks. Five of the twelve resolutions passed at SCLC's national convention in Cleveland, Ohio in August 1980 spoke pointedly to questions of violence and militarism.[44]

Foreign Policy and Black-Jewish Differences

SCLC's criticism of violence extended into its pronouncements on American foreign policy. A specific catalyst was the resignation of United Nations Ambassador Andrew Young in August 1979. Young had met informally with Palestine Liberation Organization UN observer Zehdi Labib in late July, and this infuriated the State Department and put President Carter in a very awkward position. Jews protested vehemently, and Young tendered his resignation to avoid trouble in the administration and to nip in the bud any increase of tensions between blacks and Jews, already alienated by their differing stands of affirmative action. But many black leaders, among them Walter Fauntroy, Julian Bond, Coretta King, Jesse Jackson and Benjamin Hooks—to mention only a small sampling—considered Young's exit as a dismissal. Fauntroy forcefully defended

Young's meeting with the PLO. "If we are to have peace," he said, "somebody had better talk to them."

Carter tried desperately to dampen the furor over Young's resignation and dispel the image that American foreign policy was in disarray. He sensed the gravity of the growing black-Jewish cleavage and spoke out frequently to both sides in an effort to mend it. "Black Americans and Jewish Americans," he proclaimed in Atlanta, "have worked side by side in the service of human rights, social justice and the general welfare. Both groups have a particular call on the conscience of each other and on the conscience of us all. Both groups have suffered too much pain, too much persecution, and too much bigotry to compound that suffering in any way."[45] The President also continued to praise Young despite the widespread criticism of his outspoken style and the meeting with the PLO representative. HEW Secretary Patricia Roberts Harris tried to promote black-Jewish harmony as well, comparing the two groups to brothers and sisters who fight occassionally but are actually on the same side.

The problem deepened in late 1979, however, as SCLC sent a mission to Lebanon to make its own move in behalf of Middle East pacification. In mid-September Dr. and Mrs. Lowery, Congressman Fauntroy, C. T. Vivian, Albert Sampson, former executive director Bernard Lee, Rev. Harry T. Gibson of the United Methodist Church Global Ministries, and photographer Elaine Tomlin left for a five-day trip to the unsettled country to confer with officials and present a proposal for a cease-fire. Traveling with the group at his own expense was columnist Samuel F. Yette of the *Afro-American*. Lowery and Fauntroy were the principal spokesmen as they met with private citizens and officials, including President Elias Sarkas and PLO chief Yasir Arafat.

Upon returning in late September Lowery stated that he considered the mission a success. It had opened some dialogue with the Palestinian refugees and more insight had been gained into the problems of Lebanon. The message of "peace through nonviolence" had been carried directly to an area where it was surely needed. Lowery noted that Arafat had agreed to give

SCLC's cease-fire proposal "serious consideration."[46] The SCLC president pledged to work further at securing a Middle Eastern peace through educational forums, a World Day of Prayer, pressure on Congress and the administration, and disclosure of what he had seen and heard in Lebanon.

Considerable support was forthcoming from black leaders, but critics abounded too. Among the prominent blacks who questioned SCLC's trip were Bayard Rustin and Vernon Jordan. Rustin had expressed in late August his opposition to dealings with the PLO and continued to warn against such implicit cooperation with terrorists. In a hard-hitting critique the veteran civil rights advocate said, "Naturally, this talk about the PLO as a 'civil rights' group or a minority movement within Israel has generated sympathy for Palestinians among black people. But this identification and even solidarity with the PLO is based on a terrible perversion of the truth, not only the truth about the PLO but the truth about our own movement as well."[47]

What Rustin meant was that the PLO had never uttered a word in behalf of nonviolence while the basic essence of the black movement was nonviolence. Nor had the Palestinian organization expressed any friendly disposition toward Israel, whereas American blacks had often done so. In Rustin's view, "any links, no matter how limited, would tacitly approve the rule of the gun."

For several weeks, Jordan decried the SCLC contacts with Arafat and the PLO. To a Catholic assemblage in October he urged black-Jewish harmony, stating that the only people who would gain from tensions between the two peoples "are the enemies of both groups."[48] He called to task those who made the trip, suggesting that the mission was inimical to the nonviolent tradition. "Black-Jewish relations should not be endangered by ill-considered flirtations with terrorist groups devoted to the extermination of Israel. The black civil rights movement is based on nonviolent moral principles. It has nothing in common with groups whose claim to legitimacy is compromised by cold-blooded murder of innocent civilians and school children."[49]

Such criticism put SCLC in an awkward position. Some

response was necessary to clarify just what the leadership conference was hoping to accomplish by dealing with a group like the PLO which had an undeniable record of terrorism. Lowery's replies were not very convincing to some, but he linked his Middle East trip to Christian witness and to questions about foreign policy priorities. He insisted that the contacts were "missional" not political. "We are not called upon to draw lines on maps, but to preach moral principles upon which those who will negotiate should base the maps."[50]

In truth SCLC was not anti-Semitic, but there were several past and present leaders who opposed Zionism and wanted a more even-handed American approach to dealing with Israel and the Arab peoples.[51] To some, Arafat was more of a "freedom fighter" than a terrorist. Wyatt Tee Walker, SCLC's contact person with the United Nations in New York, as well as Jesse Jackson expressed strong sentiments for the Arab cause without repudiating Israel.[52]

Lowery held to his position, but noted from time to time that he "had trouble getting (Jews) to understand" what he was attempting. He compared his efforts to those of King during the Vietnam War. Other black leaders reinforced SCLC's stand and even some who disagreed with the approach argued in behalf of SCLC's right to do what it did. NAACP head Benjamin Hooks spoke in favor of contacts with the PLO on the grounds that communication with them might help the American people to determine whether the organization was willing to abandon its terrorism and its official opposition to Israel's right to exist. Hooks also expressed concern about alleviating the tension between blacks and Jews by clarifying the reasons blacks strongly supported affirmative action.[53]

Thus, the SCLC mission to the Middle East was caught in a maelstrom of conflicting interests and political cultures. If American Jews were alienated by direct contacts with the PLO, this was only part of a larger set of issues that troubled black-Jewish relations. Indeed, some of them had come into focus at the height of the campaigns of the sixties, although Jews were pivotal partners in the civil rights efforts of blacks. Black nationalism, with its Pan-African linkage, had bothered many Jews in the period when SNCC and CORE turned to a basically all-black emphasis within their organizational structures. And as the integrationist organizations like SCLC and the NAACP spoke out strongly for affirmative action, Jews had additional reasons for concern. Quotas for employment, educational opportunity, and political participation struck Jews as dangerous and unfair. For Jews, quotas had operated negatively throughout their history and brought back memories of very restrictive Nazi policies, as well as less vicious discrimination against them in other times and places. Furthermore, the cultural ethos of Jews had emphasized the point that through hard-work and suffering they had managed to overcome racist and ethnic barriers to establish themselves in jobs and education. Why should blacks be favored by preferential policies if they had not been?

But SCLC's trip was not intended as a rebuff to Israel, but rather as a gesture of support for a broader American policy in the Middle East. And within a few weeks, events there took a very negative turn that overshadowed American-Israeli relations and black-Jewish tensions. Khomeini's seizure of the American embassy in Teheran in November 1979 quickly preoccupied the media, the Carter Whitehouse, and the nation.

Lowery called for denying asylum to the ousted Shah of Iran and for a hearing before an international tribunal to allow the Iranian people to voice their grievances. He praised Khomeini's decision to release the black and most of the female members of the American staff as a humanitarian gesture, calling it "an attempt to identify with the powerless and oppressed." But he had no inclination to support Khomeini and turned down an invitation to visit the hostages and quickly dissociated himself from the actions of the "student" kidnappers and the Ayatollah himself. The release of the women and blacks, said Lowery, "was rendered meaningless as long as the human rights of the hostages are being violated."[54]

SCLC spokesmen, including Lowery, praised the Carter administration's diplomatic efforts to free the prisoners and criticized American backlash against Iranian students in the United

States. Lowery argued that Americans had the opportunity in the crisis to show more humaneness toward Iranians in the United States than the Iranian government had displayed toward the hostages.

As it turned out, the Iranian crisis dragged on for more than 400 days, severely damaging the Carter administration and adding to the growing burdens on American self-image. At the same time, Soviet-American relations worsened in the wake of the December 1979 invasion of Afghanistan by Soviet troops to bolster a faltering puppet government. This caused the Carter administration to cancel grain sales agreements with the USSR and to prohibit American participation in the Olympic Games scheduled for Moscow in the summer of 1980. And NATO decided that same month, although not precisely because of Afghanistan, to deploy some 572 American Pershing II and cruise missiles in Europe, beginning in late 1983. That decision by Carter and the European allies stirred much debate at home and abroad, and within SCLC it engendered a new round of criticism of American foreign policy. It appeared that the U.S. was matching force with force and failing to see the dangers therein. When U.S. commitment to conventional and nuclear deterrence increased after Reagan's inauguration, SCLC became even more critical of this aspect of American international policy.[55]

Specifically, SCLC favored a freeze on nuclear testing by both the United States and the Soviet Union, and bold efforts by the American government to move forward on arms reductions. It also called at a more generic level for a redirection of foreign policy to give higher regard to the possible efficacy of nonviolence in international relations. At a Richmond, Virginia rally Lowery told the National Conference on a Black Agenda for the Eighties in early 1980 that blacks played too small a role in shaping American international relations. And part of the cost of that was a stifling of their experience and deep interest in nonviolent solutions to tensions. A 'new power' was needed, one based not on "bombs and bullets, macho and missiles, white and might" but one that was "sensitive and not arrogant, compassionate and not paternalistic, moral and not materialistic."[56] He and other speakers urged the State Department and White House to shift markedly to other than military answers.

The current, however, was flowing in a different direction. Philosophically, people of divergent political persuasions were united on the common core of this approach. That is, public opinion and official pronouncements alike sharply opposed war and the terrible prospect of using nuclear weapons. But even major religious leaders, especially from the new right, were supporting stronger deterrence and, interestingly, on grounds of love. To them it was imperative not to allow an evil force to overrun the innocent and endanger the institutions of democracy.[57] As the 1980 presidential election campaign developed during the spring and summer, it became apparent that the United States would put more, not less, emphasis upon a strong deterrent power. Candidate Ronald Reagan, especially, emphasized the need to upgrade American and NATO forces and spoke very negatively about recent Soviet actions and arms increases.

SCLC's primary focus remained on economics and social justice, but with a clear linkage to foreign policy. When the board of directors met in Tallahassee in the spring of 1980 it did not neglect international matters, yet most of its deliberations dealt with budget priorities. Again, SCLC challenged the Carter administration and Congress on their attitudes toward the poor and questioned the realism of budget-cutting as an answer for inflation.

> . . . the Carter Administration's and Congress' proposed budget cuts will not fight inflation. The cuts stress a balanced budget at the expense of social services. The contention. . . that balancing the budget by cutting food programs, welfare programs and jobs is based on political rhetoric and emotionalism and only serves to create false hopes for an end to present economic woes.[58]

Throughout the rest of 1980 SCLC articulated this kind of message while watching closely the presidential and congressional election trends. There was no endorsement of any of the presidential candidates. Democratic or Republican. SCLC's official position was to remain basically neutral so that the Democratic Party would not assume black support without earning it and the Republicans would not write off blacks. SCLC argued that blacks would be ready "to call upon whoever won the White House." Independent candidate John Anderson had strong appeal and was the only one to appear at SCLC's national convention in August 1980. But even he did not receive an SCLC endorsement.[59]

There was a certain paradox in the fact that SCLC criticized Carter but did not favor Reagan's election. SCLC representatives made an appearance at both political conventions, but as Carter and Reagan emerged as the nominees the prospects that either party would strongly support the Black Agenda seemed remote. Furthermore, the Moral Majority and other conservative religious groups targeted many liberals and moderates for defeat, among them people who had strongly supported civil rights over the years. As Reagan won by landslide proportions in the November elections, several of them fell, including George McGovern, Birch Bayh, and Frank Church.

As it became clear that conservatives gained across the board, SCLC was quick to lament the outcome. The Conference on Black Agenda for the Eighties and the Congressional Black Caucus—to which SCLC had ties, especially through Walter Fauntroy—had called for the election of a president and legislators who would support full employment and continuance of basic development and aid programs. But the new Reagan administration was motivated by what was called the 'supply side' economic theory that stressed less government involvement and more free play of capital producing investments, tax cuts, and slowing the pace of social program growth. In some cases, extensive cutbacks in programs were envisaged. Soon, "Reaganomics" appeared to SCLC and others as a very negative indicator for the future of social reform.[60]

Now the civil rights setting was altered even more. Reagan's inauguration was hailed by most as a victory for traditional values and American strength. The media spoke of an 'upbeat mood' in the United States, and conservatives felt that the traditional liberal Democratic coalition basis had been wrecked and people like William F. Buckley, Jr. rejoiced that the nation had perhaps at last moved 'up from liberalism.' Thus, the efforts at resurgence as defined by the agendas of SCLC and related organizations of the late seventies ran up against a formidable wall. At first, the U. S. Civil Rights Commission remained essentially the same, but gradually it also felt the pressure of the new conservatism and the administration's 'color blind' approach to civil rights, by which was meant opposition to both discrimination and reverse discrimination. Neither blacks nor whites would receive special consideration, although the Justice Department continued to affirm its commitment to enforcing vigorously the laws on civil rights.

Much rethinking was required, both in civil rights circles and beyond. Proponents of the new conservatism argued that the changes would actually help blacks, and as we have seen, some black writers agreed. The key, they felt, was to improve the economy, not to seek more and more from the public sector. Again, there was philosophical unity on the basic premise and political division on the means. Blacks who led organizations like SCLC were also speaking of more self-help and independence. But they also believed that it was crucial to hold the line on the basic laws on civil and human rights and for the government not to back away from its past commitments.

The Pilgrimage to Washington 1982

Positions were clarified somewhat in 1981 as Congress began to implement, if somewhat grudingly, much of the Reagan program for budget and tax cuts. The Reagan administration did not get all of the cuts it wanted, but substantially the new course was set. Governmental input into aid programs would be significantly lower and the attitude in Washington would be more negative toward anything smacking of liberalism.

Black advocacy leaders adjusted, although with major reservations. One can see this in comments by prominent spokesmen like Jesse Jackson to the effect that blacks would have to do more on their own. "White allies are good to have, said the

377

PUSH leader, "and are much needed, but we can only look to them for support not leadership." And in New Orleans in August 1981, SCLC officials and panelists said much the same thing. SCLC would try to launch a "new moral movement to redeem the soul of America." This was precisely the original theme of SCLC in the late 1950s, and it is quite instructive to see its reiteration in 1981, just one year before SCLC's silver anniversary.[61]

By then, the question of extending the 1965 Voting Rights Act had become the preoccupation of all the major civil rights organizations, including SCLC. This was basic to all other objectives since it affected the political potential of minority voters at a time when the ideological pendulum had swung markedly to the right. Virtually every black spokesperson and public official ardently urged passage of a strong extension bill.

Much more was involved than simply extending the life of the act. Already the 1964 law had been renewed twice and had been broadened beyond its original scope. Revisions of 1970 and 1975 had removed literacy tests and other barriers to voting and had demanded more from states where the act applied, including Justice Department prior approval for any changes in electoral laws.[62] Chances for extending the act beyond 1982 were good, but there were problems with certain important features of it. The central debate concerned whether the 'intent' or 'effect' criterion would be used to define violations.

If intent were the standard, black leaders feared that many restrictive practices might get by without legal reprisal. If a state law on voting did not visibly 'intend' to discriminate, there would be nothing the federal act could do to reverse it. On the other hand, those who favored the intent standard felt that the 'effects' approach was tantamount to a quota system. It would, they felt, open the door to using federal authority to force a certain percentage of black officials and thereby promote reverse discrimination.[63] The House of Representatives passed the renewal bill in October 1981 on the basis of the effects criterion, but in the Senate it met adamant resistance from Jesse Helms and other conservative opponents.[64]

378

President Reagan began an inquiry into the renewal question as early as June 1981, but for some months he waited for the Attorney General's report before airing his policy. In October Reagan strongly endorsed renewal saying that he was "whole-heartedly in favor. . . in principle of the Voting Rights Act."[65] But he had reservations about the intent criterion and called the House version "pretty extreme." Reagan was not certain that it was appropriate to apply the act only to specified states or to punish them for "sins that are no longer committed."[66] This was sharply opposed to what many black leaders were saying, since they not only saw evidence of continuing restrictions on voting but also because, to them, it was imperative for the nation to make an irreversible commitment to strong voting rights guarantees. Nor did black spokespersons want to see an easing of 'bail out' provisions that would facilitate a complying state's removal from the Voting Rights Act's jurisdiction.[67]

The list of black leaders who appeared before committees of the House and Senate in support of strong renewal is long. Coretta King, Ralph Abernathy, Jesse Jackson, Vernon Jordan, Julian Bond, and a host of others gave testimony in behalf of the bill.[68] SCLC officials were among them. In June 1981 Lowery spoke to the House Sub-Committee on Civil and Constitutional Rights, pointing to the "terrible price for these wares of freedom" paid by men and women of both races. He appealed to the legislators' sense of national welfare. "The so-called conservative tide in the nation need not be identified with racism. The nation needs the extension of this Act as support for those moral forces working daily to insure brotherhood and peace."[69]

Alabama SCLC state president John Nettles also made a hard-hitting appeal to the Congress. Intensely aware of resurgent racial tensions in his state, Nettles cited cases from 1980 and 1981 in which what he called "the iron hand" of resistance had succeeded in "blocking and impeding black registration efforts." Nettles expressed fear that if a strong act with prior approval of electoral law changes were not passed, there might be a "reign of terror in Alabama as unforgettable and as inglorious as our dark history following Reconstruction." While

Nettles' words were perhaps somewhat disturbing to the committee, his statement was couched in terms of interracial cooperation.

> You've enabled us through the Voting Rights Act to begin climbing towards the top of a very deep pit. We've been climbing steadily but we have not yet reached the top. The pit is twenty feet deep. The pole, the Voting Rights Act, is only fifteen feet. We're only ten feet from the top—half way. Taking the pole from us now—the Voting Rights Act—would cause us to descent rapidly to the bottom. I plead with you today to extend the pole ten additional years.[70]

There was much remaining debate throughout 1981 and part of 1982 as the Senate heard arguments for and against extending the Bill. Senator Helms and his associates worked hard to prevent passage. But blacks were moving simultaneously to pressure the Senate to pass a strong extension bill. Indeed, as SCLC's twenty-fifth anniversary approached, the Voting Rights Act became its primary political interest. In early 1982 the leadership conference joined an effort to free two black women, Julia Wilder and Maggie Bozeman, who had been convicted and sentenced to four-year and five-year prison terms in Alabama for violation of voter registration terms. Wilder, 69, and Bozeman, 51, had helped elderly and shut-in blacks to register. Their case triggered a major SCLC operation.

On January 9, 1982, Lowery, Cottonreader, Nettles, and several other experienced march leaders went to Carrollton, Alabama to demonstrate their support for Bozeman and Wilder, arguing that the women were simply trying to assist disadvantaged people to vote and certainly were not criminals in any equitable application of the term. Some twenty-nine organizations gathered there two weeks later in behalf of the two women, and the state Board of Pardons and Paroles agreed to transfer them to a work release program in Tuskegee. This plan, however, was unsatisfactory to SCLC and to the "National Coalition to Save the Voting Rights Act and Free Maggie Bozeman and Julie Wilder".[71] Other organizations, including the NAACP, were also involved.

The next month SCLC co-sponsored a 160-mile march from Carrollton to Montgomery, via Selma. Again, civil rights marchers crossed the Edmund Pettus Bridge in Selma as some of them had done seventeen years earlier. An impressive array of blacks and whites turned the 1982 march into a major affair. Among the participants were Dr. Martin Luther King, Sr., Mrs. Coretta King, John Lewis, Angela Davis, Andrew Young, Martin Luther King, III, Fred Shuttlesworth, and Tony Liuzzo, whose mother had died while assisting the 1965 marchers. Memories of 1965 were vivid as they began the long walk to the state capital. Prayer vigils, rallies, speeches, songs, and more than fifty miles of walking brought something of the sixties back to life.

In April, SCLC extended the march into a much longer one known as the Pilgrimage to Washington for Voting Rights, Jobs, and Peace. The 2,700 mile journey began on April 19 in Tuskegee and traced a path across Alabama, Georgia, the Carolinas, and Virginia before culminating with ceremonies on the steps of the Capitol in late June 1982. "Fired up" by a youthful enthusiasm, the nucleus of about six dozen pilgrims was joined at various points along the route by both private citizens and dignitaries. Everywhere they shouted "Fired up!" They sang songs, encouraged people to register and vote, and for three months got a taste of what it was like in the days of the extended voter registration campaigns.[72]

The Pilgrimage was more than a demonstration or an exciting summer vacation for the students, and the emotional and spiritual impact upon them was profound in many cases. The route was carefully planned to take the marchers through electoral districts where blacks comprised more than 30% of the population.[73] In many counties and cities the marchers assisted with registration and encouraged those already on the voting lists to effectively use their votes. All the while, the group was briefed on what was happening in the Congressional debate on the extension bill. With the pilgrims constantly was Mrs. Evelyn Gibson Lowery, and periodically her husband and other SCLC officers would join them at various junctures to bring information, encourage them when things did not go well, and to share in what was becoming a more intense experience than anyone imagined at the outset.[74]

Many of the young people on the 1982 pilgrimage had never done anything quite like it. Several, including Brenda Davenport and Kim Miller, had worked with the King Center training programs or local civil and human rights activities, but the long summer journey of 1982 gave them an upclose look at the best and the worst of black experience in the 1980's. Some of the dwellings which they visited along the route were barely tolerable, like islands of poverty in the midst of plenty. Both young ladies, who at this writing are working with SCLC national headquarters in youth activities and promotion, report the depths of feeling they had as they saw homes where safety and comfort were almost totally lacking and where people's spirits were drained by constant reminders that they had little political power and virtually no economic leverage. It was a far cry from their own homes and dormitory rooms. They, like many others, were moved and cared. In the final analysis, this was as important as anything else that summer. It became apparent that sensitivity could still be stirred when human need was viewed without the distortions of distance and purely factual reporting. Many of the participants were dedicated Christians who found in what they saw a way to express that faith through direct service.[75]

Young people enjoy fellowship and *esprit de corps*. And on this trip, there was much reminiscing about the spirited kick-off rally in Tuskegee where gospel singer Cleophus Robinson had electrified the group and John Conyers and others had sent them off like a team into a tough game.[76] Along the way there were opportunities to stay in a wide range of homes and witness the variety of experience of southern blacks in rural communities, cities, and small towns on the eastern fringes of the South.

Like any extended campaign this one had its good and bad moments. At times there was indifference, but most of the communities received the group well. Gradually the number of new voting registrants grew to the hundreds. Efforts were made also to follow up with subsequent programs to see to it that the summer's activities would not be lost to apathy later. In some cases SCLC was able to establish a local presence that developed into an affiliate group.

There were problems at various times. James Orange was arrested in Wilmington, North Carolina on a warrant dating from 1973 when he was charged in Edenton with failing to obey a police order to disperse during a demonstration. Actually Orange had turned himself in to the Atlanta police after his conviction *in absentia* in 1973, and because he was not extradited, assumed the case had been closed. But as some of the marchers demonstrated against Senator Jesse Helms in June, Orange was taken into custody. He was then taken to the North Carolina State Prison in Raleigh where he spent almost two weeks, refusing to eat for the duration. Governor James Hunt ordered his release, heading off a major demonstration in North Carolina's capital city.[77]

Meanwhile Senator Helms and a few others continued their determined effort to prevent passage of the House version of the Civil Rights Act extension. The Senate was struggling in the late spring with the question of whether to follow the proposals supported by Senator Oran Hatch and staunch conservatives like Helms. Hatch doubted that the Senate should accept the premise of black organizations that the House version was the best approach.[78] Helms was even more opposed to it and attempted a filibuster.

As the Pilgrimage neared Washington in mid-June and the momentum of the filibuster seemed to be intensifying, a compromise bill was brought about largely through the work of Republican Senator Robert Dole of Kansas. Dole's amendments retained the effects criterion but required that judges evaluate "the totality of circumstances" including the history of a particular locale's electoral standards to determine whether discrimination had been present. The compromise bill thus was a strong one that offered some comfort to those who feared that a quota system was in the offing. On June 16, the Senate choked off the filibuster and two days later renewed the Civil Rights Act for twenty-five years, extending it into the twenty-first century.

The renewed act contained strong provisions not unlike those passed by the House.[79]

As critics lamented the new act, SCLC and many other blacks across the nation rejoiced. Lowery hailed the Senate bill as a wise one and a victory for justice. When the SCLC marchers reached Washington a few days later, they were greeted in front of the Capital by Congressional leaders who informed them officially that the House had just unanimously passed the Senate's compromise bill. Lowery then urged the beneficiaries of the bill, "Now that we have extended our voting rights, let's extend our voting—Right!"

In at least four ways, the 1982 Pilgrimage to Washington was important to the Southern Christian Leadership Conference. First, it was the kind of activity SCLC had excelled in throughout its history and thus underscored the continuity that had been questioned by some observers and by certain key figures in the earlier campaigns. Historically, the SCLC ethos was based on direct-action, and this long journey across the South qualified in both a strategic and a substantive sense. Voting rights, jobs, and peace were abiding themes of SCLC's message, so that the pilgrimage flowed fundamentally from the organization's true identity.

Furthermore, the pilgrimage and other demonstrations contributed to the actual passage of the extension bill, although this is difficult to evaluate objectively. One thing is clear. The Congress knew of it and the other pressures being put on the Senate to pass a strong bill. The final version was passed, as it turned out, just a few days before completion of the SCLC campaign, but whatever disappointment was felt over not arriving in Washington before that was offset by the delight over the realization that the Voting Rights Act was secured till after the year 2000.

Thirdly, the 1982 campaign strengthened ties between the older and more experienced adults like James Orange, E. Randel T. Osburn, the Lowerys, and others, and the young people who provided so much of the energy of the long summer activity. This was important, indeed much more so than was known generally. Like all other activist organization, SCLC was in need of a sense of continuity with an emerging young generation of adults. The relative lack of drama in the movement had militated for years against drawing them in as the sit-ins had earlier. There is good evidence that what happened in 1982 was conducive to a higher personal enthusiasm for activism. Some, like Brenda Davenport and Kim Miller would not be able to let it go. The compelling memories of their work at the King Center and particularly in the summer campaign altered their personal plans, underscoring the fact that a clear sense of need could still draw young blacks into a cause deemed anachronous by outsiders. And these youth were college-educated, flexible, and in many cases deeply committed to their religious faith.[80]

A fourth element was of equal importance. The 1982 Pilgrimage to Washington brought the rebuilding of SCLC to a new plateau. It was the most ambitious undertaking of the national officers since the 1968 Poor People's Campaign of Abernathy's first year. The question of its relative weight in the complicated process of renewing the Voting Rights Act is less crucial than this aspect. SCLC had a good feeling about the 1982 effort, and that translated into encouragement of strengthening the affiliate structure, public education on the aims of the organization, and the inter-organizational connections of the leadership conference. Already that aspect of SCLC's situation was improving. Lowery was tied to a number of cooperative undertakings like the Leadership Forum, over which he presided, the Anti-Klan Network, and more. He still had to contend to some degree with a middle-class image, but the pilgrimage certainly demonstrated that he and his wife could sincerely plunge into a sustained direct-action effort as vigorously as anyone.

Finally, it should be noted that this southern campaign coincided with, and contributed to, what may be viewed as a revitalization of the "new movement" mentality that had come temptingly close in the past only to be lost to a return of indifference or discouragement. That dimension will be the subject of the final chapter.

"The black church must be returned to as the source of our spiritual life and taproot of our culture. Most of our black leaders gained their strong convictions in those hallowed halls. . .

Michelle Alexander

13

A Clearer Vision

Morale was still high as SCLC met for its silver anniversary convention in Birmingham. The young marchers chanted approval of James Orange and the Lowerys, and they responded warmly. Anyone could see that the Pilgrimage had given all of them an emotional lift and a sense that something important had been accomplished. Julia Wilder was there and was honored. And both Evelyn Lowery and James Orange received special awards for their pivotal roles in the entire operation.[1] The trek through some seventy cities and towns now ended in celebration in Birmingham where SCLC had turned the corner toward genuine effectiveness in 1963.

Throughout the 1982 annual convention, history and the idea of an "ongoing dream" were closely linked. Mayor Richard Arrington welcomed the delegates to the city and could be seen in several of the sessions. As the first black to hold the city's highest office, he symbolized how far the movement had come in two decades and he made it clear that he considered nonviolent direct-action a major catalyst in his career. But he also underscored the fact that neither Birmingham nor the rest of the nation could rest on mere symbolism or tokenism.

Naturally, it was a time for memories and reflections on the meaning and experiences of the 1963 Birmingham campaign. A memorial march from Kelly Ingram Park and a candlelight vigil at city hall recalled the deaths of four little black girls at the

Sixteenth Street Baptist Church that fateful September. Repeatedly, speakers alluded to them and to the many other human costs of the Birmingham campaign. Fred Shuttlesworth's injuries, the water hoses, dogs, and police barricades, the huge marches and rallies, the crowded jails. . .all strangely distant now but deeply embedded in collective and individual memories.

"Hold Fast to Dreams: Economic Justice, Political Justice, and Peace" were the words printed in bold letters on convention signs and programs, indicating the theme the board had chosen to mark this twenty-fifth year of SCLC. Langston Hughes provided the poetic backdrop to what was considered a still urgent matter. Several of the stalwarts of the past were honored, including Claudette Mathews, Hattie Brooks, and "Big Lester" Hankerson. Collins "Pop" Harris, who had been with the movement for thirty years and was ill at the time, received a special award accepted in his behalf by his daughter Mrs. Louise Evans. And present in various sessions were virtually all of the dignitaries of SCLC and the King Center: Mrs. Coretta King, Ralph Abernathy, Wyatt Tee Walker, Dorothy Cotton, Jesse Jackson, Andy Young, all four of the King children, and several others. A. G. Gaston welcomed the board to Hilton lounge, a gesture reminiscent of his provision of headquarters for the 1963 campaign at his motel.[2] At one point, Jesse Jackson, Wyatt Walker, Dr. Abernathy, and Dr. Lowery were pictured smiling and arms interlocked, suggesting that whatever differences had divided them in the past were now forgotten.[3]

Andrew Young was the principal speaker for the annual banquet, a well-attended affair that brought out many local blacks. Already mayor of Atlanta, Young had a long distinguished career behind him and seemed ready for much more. He recalled some of the humorous moments of the Birmingham struggle of 1963 but also some of the frightening and inspirational ones. Throughout his speech he affirmed the integrity of nonviolence and criticized the increasing reliance of the United States on weapons of war, not just under Reagan but over many years.

There was an alternative, Young argued, and in a world where global human needs were severely pressing, it was the only one. It was time, said the former United Nations Ambassador, for the United States to take the lead in a bold new experiment in international relations. It was not, he suggested, a romantic, idealistic vision, but a tangible imperative. And it had worked in Birmingham in 1963. To an audience that included Wyatt Walker and Dorothy Cotton, who served as co-toast masters for the banquet, and hundreds more with vivid memories of the Birmingham campaign, Young averred that there was a generic linkage between nonviolence as the effective method of black liberation and the potential of nonviolent perspectives on foreign policy.[4] With that he underscored a fundamental theme of SCLC in the eighties.

Celebrating and remembering were only part—albeit the most visible part—of the twenty-fifth annual gathering. Walter Mondale spoke during one of the plenary sessions and was well received. Cries of "Mr. President" could be heard in the church as he addressed the delegates, indicating that at least some present looked forward to his challenging Reagan in 1984. Interestingly, George Wallace also appeared in another session, arguing that he had changed his mind on racial matters and was now a true believer in integration and interracial cooperation.

In a workshop on world peace, spokesmen for Haitian refugees called for black collaboration against white imperialism. Little confidence was expressed that whites would help the Haitians or any victimized blacks. Wyatt Walker and Jesse Jackson blasted the white power structure. Jackson spoke of "stupidity" of white foreign policy formulators and decried the apparent deterioration of racial relations in many parts of the world. Only a handful of whites were in the audience, but they could be seen joining hands with the others and singing "We Shall Overcome." If the spirit of interracial fellowship seemed strained, the symbolism was still there.[5]

Nobody is Going to Do It For Us

As the 1982 convention ended and SCLC began its twenty-sixth year, the storm over civil rights was just beginning to peak.

389

The following months would bring news of major changes in the philosophy and personnel of the U. S. Civil Rights Commission, moving it to a less independent position and more into line with the official 'color blind' policy of the administration. Increasingly, black spokespersons emphasized the fact that blacks had always taken the lead in their own liberation and would have to continue, and even intensify, their efforts. Whatever the specific items on the general agenda, the key to success would be a 'coming together' of the black community as never before. A 'new moral movement' had to be launched, as SCLC stated in 1981 and re-affirmed in 1982.[6] A clue to this mood was Andrew Young's comment at an economic summit conference that summer in Gary, Indiana, that blacks should not "bemoan and despair and wallow in our frustrations." And Lowery added that "We must have the courage to grab America and wrestle with this problem. If not Black America, then who? If not now, when?"[7]

The "action-agenda" outlined in Birmingham contained some familiar items such as continued use of Operation Breadbasket to promote black businesses and job opportunities for the poor, as well as several thrusts in foreign policy. SCLC committed itself to helping Haitian refugees, opposing South Africa's *apartheid* system, and urging a summit conference on the recent Israeli occupation of Lebanon and a framework for general peace in the Middle East. As a whole, the positions taken by the leadership conference were at odds with administration policies and were easy to characterize as "liberal" and "dependent upon the government." Whereas in the days of Black Power militants SCLC was viewed by alarmed whites as "moderate" in comparison, as Lewis Killian has noted, the altered ideological spectrum placed them closer to the left.[8]

The truth is that SCLC was left of center on some matters but quite traditional, or even conservative in the broadest sense, on others. The programs of SCLC in the 1980s included many that reaffirmed traditional moral values and sought to preserve the black family, black colleges, and black businesses as essential elements of their culture and political leverage. Well before the "crisis of the black family" once again became an intense public concern, SCLC was giving it close attention. In particular, SCLC/WOMEN viewed the problems of black families as crucial issues for the Southern Christian Leadership Conference and indeed the nation as a whole. Although only in its third year in 1982, SCLC/WOMEN had already implemented several programs to support family life, black heritage, and education of both children and parents in the basics of family relationships.

To understand this, it is helpful to know the origins and logic of the women's organization. SCLC/WOMEN (Women's Organizational Movement for Equality Now) was conceived by Mrs. Evelyn G. Lowery and a small group of women who worked with her in its formation. She first seriously proffered the concept at the annual convention in Norfolk, Virginia in August 1979, the same meeting that initiated the "survival agenda" theme and the counter-attack on negative trends in race relations. Although related, Mrs. Lowery's objective was broader. Keenly aware that women had been deeply involved in black liberation from the beginning, and from the early days of SCLC had played key roles, Mrs. Lowery felt that it was time for SCLC women, along with others who might be drawn in, to organize. Response was good in Norfolk, and the convention left her with a charge to explore the idea further.[9]

After thinking and praying about it over the following two months, she recalls, Mrs. Lowery decided to bring together a group of women who seemed to have the time to give to the work and who represented something of a cross-section of black women's experience. They met at the Lowery home on October 12, 1979 to begin the process of organizing. Enthusiasm was high, and in a second meeting six days later, the formal name was adopted and the initial goals outlined. As the new group began to function, work was sectioned into a number of task forces that steadily grew in number.* A 'womanpower network'

* Child and Youth Enrichment, Legislative Affairs, International Affairs, Heritage, Media, Direct Action, Health Education, Membership, Voter Registration and Education, Womanpower Network, and Womanpower Forum.

was added in 1982 to support the Bozeman-Wilder campaign, and it became permanent.[10]

Although the principal interest of SCLC/WOMEN was collectively the issues of women, families, and childhood, its focus was much broader. Its statement of purpose incorporated the larger framework of SCLC and tied it closely to the parent body:

> Our purpose is to support and complement the work of the Southern Christian Leadership Conference in its efforts to "improve the civic, cultural, economic, and religious conditions in the nation," and to "aid in the restructuring of our society in such a way that all citizens will be afforded equal opportunities and a chance for fulfillment as persons. . ."
>
> We shall particularly assist and support the Southern Christian Leadership Conference in dealing with those issues related to achieving full and equal rights and opportunities for women.
>
> SCLC/WOMEN not only supports SCLC in on-going projects, it initiates projects and programs of its own. It also serves to encourage women in shaping their own destinies and protecting the rights of others to self-determination.[11]

Clearly under the constitutional authority of SCLC, SCLC/WOMEN did not attempt an independent status. Mrs. Lowery was designated National Convener, rather than president or chairman. And SCLC/WOMEN could soon be seen working in conjunction with the leadership conference during the Atlanta crisis, the 1982 Pilgrimage, and several other conference-wide projects. Yet, it also made addenda of its own. In its first year, SCLC/WOMEN spearheaded what proved to be a permanent series of banquets for presentation of Martin Luther King, Jr. Memorial Awards designated as "Drum Major" awards and covering various fields of contribution such as education, entertainment, and public service. The first was held in April 1980 in conjunction with observances of the anniversary of King's assassination, and that became the annual pattern. Bill Cosby and board member Dick Gregory were among the first winners, as was baseball star Hank Aaron.*

* A complete list of the Drum Major Award recipients from 1980 to 1985 is found in Appendix III.

392

One of its most successful undertakings was an oratorical contest for youth. Top winners received substantial scholarship aid for college study, and the themes were deliberately chosen to encourage reflection on the meaning for the contemporary world of the nonviolent tradition and the life and work of Dr. King. Winners were formally recognized at a plenary session of the annual convention. As the contest grew in popularity, it became a major affair. Local schools cooperated by announcing the annual topics and providing forums for the competition that led to regional and eventually national winners. By the middle eighties, it was decided that contest themes would cover international issues as well as the conceptual framework of the nonviolent tradition.[12]

SCLC/WOMEN also sponsored sporting tournaments in tennis and eventually golf to coincide with their other King memorial activities. These individual, life-time sports often considered middle or upper class hobbies were in line with the other role-model emphases of SCLC/WOMEN. The tournaments drew black dignitaries like Andrew Young and golf professional Lee Elder, whose wife Rose Harper Elder directed the early 'Drum Major for Justice' golf competition. Both of the Elders were given the Drum Major Award in sports in 1985.

Mrs. Lowery's organization was also involved in numerous efforts to support the black family at a time when several negative trends were working against it. Apart from the fact that television portrayals of the black family in situation comedies and dramatic series were distorting in some ways the real strengths of black family life, there was a growing crisis of teenage pregnancies outside of marriage. And this was one of the central foci of SCLC/WOMEN's seminars and conferences of the eighties.

The unwed teen mother problem affected all races. Between 1970 and 1982, births by white teenagers who were unmarried increased dramatically from 18% of the total births by that age group to some 37%. For black teenage girls the statistics were even more sobering, jumping from 64% to about 87%. Some 42% of black households were headed by unmarried females, and roughly half of all black babies were born outside of marriage. A deeply concerned NAACP and Urban League leadership organized a Black Family Summit at Fisk in 1984, and by then SCLC/WOMEN had been sponsoring pro-family conferences for over three years.[13] And while there was much emphasis upon reinvigorating waning moral discipline as an essential requisite for a genuine solution, the social and political factors that militated against morality were extensively probed. Problems of drug and alcohol addiction, unemployment, welfare dependency, and self-images of black children were addressed by social science experts and ministers. Teenagers were provided forums, not only in Atlanta but in several other cities in the SCLC network, for frankly discussing sensitive matters of sexuality and parenting.[14]

If talking about such problems did not in itself solve them, the open discussions by SCLC/WOMEN and many other organizations around the country did serve to raise public awareness and to dispel simplistic views such as blaming everything on welfare policy. Much more was involved, as became apparent from the data amassed in the eighties. Black males were not reinforced in their instincts to be good husbands and fathers, and black women often found having more children an asset in circumstances where welfare laws militated against earning wages or attending school while getting temporary aid. It was also emphasized in many circles that the long history of discrimination and the technological revolution had left millions of blacks with neither the hope nor the means to change their lives. That journalists pointed to success stories like that of Glenn Loury, who had risen from poverty on Chicago's South Side to become a voice in American scholarship, did not change the fundamental fact that many could not or did not do the same.[15] Neither SCLC nor SCLC/WOMEN ignored the moral challenge. Joseph Lowery began to call for "liberation lifestyles" without drugs, alcohol abuse, or sexual license. And Dick Gregory used his wit and quite serious platform style to say that it was time to upgrade personal lifestyles. "You've got more respect for your automobile," said Gregory, "than for that temple of God that is your body."[16]

Some aspects of the work of SCLC/WOMEN cannot yet be adequately evaluated. But clearly, the new subsidiary of the Southern Christian Leadership Conference appeared to be one of the most creative parts of the total program. The Womanpower Network initiated during the Bozeman-Wilder campaign continued to grow. By 1984 it had added a Womanpower Forum to deal with a wide range of women's issues and world problems. Dr. Shirley Chisholm, former member of Congress and a 1972 presidential nomination candidate, was the keynote speaker for the first one. Chisholm praised the work of black women in the civil rights movement, but noted that they had never had their full recognition as standardbearers in political elections. It was time, she said, for black women to "stop being shrinking violets and rise to the challenge and remember the old adage that 'God helps those who help themselves'." She was given the first Trailblazer Award for her outstanding record in politics.

SCLC/WOMEN did indeed get more deeply into political issues and could be seen supporting product safety, opposing dumping of toxic wastes, demonstrating against *apartheid*, and in many more local and national campaigns. The 1982 Pilgrimage had given it more visibility, and as the eighties progressed, the organization was looking to the future of black women's role in both family and public affairs. It encouraged women to seek elective offices.

At the same time, the chapter and affiliate structure was broadened, the youth activities expanded, and the agenda refined in some ways. SCLC listed 380 affiliates, now led by E. Randel T. Osburn. It was impossible to specify a membership number because SCLC remained an affiliated structure rather than a strictly membership organization.[17] As always, the backbone of the conference was its local activities. In Wrightsville, Los Angeles, Louisville, Birmingham, and many other cities and towns, these groups were involved with local churches, high schools, colleges, and labor organizations.[18] College and university campuses organized SCLC chapters, thus enhancing the participation of young people. Joseph Lowery told a Spelman College student body in late 1982 that "You have come to this historic setting—this place of challenge—to serve the present age; and through your enrichment, you must help America to move forward ethically, and economically . . . and not only Black America."

There was wide divergence of opinion within the black community on what serving the present age meant. But leaders as different as Coretta King, Vernon Jordan, NAACP head Benjamin Hooks, Jesse Jackson, and Eleanor Holmes Norton were calling for more participation by blacks themselves, public sensitivity to the poor, and reconsideration of features of American foreign policy. The key was an aroused conscience, and while there were difficulties in realizing that, evidence suggests that there was something of a revival of awareness that self-centered economic concerns were not enough for a full and rewarding life.

In 1983, several civil and human rights organizations led a commemorative march on Washington reminiscent of the historic 1963 demonstration. It was spearheaded by a group called the "Coalition of Conscience," led chiefly by the King Center and SCLC but involving several other groups and individuals. It began in 1982 with observances in honor of Martin King at a time when the King holiday proposal was picking up momentum. The election of Congresswoman Katie Hall, the continuing efforts of singer Stevie Wonder, and a growing coalition that lobbied and campaigned for the King holiday bill all served to make the national holiday bill a more compelling one in both Houses.

The hope was that another march on Washington would enlarge the "coalition of conscience" to national scope. That political factors influenced it was quite clear. Many black leaders looked upon Reagan administration policies as hostile to black interests, and this became a factor in the 1983 demonstration. But the underlying premise was that it would help to evoke "the high point of the civil rights struggle at a time of growing despair. . . ." Representative Walter Fauntroy, still chairman of

SCLC's board of directors, was the chairman of the Twentieth Anniversary Mobilization Committee. Platform masters of ceremony included Maya Angelou, who once worked in SCLC's early New York office.

The 1983 March on Washington

"If the dream was there," wrote one journalist who covered the 1983 march, "the fire was not. The reprise had a forced quality, as if the participants had been jaded by all the marches and speeches of the intervening two decades."[18] He noted the bewildering array of organizations and causes carrying banners and making speeches to the quarter of a million people who gathered at the same site where King had electrified a crowd of similar size twenty years earlier. In the 1983 throng were advocates of women's rights, gay rights, animal protection, nuclear freeze and myriad other specific causes. The reporter could not avoid concluding that the cliqueish make-up of the demonstration detracted from a clear, unified sense of purpose.

That much was certainly true. Being in the demonstration did indeed mean different things to different people. There was much criticism of the Reagan administration. Many speakers called for defeating Reagan in his expected 1984 re-election bid. Folk singers like Pete Seeger satirized the President, and major speakers jabbed at his California ranch life. Jesse Jackson, who was beginning to mount a presidential nomination bid of his own, insisted that "Our time has come," and he averred that "We will march on! March on! Voices could be heard in the crowd urging him to go for the presidential nomination.

Close to half those present were white, marking another difference between the 1963 and 1983 marches. Many were young, too young in fact to have any memories of the 1963 demonstration. Buses brought them from as far away as California, and it is intriguing to speculate on what the thousands of young people were thinking as they marched in the carefully prepared and officially secured commemorative march. How much of the realism of the days of Birmingham could they capture, or of the steamy afternoon when King spoke about a dream when there was as yet no Civil Rights Act or Voting Rights Act? No one, not even those who were with King in the Birmingham campaign or heard him speak at the Lincoln Memorial, could transfer that to them.

Of course, the fire was not as intense as in 1963. The hastily prepared articles and editorials on the march might have profitably considered more realistically that no one expected it to be. Time had changed the movement and the people in it. Some who were key figures in the 1963 march disavowed the 1983 demonstration. Bayard Rustin, who was a pivotal organizer of the original march, would not support the commemorative march. He stated on national television that marching on the capital in 1983 was not the best way to help solve the many pressing problems facing blacks and the poor. He was convinced that class, not race, was the key determinative factor by 1983 and that tackling "structural problems in the economy" was the crying need of the times. Any "black agenda," Rustin argued, had to be "part and parcel of an agenda for all Americans." A huge demonstration in Washington, he felt, was essentially anachronistic.[19]

Mrs. King, who was co-chairperson of the Coalition of Conscience with Joseph Lowery, spoke to the huge crowd. She told them in measured words that she could feel her husband's presence. The dream must be kept alive, she told the crowd in words similar to her address the night before at the SCLC national convention. She did not share Rustin's estimation of the march or the precise means he would use to continue the movement.

Nor did SCLC. The leadership conference came to the march on Saturday morning from its two-day twenty-sixth annual convention at the New Bethel Baptist Church in Washington where Walter Fauntroy pastored. The somewhat shorter than usual convention had adopted the memorial march theme "For Jobs, Peace, and Freedom," essentially the original theme of the 1963 demonstration but with an emphasis on peace encouraged by SCLC. Friday evening had been filled with short, spirited addresses by Coretta King, Dick Gregory, James Lawson, Fred

Shuttlesworth, Benjamin Hooks, Andrew Young, and others who stirred up enthusiasm for the march and reviewed some of the highlights of the nonviolent movement. At midnight Dick Gregory still had the overflow crowd laughing, crying, and anticipating.[20]

On the morning of the march SCLC walked behind a huge banner proclaiming in bold letters "Working to Fulfill the Dream." Before the day was over, several SCLC speakers, including Lowery, mounted the platform in front of the Lincoln Memorial. Lowery criticized administration policies and seeming indifference to civil rights. President Reagan was not in the city, again a difference from 1963 when Kennedy had cars waiting to carry some of the major march leaders to the White House for a conference. But this time, there was much less political pressure to deal directly with black leaders.[20]

The parade of supporters of diverse causes did not go unnoticed by either the participants or the press. King's dream seemed to be swallowed up in a heterogeneous array of *ad hoc* issues, some of questionable linkage with the nonviolent movement. Organizers of the 1983 march had worried about that possibility from the beginning, and there had been several clashes of opinion about who should participate. Jewish leaders had been reluctant to participate for fear of an anti-Israel contingent in the demonstration. Ultimately some Jewish leaders did march, but only after securing an agreement to avoid any anti-Israel treatment of the Middle East question.

In microcosm, the 1983 march reflected not only the changing times but also the multi-faceted impact of the black liberation movement. Political cartoonists displayed Martin Luther King, Jr. with his placard raised high to proclaim his dream, but with his eyes glancing in dismay at the multitude of slogans in behalf of homosexuals, feminists, workers, children, and all the rest. The implication was that the "dream" by 1983 was too diffuse to have any real substance. But this was misleading.

Underlying the complexity of the 1983 march, and indeed the entire nonviolent movement, was the fact that one of the cardinal tenets of the movement was free expression of ideas.

Without it, there could have been no effective organization in the past. Its success in gaining rights such as access to public facilities and guarantees of the franchise had affected all people, not blacks alone, and in more than legal or circumstantial ways. The psychology of "standing up for one's rights" became more deeply embedded in the American political culture and that of many other countries as well. David Lewis has seen this as clearly as anyone.

> Even as the nation recoils into conservatism from the activism of the late sixties, the legacies of this period persist. . .It has become possible for others—women, Hispanics, Indians, homosexuals, the mentally and physically impaired, battered wives and children to make their legitimate grievances hear.[21]

Thus, any fair appraisal of the 1983 march on Washington or the movement as a whole must take this into consideration. Neither SCLC nor the other leading participants endorsed all of the cacophononous causes on display in the march. What they did endorse was the right to speak one's mind and express one's needs. It is doubtful that the march had a significant impact on the administration. But it did demonstrate the determination of many people to keep the moral vision alive, even if others used it for their own purposes. Many people in SCLC circles, including Fred Shuttlesworth, felt that marching was still relevant but that in the future large numbers of concentrated local demonstrations would be more effective. Dr. King, Sr., in response to Rustin's criticism of the march, said that there just might be much more direct-action demonstrating if the situation of blacks did not improve.

Where Do We Go From Here?

The following months presented a mixed picture. It became obvious by late 1983 that the U.S. Civil Rights Commission would play less of an advocacy role and, some felt, might be in its dying days. In October 1983 President Reagan fired three Jimmy Carter appointees to the commission: Mary Frances Berry, Blandina Cardenas Ramirez, and Rabbi Murray Saltzman. But they appealed to the courts and their dismissal was barred. Berry remained an outspoken critic of administration policies as the commission changed dramatically. It vowed to "reassess" civil rights, which meant less regard for affirmative action and government intervention than was typical over the previous three decades. Later, in 1984, Reagan decided to nominate Edwin Meese to head the Justice Department, which was taken by many to indicate that the administration would back away even more from moderate and liberal views of civil rights. Reagan, however, continued to insist that his people would vigorously pursue enforcement of rights laws. Meese's nomination was controversial and took many months to complete, but eventually in 1985 the Senate approved his appointment.

"Despite contrary myths," wrote John W. Blassingame of Yale University's Afro-American Department, "revolutions can go backwards." He felt that the so-called civil rights revolution had not accomplished anything like what it sought or was supposed to have achieved. He did credit the nonviolent movement with some important successes and a "reformist zeal" that was built on a sense of truth. "King and the other members of SCLC acted on their convictions and their certainty," he wrote. But regression had been the trend of the seventies and eighties, and the "revolution" had not yet happened. If America was "closer than it had ever been" to a genuinely egalitarian society, the "latest onslaught on civil rights" underscored the need to re-establish a coalition that can rise above temporary defeats and go on with the task.[22] Blassingame wrote these words a few months before the reorganization of the Civil Rights Commission and was thus not thinking precisely of that, but of the general erosion of a sense of movement shared by blacks and non-blacks alike.

On the surface at least, the passage of Public Law 98-144 in late October 1983 and its signing a few days later by President Reagan was a positive sign. After fifteen years of debate on versions supported by lawmakers from Brooke and Conyers to Katie Hall, the King national holiday became a reality. The third

Monday in January, beginning in 1986, would officially recognize King as part of a company that included only one other American, George Washington. But even some of the staunch advocates of the holiday wondered whether it would mark a more formal institutionalization of King at a time when his vision of society was far from reality. In any case, he and several other late heroes of the movement were remembered in a variety of memorial activities between 1983 and 1986. By the middle eighties a sizable number of the historical leaders had died: Dr. King, Sr., C. K. Steele, Benjamin Mays, Roy Wilkins, Kelly Miller Smith, and several more. These were important losses and were viewed as such. Of necessity, a middle and younger generation had to pick up the threads of continuity. In that light, King's holiday was especially meaningful. By it a race, a movement, and a nation were symbolically interlocked.

The circumstances that had produced leaders like King and Asa Philip Randolph could not, of course, be duplicated. Whether their kind of faith could depended upon a number of factors, one of which was a proper historical appreciation for them. And that, as much as personal glory, was what the King holiday was all about. That there was some apprehension about it is understandable. King on an official pedestal was appropriate enough, but the King of the streets, the planner of the Poor People's Campaign, indeed the King who had died while aiding a labor strike, had to be preserved as well.

SCLC remained critical of administration budget priorities, several aspects of its foreign policy in general, and its less than vigorous opposition to South African *apartheid*. In 1984 the leadership conference helped write and promulgate a 'People's Platform' agreed upon by the National Black Coalition for 1984 and the National Black Leadership Forum. It called for repairing the "tattered safety net" for the truly needy and supported tax reforms to raise additional revenues to go into social programs such as maternal and child care, aid to families with dependent children, and job retraining. There was also a section on minority business development and others on urban and educational reform. The defense and foreign policy planks called for nuclear disarmament, a replacement of the constructive engagement approach to South Africa with a more "stringent and compelling stand. . ."[23]

Basically SCLC opposed Reagan's re-election but did not close the door to working with the Republican Party. The GOP still controlled the Senate and had a more powerful voice in the House than at any time in recent history. It was imperative, as in 1980, to maintain links with both parties. For many years SCLC leaders had warned against either letting Democrats assume black support without earning it, or Republicans write it off as predictably impossible. That view was reasserted in 1984.

As it turned out, Reagan won almost every state and began a second term with high levels of public approval which included some shifting of blacks' opinion to the conservative side. SCLC began to look ahead to the next round of Congressional elections and to the prospect of another black candidate's participation in the presidential race comparable to the serious bid put forth by Jesse Jackson in 1984.

SCLC's major operations were in the direction of economic justice, often linked, as in the case of its four-month boycott of Winn-Dixie, to *apartheid*. Encouraged by agreements with Macy's, Zales, and other distributors of South African goods, SCLC continued its pressure on the Winn-Dixie system. It worked in conjunction with labor unions to effect first a pledge not to buy more of the products, and later an agreement whereby the huge grocery chain would pull all of the products from their shelves. A press conference in Atlanta on King's birthday, January 15, 1986, publicized the agreement.[24] Lowery emerged from a week's stay in the hospital happy about it all.

In the meantime, SCLC remained critical of federal civil rights policy. The changing mood of the Civil Rights Commission and the appointment of Edwin Meese to head the Justice Department were viewed negatively. As Lowery often put it, the new policy was to "overturn rather than overcome." Yet, even this was expressed with a certain amount of humor and certainly with the realization that appeals would have to be made to Republicans as well as Democrats if effective relationships were to be preserved. A purely partisan approach would be politically suicidal, SCLC leaders realized.

Actions taken by the SCLC board in the middle eighties reflected the concerns of the time. In 1984 and 1985, the board condemned *apartheid*, called for continuance of affirmative action programs, expressed support for Bishop Desmond Tutu and the Mandellas, and called for an end to American military support of the Nicaraguan Contras. It also affirmed support for a nuclear freeze and negotiations with the Soviet Union and was pleased with the Reagan-Gorbachev Summit in Geneva in 1985. Overall, the board and the Atlanta administration persisted with several of its survival themes related to economic progress of blacks and poor people.[25]

Consideration was given to establishing full-time paid executive directors or administrators of chapters around the country, though financing them would be difficult. A major financial pledge by Dick Gregory at the Charlotte convention in 1984 was a big boost, as was the growing membership. If such could be accomplished this would give SCLC a clearer presence in local areas and likely facilitate unity of action.[26]

It was the inner dynamic that was most challenging. Could the sense of continuity with the spiritual roots be transferred to the present? That depended upon several factors, one of which was the inter-organizational cooperation necessary to mount a new movement. Youth were also a key, and in that regard we have seen some real progress both within SCLC and in other structures. Most of the concern in this regard was with blacks themselves, but it also extended to whites and other Americans. Somehow, the "flame within," as communications officer Michelle Alexander put it, had to be rekindled. Too many successful blacks had forgotten where it had all originated: in the churches, in the streets of segregated cities and, in a very real sense, in the hearts of people determined to be free, but without violence.[27]

Real differences of view and personality were still present. But as Rev. Osburn said in 1985:

> SCLC has always been a family. And in any family there will be fights between brothers and sisters, brothers and brothers, and sisters and sisters. . .but in the final analysis they are all family. In the black experience we have an expression that "blood is thicker than water," so while our sisters and brothers might fight each other, nobody else can expect to come in and receive the benefits of that kind of "fighting."[28]

The thrust of this comment was valid enough. Many of the internal disputes had been overworked in public treatments. But it remained to be seen how much of the broader black and white communities could, as many still hoped, join hands in the eighties and say in life what King symbolized in death, "Free at last, free at last. Thank God Almighty, we are free at last."

Conclusion

This history has focused primarily on the national leadership and campaigns of the Southern Christian Leadership Conference. Some readers will be aware, as I am, that the full story involved much more at the local level. But one must begin with a frame of reference. The complex local and state history of SCLC should be recorded soon, but that will take two volumes and the cooperation of many scholars and participants. Perhaps what has been done here will facilitate that undertaking.

In a deeper sense we have reviewed the fundamental substance of SCLC's history—shared by several other organizations—by examining the evolution of what has usually been called a "dream." More precisely, it is a concept of justice set in a prophetic style of Christian activism, a term used here broadly enough to include Jews and others with a sense of divine intervention in history. At the time King expressed his version of this dream, external circumstances needed to be changed, though he never accepted a visionary or "gnostic" view that changing the outer world was tantamount to human redemption. But in those formative days, millions of blacks could not vote or even sit beside a white person in a restaurant or use the same restrooms. Changing the external order was imperative but not an end in itself.

Nor did the tenets of Marxism appeal very much to King or his followers, despite the excessive emphasis upon that possibility in our time. Class struggle as defined by Marx meant next to nothing to blacks who wanted both freedom and dignity within the American mainstream. Theirs was a dual awakening, of freedom and racial-cultural pride, and its dynamic altered but did not reject the American democratic political system. SCLC's constitution as well as King's 1963 dream speech were premised on the concept that theirs was a goal actually derived from the American dream. "I have a dream," King said in 1963, ". . . deeply rooted in the American dream."

However, the key to the meaning of the nonviolent movement was a related dictum, namely, that the basic assumptions of morality cannot be segregated. Especially crucial in King's thinking was the view that the political-social order must be judged by the same standards that apply to the rightness and wrongness of personal actions. He told a college audience in the sixties that "There cannot be two consciences, one in civil and another in political life." King's concept of justice shared with Plato's an emphasis upon the organic whole, but countered the famous Athenian philosopher's view of social stratification. To the founder of SCLC and to many of his followers, justice entailed a synthesis of personal integrity and political order. King did not dream of a world which could totally eliminate injustice, hatred or inequity. Biographers have amply demonstrated that King struggled throughout his career with the contradictory impulses of human nature and certainly did not naively pursue a perfect world created by modifications of the social system. Indeed, King was poles apart from this approach.

To King evil in the world was quite real, but he saw it as penultimate and defeated already by God's intervention in history. "The cross is the external expression of the lengths to which God will go in order to restore broken community. The resurrection is a symbol of God's triumph over all the forces that seek to block community. The Holy Spirit is the continuing community-creating reality that moves through history," King said at the Prayer Pilgrimage ceremonies in Washington in 1957. His use of "community" in this context had special meaning for King, and was quite different from the use of community in socialist or welfare state theories. Community to King was basically a proper relationship, based on love and mutual recognition of selfhood. Community was the ultimate end of existence, as well as its beginning. Evils that obstructed it could not endure permanently. King liked to quote James Russell

Lowell's aphorism: "Truth forever on the scaffold, wrong forever on the throne. Yet, that scaffold sways the future, and behind the dim unknown stands God—within the shadow keeping watch above His own."

Specific application of this conviction to societal ills was no simple matter. In the early days of SCLC, physical abuse, deprivation and discrimination were blatant enough to elicit strong morally-inspired resistance to them. People could be moved to shame over such obvious violations of community. King could contrast the official American policy of supporting free elections in eastern Europe after World War II with the lack of free elections in Mississippi or Alabama. He could speak of the universalism of America's social vision and use it to good advantage in bringing domestic social oppression into sharp relief.

As we have seen, however, going beyond that level of application of community was more difficult. When the issues became world peace, economic opportunity, and a mutually respectful relationship among races and classes, other considerations dampened the enthusiasm for community which had effectively removed physical segregation and disenfranchisement from American society.

King was disillusioned by the hardness of the barriers as he faced the challenges of the late sixties. Earlier he had accentuated the fact that blacks had been loyal to the nation, "even in the moments of your greatest denial of our freedom." Black Americans had, he said in the late fifties, "mingled their blood with other Americans in defense of the Republic" from the Revolution to the present. All they were asking was to be free. "We are not seeking to dominate the nation politically or hamper its social growth; we just want to be free. . ." King believed that the achievement of this freedom—which worked both ways, for blacks and all others—would be beneficial to the entire world. "If this is done, we will be able to emerge from the bleak and desolate midnight of man's inhumanity to man into the bright and glittering day of freedom and justice."

Near the end of his life King had less confidence in the

proximity of this kind of community and wrote that racism and segregation were a "congenital deformity" in American life. Nonetheless, the late King was even more emphatic upon the necessity for nonviolence, the need for a rededication to the quest for justice, and a bold critique of world militarism. It was not precisely the United States he criticized, but the inertia of forces that maintained traditional patterns of discrimination and violence. It is important that despite his discouragement King went on preaching his dream.

King's successors lived with this paradox. While the nonviolent social vision appeared to them to be more indispensable than ever, the circumstances in which it had to operate worsened. Ralph Abernathy often found himself speaking out against a variety of practices and attitudes. This did not abate much in the late 1970s and early 1980s. Everywhere, "injustice" seemed to block progress. It became easier to blame social problems on general lack of concern for justice and to measure public policy by criteria derived from the concept of justice identified with King's movement.

On the other side, it was also simpler for many people to write off this view of justice as idealistic and misleading. The "real problems" and the "real solutions" lay elsewhere, some judged. Pressing national economic problems displaced concern for the rights of particular groups. Arguments in favor of protecting those unable to fend adequately for themselves were countered by rebuttals stressing economic necessity. Arguments favoring reduced military spending ran up against the easy to document neo-imperialism of the Soviet Union, Cuba, and Libya.

What King really meant by the dream in 1963 is debatable. Likely what one sees in it corresponds to his or her perception of society and ethics. We do know that at the time he made the speech King was suffering personally. The Birmingham settlement was tenuous. There was no guarantee that the civil rights bill would pass and even less certainty that substantive change could be brought about in local communities. King's own family was facing problems in dealing with the local school system in Atlanta and he was hardly convinced that a speech could turn a nation around. But he did make the speech. He did say that he dreamed of a day when his children would be judged "by the content of their character." King did say that the American dream demanded living out the true meaning of the nation's creeds. He did declare that the "glory of the Lord" would be seen by all people.

That, in itself, was historically significant. The dream—and what SCLC and its fellow organizations had done up to that time—became part of American history in a deeper sense than before. Someone actually stood at the Lincoln Memorial and said that "the sons of former slaves and the sons of former slave owners" could sit down at a "table of brotherhood." No retrospective judgment, however scholarly in appearance, that King's vision of society was too ambitious or based on too much idealism can change the fact that it was registered in the historical annals of the United States.

Beyond the fact of its articulation, the dream also served to unite sufficient numbers of people to bring about historic changes in American society both for blacks and others. In that sense the "dream" was translated into action. In fact, the efficacy of the social vision suggested by the concept of the dream can be measured in part by tangible results. Evidence that shows greater black participation in elections, for example, gives credence to the dream insofar as it embodied the importance of active citizenship. Fair housing laws and employment practices can also be seen in this light. They are concrete manifestations of greater mobility and opportunities for economic advancement. Furthermore, as blacks and whites establish friendships, engage in joint political and economic activities, or simply live side by side as neighbors in a community without malice, they give substance to the dream.

Much more is involved, however. In an address to the National Conference on Religion and Race in Chicago in January 1963, King enumerated five major challenges to religious leaders representing Catholics, Jews, and Protestants. He prefaced his list by making a distinction between neighborhood and brotherhood. "Through our scientific genius we have made of our nation—and even the world—a neighborhood, but we have failed to employ our moral and spiritual genius to make of it a brotherhood.''[1] Then he listed the critical areas that needed attention:

1. enhancement of human dignity since "the image of God is universally shared in equal portions by all men."
2. uprooting prejudice because prejudice is based on fears, suspicions and misunderstandings. . . .
3. supporting social justice; the church or synagogue should take the lead in social reform. . . .
4. encouraging nonviolent direct-action because violence is both impractical and immoral. . . .
5. promoting universal love. Court orders and federal enforcement agencies are of inestimable value in achieving desegregation, but desegregation is only a partial, though necessary, step toward the final goal which we seek to realize—genuine intergroup and interpersonal living. . . .[2]

At this level the dream appears in a different light, challenging the assumptions that the unresolved issues of the nonviolent movement can be settled by a free market economy that shifts the emphasis of criticism away from injustice and racism to practical policies. It is true, as Walter E. Williams has written, that political decisions have led to results that are more "antipeople" than anti-black, as such (monopolies that severely restrict opportunities, for example), but it is also true that many of the problems faced by blacks result from other causes than lack of free market conditions.[3] On the other hand, the dream construed in terms of these far-reaching relational values calls into question an unrelenting emphasis upon the United States as a "racist, sin-sick society" or upon the advanced industrial states as the central cause of the problems of the Third World.

Although they are inescapable at times, the historian ventures into value judgments at some risk. No one can confidently conclude from the facts of history whether the dream SCLC has continued to express is realizable. Certainly it should not be dismissed as mere rhetoric or misguided emotionalism. It has earned a larger place in history than that because of the changes it has helped to effect. Many Americans have benefitted from the

Civil Rights Act and the Voting Rights Act, and perhaps all have been moved to higher levels of decency by the example of Coretta and Martin Luther King, Viola Liuzzo, Fred Shuttlesworth, and Andrew Young, as well as myriad others who have been part of the nonviolent movement. That the McNairs remained in Birmingham after the violent death of their eleven-year-old daughter Denise in the bomb blast of September 1963 and that Chris McNair became a member of the Alabama state legislature says a great deal about the substance of nonviolent thinking.

It is true that SCLC's language suggests final answers and teleological notions that cannot be applied to specific problems without some difficulty. The organization has at times, some say, overly generalized about whites, about capitalism, and about the foreign policy objectives of the United States. Yet, its insistence on a standard resting on morality and human brotherhood is essential as a framework for social transformation. Political or economic systems—whether based on free market or welfare state or other models—are not final answers to problems of human relations. The "dream" we have reviewed is concerned with human relations understood in a Beloved Community context.

King argued that the nonviolent dream, in the final analysis, is the American dream. To the rest of the world, the American dream has always been fascinating. While many have criticized it, even insulted it, the United States has remained a symbol of freedom and democracy, and to its shores have come refugees from all parts of the world. Perhaps the boldness and seeming foolishness of the notion that all people can be free and equal in importance is part of the reason for this. One white clergyman who once worked with King and SCLC wrote in 1982:

Revivifying what is unique about this kind of polity, this kind of democratic aspiration, revitalizing it and dreaming it anew, it seems to me is the great and invigorating challenge of our generation and of the generations to come. For I do believe that it is not with embarrassment, but with a profound sense of accountability to the transcendent judgment of God, that we can say it remains true today that this America, this proposition, this experiment, is the last best hope of the earth.[4]

SCLC has been a student, as well as a teacher of this American dream. King's followers included well-educated scholars and pastors, but also people like Leon Hall who were pushed out of formal education early yet continued to learn. King's staff carried books with them on their trips and discussed them. Among themselves they engaged in spirited competition with one another and with King, trying to do in his absence a better job than he could have done if physically present. They were widely different kinds of people, some from rough street backgrounds, others from prestigious academic institutions. That was what made SCLC work. King's movement related to the actual chemistry of the black population in all of its variety. The intellectual and political composition changed over the years, as did that of white America. The real question became not how the climate was changing around the movement but, rather, was there enough commitment, tolerance, and active love to keep the sense of community alive.

King asked in the middle sixties, "Where do we go from here?" He spent much of his remaining life, in effect, asking "Where are we?" The Vietnam War, Watergate, and the economic crisis of the late seventies forced the nation to struggle with the same question. Although the prevailing mood became conservative, some conservatives were asking themselves what they really wanted to conserve. And some liberals looked again at the past and wondered how their view of society could be refined. Churches torn by internal divisions pored over their social responsibilities in the light of a resurgent interest in the Bible. In a sense, many people were trying to hold fast to dreams, sensing as Langston Hughes had that "when dreams go, life is a barren field frozen with snow."

414

Appendix I

"I Have a Dream"

August 28, 1963
Lincoln Memorial, Washington, D.C.

I am happy to join with you today in what will go down in history as the greatest demonstration for freedom in the history of our nation.

Fivescore years ago, a great American, in whose symbolic shadow we stand today, signed the Emancipation Proclamation. This momentous decree came as a great beacon light of hope to millions of Negro slaves who had been seared in the flames of withering injustice. It came as a joyous daybreak to end the long night of their captivity.

But one hundred years later, the Negro still is not free; one hundred years later, the life of the Negro is still sadly crippled by the mannacles of segregation and the chains of discrimination; one hundred years later, the Negro lives on a lonely island of poverty in the midst of a vast ocean of material prosperity; one hundred years later, the Negro is still languished in the corners of American society and finds himself in exile in his own land.

So we've come here today to dramatize a shameful condition. In a sense we've come to our nation's capital to cash a check. When the architects of our republic wrote the magnificent words of the Constitution and the Declaration of Independence, they were signing a promissory note to which every American was to fall heir. This note was the promise that all men, yes, black men as well as white men, would be guaranteed the unalienable rights of life, liberty, and the pursuit of happiness.

It is obvious today that America has defaulted on this promissory note in so far as her citizens of color are concerned. Instead of honoring this sacred obligation, America has given the Negro people a bad check; a check which has come back marked "insufficient funds." We refuse to believe that there are insufficient funds in the great vaults of opportunity of this nation. And so we've come to cash this check, a check that will give us upon demand the riches of freedom and the security of justice.

We have also come to this hallowed spot to remind America of the fierce urgency of now. This is no time to engage in the luxury of cooling off or to take the tranquilizing drug of gradualism. Now is the time to make real the promises of democracy; now is the time to rise from the dark and desolate valley of segregation to the sunlit path of racial justice; now is the time to lift our nation from the quicksands of racial injustice to the solid rock of brotherhood; now is the time to make justice a reality for all God's children. It would be fatal for the nation to overlook the urgency of the moment. This sweltering summer of the Negro's legitimate discontent will not pass until there is an invigorating autumn of freedom and equality.

Nineteen sixty-three is not an end, but a beginning. And those who hope that the Negro needed to blow off steam and will now be content, will have a rude awakening if the nation returns to business as usual. There will be neither rest nor tranquility in America until the Negro is granted his citizenship rights. The whirlwinds of the revolt will continue to shake the foundations of our nation until the bright day of justice emerges.

But there is something that I must say to my people, who stand on the warm threshold which leads into the palace of justice. In the process of gaining our rightful place, we must not be guilty of wrongful deeds. Let us not seek to satisfy our thirst for freedom by drinking from the cup of bitterness and hatred. We must forever conduct our struggle on the high plain of dignity and discipline. We must not allow our creative protest to generate into physical violence. Again and again we must rise to the majestic heights of meeting physical force with soul force; and the marvelous new militancy, which has engulfed the Negro community, must not lead us to a distrust of all white people. For many of our white brothers, as evidenced by their presence here today, have come to realize that their destiny is tied up with our destiny. And they have come to realize that their freedom is inextricably bound to our freedom. We cannot walk alone. And as we talk, we must make the pledge that we shall always march ahead. We cannot turn back.

There are those who are asking the devotees of Civil Rights, ''When will you be satisfied?'' We can never be satisfied as long as the Negro is the victim of the unspeakable horrors of police brutality; we can never be satisfied as long as our bodies, heavy with the fatigue of travel, cannot gain lodging in the motels of the highways and the hotels of the cities; we cannot be satisfied as long as the Negro's basic mobility is from a smaller ghetto to a larger one; we can never be satisfied as long as our children are stripped of their selfhood and robbed of their dignity by signs stating ''For Whites Only''; we cannot be satisfied as long as the Negro in Mississippi cannot vote and a Negro in New York believes he has nothing for which to vote. No! no, we are not satisfied, and we will not be satisfied until ''justice rolls down like waters and righteousness like a mighty stream.''

I am not unmindful that some of you have come here out of great trials and tribulations. Some of you have come fresh from narrow jail cells. Some of you have come from areas where your quest for freedom left you battered by the storms of persecution and staggered by the winds of police brutality. You have been the veterans of creative suffering. Continue to work with the faith that unearned suffering is redemptive. Go back to Mississippi. Go back to Alabama. Go back to South Carolina. Go back to Georgia. Go back to Louisiana. Go back to the slums and ghettos of our Northern cities, knowing that somehow this situation can and will be changed. Let us not wallow in the valley of despair.

I say to you today, my friends, so even though we face the difficulties of today and tomorrow, I still have a dream. It is a dream deeply rooted in the American dream. I have a dream that one day this nation will rise up and live out the true meaning of its creed, ''We hold these truths to be self-evident, that all men are created equal.'' I have a dream that one day on the red hills of Georgia, sons of former slaves and the sons of former slave owners will be able to sit down together at the table of brotherhood. I have a dream that one day even the state of Mississippi, a state sweltering with the heat of injustice, sweltering with the heat of oppression, will be transformed into an oasis of freedom and justice. I have a dream that my four little children will one day live in a nation where they will not be judged by the color of their skin, but by the content of their character.

416

I have a dream today!

I have a dream that one day down in Alabama—with its vicious racists, with its Governor having his lips dripping with the words of interposition and nullification—one day right there in Alabama, little black boys and black girls will be able to join hands with little white boys and white girls as sisters and brothers.

I have a dream today!

I have a dream that one day "every valley shall be exalted and every hill and mountain shall be made low. The rough places will be made plain and the crooked places will be made straight, and the glory of the Lord shall be revealed, and all flesh shall see it together."

This is our hope. This is the faith that I go back to the South with. With this faith we shall be able to transform the jangling discords of our nation into a beautiful symphony of brotherhood. With this faith we will be able to work together, to pray together, to struggle together, to go to jail together, to stand up for freedom together, knowing that we will be free one day. And this will be the day. This will be the day when all of God's children will be able to sing with new meaning, "My country 'tis of thee, sweet land of liberty, of thee I sing. Land where my fathers died, land of the pilgrim's pride, from every mountain side, let freedom ring." And if America is to be a great nation, this must become true.

So let freedom ring from the prodigious hilltops of New Hampshire; let freedom ring from the mighty mountains of New York; let freedom ring from the heightening Alleghenies of Pennsylvania; let freedom ring from the snowcapped Rockies of Colorado; let freedom ring from the curvaceous slopes of California. But not only that. Let freedom ring from Stone Mountain of Georgia; let freedom ring from Lookout Mountain of Tennessee; let freedom ring from every hill and molehill of Mississippi. From every mountainside, let freedom ring.

And when this happens, and when we allow freedom to ring, when we let it ring from every village and every hamlet, from every state and every city, we will be able to speed up that day when all God's children, black men and white men, Jews and gentiles, Protestants and Catholics, will be able to join hands and sing in the words of the old Negro spiritual: "Free at last. Free at last. Thank God Almighty, we are free at last."

Appendix II

National Conventions

Year	Location	Theme
1957	Montgomery, Alabama	"To Redeem the Soul of America"
1958	Clarksdale, Mississippi	"Stride Toward Freedom"
1958	Norfolk, Virginia	"The Crusade for Citizenship"
1959	Columbia, South Carolina	"Social Change Through Nonviolent Direct Action"
1960	Shreveport, Louisiana	"The Southern Struggle and the American Dilemma"
1961	Nashville, Tennessee	"The Deep South in Social Revolution"
1962	Birmingham, Alabama	"The Diversified Attack on Segregation"
1963	Richmond, Virginia	"Freedom Now!"
1964	Savannah, Georgia	"New Directions in the Quest for Freedom"
1965	Birmingham, Alabama	"Human Rights—Basic Issues—The Grand Alliance"
1966	Jackson, Mississippi	"Human Rights: The Continuing Struggle"
1967	Atlanta, Georgia	"Where Do We Go From Here?"
1968	Memphis, Tennessee	"New Life for Poor People"
1969	Charleston, South Carolina	"America's Dilemma: Billions for the Moon, Pennies for the Poor"
1970	Atlanta, Georgia	"We the People. . .for People's Government"
1971	New Orleans, Louisiana	"The Politics of Poor People"
1972	Dallas, Texas	"Politics '72: The Challenge of Poor People"
1973	Indianapolis, Indiana	"A Nation in Crisis Moving Forward"
1974	Philadelphia, Pennsylvania	"New Directions to Redeem the Soul of America"
1975	Anniston, Alabama	"A Movement of People"
1976	Biloxi, Mississippi	"Politics and Economics '76"
1977	Atlanta, Georgia	"Achieving Human Rights: the Priority of Our Time"
1978	Birmingham, Alabama	"Economic Justice: Basic to the Dream"
1979	Norfolk, Virginia	"Agenda for Survival—the Critical '80's"
1980	Cleveland, Ohio	"A Moral Agenda for the Nation and the World Community"
1981	New Orleans, Louisiana	"Toward a Positive Future: Countering the Assault on Black Life"

418

1982	Birmingham, Alabama Silver Anniversary	"Hold Fast to Dreams: Economic Justice, Political Justice and Peace"
1983	Washington, D. C.	"March on Washington For Jobs, Peace, and Freedom"
1984	Charlotte, North Carolina	"Turning to Each Other to Turn the Nation to Jobs, Peace, and Freedom"
1985	Montgomery, Alabama	"Finishing the Unfinished Task: Voting Rights, Jobs, Peace and Justice"

Appendix III

**Drum Major Awards
Given by
SCLC/WOMEN
April 4—the anniversary of the assassination of
Martin Luther King, Jr.**

1980

American Government	Rep. Parren Mitchell (Maryland)
Education	United Negro College Fund
Entertainment	Bill Cosby Dick Gregory
Law and Justice	U. W. Clemon Fred D. Gray
Sports	Henry "Hammering" Hank Aaron John Carlos Lee Evans Tommie Smith

1981

Business	Cornell McBride Charles Wallace
Communications	Max Robinson
Education Government	Dr. Alvin F. Poussaint Maynard Jackson Ron Dellums
Law and Justice	Clauncey Eskridge
Performing Arts	Ruby Dee Ossie Davis
Special Award	Dr. Septima P. Clark

420

Business	Herman J. Russell
Communications	John H. Johnson
	Chuck Stone
Education	Morehouse School of Medicine
	Mrs. Marva Nettles Collins
Government	Mayor Richard Hatcher
Law and Justice	Wrightsville
	lawyers: Ed Augustine
	Katrina Breeding
	Albert Mitchell
	Celeste Owens
	Brian Spears
	Charles Thornton
	Roosevelt Warren
	Tom West

Special Awards:
  Pioneers in Education: James Meredith
                         Mrs. Vivian Malone Jones
                         Dr. Hamilton Holmes
                         Mrs. Charlayne Hunter-Gault

  Political Awareness: Mrs. Maggie Bozeman
                         Mrs. Julia Wilder

1983

Business	Jesse Hill, Jr.
	Robert J. Brown
	Thomas C. Cordy
Communications	Tony Brown
	Zernona Clayton
	Roy Patterson

Government: Black Women in State Legislatures in the South:

Alabama: Rep. Patricia Davis
         Rep. Sundra E. Escott
         Rep. Yvonne Kennedy
         Rep. Jarushia Thornton

Kentucky: Sen. Georgia M. Powers
          Rep. Mae Street-Kidd

Florida: Rep. Corinne Brown

Georgia: Rep. Betty J. Clark
         Rep. Diane Harvey Johnson
         Rep. Mary Young
         Rep. Grace Hamilton
         Rep. Georganna T. Sinkfield

Louisiana: Rep. Diane E. Bajoie	N. Carolina: Rep. Annie Brown Kennedy

South Carolina: Rep. Mary Miles

Peace with Justice	Randall Robinson
Arts	Lou Rawls
Special Citation in Sports	Alfred Jenkins
Special Citation in the Arts	Mrs. Altovise Davis

1984

Business	Mrs. Patricia Walker Shaw
	Mr. & Mrs. Edward G. Gardner

Communications	Tracy Gray
	Ron Sailor

Government: Black Women Mayors

Alabama: Diane Kirkland, Emelle
Willie M. Snow, Hobson
City
Essie B. Madison,
McMullen

Florida: Helen Miller, Opa-Locka

Georgia: Carrie Kent, Walthourville

Illinois: Callie Mobley, Alorton

Mississippi: Violet Leggette, Gunnison
Fannie Smith, Falcon

Missouri: Hary Hall, Pagedale

S. Carolina: Janie G. Goree, Carlisle
Hazel Parsons, Ridgeville

Special Government	Katie Hall
Labor	Joe Davis
Arts	Marilyn McCoo
	Billy Davis, Jr.
Faithful Servant Award	Samuel Butts
	Andrew Bernard Snead

1985

Arts	The Staple
	Singers: Roebuck "Pop" Staples
	Cleotha Staples
	Mavis Staples
	Yvonne Staples

Business and Economic Development	Dick Gregory
	Dr. David Allen
	LeBaron Taylor

Communications	Jay Harris
	Percy Sutton
Government	Congressman Mickey Leland
	Sheriff Richard Lankford
Sports	Mrs. Rose Harper Elder
	Lee Elder
	Carl Lewis

Law and Justice: Black Women in Federal Judiciary

Joyce L. Alexander	Amalya L. Kearse
Consuela B. Marshall	Anna Diggs Taylor
Ruth Washington	

Special Award: Afro-American Heritage
         Dr. Cheikh Anta Diop

Notes

Introduction

[1] Ralph David Abernathy interview with the author, Atlanta, Georgia, April 22, 1983, p. 8 of typescript.

[2] Martin Luther King, Jr., *Stride Toward Freedom: The Montgomery Story* (New York: Harper and Row, 1958), p. 177.

[3] Hosea Williams interview with the author, March 31, 1983, p. 3 of typescript; and Abernathy/Peake interview, April 22, 1983, pp. 1–2 of typescript.

[4] King, *Stride Toward Freedom*, p. 216.

[5] For a highly useful treatment of this theme see C. Eric Lincoln, editor, *The Black Experience in Religion* (Garden City: Anchor/Doubleday, 1974).

[6] SCLC, *Hold Fast to Dreams: Economic Justice, Political Justice, and Peace*, Program of the 25th Annual Convention, Birmingham, 1982, p. 6.

Chapter One

[1] SCLC/NH, National Conventions, *Twenty-Second Annual Convention*, Cleveland, Ohio, August 10, 1980.

[2] Stephen B. Oates, *Let the Trumpet Sound: The Life of Martin Luther King, Jr.* (New York: Harper and Row, 1982), p. 47.

[3] See the suggestion of caution on the point of explaining King's career on the basis of his unusual background in C. Eric Lincoln, *Martin Luther King, Jr.: A Profile* (New York: Hill and Wang, 1970), p. vii.

[4] King, *Stride Toward Freedom*, pp. 19–21.

[5] Benjamin E. Mays, Conversation with author, January 21, 1979 at Mays' home in Atlanta. Mays clearly remembered King as a precocious, sensitive scholar.

[6] Cited in *Martin Luther King, Jr., 1929–1968: An Ebony Picture Biography* (Chicago: Johnson Publishing Company, 1968), p. 4.

[7] Lerone Bennett, *What Manner of Man: A Biography of Martin Luther King, Jr.*, 4th revised edition (Chicago: Johnson Publishing Co., 1976), p. 27.

[8] King, *Stride Toward Freedom*, p. 97.

[9] *Ibid.*, pp. 90–91.

[10] From King's "Letter from a Birmingham Jail" (1963).

[11] Martin Luther King, Jr., *Strength to Love* (New York: Pocket Books, 1964), p. 99.

[12] King, *Stride Toward Freedom*, p. 99; John J. Ansbro, *Martin Luther King, Jr.: The Making of a Mind* (Maryknoll: Orbis Books, 1982), pp. 160–162.

[13] Hanes Walton, Jr., *The Political Philosophy of Martin Luther King, Jr.* (Westport: Greenwood Publishing Corporation, 1971), p. 46.

[14] See Nat Hentoff, *Peace Agitator: The Story of A. J. Muste* (New York: Macmillan, 1963), pp. 17–18.

[15] Walter Rauschenbusch, *Christianizing the Social Order* (New York: Macmillan, 1919), p. 431.

[16] King, *Stride Toward Freedom*, pp. 18–19.

[17] Ansbro, *Martin Luther King, Jr.*, pp. 183–86.

[18] King, *Stride Toward Freedom*, p. 95.

[19] *Ibid.*, pp. 205–07.

[20] August Meier and Elliott Rudwick, *CORE: A Study in the Civil Rights Movement, 1942–1968* (New York: Oxford University Press, 1973), p. 18.

[21] Martin Luther King, Jr., "Nonviolence and Racial Justice," *Christian Century*, v. 74 (February 6, 1957), p. 166.

[22] Walton, *The Political Philosophy of Martin Luther King, Jr.*, pp. 109–16.

[23] See David Levering Lewis, *King, a Biography*, second edition (Urbana: University of Illinois Press, 1978), pp. 32–33; and Oates, *Let the Trumpet Sound*, pp. 42–43.

[24] Coretta Scott King, *My Life with Martin Luther King, Jr.* (New York: Holt, Rinehart, and Winston, 1969), p. 97.

[25] *Ibid.*, p. 98.

[26] King, *Stride Toward Freedom*, pp. 31–42.

[27] Oates, *Let the Trumpet Sound*, pp. 58–59.

[28] Ralph David Abernathy, Interview with author, March 31, 1983, p. 2 of typescript.

[29] See Carl E. Ellis, Jr., *Beyond Liberation: The Gospel in the Black American Experience* (Downers Grove, Illinois: InterVarsity Press, 1983), pp. 78–81.

[30] Lawrence Dunbar Reddick, *Crusader Without Violence: A Biography of Martin Luther King, Jr.* (New York: Harper and Brothers, 1959), p. 118.

[31] E. D. Nixon, Conversation with author, May 3, 1983, p. 1 of typescript.

[32] Oates, *Let the Trumpet Sound*, p. 64.

[33] King, *Stride Toward Freedom*, p. 69.

[34] For an interesting account by E. D. Nixon, see Howell Raines' interview with him in *My Soul Is Rested* (New York: G. P. Putnam's Sons, 1977), pp. 37–39.

[35] King, *Stride Toward Freedom*, p. 46.

[36] *Ibid.*, pp. 46–51.

[37] Abernathy/Peake Interview, March 31, 1983, p. 5 of typescript.

[38] Oates, *Let the Trumpet Sound*, pp. 68–69.

[39] King, *Stride Toward Freedom*, pp. 62–63.

[40] Lamont H. Yeakey, "Black Women in Struggle: The Montgomery Movement," *National Council for Black Studies, 6th Annual Conference: Proceedings*, Chicago, 1982, Unit III.

[41] Warren D. St. James, *NAACP: Triumphs of a Pressure Group, 1909–1980* (Smithtown, New York: Exposition Press, 1980), pp. 200–203; *New Republic*, v. 124 (June 18, 1956), p. 5; *America*, v. 96 (October 27, 1956), p. 88; and NAACP, *Annual Report, 1978*, p. 12.

[42] Joseph E. Lowery interview with the author, Atlanta, Georgia, October 23, 1984, pp. 2–3 of typescript.

[43] SCLC/KC, Martin Luther King, Jr. Center for Nonviolent Social Change, *Twenty-Two Years of the Human Rights Struggle: The Nonviolent Social Change Movement of Martin Luther King, Jr.* (Atlanta, 1978), pp. 12–13.

[44] See the *Time* cover story on King, February 18, 1957.

[45] Bayard Rustin, *Strategies for Freedom; The Changing Patterns of Black Protest* (New York: Columbia University Press, 1976), p. 38.

[46] Coretta Scott King, *My Life with Martin Luther King, Jr.*, p. 152.

[47] Lincoln, *Martin Luther King, Jr.*, p. xiii.

Chapter Two

[1] King, *Stride Toward Freedom*, p. 201.

[2] *Ibid.*, pp. 69–70.

[3] *Ibid.*, p. 190.

[4] Reddick, *Crusader Without Violence*, p. 183.

[5] Oates, *Let the Trumpet Sound*, pp. 108–09.

[6] King, *Stride Toward Freedom*, pp. 174–75.

[7] *Ibid.*, pp. 134–35. See also Oates, *Let the Trumpet Sound*, pp. 88–89; and Ralph Abernathy conversations with the author, March 1983.

[8] See Oates, *Let the Trumpet Sound*, pp. 122–23; Lewis, *King*, p. 88; and Eugene Pierce Walker, *A History of the Southern Christian Leadership Conference, 1955–1965: The Evolution of a Southern Strategy for Social Change* (Unpublished Ph.D. dissertation, Department of History, Duke University, 1978), p. 31.

[9] Walker, *History of the Southern Christian Leadership Conference*, pp. 29–31.

[10] Rustin interview with Walker, *Ibid.*, p. 31.

[11] Ralph David Abernathy interview with author, March 31, 1983, p. 2 of typescript.

[12] *Ibid.*

[13] For more on Ella Baker's early role see Clayborne Carson, *In Struggle: SNCC and the Black Awakening of the 1960s* (Cambridge, Massachusetts: Harvard University Press, 1981), pp. 19–21.

[14] MLK/MBU, "A Call to Attend a Southwide Conference on Discrimination in Transportation," January 3, 1957.

[15] Abernathy interview with author, March 31, 1983, pp. 3–5 of typescript.

[16] *Ibid.* See also Oates, *Let the Trumpet Sound*, p. 109.

[17] MLK/KC, *Atlanta Conference*, Ebenezer Baptist Church, working paper no. 1, January 10–11, 1957.

[18] *Ibid.*

[19] Rustin, *Strategies for Freedom*, p. 39.

[20] *Ibid.*

[21] Coretta Scott King, *My Life with Martin Luther King, Jr.*, p. 152.

[22] MLK/KC, *Atlanta Conference*, Ebenezer Baptist Church, working paper no. 2, January 10–11, 1957.

[23] SCLC/KC, Ebenezer Baptist Church Conference, working paper no. 1, p. 2.

[24] SCLC/KC, Ebenezer Baptist Church Conference, working paper no. 5, p. 1.

[25] *Ibid.*

[26] SCLC/KC, Ebenezer Baptist Church Conference, working paper no. 1, p. 2.

[27] *Ibid.*; and Kelly Miller Smith interview with the author, Nashville, May 26, 1983, p. 3 of typescript.

[28] *To Secure These Rights: The Report of the President's Committee on Civil Rights* (New York: Simon and Schuster, 1947), pp. 99–101.

[29] *The State of the Union Messages of the Presidents*, volume III: *1905–1966* (New York: Chelsea House, 1966), p. 3071.

[30] Robert Fredrick Burk, *The Eisenhower Administration and Black Civil Rights* (Knoxville: University of Tennessee Press, 1984), pp. 165–66; Carl M. Brauer, *John F. Kennedy and the Second Reconstruction* (New York: Columbia University Press, 1977), pp. 4–6; and Thomas R. Peake conversation with Dwight Eisenhower, Washington, D.C., July 1957.

[31] SCLC/KC, Cable to Herbert Brownell, January 11, 1957.

[32] SCLC/P, King to Eisenhower, February 14, 1957.

[33] Reddick, *Crusader Without Violence*, p. 187.

[34] *Ibid.*

[35] Ralph David Abernathy interview with the author, March 31, 1983.

[36] *Amsterdam News*, May 22, 1957, p. 1.

[37] Walker, *History of the Southern Christian Leadership Conference*, pp. 39–40, and Abernathy/Peake interviews.

[38] See the *Washington Post* and the *New York Times*, June 14, 1957.

[39] Burk, *Eisenhower Administration*, pp. 221–24.

[40] Dwight David Eisenhower, *The White House Years: Waging Peace, 1956–1961* (New York: Doubleday, 1965), pp. 155–56.

[41] Douglass Cater, "How the Senate Passed the Civil Rights Bill," *The Reporter*, v. 17 (September 5, 1957), pp. 9–13.

[42] John Hope Franklin, *From Slavery to Freedom: A History of American Negroes* (New York: Alfred A. Knopf, 1947 and 1974), p. 475.

[43] Abernathy/Peake conversation, April 1983.

[44] *SCLC Constitution and By-Laws*, p. 2.

[45] *Ibid.*, pp. 4–5.

[46] *Ibid.*, p. 7.

[47] King, *Stride Toward Freedom*, p. 222.

[48] Radio and Television address by the President, September 24, 1957. See also the *New York Times* and the *Washington Post* for September 24–25, 1957.

[49] Estimated by the Southern Educational Reporting Service in 1957.

[50] The Gallup Poll survey #589 K, question 26 (October 6, 1957) in *The Gallup Poll: Public Opinion, 1935–1971*, v. 2, p. 1518. The result was comparable to other polls in the late 1950's and thus scientifically meaningful.

[51] SCLC/KC, King address to Miami rally, February 12, 1958.

[52] Samuel Lubell, *White and Black: Test of a Nation* (New York: Harper and Row, 1964), p. 94.

[53] U. S. President. *Public Papers of the Presidents: Dwight D. Eisenhower* (1958), p. 393.

[54] *New York Times* and *Washington Post*, May 13 and 14, 1958.

55 SCLC/KC, SCLC conference, May 29, 1958, letter to Dwight D. Eisenhower.

56 SCLC/P, White House Conference, June 23, 1958.

57 Coretta Scott King, *My Life with Martin Luther King, Jr.*, p. 162.

58 Mrs. King cites the full text in *My Life with Martin Luther King, Jr.*, pp. 341–43.

59 *Ibid.*, pp. 173–80.

60 Foster Rhea Dulles, *The Civil Rights Commission: 1957–1965* (East Lansing: Michigan State University Press, 1968), p. 69.

61 *The Southern Patriot*, v. 17, no. 9 (November 1959), p. 2.

62 SCLC/KC, Resolutions adopted by the SCLC Convention, Columbia, South Carolina, October 1, 1959, no. 3.

63 *Ibid.*, Resolution, no. 9.

Chapter Three

1 Septima Clark interview with the author, August 11, 1984, Charleston, South Carolina, pp. 12–13 of typescript.

2 SCLC/KC, Files of the Executive Director's Office, Correspondence 1959–1960.

3 Oates, *Let the Trumpet Sound*, p. 150.

4 See, for example, Walker, *History of the Southern Christian Leadership Conference*, p. 63.

5 Interviews with Joseph E. Lowery, Ralph D. Abernathy, Septima P. Clark, Fred Taylor, Fred Shuttlesworth, and Kelly Miller Smith by the author, 1982–1984; SCLC/KC and SCLC/NH, Files of the President's Office, Executive Director, and Treasurer's Reports, 1959–1961, Executive Director's Reports To Annual Conventions, 1959, 1960.

6 BOH/HOW, Wyatt Tee Walker Interview; Walker interview with the author; and Oates, *Let the Trumpet Sound*, p. 157.

7 Franklin, *From Slavery to Freedom*, p. 476.

8 Langston Hughes, *Fight for Freedom: The Story of the NAACP* (New York: W. W. Norton and Co., 1962), p. 186.

9 Kelly Miller Smith interview with the author, May 26, 1983, Nashville, Tennessee, pp. 8–9 of typescript.

10 "Battle for the Lunch Counters: The Latest Drive for Integration," *U.S. News and World Report*, v. 68 (March 7, 1960), p. 44.

11 Lerone Bennett, *Confrontation: Black and White* (Chicago: Johnson Publishing Company, 1965), pp. 257–59.

12 Hughes, *Fight for Freedom*, pp. 187–90.

13 SCLC/KC, Anne Braden, Address to the SCLC Annual Convention, Birmingham, 1962.

14 Ezell Blair interview with Robert Penn Warren, *Who Speaks for the Negro?* (New York: Random House, 1964), p. 358.

15 Donald R. Matthews and James W. Prothro, *Negroes and the New Southern Politics* (New York: Harcourt, Brace and World, 1966), pp. 437–39.

16 James Lawson interview with the author, May 25, 1983, pp. 2–3 of typescript; Wyatt Tee Walker interview with the author, June 9, 1983, p. 2 of typescript; Julian Bond interview with Raines, *My Soul is Rested*, p. 102.

[17] Ezell Blair interview with Warren, *Who Speaks for the Negro?*, p. 361.

[18] Carson, *In Struggle*, pp. 13 and 17.

[19] Coretta Scott King, *My Life with Martin Luther King, Jr.*, p. 197ff.

[20] Miles Wolff, *Lunch at the Five and Ten, The Greensboro Sit-ins: A Contemporary History* (New York: Stein and Day, 1970), p. 16.

[21] See Raines, *My Soul is Rested*, p. 80; Lawson/Peake interview, p. 3. Lawson said he carried the comic book, "Martin Luther King and the Montgomery Story" everywhere he went. See also Coretta Scott King, *My Life With Martin Luther King, Jr.*, p. 188.

[22] Quoted in Raines, *My Soul is Rested*, p. 79.

[23] SCLC/KC, Summary of Raleigh Conference, April 16–18, 1960; Lawson/Peake interview, May 25, 1983, pp. 1–2 of typescript.

[24] Lawson/Peake interview, p. 2; Coretta Scott King, *My Life with Martin Luther King, Jr.*, pp. 188–89; Ralph Abernathy, *Treasurer's Report*, October 1961, comments on pp. 9–10 about youth activities; conversations with C. T. Vivian and Kelly Miller Smith.

[25] Howard Zinn, *SNCC: The New Abolitionists* (Boston: Beacon Press, 1964), p. 33.

[26] Archie E. Allen, "John Lewis: Keeper of the Dream," *New South*, Spring 1971; John Lewis interview with the author, p. 2 of typescript; and Carson, *In Struggle*, p. 21.

[27] Cleveland Sellers and Robert Terrell, *The River of No Return: The Autobiography of a Black Militant and the Life and Death of SNCC* (New York: Morrow, 1973), p. 35.

[28] Septima P. Clark/Peake interview, pp. 12–13 of typescript.

[29] MLK/KC, Martin Luther King, Jr., Address to the Shaw University Conference, April 17, 1960.

[30] Lawson/Peake interview, p. 2 of typescript.

[31] C. T. Vivian conversation with the author, April 28, 1983; Kelly Miller Smith interview with the author, p. 6 of typescript.

[32] Cf. Bennett, *What Manner of Man*, p. 114; Louis E. Lomax, *The Negro Revolt* (New York: Harper and Row, 1963), p. 99.

[33] Lawson/Peake interview, p. 4.

[34] *Ibid.*, p. 3; Smith/Peake interview, p. 6.

[35] Cited in Francis L. Broderick and August Meier, *Negro Protest Thought in the Twentieth Century* (New York: Bobbs-Merrill, 1965), pp. 274–81.

[36] SCLC/KC, Ralph Abernathy, Treasurer's Report, 1961.

[37] Broderick and Meier, *Negro Protest Thought*, pp. 273–74.

[38] *Christian Century*, v. 87 (March 16, 1960), pp. 308–09.

[39] Carson, *In Struggle*, pp. 25–26.

[40] Clark/Peake interview, pp. 5–9 of typescript.

[41] U.S. President. *Public Papers of the Presidents, Eisenhower, 1960–1961* (Washington, D.C.: Government Printing Office, 1962), p. 137.

[42] Foster Rhea Dulles, *The Civil Rights Commission, 1957–1965* (East Lansing: Michigan State University Press, 1968), pp. 109–31. Also useful is Emerson and Haber, *Political and Civil Rights*, pp. 1518–23.

[43] Brauer, *John F. Kennedy*, pp. 27–28.

[44] Bennett, *What Manner of Man*, p. 116.

[45] *New York Times*, May 29, 1960, p. 42, a full-page advertisement.

[46] Walker, *History of the Southern Christian Leadership Conference*, p. 76.

[47] SCLC/KC, Ralph Abernathy, Treasurer's Report, 1960–1961, pp. 1–2.

[48] Clark/Peake interview, pp. 6–7.

[49] For a general introduction, see Carl Tjerandsen, *Education for Citizenship: A Foundation's Experience* (Santa Cruz, California: Emil Schwarzhaupt Foundation, 1980), pp. 150ff.

[50] SCLC/KC, Public Relations, Confidential Report: *General Program 1960–1961*.

[51] *Ibid.*, p. 11.

[52] Oates, *Let the Trumpet Sound*, p. 160.

[53] Gloster B. Current, "Why Nixon Lost the Negro Vote," *The Crisis*, v. 68, no. 1 (January 1961), p. 11.

[54] Coretta Scott King, *My Life with Martin Luther King, Jr.*, p. 196.

[55] Theodore H. White, *The Making of the President, 1960* (New York: Atheneum, 1961), p. 323.

[56] Martin Luther King, Jr., "Equality Now," *The Nation*, v. 192, no. 2 (February 4, 1961), p. 95.

[57] Arthur M. Schlesinger, Jr., *A Thousand Days: John F. Kennedy in the White House* (Boston: Houston Mifflin, 1965), p. 932. See also U. S. President, *Public Papers of the Presidents: John F. Kennedy, 1961*, p. 67; Robert E. Gilbert, "John F. Kennedy and Civil Rights for Black Americans," *Presidential Studies Quarterly*, v. 12, no. 3 (Summer 1982), p. 388.

[58] Schlesinger, *A Thousand Days*, pp. 932–34; Brauer, *John F. Kennedy*, pp. 92ff.

[59] Carson, *In Struggle*, pp. 37–38.

[60] See Zinn, *SNCC*, pp. 40–42 and James Peck's account, *Freedom Ride* (New York: Grove, 1962), for a broader view by a participant.

[61] Lomax, *The Negro Revolt*, pp. 147–49; Earl and Mirian Selby, *Odyssey: Journey through Black America* (New York: Putnam Sons, 1971), pp. 72–73.

[62] C. T. Vivian conversation with the author, April 1983.

[63] Fred Shuttlesworth conversation with the author, April 1983.

[64] Meier and Rudwick, *CORE*, p. 138.

[65] Lomax, *The Negro Revolt*, p. 150. See also *The Crisis*, v. 68, no. 6 (June–July 1961), pp. 328–29.

[66] *The Crisis*, v. 68, no. 6 (June–July, 1961), p. 329.

[67] SCLC/KC, Report of Atlanta conference on Freedom Rides, May 26, 1961.

[68] Walker, *History of the Southern Christian Leadership Conference*, p. 101.

[69] SCLC/KC, Program, Sixth Annual Convention, Nashville, September 1961.

[70] SCLC/KC, King address at Nashville Freedom Rally, September 1961, pp. 1–2.

[71] Pat Watters, *Down to Now, Reflections on the Southern Civil Rights Movement* (New York: Pantheon Books, 1971), pp. 152–54.

[72] SKF, Albany Movement organizational chart, 1961, II, 1.

[73] See Lewis, *King*, p. 152.

[74] SKF, Albany Movement Statement of Aims, II, 1.

[75] Laurie Pritchett interview with Raines, *My Soul Is Rested*, p. 361.

[76] Andrew Young interview with Raines, *My Soul Is Rested*, p. 425.

[77] Lomax, *The Negro Revolt*, pp. 108–09.

[78] Watters, *Down To Now*, pp. 152ff.

[79] Lewis, *King*, p. 152.

[80] Pritchett interview with Raines, *My Soul Is Rested*, p. 363.

[81] Lewis, *King*, p. 150.

[82] Coretta Scott King, *My Life with Martin Luther King, Jr.*, p. 203.

[83] Man of the Year cover story, *Time* (January 3, 1964), p. 15.

[84] SCLC/KC, materials on the Gandhi Society, May 1962; Oates, *Let the Trumpet Sound*, p. 193.

[85] Pritchett interview with Raines, *My Soul Is Rested*, pp. 362–63; SCLC/KC clippings on Albany, July–August 1962.

[86] SKF, Slater King to President Kennedy, December 16, 1962, II, 2. Slater King told the President that the "unhuman treatment" of his wife "was not an isolated case but is symbolic of a system of lawlessness perpetrated by state officials against Negroes." See also Watters, *Down To Now*, p. 18 for excerpts from a 1970 interview with Marian King.

[87] See Claude Sitton, "Negroes Defy Ban," *New York Times*, July 21, 1962, p. 1 on background; Walker, *History of the Southern Christian Leadership Conference*, pp. 122–23; *New York Times*, July 26, 1962, p. 1; James Forman, *The Making of Black Revolutionaries*, pp. 275–77; Lewis, *King*, p. 163.

[88] See Martin Luther King, Jr., "The Case Against Tokenism," *New York Times Magazine*, August 5, 1962, p. 11.

[89] Coretta Scott King, *My Life with Martin Luther King, Jr.*, pp. 205–06.

[90] Martin Luther King, Jr., "The Terrible Cost of the Ballot," *SCLC Newsletter* (September 1962), pp. 1–2.

[91] Lomax, *The Negro Revolt*, p. 110. *The Crisis* carried a very critical review of Lomax's book in October 1962, pp. 465–70.

[92] Martin Luther King, Jr., *Why We Can't Wait* (New York: Harper and Row, 1964), pp. 34–35.

Chapter Four

[1] Andrew Young interview with Raines, *My Soul Is Rested*, p. 427.

[2] Carson, *In Struggle*, pp. 63–65.

[3] Lomax, *The Negro Revolt*, pp. 110–11 and 115–32.

[4] Vincent Harding and Staughton Lynd, "Albany, Georgia," *The Crisis*, v. 70, no. 2 (February 1963), p. 76.

[5] "Reverend Martin Luther King's Diary in Jail," *Jet*, August 23, 1962, p. 18.

[6] Shuttlesworth/Peake interview, pp. 16–18 of typescript; Walker/Peake interview, pp. 1–2 of typescript; and King, *Why We Can't Wait*, pp. 44–47.

[7] See King, *Stride Toward Freedom*, pp. 223–24; *Crisis*, v. 5, no. 4 (April 1968), pp. 114–15; King, *Where Do We Go From Here: Chaos or Community?* (New York: Harper and Row, 1967), pp. 188–91.

[8] Martin Luther King, Jr., "Fumbling on the New Frontier," *The Nation*, v. 194 (March 3, 1962), p. 190.

[9] *Ibid.*, pp. 191–92.

[10] See *New York Times*, January 3, 1962, p. 1; and *The Crisis*, v. 69 (May 1962), p. 277; and Brauer, *John F. Kennedy*, pp. 176–79.

[11] SCLC/KC, Ebenezer Baptist Church conference, Atlanta, January 10–11, 1957, working papers no. 1 and 3; SCLC/P, Areas of Concern defined by the SCLC Committee on Resolutions, October 1959, no. 11; Leadership Training Program materials, 1960; and Clark/Peake interview, pp. 1–3 of typescript.

[12] *SCLC Newsletter*, May 1961, p. 2; Septima Clark, "The Citizenship School: A Lamp Unto Their Feet," *The SCLC Story*, p. 53.

[13] William S. Kennedy, "Highlander Praxis: Learning with Myles Horton," an interview with Horton in *Teachers College Record*, v. 83, no. 1 (Fall 1981), pp. 105–19; Mike Clark, "Meeting the Needs of the Adult Learner," *Tennessee Adult Educator*, v. 11, no. 2 (Spring–Summer 1981), pp. 15–25; Frank Adams, *Unearthing Seeds of Fire: The Highlander Idea* (Winston Salem, N. C.: Blair Publishers, 1975), pp. 1–20; Aimee Horton, "The Highlander Folk School: Pioneer of Integration in the South," *Teachers College Record*, v. 68, no. 3 (December 1966).

[14] See Walker, *History of the Southern Christian Leadership Conference*, pp. 90–91.

[15] SCLC/P, SCLC Annual Convention, Resolutions Adopted, October 1959, Resolution no. 5.

[16] King, "Leadership Training Program and Citizenship Schools," memorandum, n.d. (after October 1960), cited in part in Carl Tjerandsen, *Education for Citizenship*, p. 181; see also *SCLC Newsletter*, May 1961, p. 2; and Clark/Peake interview, pp. 1–2 of typescript.

[17] SCLC/KC, Ralph Abernathy, Treasurer's Report, October 1961; Wyatt Tee Walker, Executive Director's Report, 1961; *SCLC Newsletter*, May 1961, p. 2; Clark/Peake interview, pp. 2–5; and Tjerandsen, *Education for Citizenship*, pp. 181–82.

[18] Clark/Peake interview, pp. 3–8 of typescript.

[19] See Lewis, *King*, pp. 136–37; Zinn, *SNCC*, pp. 58–59; and Oates, *Let the Trumpet Sound*, p. 179.

[20] United States Census Data, cited in Matthews and Prothro, *Negroes and the New Southern Politics*, p. 18, Table 1–1.

[21] Meier and Rudwick, *CORE*, pp. 179–81; and Carson, *In Struggle*, pp. 70–71; SCLC/KC, President's Annual Report, 1963, pp. 2–5.

[22] SCLC/KC, President's Annual Reports, 1963 and 1964.

[23] SCLC/P, Administrative Council, Minutes of quarterly meeting, March 6–9, 1961.

[24] SCLC/KC, Dorothy Cotton, Description of the Citizenship Education Program, Records of the Program Department, 1962.

[25] *SCLC Newsletter*, August 1963, p. 3 and September 1963, p. 12; President's Annual Report, 1963, pp. 3–4.

[26] SCLC/KC, President's Annual Report, 1966, pp. 6–7.

[27] Cited in Barbara A. Reynolds, *Jesse Jackson: the Man, the Movement, the Myth* (Chicago: Nelson-Hall, 1975), p. 107.

[28] SCLC/KC, President's Annual Report, 1966, p. 9.

[29] SCLC/KC, Fred C. Bennette, Jr., Operation Breadbasket, Report to SCLC, 1966, pp. 3–5.

[30] SCLC/KC, Wyatt Tee Walker, Report to the SCLC Annual Convention, September 1962, pp. 1–9.

[31] Walker/Peake interview, p. 1 of typescript.

[32] Cited in Lewis, *King*, pp. 173–74; see also *I Have a Dream: The Story of Martin Luther King in Text and Pictures* (New York: Time-Life, 1968), pp. 37–8; *Why We Can't Wait*, pp. 88–9.

[33] Shuttlesworth/Peake interview, p. 5 of typescript.

[34] *Ibid.*; and King, *Why We Can't Wait*, p. 47.

[35] SCLC/KC Board of Directors meeting, Chattanooga, Tennessee, May 1962; King,

Why We Can't Wait, p. 45; Shuttlesworth/Peake interview, Cincinatti, April 8, 1983, p. 5 of typescript.

[36] *Why We Can't Wait*, pp. 6–11; King, "Emancipation Proclamation," *Amsterdam News*, November 10, 1962, p. 1: SCLC/KC, King address to the Interfaith Conference on Civil Rights, Chicago, January 15, 1963.

[37] King, *Why We Can't Wait*, pp. xi–xii; Coretta Scott King, *My Life with Martin Luther King, Jr.*, p. 215.

[38] Martin Luther King, Jr., "Bold New Design for a New South," *The Nation*, v. 196, no. 13 (March 30, 1963), p. 259.

[39] Ed Gardner interview with Raines, *My Soul is Rested*, pp. 139–40.

[40] Shuttlesworth/Peake interview, pp. 18–19 of typescript.

[41] Martin Luther King, Jr., *SCLC Newsletter*, July 1963, pp. 1 and 4.

[42] See Oates, *Let the Trumpet Sound*, pp. 211–12 for a recent version of this view. Oates argues that King's thinking on nonviolent resistance was changing, but he does not discriminate between strategy and philosophy as seems desirable. Cf. Bennett, *What Manner of Man*, pp. 137–51; David J. Garrow, *Protest at Selma: Martin Luther King, Jr. and the Voting Rights Act of 1965* (New Haven: Yale University Press, 1978), pp. 221–25.

[43] Cited in Lewis, *King*, pp. 173–74; see also *I Have a Dream: The Story . . . in Text and Pictures*, pp. 37–8; King, *Why We Can't Wait*, pp. 88–9.

[44] SCLC/KC, King address to the Sixth Annual Convention, Birmingham, September 28, 1962, pp. 3–4.

[45] SCLC/KC, Anne Braden address to the Sixth Annual Convention, Birmingham, September 27, 1962, pp. 1–4.

[46] SCLC/KC, Jackie Robinson address to the Sixth Annual Convention, September 28, 1962, pp. 1–3; Otis Moss address, p. 1.

[47] See King's address to the Birmingham Convention; Oates, *Let the Trumpet Sound*, p. 206; King, "Who Is Their God?," *The Nation*, v. 195 (October 13, 1962), pp. 209–10.

[48] King already assumed this and preparations were continuing for launching the campaign in conjunction with the spring shopping season. See King, *Why We Can't Wait*, pp. 47–8 and *New York Times*, March 1, 1963, p. 1.

[49] King, *Why We Can't Wait*, pp. 49 and 63ff.

[50] Walker, Shuttlesworth, and Abernathy interviews with the author; Walker, *History of the Southern Christian Leadership Conference*, pp. 133–4; BOH/HOW, Walker interview; King, *Why We Can't Wait*, pp. 47–8; David Brown, "Birmingham, Alabama: A City in Fear," *Saturday Evening Post*, March 2, 1963, pp. 16–17; Cf. Garrow, *FBI and Martin Luther King, Jr., from 'Solo' to Memphis* (New York: W. W. Norton, 1981), p. 58, and note the divergent treatment.

[51] Shuttlesworth/Peake interview, pp. 20–24 of typescript. See also King, *Why We Can't Wait*, p. 63; Lewis, *King*, p. 175.

[52] SCLC/KC, Birmingham campaign, organizational plans; King, *Why We Can't Wait*, p. 60.

[53] King, *Why We Can't Wait*, p. 49.

[54] SCLC/P, Birmingham pledge cards; King cites them in *Why We Can't Wait*, pp. 61–2; also Coretta Scott King, *My Life with Martin Luther King, Jr.*, pp. 218–19.

[55] SCLC/P, "Birmingham Manifesto," April 3, 1963; also cited in *SCLC Newsletter*, July 1963, pp. 2 and 4.

434

56 SCLC/P, Statement of Birmingham Campaign aims, April 4, 1963; *New York Times*, April 5, 1963, p. 16.

57 King, *Why We Can't Wait*, p. 67; see also *Washington Post*, April 7, 1963, p. 1ff; *New York Times*, April 7, 1963, p. 55.

58 King, *Why We Can't Wait*, p. 57.

59 See Ed Gardner interview with Raines, *My Soul Is Rested*, p. 143; Shuttlesworth/Peake interview, p. 10 of typescript.

60 SCLC/KC, King press conference, April 11, 1963.

61 Abernathy/Peake interview, April 4, 1983, p. 14 of typescript.

62 See *New York Times*, April 13, 1963, p. 15.

63 King, *Why We Can't Wait*, pp. 70–1.

64 Abernathy/Peake interview, April 4, 1983, pp. 14–15 of typescript.

65 Coretta Scott King, *My Life with Martin Luther King, Jr.*, pp. 222–23.

66 King, *Why We Can't Wait*, pp. 74–5.

67 Shuttlesworth/Peake interview.

68 King, *Why We Can't Wait*, p. 102.

69 SCLC/P, Andrew J. Young, Address to the SCLC Annual Convention Banquet, Birmingham, August 11, 1982.

70 Coretta Scott King, *My Life with Martin Luther King, Jr.*, p. 230; Abernathy/Peake interview, April 22, 1983, p. 15 of typescript; SCLC/P, Young, Address to the Twenty-Fifth SCLC Annual Convention Banquet, August 11, 1982.

71 Schlesinger, *A Thousand Days*, p. 959.

72 *Washington Post*, May 5, 1963, p. 1.

73 King, *Why We Can't Wait*, p. 109.

74 See Claude Sitton, "Rioting Negroes Routed by Police," *New York Times*, May 8, 1963, p. 28; Shuttlesworth/Peake interview, pp. 17–18 of typescript.

75 Shuttlesworth/Peake interview, p. 21 of typescript.

76 *Ibid.*, pp. 21–25; see also Shuttlesworth interview, BOH/HOW and in Raines, *My Soul Is Rested*, pp. 154–61.

77 Shuttlesworth/Peake interview, p. 21 of typescript. One must note that the Kennedys were attempting all along to stop the violence in Birmingham, which is a somewhat different concern from that of the black leaders, albeit overlapping with theirs. Sid Smyer, a Birmingham real-estate executive and admittedly a segregationist, was one local leader who saw the pragmatic necessity of coming to terms. He reports that he was called to Washington by Kennedy in the spring of 1963 to discuss the problem. Smyer says that he discouraged the President from sending federal forces so that they could work it out locally. On May 7, says Smyer, he urged King to stop the demonstrations and get out of Birmingham. See Raines, *My Soul Is Rested*, pp. 162–66.

78 *Ibid.*

79 King, *Why We Can't Wait*, p. 115.

80 John Lewis interview with the author, June 20, 1983, pp. 1–2 of typescript. See also "On The March," *Newsweek*, v. 61, no. 19 (September 2, 1963), photograph of leaders, p. 18.

81 Schlesinger, *A Thousand Days*, p. 969; and Lewis/Peake interview, June 20, 1983, p. 1 of typescript; Anderson, *A. Philip Randolph*, p. 326.

82 *Ibid.*

[83] Schlesinger, *A Thousand Days*, p. 970.

[84] *New York Times*, July 1, 1963, p. 1.

[85] SCLC/KC, King interview with Robert Penn Warren, March 18, 1964, p. 2.

Chapter Five

[1] *New York Times*, June 24, 1963, p. 20.

[2] *Ibid.*; see also James Alonzo Bishop, *The Days of Martin Luther King, Jr.* (New York: G. P. Putnam's Sons, 1971), p. 316.

[3] Lewis/Peake interview, p. 2.

[4] All quotations are from King's "I Have a Dream" speech, text in SCLC/KC. For full copy of text see Appendix.

[5] Coretta Scott King, *My Life with Martin Luther King, Jr.*, p. 241.

[6] Malcolm X and Alex Haley, *Autobiography of Malcolm X* (New York: The Grove Press, 1963), p. 281.

[7] See Arthur Meier Schlesinger, *Robert Kennedy and His Times* (Boston: Houghton Mifflin, 1978), pp. 358–61.

[8] *The Crisis*, v. 70, no. 6 (June–July 1963), p. 327.

[9] Coretta Scott King, *My Life with Martin Luther King, Jr.*, p. 243.

[10] King, *Why We Can't Wait*, pp. 113–14.

[11] King, *Stride Toward Freedom*, p. 207.

[12] SCLC/KC, Wyatt Tee Walker, "The Meaning of Birmingham," *The SCLC Story in Words and Pictures*, edited by Edward T. Clayton (Atlanta: SCLC, 1964), p. 31.

[13] *Ibid.*

[14] King, *Why We Can't Wait*, p. 121.

[15] Walker interview with Warren, in Robert Penn Warren, *Who Speaks for the Negro?*, pp. 224–25; King, *Why We Can't Wait*, pp. 165–67.

[16] SCLC/KC, Walker address to the Seventh Annual SCLC Convention, Richmond, Va., September 25, 1963.

[17] SCLC/KC, King address to the Seventh Annual SCLC Convention, Richmond, Va., September 25, 1963.

[18] SCLC/KC, Walker address to the Seventh Annual SCLC Convention.

[19] MLK/KC, King comments to the press, September 27, 1963; see also the *Richmond Times*, September 28, 1963, p. 1

[20] Kenneth B. Clark interview with Malcolm X in the television series "The Negro and the American Promise," National Educational Television, 1963, Videofilm in the National Archives, Washington, D.C. See also Kenneth B. Clark, *The Negro Protest* (Boston: Beacon Press, 1963).

[21] Many of the official details of the FBI's investigations of King and SCLC are available in U. S. Congress, House of Representatives, *Investigation of the Assassination of Martin Luther King, Jr.: Hearings Before the Select Committee on Assassinations of the U. S. House of Representatives, 95th Congress, Second Session* (Washington, D.C.: Government Printing Office, 1978), hereinafter cited as HRSCA: King. But for perspective one must also see Garrow, *The FBI and Martin Luther King, Jr.*; and Andrew Young interview with Howell Raines, *My Soul Is Rested*, pp. 430–31.

[22] See Oates, *Let the Trumpet Sound*, pp. 282–85 on King's relations with women, but be cautious about any account, however well researched, on such a personal and elusive matter.

[23] Julius Lester, "The Martin Luther King I Remember," *Evergreen Review*, v. 74 (January 1970), pp. 20–21. See King, *Strength to Love* for a number of pertinent sermons.

[24] James Lawson interview with the author, May 25, 1983, pp. 1–2 of typescript.

[25] SCLC/KC, Ralph D. Abernathy, Treasurer's Report to the SCLC Board of Directors, October, 1963.

[26] Tyrone Brooks interview with the author, Georgia State Capitol, April 1, 1983, pp. 2–3 of typescript; Hosea Williams interview with the author, March 31, 1983, pp. 10–13 of typescript; and Williams interview with Raines, *My Soul Is Rested*, pp. 435–45.

[27] Williams interview with the author, p. 2 of typescript.

[28] C. T. Vivian conversations with the author, February 16 and March 31, 1983.

[29] Martin Luther King, "In a Word—Now," in "What Next?: Five Negro Leaders Reply," *New York Times Magazine*, September 29, 1963, p. 92.

[30] Chris McNair interview with Raines, *My Soul Is Rested*, pp. 184–85; McNair was the father of eleven-year-old Denise McNair, one of the victims of September 1963.

[31] *Atlanta Constitution*, December 16, 1963, p. 1; Lewis, *King*, pp. 233–34.

[32] Coretta Scott King, *My Life with Martin Luther King, Jr.*, p. 244.

[33] Martin Luther King, "It's a Difficult Thing to Teach a President," *Look*, v. 28 (November 17, 1964), p. 61.

[34] King, *Why We Can't Wait*, pp. 158–60.

[35] *Ibid.*, p. 161.

[36] *Ibid.*

[37] See Watters, *Down to Now*, pp. 276–77.

[38] U. S. President, *Public Papers: Lyndon B. Johnson, 1963–1964*, v. 1, p. 10.

[39] *State of the Union Messages of the Presidents*, Lyndon B. Johnson, First Annual Message, January 8, 1964, pp. 3156–61; and Lyndon B. Johnson, *My Hope for America* (New York: Random House, 1964), pp. 52–54; and Doris Kearns, *Lyndon Johnson and the American Dream* (New York: Harper and Row, 1976), p. 192.

[40] Martin Luther King, "The Hammer of Civil Rights," *The Nation*, v. 198, no. 11 (March 9, 1964), pp. 230–34.

[41] See "The Dirksen Amendments," *The New Republic*, v. 150, no. 23 (June 6, 1964), pp. 3–4. For a complete list of Senators and how they voted, see *The Crisis*, v. 71, no. 7 (August–September, 1964), pp. 432–33.

[42] U. S. President, *Public Papers: Johnson, 1963–1964*, v. 2, pp. 842–44.

[43] *The Crisis*, v. 71, no. 7 (August–September, 1964), p. 434.

[44] "With New Civil-Rights Law—How Negroes See the Future," *U. S. News and World Report*, v. 56, no. 26 (June 29, 1964), p. 39.

[45] SCLC/KC, King, Statement before the Republican Platform Committee, July 7, 1964 at the San Francisco National Convention.

[46] Kearns, *Lyndon Johnson*, p. 228.

[47] King, *Why We Can't Wait*, p. 155.

[48] *Ibid.*, p. 168.

[49] Carson, *In Struggle*, pp. 142–44.

[50] SCLC/KC, Materials on the Black Mountain Retreat, January 1964; SCLC Board of Directors Meeting, April 16, 1964.

[51] See Oates, *Let the Trumpet Sound*, pp. 291–92 for a brief treatment; also SCLC/KC, Board of Directors meeting, April 16, 1964; Willie Bolden interview with Raines, *My Soul Is Rested*, pp. 451–52; Abernathy conversation with the author, March 31, 1983.

[52] See Garrow, *The FBI and Martin Luther King, Jr.*, pp. 116ff.

[53] SCLC/KC, Ponder to King, January 28, 1964.

[54] *Ibid.*, and William McCord, *Mississippi: The Long, Hot Summer* (New York: W. W. Norton, 1965), p. 23.

[55] BOH/HOW, Hayling interview with John H. Britton, August 16, 1967; Watters, *Down To Now*, pp. 278–82; Lewis, *King*, pp. 240–42; John Dillin, "The Story of St. Augustine," *Christian Science Monitor*, July 13, 1964.

[56] Martin Luther King, Interview in *Playboy Magazine*, January 1965, reprint by HMH Publishing Co., 1965, p. 4.

[57] *Ibid.*

[58] See Bennett, *What Manner of Man*, p. 210.

[59] *New York Times*, November 7, 1963, p. 30.

[60] See Bishop, *The Days of Martin Luther King, Jr.*, p. 343.

[61] Larry Goodwyn, "Anarchy in St. Augustine," *Harper's Magazine*, v. 230. no. 1376 (January 1965), p. 78.

[62] *Ibid.*, p. 79.

[63] See "Civil Rights: Fantasy's End," *Newsweek*, v. 64, no. 7 (August 17, 1964), p. 28.

[64] SCLC/KC, King, Statement before the Republican Platform Committee, July 7, 1964, p. 8.

[65] SCLC/KC, King, Statement before the Democratic Platform Committee, August 22, 1964, p. 3.

[66] Rowland Evans and Robert Novak, *Lyndon B. Johnson: The Exercise of Power* (New York: New American Library, 1966), pp. 452–55.

[67] King, *Where Do We Go From Here?*, pp. 146–47.

[68] *New York Times*, July 30, 1964; "Negro Leaders Ban Demonstrations," *Christian Century*, v. 81, no. 33 (August 12, 1964), p. 1005.

[69] Coretta Scott King, *My Life with Martin Luther King, Jr.*, p. 246; King, *Where Do We Go From Here?*, pp. 146–47; Hosea Williams, "SCLC Puts Might of Its Organization Against Goldwaterism," *SCLC Newsletter* (October–November, 1964), pp. 1–2; SCLC/KC, July–August 1964 newsclippings on political campaign.

[70] See excerpts from Farmer's report to the 1965 CORE Convention in Meier and Rudwick, *CORE*, pp. 230–31.

[71] *Ibid.*

[72] SCLC/KC, Eighth Annual Convention, Savannah, Georgia, October 1, 1965, Presidential Address, pp. 2–3; see also King, *Where Do We Go From Here?*, pp. 152–57 for a more fully synthesized commentary.

[73] See King's comments to Robert Penn Warren in *Who Speaks for The Negro?*, p. 216.

[74] *Ibid.*, pp. 209–210.

[75] King, *Where Do We Go From Here?*, pp. 159–61; "A Need for Soul Searching," *SCLC Newsletter* (October–November, 1964), p. 7.

[76] "The Big Man is Martin Luther King, Jr.," *Newsweek*, v. 62, no. 5 (July 29, 1963), p. 31.

[77] For an inside account see Coretta Scott King, *My Life with Martin Luther King, Jr.*,

pp. 2–3 and 247–53; a good brief account with pictures is in Bennett, *What Manner of Man*, pp. 224–28; *New York Times*, October 15, 1964, p. 1.

78 SCLC/KC, King, Statement in response to the Hoover comments, November 19, 1964.

79 Garrow, *The FBI and Martin Luther King*, p. 130.

80 *Ibid.*, pp. 173–74.

81 Oates, *Let the Trumpet Sound*, p. 365.

Chapter Six

1 Oates, *Let The Trumpet Sound*, p. 365.

2 David J. Garrow, *Protest at Selma*; p. 31; Carson, *In Struggle*, pp. 157–58; Zinn, *SNCC*, pp. 149–66; and Charles E. Fager, *Selma 1965* (New York: Charles Scribner's Sons, 1974), pp. 1–7.

3 Julian Bond interview with Raines, *My Soul Is Rested*, pp. 213–14.

4 Martin Luther King, Jr., "Behind the Selma March," *Saturday Review*, v. 68, no. 14 (April 3, 1965), pp. 16, 17, and 57; Watters, *Down To Now*, p. 323.

5 *New York Times*, January 20, 1965, p. 18; and *Washington Post*, January 20, 1965, p. 10.

6 *New York Times*, February 5, 1965, p. 15.

7 Garrow, *Protest at Selma*, pp. 58–60.

8 Raines, *My Soul Is Rested*, pp. 206–08.

9 Flip Schulke, *Martin Luther King, Jr.: A Documentary, Montgomery to Memphis* (New York: Norton, 1976), pp. 141–42.

10 Lewis, *King*, pp. 284–85.

11 Eldridge Cleaver, *Soul On Ice*, seventh edition (New York: Dell, 1972), p. 76.

12 Garrow, *Protest at Selma*, p. 223.

13 Kenneth L. Smith and Ira G. Zepp, Jr., *Search for the Beloved Community: The Thinking of Martin Luther King, Jr.* (Valley Forge: Judson Press, 1974), p. 120.

14 Ansbro, *Martin Luther King, Jr.*, p. 186.

15 King, *Where Do We Go From Here?*, p. 137.

16 *Ibid.*, p. 148.

17 *Ibid.*, p. 157.

18 *Ibid.*

19 *Ibid.*, p. 160.

20 *Ibid.*, p. 157.

21 Harold A. Nelson, "Whither the Civil Rights Struggle?," *The Crisis* v. 72, no. 9 (November 1965), pp. 556–57.

22 King, "Let Justice Roll Down," *The Nation*, v. 200, no. 11 (March 15, 1965), p. 273.

23 See *U. S. News and World Report*, March 29, 1965, p. 8.

24 King, "Let Justice Roll Down," p. 271.

25 SCLC/KC, President's report to the Board of Directors, Baltimore, April 1, 1965.

26 SCLC/KC, Records of the SCLC Board meeting in Baltimore, Maryland, April 1–2, 1965.

[27] *SCLC Newsletter*, April–May 1965, pp. 1–2.

[28] King, *Where Do We Go From Here?*, p. 145.

[29] Cited in Ansbro, *Martin Luther King, Jr.*, opposite title page.

[30] SCLC/P, Martin Luther King, Jr., Address to the Association of the Bar of the City of New York, *The Record of the Association of the Bar of New York*, May 1965, pp. 5–7.

[31] *Ibid.*, p. 19.

[32] King, *Where Do We Go From Here?*, p. 3.

[33] *Ibid.*, p. 4.

[34] *Ibid.*, p. 6.

[35] SLCL/KC, Ralph Abernathy, Treasurer's Reports, 1964–1965, and 1965–1966.

[36] SCLC/KC, Walter E. Fauntroy, Director of the Washington Bureau, Staff Report, September 1964, p. 1

[37] SCLC/KC, Walter E. Fauntroy, Director of the Washington Bureau, Staff Report, August 1965; p. 1.

[38] SCLC/KC, Martin Luther King, Jr., Presidential Report to the Ninth Annual SCLC Convention, Birmingham, Alabama, August 11, 1965, p. 7.

[39] SCLC/KC, Harry G. Boyte, Address on Dialogue to the SCLC National Convention, Birmingham, August 1965.

[40] *Ibid.*

[41] SCLC/KC, King, Presidential Report to the Ninth Annual SCLC Convention, p. 7.

[42] Dialogue Brochure, "A Search for Reconciliation," 1965, p. 4.

[43] SCLC/KC, Martin Luther King, Jr., Address to the SCOPE Conference, Atlanta, June 16, 1965, p. 1.

[44] Carson, *In Struggle*, pp. 186–87.

[45] SCLC/KC, Hosea Williams, SCOPE Director, Report to Martin Luther King, Jr., November 6, 1965, p. 1. Leon Hall, interview with the author, 1986, pp. 25–28 of typescript.

[46] *Ibid.*

[47] SCLC/KC, Ralph Abernathy, Treasurer's Reports, 1963–1965; Records of the Program Director, 1964 and 1965.

[48] SCLC/KC, Fred Shuttlesworth, Greetings to the SCLC Convention, August 11, 1965, Birmingham, Alabama, Program, pp. 2–3.

[49] SCLC/KC, Andrew J. Young, "An Experiment in Power," Keynote Address to the Ninth Annual SCLC Convention, Birmingham, August 11, 1965, p. 2.

[50] *Ibid.*

[51] SCLC/P, Martin Luther King, SCLC Ninth Annual Convention, Birmingham, Program, p. 5.

[52] Franklin, *From Slavery to Freedom*, p. 360.

[53] Rustin, *Strategies for Freedom*, p. 61.

[54] See Bishop, *Days of Martin Luther King*, pp. 405–13.

[55] SCLC/NH, Martin Luther King Statement in Los Angeles on the Watts riots, August 17, 1965, p. 1.

[56] *Ibid., passim.*

[57] SCLC/KC, Report of the Committee on Resolutions, Ninth SCLC Convention, Birmingham, August 1965, Program, p. 16.

[58] Carson, *In Struggle*, pp. 186–87.

[59] Bishop, *Days of Martin Luther King*, p. 404.

⁶⁰ "King Acts for Peace," *The Christian Century*, v. 82, no. 39 (September 29, 1965), p. 1181.

⁶¹ Garrow, *FBI and Martin Luther King, Jr.*, p. 179.

⁶² Stoney Cooks, Interview with the author, Atlanta, July 1983, p. 4 of typescript. Leon Hall/Peake interview, pp. 28–31 of typescript.

⁶³ "King Comes to Chicago," *The Christian Century*, v. 82, (August 11, 1965), p. 979.

⁶⁴ Lewis, *King*, p. 318.

⁶⁵ Martin Luther King, Jr., "The Last Steep Ascent," *The Nation*, v. 202, no. 11 (March 14, 1966), p. 288.

Chapter Seven

¹ SCLC/KC, Spring Board of Directors Meeting, Miami, Florida, April 10, 1966.

² SCLC/KC, Andrew J. Young, Report to the SCLC Board of Directors, Miami, April 10, 1966.

³ King, *Where Do We Go From Here?*, p. 50.

⁴ *Ibid.*, p. 59.

⁵ *Ibid.*, p. 51.

⁶ See the *Chicago Tribune*, May 27, 1966, p. 1.

⁷ Carson, *In Struggle*, p. 207.

⁸ Lewis resigned in late June 1966, after hearing of SNCC officials subterfuge in getting SCLC officials arrested. He did not renounce Black Power but offered his "personal commitment to nonviolence." See Carson, *In Struggle*, p. 231 and the *Los Angeles Times*, June 29, 1966.

⁹ King, *Where Do We Go From Here?*, pp. 31–32.

¹⁰ Stokely Carmichael and Charles V. Hamilton, *Black Power: the Politics of Liberation in America* (New York: Random House, 1967), p. 50.

¹¹ *Ibid.*, p. 53.

¹² Floyd B. Barbour, *The Black Power Revolt* (Boston: Porter Sargent, 1968), pp. 63–65.

¹³ "Black Power: Politics of Frustration," *Newsweek*, v. 68, no. 2 (July 11, 1966), p. 26.

¹⁴ Flip Schulke, *Martin Luther King, Jr.*, p. 174.

¹⁵ King, *Where Do We Go From Here?*, pp. 30–35.

¹⁶ SCLC/KC, "I Have a Dream" tape.

¹⁷ Schulke, *Martin Luther King, Jr.*, p. 182.

¹⁸ King, *Where Do We Go From Here?*, p. 50.

¹⁹ Coretta Scott King, *My Life with Martin Luther King, Jr.*, p. 278.

²⁰ Oates, *Let the Trumpet Sound*, p. 405.

²¹ King, *Where Do We Go From Here?*, p. 37.

²² Cited in Paul Good, "A White Look at Black Power," *The Nation*, v. 203 (August 8, 1966), p. 115.

²³ Stokely Carmichael, "Toward Black Liberation," *Massachusetts Review*, v. 7 (Autumn 1966), p. 642.

[24] U. S. Congress. Senate. Permanent Subcommittee on Investigation, Committee on Government Operations, *Riots, Civil and Criminal Disorders*, 91st Congress, First Session, Part 2, November 21, 1967, pp. 683–84.

[25] Carmichael, "Toward Black Liberation," pp. 642–51.

[26] King, *Where Do We Go From Here?*, p. 57.

[27] See Carson, *In Struggle*, pp. 192, 198, and 235.

[28] SNCC after this became more nationalistic and eventually was led by H. Rap Brown, a man often in trouble with authorities for inciting riots and committing crimes. For Carmichael's speech in Jackson, see Lester A. Sobel, editor, *Civil Rights 1960–1966* (New York: Facts on File, 1967), p. 396. Cf. King, *Where Do We Go From Here?*, pp. 27–32.

[29] See *Newsweek*, v. 68 (August 22, 1966), p. 58.

[30] Interview with Rev. Jesse Jackson in Schulke, *Martin Luther King, Jr.*, p. 186.

[31] SCLC/KC, "King Address on Freedom Sunday," July 10, 1966, pp. 2–3.

[32] See *New York Times*, July 11, 1966, p. 1.

[33] *Chicago Tribune*, July 12, 1966, p. 2.

[34] "West Side Story," *Newsweek*, v. 68 (July 25, 1966), pp. 17–18.

[35] See *Chicago Tribune*, August 6, 1966, p. 1.

[36] Lewis, *King*, p. 348.

[37] "Still King," *Christian Century*, v. 83 (September 7, 1966), pp. 1071–72.

[38] Mike Royko, *Chicago Daily News*, April 5, 1967.

[39] Barbara A. Reynolds, *Jesse Jackson*, pp. 9–10.

[40] SCLC/KC, Transcript of Face the Nation Broadcast, August 1965.

[41] King, *Where Do We Go From Here?*, p. 86.

[42] For a useful critique see "The Hard Choice," *The New Republic*, v. 156 (February 4, 1967), pp. 7–8.

[43] Coretta Scott King, *My Life with Martin Luther King, Jr.*, pp. 292–93.

[44] SCLC/KC, SCLC Board of Directors Meeting, April 1966, Miami.

[45] Emmet John Hughes, "A Curse of Confusion," *Newsweek*, v. 69 (May 1, 1967), p. 1.

[46] Carl T. Rowan, "Martin Luther King's Tragic Decision," *Reader's Digest*, v. 90 (September 1967), p. 37.

[47] Garrow, *FBI and Martin Luther King, Jr.*, pp. 181–83.

[48] David Halberstam, "The Second Coming of Martin Luther King," *Harper's Magazine*, v. 235, no. 1407 (August 1967), pp. 47–50.

[49] See *New York Times*, April 13, 1967; SCLC/KC, clippings on King's responses and "Proposed Vietnam Form Letter;" and Ansbro, *Martin Luther King*, Jr., pp. 256–65.

[50] Reinhold Niebuhr, cited in Committee of Clergy and Laymen Concerned About Vietnam, *Dr. Martin Luther King, Jr., Dr. John C. Bennett, Dr. Henry Steele Commager, Rabbi Abraham Herschel Speak on the War in Vietnam* (1968), p. 3.

[51] See King, "Vietnam is Upon Us," February 6, 1968, Reprint by Clergy and Laymen Concerned About Vietnam, pp. 23–24; King, "The Domestic Impact of the War in Vietnam," November 11, 1967; SCLC/KC, clippings on King's speeches on Vietnam; King, "The Casualties of the War in Vietnam," *The Nation Institute*, February 25, 1967, Reprint by Clergy and Laymen Concerned About Vietnam, pp. 5–6; and for a comprehensive examination see Ansbro, *Martin Luther King, Jr.*, pp. 256–65.

[52] King, *The Trumpet of Conscience* (New York: Harper and Row, 1968), p. 72.

[53] Halberstam, "The Second Coming of Martin Luther King," pp. 47–50.

442

⁵⁴ Cited in "Negroes Go National with Demands for Jobs," *Business Week*, no. 1981 (August 19, 1967), p. 37.

⁵⁵ SCLC/KC, Sidney Poitier, "Keynote Address," Tenth Anniversary Convention of SCLC, Atlanta, August 14, 1967, p. 3.

⁵⁶ SCLC/KC, King, "President's Message," Tenth Anniversary Convention of SCLC, Atlanta, Georgia, p. 1.

⁵⁷ King, "A Proper Sense of Priorities," address, February 6, 1968, in Martin Luther King Speaks series; King, "Showdown for Nonviolence," *Look*, v. 32, no. 8 (April 16, 1968), p. 24; and SCLC/NH, Poor People's Campaign files.

⁵⁸ "Challenge/Response," *New Republic*, v. 156 (March 16, 1968), pp. 5–6.

⁵⁹ George Goodman, "He Lives, Man!" *Look*, v. 33 (April 15, 1969), p. 29.

⁶⁰ SCLC/KC, King, "Plans for the Poor People's Campaign," Staff Meeting, Atlanta, February 12, 1968.

⁶¹ SCLC/KC, Poor People's Campaign files, 1968; and Abernathy/Peake interviews.

⁶² Cited in *Martin Luther King, Jr., 1929–1968; An Ebony Picture Biography*, p. 75; also copies in King's sermons and speeches, SCLC/KC.

Chapter Eight

¹ "SCLC on the Couch," *Newsweek*, v. 73, no. 24 (December 9, 1968), p. 34.

² Bernita (Mrs. Fred C.) Bennett, Interview with the author, December 16, 1981, at the King Center in Atlanta, p. 2 of typescript.

³ "Coretta King reveals What's Happening to the Martin Luther King, Jr. Memorial Center," *Jet*, v. 29, no. 5 (November 5, 1970), p. 12.

⁴ Bernita Bennett/Peake interview, p. 3 of typescript.

⁵ Martin Luther King, Sr., *Daddy King: An Autobiography* (New York: William Morrow, 1980), p. 190.

⁶ SCLC/KC, Clippings on King's death; also cited in Coretta Scott King, *My Life with Martin Luther King, Jr.*, p. 345.

⁷ "Johnson, King, and Ho Chi Minh," *Christianity Today*, v. 12, no. 15 (April 26, 1968), p. 24.

⁸ Ralph D. Abernathy, Editorial, *Soul Force*, v. 1, no 6 (August 15, 1968), p. 24; Abernathy/Peake interview, April 22, 1983, pp. 4–5 of typescript; SCLC/ND, Poor People's Campaign Leaflets, 1968; SCLC/KC, Poor People's Campaign Papers.

⁹ "The Martyrdom of Martin Luther King, Jr.," *The Crisis*, v. 5, no. 4 (April 1968), pp. 114–15.

¹⁰ Carlyle C. Douglas, "Ralph Abernathy: the Man Who Fights to Keep King's Dream Alive," *Ebony*, v. 25 (January 1970), pp. 40–44; Abernathy/Peake conversations March and April 1983.

¹¹ For a general treatment of Abernathy's situation in the aftermath of King's death, see Paul Good, "No Man Can Fill Dr. King's Shoes—But Abernathy Tries," *New York Times*, May 26, 1968, pp. VI, 28ff.

¹² King, *Stride Toward Freedom*, p. 74.

¹³ Abernathy/Peake interview, April 22, 1983, p. 1 of typescript.

[14] Coretta Scott King, *My Life with Martin Luther King, Jr.*, pp. 318–20.

[15] Abernathy/Peake interview, April 22, 1983, p. 2; Hosea Williams/Peake interview, March 31, 1983, p. 2 gives substantially the same account.

[16] Abernathy/Peake interview, April 22, 1983, p. 2.

[17] *Ibid.*, p. 3.

[18] *Ibid.*, p. 4.

[19] Coretta Scott King, *My Life with Martin Luther King, Jr.*, pp. 328–29.

[20] Abernathy/Peake interview, April 22, 1983, p. 8.

[21] See "The Belated Civil Rights Legislation of 1968," *The New Republic*, v. 158, no. 13 (March 30, 1968), pp. 11–12 on the House version, and the *New York Times*, April 11, 1968, pp. 1 and 34 on the final passage and contents. See also Clarence Mitchell, "Civil Rights and Economic Rights," *The Crisis*, v. 5, no. 4 (April 1968), pp. 117–21.

[22] For a summary of urban problems in 1968 see the December 1968 issue of *Current History* (v. 55, no 328). Particularly useful on the Johnson administration's urban renewal efforts is Robert C. Weaver, "Rebuilding American Cities: an Overview," pp. 321–26 and 364.

[23] *New York Times*, April 5, 1968, p. 24; SCLC/NH, Clippings on Poor People's March on Washington.

[24] "A Nation Within a Nation," *Time*, v. 91, no. 20 (May 17, 1968), pp. 24–37.

[25] "A Year of SCLC," *Soul Force*, v. 1, no. 6 (August 15, 1968), p. 21; Abernathy/Peake interview, April 22, 1983, pp. 4–5; SCLC/NH, Poor People's Campaign, 1968.

[26] *Washington Post*, May 12, 1968, pp. 1 and 6.

[27] Abernathy, Editorial, *Soul Force*, v. 1, no. 6 (August 15, 1968), p. 21.

[28] See Reynolds, *Jesse Jackson*, pp. 314–15; and Hosea Williams/Peake interview, March 31, 1983, p. 2.

[29] *Washington Post*, May 26, 1968, pp. 1 and 70.

[30] "Let No One Be Denied: But In Resurrection City 'Someday' is Not at Hand," *Newsweek*, v. 72, no. 1 (July 1, 1968), pp. 20–21.

[31] Cited in *Washington Post*, June 20, 1968, p. A-5.

[32] "Poverty: End of the Dream," *Newsweek*, v. 72, no. 2 (July 8, 1968), p. 19.

[33] SCLC/NH, Ralph D. Abernathy, "Statement before the Sub-Committee on Equal Opportunity in Urban Society," Republican Party Platform Committee, Miami, July 31, 1968, p. 1.

[34] *Ibid.*, p. 2.

[35] Republican Party Platform, 1968, cited in Arthur Meier Schlesinger, Jr., *History of American Presidential Elections, 1789–1968* (New York: McGraw-Hill Book Co., 1971), v. 4, pp. 3781–84.

[36] SCLC/NH, Eleventh Annual Convention, August 1968, Programs and Clippings; see also John Osborne, "King's Men Return to Memphis: What Will Become of His Dreams?," *New Republic*, v. 159 (August 24, 1968), pp. 12–14.

[37] SCLC/NH, "Presidential Address to the Eleventh Annual Convention," August 15, 1968, pp. 1–3; news conference clippings, August 16–17, 1968; see also *New York Times*, August 16, 1968, p. 14 and August 18, 1968, p. 18.

[38] SCLC/NH, "Presidential Address to the Eleventh Annual Convention."

[39] Schlesinger, *History of American Presidential Elections*, v. 4, p. 3770.

[40] Richard Milhous Nixon, *The Memoirs of Richard Nixon* (New York: Warner Books, 1978), v. 1, pp. 538–39.

⁴¹ Rowland Evans and Robert Novak, *Nixon in the White House: The Frustration of Power* (New York: Random House, 1971), p. 134.

⁴² U.S. President. *Public Papers of the Presidents: Richard Nixon, 1969* (Washington: Government Printing Office, 1971), pp. 1–3.

⁴³ Nixon, *Memoirs*, v. 1, p. 539.

⁴⁴ Evans and Novak, *Nixon*, pp. 142–44.

⁴⁵ See "Nixon's Moves in Civil Rights," *U.S. News and World Report*, v. 66, no. 16 (April 21, 1969), p. 15.

⁴⁶ For text see Thomas R. Frazier, *Afro-American History: Primary Sources* (New York: Harcourt, Brace & Jovanovich, 1971), pp. 270–76.

⁴⁷ Ralph D. Abernathy, "Honoring Dr. King. America: Promises and Realities," *Soul Force*, v. 2, no. 1 (April 4, 1969), p. 2.

⁴⁸ *Washington Post*, April 5, 1969, p. 1.

⁴⁹ *Ibid.*, p. A-10.

⁵⁰ *New York Times*, April 5, 1969, p. 13.

⁵¹ Andrew J. Young, "Historic Charleston," *Soul Force*, v. 2, no. 2 (June 1969), p. 4.

⁵² Walter E. Fauntroy, "Poor People's Campaign," *Soul Force*, v. 2, no. 3 (August 13, 1969), p. 3.

Chapter Nine

¹ See Martin Luther King, Jr., "A New Sense of Direction," reprinted in *Drum Major* (August 1971), pp. 1–5.

² SCLC/NH, Files of the Program Department, 1969–1971; interviews by the author with Kelly Miller Smith, Ralph Abernathy, Bernita Bennette, Bernard Lafayette, and Hosea Williams.

³ Cf. Garrow, *The FBI and Martin Luther King, Jr.*, p. 215 and interviews with Abernathy, Walker and Williams.

⁴ C. T. and Octavia Vivian conversations with the author, January and March 1983 and interview, July 7, 1983, p. 2 of typescript; many other interviews with SCLC leaders, especially Fred Shuttlesworth, James Lawson, Bernard Lafayette, E. Randel T. Osburn, Ralph Abernathy, and Hosea Williams, 1979–1983.

⁵ Carl F. Ellis, *Beyond Liberation, The Gospel in the Black American Experience* (Downers Grove, Illinois: InterVarsity Press, 1983), p. 84.

⁶ Ralph David Abernathy interview with Dorothy Cotton in Paul H. Sherry, "Hope in a Time that Invites Despair," *United Church of Christ Journal*, v. 9, no. 3 (November–December 1970), p. 2.

⁷ Abernathy/Peake interview, April 22, 1983, p. 24 of typescript.

⁸ SCLC/NH, Andrew J. Young, "And Birmingham," in *Drum Major* (Winter 1971), p. 21.

⁹ *Ibid.*, p. 27.

¹⁰ See Michael Novak, *The Spirit of Democratic Capitalism* (New York: Simon & Schuster, 1982), pp. 266, 272–76.

¹¹ Charles E. Silberman, "Negro Economic Gains—Impressive but Precarious," *Fortune*, v. 82, no, 1 (July 1970), pp. 74–77ff.

[12] Nixon, *Memoirs*, v. 1, p. 544.

[13] Cited in *The Crisis*, v. 76, no. 7 (August–September 1969), p. 276.

[14] SCLC/NH, Ralph Abernathy, Statement at the White House conference, May 13, 1969; *Soul Force*, v. 2, no. 2 (June 1969), pp. 2–3; Williams/Peake interview, July 5, 1983, p. 5 of the typescript.

[15] Nixon, *Memoirs*, v. 1, p. 539.

[16] SCLC/P, clippings on the May 13 White House meeting, May 14–15, 1969; see *Washington Post*, May 14, 1969, p. A-1.

[17] "The President and the Preacher," editorial, *Washington Post*, May 15, 1969, p. A-18; copies in SCLC/NH.

[18] SCLC/NH, Labor coalition leaflets; *Soul Force* commentaries, May to July 1969; Abernathy/Peake interview, April 22, 1983, pp. 11–13.

[19] Abernathy/Peake interview, April 22, 1983, pp. 8–9, and "A Rush of Action to Get More Jobs for Negroes," *U.S. News and World Report*, v. 92 (September 15, 1969), p. 67.

[20] SCLC/KC and SCLC/NH, Poor People's Campaign plans, statement of purpose, and staff data sheets, January through June 1968. The model of Selma was clearly in view. The idea of opening the issues of poverty to the full view of the public was an emphasis in the Statement of Purpose, January 1968, p. 3.

[21] SCLC/P, Andrew Young, Executive Vice President's Report to the Board of Directors, August 13, 1969, pp. 1–2.

[22] *Ibid.*, pp. 2–5.

[23] U. S. President. *Public Papers of the Presidents, Nixon, 1969*, pp. 324–25.

[24] SCLC/P, Statement of Rev. Ralph David Abernathy on the Goals of the Poor People's Campaign, June 1968; and Poor People's Campaign Second Chapter, goals and planning materials, February to May 1969; Abernathy/Peake interviews.

[25] SCLC/P, Thomas E. Kilgore, Keynote address to the Twelfth Annual SCLC Convention, Charleston, South Carolina, August 13, 1969, pp. 1–3.

[26] *Ibid.*, pp. 3–5.

[27] James Forman, "Black Manifesto" address at Riverside Church, May 4, 1969, reprinted in Thomas R. Frazier, *Afro-American History*, pp. 270–76.

[28] See reprint of *Christian Century* article and commentary in *Soul Force*, v. 2, no. 4 (November 1969), p. 11.

[29] Abernathy/Peake interview, April 22, 1983, pp. 8–9 of typescript; Williams/Peake interview, July 5, 1983, p. 8 of typescript. Williams was working in Mississippi at the time but was called to Charleston to accompany Abernathy in jail. After several days, they were given the privilege of signing themselves out on their own recognizance. Williams, weary of the ordeal, decided to sign, but Abernathy refused, so Williams retracted his signature. The doors of the jail were then left open for them to walk out, and they did.

[30] *SCLC/Operation Breadbasket News*, v. 1, no. 4 (January 1970), pp. 6–9; *New York Times*, August 21, 1969, p. 36; *Washington Post*, August 14, p. A-1; SCLC/P, "Twelfth Annual Convention Program."

[31] SCLC/NH, Ralph David Abernathy, President's Report to the Board of Directors of the Southern Christian Leadership Conference, Birmingham, Alabama, April 14–15, 1970, p. 3.

[32] *Ibid.*, p. 4.

[33] "Civil Rights: A New Approach," *U.S. News and World Report*, v. 71, no. 8 (August 23, 1971), p. 27.

[34] *Ibid.*, p. 28.

[35] George C. Herring, *America's Longest War: the United States and Vietnam, 1950–1975* (New York: John Wiley and Sons, 1979), p. 226.

[36] See *New York Times*, May 12, 1970, pp. 1 and 11.

[37] See Evans and Novak, *Nixon*, pp. 322–27, for an analysis.

[38] SCLC/NH, SCLC News Release of May 17, 1970, p. 1; March Against Repression materials.

[39] SCLC/NH, Hosea L. Williams, Address to the March Against Repression participants, Perry, Georgia, May 19, 1970.

[40] *New York Times*, May 16, 1970, p. 19; and May 19, 1970, p. 35.

[41] SCLC/NH, Ralph David Abernathy, Address to the March Against Repression Rally, Atlanta, Georgia, May 23, 1970, p. 9.

[42] SCLC/NH, Ralph David Abernathy, President's Report to the Thirteenth Annual SCLC Convention, Atlanta, August 14, 1970.

[43] SCLC/NH, Young campaign posters, leaflets, statements, and clippings, 1970.

[44] "The South; New Black Politics," *Soul Force*, v. 3, no. 2 (December 4, 1970), pp. 1 and 4.

[45] "The Young Campaign," *Soul Force*, v. 3, no. 2 (December 4, 1970), pp. 2 and 4.

[46] "Civil Rights: A New Approach," *U.S. News and World Report*, v. 71, no. 8 (August 23, 1971), p. 28.

[47] "1971 in Review," *Soul Force*, v. 5, no. 6 (November–December 1971), p. 13.

[48] SCLC/NH, 'Politics '72' materials; "Politics is Power," *Drum Major* (Winter Issue, 1971), pp. 6–8.

[49] Rustin, *Strategies for Freedom*, p. 73.

[50] SCLC/NH, Ralph Abernathy statement at a birthday tribute for Angela Davis, New York, February 1971, p. 2.

[51] SCLC/P, Photographs and notes by the author in the Soviet Union and the German Democratic Republic, January 1972.

[52] SCLC/NH, Ralph David Abernathy, President's Report to the 13th Annual SCLC Convention, Atlanta, August 14, 1970; see also *Soul Force*, v. 4, no. 2 (March 1971), p. 3.

[53] SCLC/P, Coretta Scott King, Address to the Anti-War Rally in Washington, D.C., Saturday, April 24, 1971.

[54] *Washington Post*, April 25, 1971, pp. a and A-19.

[55] *Soul Force*, v. 4, no. 5 (May 1971), pp. 3 and 15.

[56] Cornish Rogers, "SCLC: Faithful to Its Function," *Christian Century*, v. 88, no. 18 (May 5, 1971), p. 550.

[57] *Ibid.*

[58] See *Soul Force*, v. 5, no. 4 (October 1971), p. 4.

[59] Carson, *In Struggle*, p. 305.

[60] *Soul Force*, v. 5, no. 4 (October 1971), p. 11.

[61] SCLC/NH, Walter E. Fauntroy, "The Arithmetic of Power Politics," Keynote Address to the 14th Annual SCLC Convention, New Orleans, August 12, 1971, p. 6.

[62] *Ibid.*

[63] SCLC/NH, Resurrection City II, Miami 1972, programs; see also *Soul Force*, v. 6, no. 6 (July 1972), pp. 4–9.

447

[64] SCLC/NH, Abernathy, President's Report, April 12, 1972, p. 2.

[65] Roy Reed, "Dr. King's Followers Modify his Approach in Their Continuing Pursuit of Justice," *New York Times*, January 7, 1972, p. 9.

[66] *New York Times*, September 20, 1971, pp. 4–8.

[67] SCLC/NH, Ralph Abernathy, Report to the SCLC Board of Directors, Atlanta, April 12, 1972, pp. 2–3.

[68] Richard Nixon, Annual Message to the Congress: The Economic Report of the President, January 30, 1973, *Public Papers of the Presidents, Richard Nixon, 1973*, p. 49.

[69] Figures from VEP Totals, November 1972.

[70] *Soul Force*, v. 6, nos. 10–11 (November–December 1972), p. 4.

[71] King, *Where Do We Go From Here?*, p. 188.

Chapter Ten

[1] Reynolds, *Jesse Jackson*, p. 359.

[2] Williams/Peake interviews, 1983.

[3] Williams/Peake interviews, 1983; conversations with Abernathy, C. T. Vivian.

[4] Cited in "Atlanta-DeKalb Metro SCLC," *Soul Force*, v. 6, no. 9 (September-October 1972), p. 10; also Abernathy/Peake and Williams/Peake interviews, 1983; C. T. Vivian/Peake conversations, 1983.

[5] On the development of the Black Expo see "Black Expo Comes of Age," *Ebony*, v. 27, no. 2 (December 1971), pp. 64–72.

[6] Interviews with Joseph E. Lowery, 1983, 1985; conversation with E. Randel T. Osburn, 1985; see also, Reynolds, *Jesse Jackson*, pp. 325–334.

[7] Thomas A. Johnson, "Jesse Jackson is Rising as a Black Leader," *New York Times*, October 12, 1971, p. 14.

[8] SCLC/NH news clippings, interview with Lowery 1985, *New York Times*, December 5, 1971, p. 70.

[9] Reynolds, *Jesse Jackson*, pp. 312–13.

[10] "Split in SCLC," *Newsweek*, v. 78, no. 25 (December 20, 1971), pp. 27–28.

[11] Stoney Cooks interview with the author, June 29, 1983, pp. 9–11 of typescript.

[12] Hosea Williams/Peake interviews; Abernathy/Peake interviews; Joseph Lowery/Peake conversations; Reynolds, *Jesse Jackson*, p. 362; Chauncey Eskridge conversation with the author, July 1983.

[13] John Dean's testimony and evidence on the 'Special Service Group' of the Internal Revenue Service in U. S. Senate, *Hearings Before the Select Committee on Presidential Campaign Activities: Ninety-Third Congress, First Session*, Book 3, pp. 1338–45. Also Cooks/Peake interview; Eskridge/Peake conversation; and "Milk Fund . . . IRS . . . Bugging . . . Highlights of the Evidence," *U.S. News and World Report*, v. 77 (July 29, 1974), pp. 19–21.

[14] Reynolds, *Jesse Jackson*, pp. 318–21.

[15] Williams, Vivian, Shuttlesworth and Smith interviews with the author.

[16] Private interviews with former SCLC officials.

[17] SCLC/NH, Ralph David Abernathy to Dr. Joseph Echols Lowery, July 5, 1973.

[18] SCLC/NH, Ralph David Abernathy, Press Release, July 9, 1973, p. 4.

[19] "Abernathy Steps Down," *Time*, v. 102, no. 4 (July 23, 1973), p. 31.

[20] Walker/Peake interview, p. 3.

[21] Lowery/Peake interview, June, 1985, pp. 14–15; SCLC/NH Presidential Search Committee, August 1973; conversations with C. T. Vivian, 1983. The national press provided some coverage, but it was limited by the relatively superficial investigation of the underlying issues. A reasonably good but brief account can be found in the *New York Times*, August 14, 1973, p. 39. Several other clippings can be found in SCLC/NH records on the Abernathy resignation and re-election.

[22] Reynolds, *Jesse Jackson*, p. 363.

[23] SCLC/NH, Reorganization Plan, August 1973; conversations with Lowery, 1981–1983; financial reports, 1973–1974. From this point one can see in SCLC fund-raising operations a more selective targeting and use of a wider range of appeals.

[24] SCLC/NH press releases; see also *New York Times*, August 16, 1973, p. 36. Lowery/Peake interview; conversations with Hosea Williams and C. T. Vivian.

[25] SCLC/P, SCLC Sixteenth Annual Convention, Indianapolis, August, 1973, notes. Abernathy/Peake conversation, 1983.

[26] Reynolds, *Jesse Jackson*, p. 365. While there is some truth in this, it misses the deeper implications of Abernathy's move. Not only his presidency, but the future of SCLC was also in crisis. That the board supported him for continuance was part of a broader move to rejuvenate the organization. They did simply go on with business as usual.

[27] *New York Times*, August 16, 1973, p. 36.

[28] SCLC/P, Abernathy acceptance speech at the Sixteenth Annual SCLC Convention, Indianapolis, August 15, 1973.

[29] "SCLC's Leadership Crisis," *Christian Century*, v. 90, no. 31 (September 5, 1973), p. 844.

[30] *New York Times*, August 29, 1973, p. 1.

[31] Terry Wingate interview with the author, p. 3. of typescript; Charles Kirby conversation with the author; Fred Taylor interview with the author, February 17, 1983, p. 2 of typescript.

[32] Taylor/Peake interview, p. 1 of typescript.

[33] SCLC/NH, Biographical sketch of the Reverend Fred D. Taylor; Taylor/Peake interview, p. 1; E. Randel T. Osburn and C. T. Vivian conversations with the author.

[34] SCLC/NH, Chapter of the Year Award to Louisville, Kentucky Chapter, 1973–1974; Kirby/Peake interview, p. 4 of typescript.

[35] See, for example, SCLC/NH, *Movement: The Story of SCLC* (August 1974), p. 11.

[36] SCLC/NH, Reports by the Director of Chapters and Affiliates, 1974, 1975.

[37] Fred Taylor, Charles Kirby, Terry Wingate interview with the author.

[38] See SCLC/NH, *Movement: The Story of SCLC*, p. 24; Albert Love interview with the author, February 17, 1982, p. 1 of typescript.

[39] *Ibid.*

[40] SCLC/NH, National Amnesty Program, April 4, 1974.

[41] American Revolutionary Bicentennial Administration, *The Bicentennial of the United States of America: A Final Report to the People*, 5 volumes (Washington, D.C.: Government Printing Office, 1977), v. 1, "Introduction," unpaged.

[42] "A New President: An End to a Nation's Agony," *U.S. News and World Report*, v. 77, no. 8 (August 19, 1974), p. 15.

[43] For the final months and the immediate post-war period, see George C. Herring, *America's Longest War*, pp. 270–72.

[44] SCLC/NH, Program of the Seventeenth Annual SCLC Convention, Philadelphia, August 13–16, 1974.

[45] *New York Times*, August 17, 1974, p. 24.

[46] SCLC/NH, Abernathy interview with the press, August 16, 1974; clippings on the Philadelphia convention.

[47] SCLC/NH, Dick Gregory address to the Seventeenth Annual SCLC Convention, August 16, 1974.

[48] Cited in Elizabeth Hardwick, "The Apotheosis of Martin Luther King," in *Bartleby in Manhattan and Other Essays* (New York: Random House, 1983), p. 15.

[49] *Ibid.*, p. 19.

[50] Interviews by the author with James Lawson, C. T. and Octavia Vivian, Albert Love, Fred Taylor, Kelly Miller Smith, and Wyatt Tee Walker.

[51] Abernathy/Peake interviews, March and April 1983.

[52] SCLC/NH, press clippings on the 1973 annual convention.

[53] For such a negative conclusion about SCLC's viability after 1968, see Adam Fairclough, "The Southern Christian Leadership Conference and the Second Reconstruction, 1957–1973," *South Atlantic Quarterly*, v. 80, no. 2 (Spring 1981), pp. 177–94. The study has merit, especially in its treatment of the implications of the Chicago campaign, but is based on mostly secondary materials and is strongly influenced by C. Vann Woodward's judgments on the failure of the post-1965 civil rights movement.

[54] Cited in Meier and Rudwick, *CORE*, p. 329.

[55] Nick and Mary Lynn Kotz, "Welfare Mothers and the Civil Rights Movement," excerpted from *A Passion for Equality*, in *Civil Liberties Review* (April 4, 1977), p. 83.

[56] Fairclough, "The Southern Christian Leadership Conference," p. 192.

[57] SCLC/NH, Office of the President, Voter Education Project Report on Political Participants, 1960; United States Civil Rights Commission, Report, May 1968; and Southern Regional Council Fact Sheet, 1970, p. 4.

[58] Voter Education Project Report, 1966.

[59] Voter Education Project Report, *National Roster of Elected Black Officials*, 1974; SCLC/NH, Voter Registration Campaigns, 1974–1975.

[60] SCLC/Atlanta-Dekalb Chapter, campaign materials, 1974.

[61] Diana Jones and Bill Burton to Bernard Lee, November 27, 1974, in SCLC/NH, Executive Director's Office files.

[62] SCLC/NH, Files of the President's Office; Executive Vice-President's Office, and Director of Chapters and Affiliates.

[63] King, *Where Do We Go From Here?*, p. 202.

[64] C. T. Vivian, Ralph Abernathy, Stoney Cooks, Terry Wingate, Bernard Lafayette, and John Lewis interviews with the author.

[65] Cooks/Peake interview, July 1983, p. 3 of typescript; SCLC/KC, Poor People's Campaign, 1968–1969.

[66] This position has been maintained by Abernathy for over fifteen years.

[67] Coretta Scott King, "Twenty Years Later," *Family Weekly* (August 14, 1983), p. 5.

[68] Cooks/Peake interview; *Movement* series, 1974, 1975, 1976; SCLC/NH, flyers on black poverty, 1975–1976.

[69] Kotz, "Welfare Mothers and the Civil Rights Movement," pp. 82–83.

[70] SCLC/NH, Materials on Black Economic Summit Meeting, November 21–22, 1974.

[71] SCLC/NH, Letter to Governor Jimmy Carter, January 5, 1975; Statements by communications director Tyrone Brooks, January and February, 1975.

[72] "Joan Little's Story," *Time*, v. 106, no. 8 (August 25, 1975), p. 14; SCLC/NH, Abernathy statement on the Little case, March 1975, p. 2; SCLC news release, March 17, 1975.

[73] *Ibid.; New York Times*, March 18, 1975, p. 74; and "A Case of Rape or Seduction," *Time*, v. 106, no. 4 (July. 28, 1975), p. 19.

[74] "Joan Little's Story," *Time*, v. 106, no. 8 (Aug. 25, 1975), p. 14.

[75] SCLC/NH, *Movement: The SCLC Story, 1976*, p. 11.

[76] *New York Times*, August 3, 1975, p. 24 and October 10, 1975, p. 14; Abernathy/Peake interview, 1983.

[77] SCLC/NH, SCLC Amnesty position paper, April 4, 1974, p. 1.

[78] *Ibid.*, p. 4.

[79] SCLC/NH, Abernathy statement on amnesty and the Johnson case, January 9, 1975, pp. 1–2.

[80] Tyrone Brooks/Peake interview, p. 6; Abernathy/Peake conversation, April 22, 1983.

[81] Conversations with SCLC office personnel and Chapter and Affiliates Director Fred Taylor by the author; examination of files at the SCLC National Headquarters; and conversations with Ralph Abernathy.

[82] SCLC/NH, Petitions and files on the campaign for a Martin Luther King, Jr. national holiday; *Congressional Record*, and interviews with King Center personnel.

[83] Garrow, *The FBI and Martin Luther King, Jr.*, p. 213.

[84] U.S. Congress. Senate, *Select Committee to Study Governmental Operations with Respect to Intelligence Activities, Final Report*, especially Book III: *Supplementary Detailed Staff Reports on Intelligence Activities and the Rights of Americans*, 1976; *New York Times*, October 3, 1975, p. 1; October 5, 1975, p. 2; and November 19, 1975, p. 16.

[85] SCLC/NH, National Task Force on the Black Economic Agenda, Position Paper discussed at the Eighteenth SCLC Annual Convention, Anniston, Alabama, August 12, 1975, Part II: *The Challenge*, p. 1.

[86] *Ibid.*, p. 45.

[87] *Ibid.*, p. 46.

[88] *Ibid.*, p. 5.

[89] "Can Capitalism Survive?," *Time*, v. 106, no. 2 (July 14, 1975), p. 63.

[90] *New York Times*, December 7, 1975, p. 37.

[91] SCLC/NH, Report of National Task Force on the Black Economic Agenda, December 5–7, 1975.

[92] Abernathy, Lewis, and Williams interviews with the author; Septima P. Clark, "Citizenship and Gospel," *Journal of Black Studies*, v. 10, no. 4 (June 1980), pp. 461–66.

[93] SCLC/P, Notes, conversations, and tapes from SCLC conventions; examination of SCLC convention records.

[94] Randell Frame, "Why Black Brethren Embrace Politics," *Christianity Today*, v. 27, no. 9 (May 20, 1983), p. 34.

[95] SCLC/NH, Halifax, North Carolina demonstration, April 12, 1976.

[96] Vickie Leonard and Tom MacLean, editors, *The Continental Walk for Disarmament and Social Justice* (New York: Continental Walk for Disarmament and Social Justice Organization, 1977), p. 1.

[97] SCLC/NH, Bernard Lee, Address to Southern Walk Rally, April 4, 1976.

[98] Leonard and MacLean, *The Continental Walk*, p. 53.

[99] *New York Times*, October 19, 1975, p. 38; and *Washington Post*, October 17, 18 and 19, 1975.

[100] See Clarence Mitchell, "Mr. Ford and Civil Rights: A Mixed Record," *The Crisis* (January 1974), pp. 7–11; *New York Times*, February 8, 1976, p. 1; April 7, 9, 10, 11, 1976; October 2, 1976, p. 1. Jimmy Carter interview with the Author, 1986, pp. 2–3 of typescript.

[101] *New York Times*, December 17, 1976, p. 1.

[102] SCLC/NH, Abernathy Announcement of Congressional race, January 5, 1977; *SCLC West*, v. 6, no. 7 (March-April 1977), pp. 6–7.

[103] *Ibid.*

[104] Private interviews by the author with various SCLC staff members, 1982–1983.

[105] *Atlanta Constitution*, February 24, 1977, p. 3.

Chapter Eleven

[1] SCLC/NH, Abernathy and Williams nominating speeches at the SCLC Twentieth Anniversary Convention, Atlanta, August 18, 1977; conversations with Williams and Abernathy, April 1983.

[2] *Atlanta Constitution*, August 19, 1977, p. 16.

[3] Williams/Peake interview and conversations, March and July 1983.

[4] See *Atlanta Constitution*, October 15, 1974, p. 9; also Williams/Peake interviews.

[5] Interviews with Abernathy and Williams, 1983; Lowery, 1981–1985; and conversations with Fauntroy, 1980.

[6] See above, Chapter Two, pp. 6–7.

[7] "SCLC Elects Lowery President," *Atlanta Voice*, v. 12, no. 1 (August 27, 1977), pp. 1 and 9; SCLC/NH, Joseph Echols Lowery biographical sketch, p. 1; *SCLC Magazine*, v. 6, no. 8 (October–November 1977), pp. 12–13.

[8] Lowery/Peake interview, June 4, 1985, p. 2 of typescript.

[9] *Ibid.*

[10] *Ibid.*, p. 4.

[11] Joseph E. Lowery, presidential address, 20th anniversary convention, Atlanta, August 1977.

[12] *Ibid.*, pp. 2 and 8.

[13] See article in *Atlanta Constitution*, April 1, 1977, p. 4; and SCLC/NH, John Lewis comments on Twentieth Anniversary Convention, August 1977; Lewis/Peake conversations, June 1983.

[14] SCLC/P, Joseph E. Lowery and John S. Nettles (secretary), Recommendations/Committee Reports, SCLC National Board of Directors Retreat, Camp Calvin, Georgia, December 5–7, 1977, pp. 1–4.

[15] SCLC/P, Joseph E. Lowery, Address to the SCLC board of directors, Camp Calvin, Georgia, December 5, 1977, p. 7.

[16] *Ibid.*, p. 2.

[17] Richard A. Viguerie, *The New Right: We're Ready to Lead* (Falls Church, Virginia:

The Viguerie Press, 1980), p. 222. Even more moderate conservatives like Michael Novak have recently shifted to a more critical view of such reform activists, Novak/Peake interview, October 1983, p. 2 of typescript.

[18] U. S. Bureau of the Census, Public Use Files of the One-in-One-Thousand Sample (1960) and 1970 and 1980 Current Population Surveys. See also the carefully reasoned analysis in Reynolds Farley, *Blacks and Whites Narrowing the Gap?* (Cambridge, Massachusetts: Harvard University Press, 1984), pp. 56–81 and *passim* also, John Herbers, "Decade After Kerner Report: Division of Races Persists," Part I of Series: "Two Societies; America Since the Kerner Report," *New York Times*, February 26, 1978, p. 1.

[19] Jon Nordheimer, "1978 Race Relations: 3 Widely Divergent Views," Part II of Series: "Two Societies; America Since the Kerner Report," *New York Times*, February 27, pp. 1 and 14; and Paul Delaney, "Middle Class Gains Create Tensions in Black Community," Part III of Series: "Two Societies; America Since the Kerner Report," *New York Times*, February 28, 1978, pp. 1 and 22.

[20] SCLC/NH, Lowery's address to the board, pp. 6–7; and Lowery/Peake interview, June 4, 1985, p. 5 of typescript.

[21] Fred Taylor/Peake interview, p. 3 of typescript; and Fred D. Taylor, "Membership Drive—Why Now?," *SCLC Magazine*, v. 7, no. 5 (July–August 1978), pp. 16–17.

[22] SCLC/NH, Fund-Raising and Budget Committee Recommendations, 1977, p. 1.

[23] *Ibid.*, and Lowery/Peake interview, June 1985, p. 5.

[24] SCLC/NH, Fund Raising and Budget Committee Recommendations, 1977, p. 3.

[25] Jesse Jackson, "Dr. King Still Lives," *SCLC West*, v. 6, no. 8, (May–June 1977), p. 3.

[26] Joseph E. Lowery, "I Remember Martin," a sermon in the 'Martin Luther King Speaks' radio series, April 1979, reprinted in condensed version in *SCLC Magazine*, v. 10, no. 1 (January–February 1981), p. 1.

[27] *Ibid.*

[28] *Ibid.*

[29] *Ibid.*

[30] Joseph E. Lowery conversation with author, January 22, 1982.

[31] Barbara A. Reynolds, "An Interview with the Rev. Dr. Joseph Lowery," *Dollars and Sense*, v. 7, no. 2 (June–July 1981), p. 104.

[32] SCLC/NH, Lowery remarks at the Twentieth Anniversary Convention, August 1977.

[33] SCLC/NH, James Lawson, Report on Issues, Priorities, and Movements, December 1977, pp. 2–3.

[34] *Ibid.*, p. 5.

[35] *Ibid.*, p. 7.

[36] SCLC/NH, Recommendations/Committee Reports, December 5–7, 1977, p. 1.

[37] *SCLC West*, v. 6, no. 8 (May–June 1977), pp. 27–28.

[38] Charles Lawrence, III, "The Bakke Case: Are Racial Quotas Defensible?," *Saturday Review*, v. 5, no. 2 (October 15, 1977), p. 11.

[39] "Reverse Discrimination: What the Supreme Court was Told in the Bakke Case," *U.S. News and World Report*, v. 83, no. 17 (October 24, 1977), p. 94.

[40] Ramsey Clark, "The Bakke Decision," *The Nation*, v. 227, no. 2 (July 8–15, 1978), p. 38.

[41] "Business Outlook at Midyear," *U.S. News and World Report*, v. 84, no. 26 (July 3, 1978), p. 22.

[42] Herbers, "Decade After Kerner Report," *New York Times*, February 26, 1978, p. 1.

[43] Joseph E. Lowery, Address to the National Leadership Conference, Chicago, May 5–7, 1978, reprinted in *SCLC Magazine*, v. 7, no. 4 (May–June 1978), p. 11.

[44] SCLC/NH, Joseph E. Lowery, "I Remember Martin," p. 1.

[45] *Ibid.*

[46] Lerone Bennett, Jr., "The Lost/Found Generation: New Group with New Values Changes Racial Dialogue," *Ebony*, v. 33, no. 10 (August 1978), p. 37.

[47] See *SCLC Magazine*, v. 6, no. 8 (October–November 1977), pp. 26–27.

[48] "Struggle in Gadsden Continues," *SCLC Magazine*, v. 7, no. 4 (May–June 1978), pp. 14–15.

[49] U. S. President. *Public Papers of the Presidents, Jimmy Carter, 1978*, v. 1, p. 582.

[50] David C. Perry and Alfred J. Watkins, "Carter's Urban Policy," *The Nation*, v. 227, no. 8, p. 238.

[51] U. S. Commission on Civil Rights, *The State of Civil Rights in 1977: A Report* (Washington, D.C.: Government Printing Office, 1978), p. 1.

[52] See for example, *SCLC Magazine*, v. 7, no. 2 (March 1978), pp. 16–17.

[53] The Supreme Court was actually seriously split in its formal Bakke decision of June 1978. Five of the Justices voted to admit Bakke to the medical school, and by the same 5–4 margin judged the Davis Medical School's quota system unacceptable. But on the question of whether race can ever be considered in deciding who should be admitted, the Supreme Court voted 5–4 in the affirmative, with the four (Burger, Stevens, Rehnquist, and Stewart) voting that it was irrelevant in this case.

[54] U. S. President. *Public Papers of the Presidents, Jimmy Carter, 1978*, v. 2, p. 1873.

[55] "The Age of Less," *Newsweek*, v. 92, no. 2 (July 10, 1978), p. 18.

[56] "Now in Prospect: A 'Pinchpenny Congress', Survey of Freshman Lawmakers," *U.S. News and World Report*, v. 86, no. 3 (January 22, 1979), p. 31.

[57] SCLC/NH, Joseph E. Lowery, SCLC news release, December 7, 1978.

[58] U.S. President. *Public Papers of the Presidents, Jimmy Carter, 1979*, v. 1, p. 29.

[59] *New York Times*, January 15, 1979, p. I-15.

[60] Cited in *SCLC Magazine*, v. 8, no. 2 (March–April 1979), pp. 11–12.

[61] "The Politics of Austerity," *Newsweek*, v. 93, no. 5 (January 29, 1979), p. 21.

[62] See "Guns vs. Butter, Battle of the Year," *U.S. News and World Report*, v. 86, no. 3 (January 22, 1979), p. 17.

[63] U. S. House of Representatives. Committee on Foreign Affairs, *Staff Report on the Assassination of Representative Leo J. Ryan and the Jonestown, Guyana Tragedy* (Washington, D.C.: Government Printing Office, 1979), pp. 3–5.

[64] SCLC/NH, Press release, January 3, 1979.

[65] *SCLC Magazine*, v. 8, no. 2 (March–April 1979), p. 42. See also pp. 43–49 for other aspects of the Conference.

[66] U. S. House of Representatives, *Jonestown Investigation*, pp. 36–37. See also *New York Times*, May 4, 1979, p. 14.

[67] Larry Riedman, "The Condition of Civil Rights Advocacy, Emerging from Despair with New Strategies for Progress," *Civil Rights Digest*, v. 2, no. 3 (Spring 1979), p. 35.

[68] "Special Ebony Poll," *Ebony*, v. 24, no. 7 (May 1979), p. 184.

[69] U. S. Commission on Civil Rights, *Twenty Years After Brown; A Report* (Washing-

454

ton, D.C.: Government Printing Office, 1975), pp. 48–55; and *The State of Civil Rights*, 1978, pp. 36–37.

70 Benjamin L. Hooks, "The '80's: Civil Rights," in "The '80's, What's Ahead for Blacks?," *Ebony*, v. 36, no. 3 (January 1980), p. 28.

Chapter Twelve

1 Riedman, "The Condition of Civil Rights Advocacy," pp. 36–37.

2 *Ibid.*

3 "Selected Yankelovich, Skelly and White, Inc. Data on Civil Rights Issues," Cited in Edward B. Keller, "A Changing Climate For Civil Rights; Five Key Trends," *Perspectives*, v. 15, no. 3 (Summer 1983), p. 13.

4 See especially Charles Murray, *Losing Ground: American Social Policy 1950–1980* (New York: Basic Books, 1984). Murray calls for scrapping of welfare programs and putting billions into "equal opportunity, not one cent for equal outcome," p. 233.

5 Walter E. Williams, *America: A Minority Viewpoint* (Stanford: Hoover Institution Press, 1982), p. 16, and for a general thesis, pp. 76–77, 85–86, 97–98, and 109–110. Williams is only one of several successful black professionals leaning toward conservative economic policies and away from the traditional notions of civil rights advocacy.

6 Viguerie, *The New Right*, p. 222.

7 See Irwin J. Suall, "The Ku Klux Klan Malady Lingers On," *New Perspectives: The Civil Rights Quarterly*, v. 12, no. 3 (Fall–Winter 1980–81), p. 11.

8 See a clear statement on this by King in *Where Do We Go From Here?*, pp. 149–157 and especially 161–166. See also Rustin, *Strategies for Freedom*, pp. 67–69.

9 SCLC/NH, Joseph E. Lowery, Address to the Senate Judiciary Committee, Washington, D.C., March 27, 1979, pp. 3–4.

10 SCLC/NH, Joseph E. Lowery, Report to the Board of Directors Conference, Washington, D.C., March 1979. See also *Atlanta Constitution*, April 1, 1979, p. B-18 and April 11, 1979, pp. 1 and 12.

11 Hosea Williams, quoted in the *Atlanta Constitution*, April 15, 1979, p. A-7.

12 Williams/Peake interview, p. 8 of typescript.

13 *Ibid.*

14 Brooks/Peake interview, pp. 1–2 of typescript.

15 Howell Raines, *New York Times*, April 8, 1979, p. 24.

16 SCLC/NH, SCLC news release, April 25, 1979, p. 1.

17 Vivian/Peake conversations.

18 SCLC/NH, Thomas Brown biographical sketch.

19 Rick Dunn conversation with the author, SCLC National Headquarters, Atlanta, June 1982.

20 Albert E. Love, interview with the author, February 1983, p. 3 of typescript.

21 E. Randel T. Osburn conversations/interviews 1983–1986, especially October 1983, pp. 6–7 and November 1985, pp. 3–4; brochure on Osburn's career (Cleveland operation); SCLC/NH, "Black American Human Rights Leader on the Move."

22 See "SCLC Pledges Solidarity to Sugar Cane Workers Head," *SCLC Magazine*, v. 8, no. 3 (May–June 1979), pp. 14–15 numerous clippings, SCLC/NH.

[23] SCLC/NH news release, May 8, 1979. See Pamela Browning, "Black Farming: the Erosion of a Scarce Resource," *New Perspectives*, v. 15, nos. 1–2 (Winter–Spring 1983), pp. 44–50.

[24] See "Twenty-Five Years of SCLC Tradition," *SCLC Magazine*, v. 11, no. 3 (August–September 1982), p. 20; and R. B. Cottonreader conversation with the author, August 26, 1983.

[25] Evelyn Gibson Lowery interview with the author, November 25, 1985, pp. 20–21 of typescript.

[26] Joseph E. Lowery, "To Hear Somebody Pray," *SCLC Magazine*, v. 9, no. 1 (January–February 1980), p. 23.

[27] SCLC/NH, Decatur March, clippings, strategy plans, summaries, 1979.

[28] *Birmingham Post-Herald*, July 17, 1979, p. 1.

[29] *SCLC Magazine*, v. 8, no. 5 (September–October 1979), p. 57.

[30] *Ibid.*

[31] SCLC/NH, Press comments, July 20, 1979.

[32] SCLC/P, Twenty-Second Annual SCLC Convention, Norfolk, Virginia, August 18, 1979, program, notes.

[33] Vivian/Peake conversations, March 1983; SCLC/NH clippings.

[34] See the series of articles by Joseph Gatlins of the *Richmond Times Dispatch*, especially April 4, 1981, pp. A1-2; April 3, 1981, p. A-1. Also E. Lowery/Peake interview, pp. 2–3 of typescript.

[35] Albert E. Love, "We Must Save Our Children," *SCLC Magazine*, v. 9, no. 5 (November–December 1980), pp. 29–31.

[36] SCLC/NH Press releases, January and February 1981; *Atlanta Constitution*, February 11, 1981, p. 1ff.

[37] E. Lowery/Peake interview, p. 4 of typescript; and SCLC/WOMEN brochure.

[38] "Gunfire in Greensboro," *America*, v. 141 (November 17, 1979), p. 292; "Shootout in Greensboro: Anti-Klan Protest," *Time*, v. 114, no. 20 (November 12, 1979), p. 31; and "Old South Anti-Klan Protest in Greensboro," *Newsweek*, v. 94, no. 20 (November 12, 1979), p. 50.

[39] *New York Times*, February 3, 1980, p. 22.

[40] SCLC/NH, Joseph E. Lowery, Presidential Address, Twenty-Third Annual Convention, Cleveland, August 1980.

[41] "The Mood of Ghetto America," *Newsweek*, v. 95, no. 22 (June 2, 1980), pp. 32–38.

[42] David S. Tatel, "New Riots, Old Reasons," *Washington Post*, May 24, 1980, p. A-15.

[43] SCLC/NH, Wrightsville Program file.

[44] SCLC/NH, Statement of Intent, SCLC Twenty-Third Annual Convention, Cleveland, Ohio, August 1980, Planks 6, 10, and 11 especially.

[45] U. S. President. *Public Papers of the Presidents, Jimmy Carter, 1979*, v. 2, p. 1564.

[46] Joseph E. Lowery, Statement, *SCLC Magazine*, v. 8, no. 6 (November–December 1979), pp. 34–39.

[47] Bayard Rustin, "To Blacks: Condemn P.L.O. Terrorism," *New York Times*, August 30, 1979, p. A-21.

[48] Vernon E. Jordan, Jr., Address to the National Conference of Catholic Charities, Kansas City, October 14, 1979, p. 3.

[49] *Ibid.*, p. 4.

[50] SCLC/P, Joseph E. Lowery, Statement on SCLC's contacts with the PLO, October 1979.

[51] SCLC/P, Notes on session on Peace and Foreign Policy, 25th Annual SCLC Convention, Birmingham, Alabama, August 12, 1982.

[52] *Ibid.*

[53] Nathaniel Sheppard, Jr., "Forum on Black-Jewish Relations Hears Vows for Initiatives on Ties," *New York Times*, October 23, 1979, p. 20.

[54] Rick Dunn, "Dr. Lowery Calls Iranian Crisis Self Defeating," *SCLC Magazine*, v. 9, no. 1 (January-February 1980), p. 34.

[55] For a supportive view, see Michael Novak, *Moral Clarity in the Nuclear Age* (Nashville: Thomas Nelson Publishers, 1983), pp. 54–67; Committee on the Present Danger, *Has America Become Number 2?* (Washington: Government Printing Office, 1982), pp. 16–22 and *passim*. On SCLC's position, see SCLC/NH, President's Report to the 23rd Annual Convention, Cleveland, August 1980, pp. 3–6; Statements by Walter Fauntroy and Lowery on the basic aspects of American foreign policy in "Blacks and U. S. Foreign Policy," *SCLC Magazine*, v. 8, no. 5 (September–October 1979), pp. 38–39; and an address by Lowery at the United Methodist Ethnic Minority Local Church Leadership Seminar, New York, December 1979; resolutions passed by the Cleveland convention.

[56] Joseph E. Lowery, Address to the National Conference on a Black Agenda for the Eighties, Richmond, Virginia (February 28–March 2, 1980), pp. 1–2.

[57] See Novak, *Moral Clarity in the Nuclear Age*, pp. 69–74 and 103–105.

[58] SCLC/P, Proceedings of the SCLC Board of Directors, Tallahassee, Florida, April 1980, Summary Statement, April 15, pp. 1–2.

[59] SCLC/P, author's notes on the 1980 convention; Lowery, Presidential Address to convention; and news releases August–November 1980.

[60] SCLC/NH, Brochures on labor and economics; Convention notes for 1981 and 1982; Interview with Lowery, Fred Taylor; Ernest P. Carson, "Reagonomics: Who Pays the Price?," *SCLC Magazine*, v. 10, no. 5 (October–November 1981), pp. 34–37.

[61] SCLC/P, Notes on the 24th annual convention, New Orleans; Program, presidential address tape; *SCLC Magazine*, v. 10, no. 5 (October–November 1981), pp. 9–11.

[62] "The Evolution of the Act," *Congressional Digest*, v. 60, no. 12 (December 1981), pp. 292–93.

[63] For a conservative view see "The Compromise: God Help Us," *National Review*, v. 34, no. 11 (June 11, 1982), p. 673.

[64] *Congressional Record: Senate 97th Congress*, v. 128, no. 76 (June 16, 1981), pp. S6841–S6842.

[65] Reagan, Press Conference, October 1, 1981.

[66] Reagan, Press Conference, October 17, 1981.

[67] U. S. President. *Public Papers of the Presidents, Reagan, 1981*, p. 1018.

[68] U. S. Congress. House of Representatives, *Hearings Before the Subcommittee on Civil and Constitutional Rights of the Committee on the Judiciary*, Ninety-Seventh Congress, May–July 1981, parts 1–3, pp. 7, 86, 224, 1866, 2070, and 2073.

[69] *Ibid.*, pp. 2068–71.

[70] *Ibid.*, pp. 841–49.

[71] See *SCLC Magazine*, v. 11, no. 2 (June–July 1982), pp. 10–17.

[72] Evelyn Lowery/Peake interview, pp. 9–11 of typescript; interviews with Brenda

Davenport and Kim Miller, November 27, 1985 and December 20, 1985, pp. 1–15 of typescript.

[73] SCLC/NH, Pilgrimage to Washington brochure, 1982; Evelyn Lowery/Peake interview, p. 14 of typescript.

[74] *Ibid.*, and Davenport and Miller/Peake interview.

[75] *Ibid.*, and Conversations with marchers, Birmingham, August 1982.

[76] *Ibid.*

[77] See *SCLC Magazine*, v. 11, no. 3 (August–September 1982), p. 32.

[78] U. S. Senate. Subcommittee on the Constitution, Committee on the Judiciary. *Hearings*, 97th Congress, 2d session, April 28, 1982 (Washington: Government Printing Office, 1982), pp. 28–29.

[79] See *Washington Post*, June 19, 1982, pp. A-1 and A-9.

[80] SCLC/P, Notes on Birmingham Convention, 1982.

Chapter Thirteen

[1] SCLC/P, Notes and tapes on the Twenty-Fifth Annual Convention, Birmingham, August 9–13, 1982.

[2] *Ibid.*

[3] See *SCLC Magazine*, v. 11, no. 4 (October–November 1982), p. 11.

[4] SCLC/NH, Andrew Young Address to the Banquet, 25th Annual Convention, Birmingham, August 12, 1982: SCLC/P, Convention notes.

[5] SCLC/P, Swords into Ploughshares workshop, SCLC 25th Annual Convention, Birmingham, author's notes and tapes.

[6] SCLC/P, Notes on Abraham Woods' presentation of the action-agenda, Birmingham, 1982; SCLC news releases and highlights summaries, August–November, 1982.

[7] See *SCLC Magazine*, v. 11, no. 4 (October–November 1982), p. 69, reprint from the *National Leader*, August 5, 1982.

[8] See Lewis M. Killian, *The Impossible Revolution*, pp. 126–128.

[9] Evelyn Lowery/Peake interview, p. 1 of typescript.

[10] SCLC/NH, Historical sketch and statement of purpose of SCLC/WOMEN.

[11] SCLC/WOMEN, Statement of Purpose, 1979 in SCLC/NH files on SCLC/WOMEN and awards programs and brochure on the organization's structure and goals.

[12] SCLC/P notes and tapes on SCLC/WOMEN's Oratorical Contests, 1980–1985; Evelyn Lowery/Peake interview, pp. 6–7; SCLC/WOMEN announcements of oratorical contest themes, 1980–1985; conversations with participants 1981–1983.

[13] For a useful summary of this and related data see Kristin A. Moore, "Teenage Pregnancy: the Dimensions of the Problem," in *New Perspectives*, v. 17, no. 3 (Summer 1985), pp. 11–15; also Evelyn Lowery/Peake interview, pp. 8–9; SCLC/WOMEN, brochures on seminars on the black male child, family relations, and convention luncheon programs, 1982–1985.

[14] Evelyn Lowery/Peake interview, pp. 9–12; SCLC/NH "Conference on the Black Teenager," materials, April 1983; William E. Cavil III, "From Family Chaos to the Cosby Show: Television Treatment of the Black Family," in *SCLC Magazine*, v. 14, no.

2 (May–June 1985), pp. 70–75; and Quentin Bradford, "Black Teens Told to Re-Establish Family Tradition . . . Take Marriage Seriously," in *Ibid.*, v. 13, no. 2 (July–August 1984), pp. 13–15.

[15] See "Redefining the American Dilemma," *Time*, November 11, 1985, pp. 33–36. Cf. "Blacks See Blacks Saving the Family," *New York Times*, May 7, 1984, p. 14: Dr. Lawford L. Goddard, "Contemporary Conditions Affecting the Black Family," in *SCLC Magazine*, v. 13, no. 5 (February–March 1985), pp. 82–85. Goddard underscores the underlying causes of the inertia in urban environments: crowded conditions, underemployment, unemployment, health care problems, and lack of recreation, as well as the psychological burden of lower-class identity in housing and jobs.

[16] Dick Gregory, address to the SCLC annual convention, Montgomery, August 1985, SCLC/NH tape; Joseph E. Lowery address to the same convention.

[17] SCLC/NH, list of chapters and affiliates; E. Randel T. Osburn/Peake interview, pp. 6–7; conversations with SCLC chapter heads in several cities, including Washington, Louisville, Wrightsville, Los Angeles, and others; *SCLC newsletters* 1983–1985.

[18] "We Still Have a Dream," *Time*, v. 122, no. 10 (September 5, 1983), p. 8.

[19] ABC Television Network, "Nightline," August 25, 1983; see also "An Interview with Bayard Rustin," in *New Perspectives*, v. 17, no. 1 (Winter 1985), pp. 27–29.

[20] Author's tapes and notes on the plenary SCLC convention session, addresses, conversations with Fred Shuttlesworth, James Lawson, Dr. Claud Young, Walter Fauntroy, Dr. Martin Luther King, Sr., R. B. Cottonreader, Rev. Abraham Woods, and SCLC/NH tapes on the convention; news clippings from the *Washington Post* and *Atlanta Constitution*. August 25–27, 1983.

[21] Lewis, *King*, p. 405.

[22] John W. Blassingame, "The Revolution that Never Was: the Civil Rights Movement, 1950–1980," in *New Perspectives*, v. 14, no. 2 (Summer 1982), pp. 3–15.

[23] SCLC/NH *The People's Platform*, 1984; interviews with SCLC staff and field workers, Lowery, and Osburn; news clippings on 1984 campaigns.

[24] Author's notes on the January 15 press conference in Atlanta; SCLC news release, January 15, 1986; conversations with participants.

[25] SCLC Board of Directors' resolutions 1984, 1985, SCLC/NH summaries and texts.

[26] E. Randel T. Osburn/Peake interview, 1985, pp. 3–4.

[27] See Michelle Alexander, "What is a BUPPIE?" *SCLC Magazine*, v. 14, no. 4 (October–November 1985), p. 101.

[28] Osburn/Peake interview, p. 5.

Conclusion

[1] Rabbi Marc H. Tannenbaum, "The Moral Legacy of Martin Luther King, Jr.," pamphlet (New York: The American Jewish Committee, 1983), p. 2.

[2] *Ibid.*, pp. 3–6.

[3] Walter E. Williams, *The State Against Blacks* (New York: McGraw-Hill, 1982), pp. 141–149.

[4] Richard John Newhaus, "Moral Leadership in Post-Secular America," *Imprimis*, v. 11, no. 7 (July 1982), p. 4.

Bibliography

I. Documentary Collections and Official Records

Martin Luther King, Jr. Collection, Mugar Memorial Library, Boston University.
Martin Luther King, Jr. Papers, Martin Luther King, Jr. Center for Nonviolent Social Change, Atlanta, Georgia.
Ralph J. Bunche Oral History Collection, Moorland-Spingarn Research Center, Howard University, Washington, D.C.
Slater King Collection, Papers, 1955–1970, Fisk University, Nashville, Tennessee.
Southern Christian Leadership Conference Records, Martin Luther King, Jr. Center for Nonviolent Social Change, Atlanta, Georgia.
Southern Christian Leadership Conference Files, SCLC National Headquarters, Atlanta, Georgia.
Student Nonviolent Coordinating Committee Records, Martin Luther King, Jr. Center for Nonviolent Social Change, Atlanta, Georgia.

II. Theses and Dissertations

Hartley, Robert Wayne. *A Long Hot Summer: The St. Augustine Racial Disorders of 1964.* Unpublished Masters Thesis, Stetson University, DeLand, Florida, 1972.
Schmeidler, Emilie. *Shaping Ideas and Actions: CORE, SCLC, and SNCC in the Struggle for Equality, 1960–1966.* Unpublished Ph.D. dissertation, Department of Sociology, University of Michigan, 1980.
Sloan, Rose Mary. *Then My Living Will Not Be in Vain: A Rhetorical Study of Dr. Martin Luther King, Jr., and the Southern Christian Leadership Conference in the Mobilization for Collective Action toward Nonviolent Means to Integration, 1954–1964.* Unpublished Ph.D. dissertation, Ohio State University, 1977.
Tinney, James S. *A Theoretical and Historical Comparison of Black Political and Religious Movements.* Unpublished Ph.D. dissertation, Howard University, 1978.
Walker, Eugene Pierce. *A History of the Southern Christian Leadership Conference, 1955–1965: The Evolution of a Southern Strategy for Social Change.* Unpublished Ph.D. dissertation, Department of History, Duke University, 1978.
Yeakey, Lamont H. *The Montgomery Bus Boycott, 1955–1956.* Unpublished Ph.D. dissertation, Columbia University, 1979.

461

III. Periodical and Newspaper Articles

Abernathy, Ralph David, "Birthday Tribute to Angela Davis," speech delivered in New York, February 1971 and reproduced in *Soul Force*, v. 4, no. 2 (March 1971), p. 3.

———, "A Black Preacher Looks at the Black Manifesto," *Soul Force*, v. 2, no. 4 (November 1969), p. 11. Also in *Christian Century*, v. 86 (August 13, 1969), pp. 1064–65.

———, "Comment: Politics '72," *Soul Force*, v. 4, no. 6 (June 1971), p. 3.

———. Editorial, *Soul Force*, v. 1, no. 6 (August 15, 1968), pp. 2 and 21.

———, "Honoring Dr. King. America: Promises and Realities," *Soul Force*, v. 2, no. 1 (April 4, 1969), p. 2.

"Abernathy Steps Down," *Time*, v. 102, no. 4 (July 23, 1973), p. 31.

"The Age of Less," *Newsweek*, v. 92, no. 2 (July 10, 1978), pp. 18–24.

"Alfred Daniel Williams King, Sr.," Obituary, *Soul Force*, v. 2, no. 3 (August 13, 1969), p. 11.

Allen, Archie E., "John Lewis: Keeper of the Dream," *New South* (Spring 1971).

Allen, Cathy, "Democracy at Home and Abroad?," *Soul Force*, v. 5, no. 4 (October 1971), p. 6.

"American Renewal," *Time*, v. 117, no. 8 (February 23, 1981), pp. 34–35.

"America's Incredible Day," *Time*, v. 117, no. 5 (February 2, 1981), pp. 8–16.

"Atlanta-DeKalb Metro SCLC," *Soul Force*, v. 6, no. 9 (September-October 1972), p. 10.

"Battle for the Lunch Counters: the Latest Drive for Integration," *U.S. News & World Report*, v. 68, (March 7, 1960), pp. 44, 46.

"The Belated Civil Rights Legislation of 1968," *The New Republic*, v. 158, no. 13 (March 30, 1968), pp. 11–12.

Bennett, Lerone, Jr., "The Lost/Found Generation: New Group with New Values Changes Racial Dialogue," *Ebony*, v. 33, no. 10 (August 1978), pp. 35–42.

Bickel, Alexander M., "Civil Rights' Dim Prospects," *New Republic*, v. 155 (September 17, 1966), pp. 17–18.

"The Big Man is Martin Luther King, Jr.," *Newsweek*, v. 62, no. 5 (July 29, 1963), p. 31.

"Black Expo Comes of Age," *Ebony*, v. 27, no. 2 (December 1971), pp. 64–72.

"Black Lawmakers in Congress," *Ebony*, v. 29, no. 4 (February 1971), pp. 115–122.

"Black Leaders Look Ahead to New Worries," *U.S. News and World Report*, v. 92, no. 5 (March 1, 1982), p. 65.

"Black Power: Politics of Frustration," *Newsweek*, v. 68, no. 2 (July 11, 1966), pp. 26–32.

"Blacks and U.S. Foreign Policy," *SCLC Magazine*, v. 8, no. 5 (September–October 1979), pp. 38–39.

Braden, Anne, "Wilmington 10 Hearing and Demonstration," *SCLC Magazine*, v. 9, no. 5 (November–December 1980), pp. 44–47.

Brown, Joe David, "Birmingham, Alabama: A City in Fear," *Saturday Evening Post*, v. 236 (March 2, 1963), pp. 16–17.

"Budapest," *Soul Force*, v. 4, no. 6 (June 1971), p. 7.

"Business Outlook at Midyear," *U.S. News & World Report*, v. 84, no. 26 (July 3, 1978), pp. 20–22.

"Can Capitalism Survive?," *Time*, v. 106, no. 2 (July 14, 1975), p. 63.

Carmichael, Stokely, "Toward Black Liberation," *The Massachusetts Review*, v. 7 (Autumn 1966), pp. 642–651.

Carson, Ernest P., "Reagonomics: Who Pays the Price?," *SCLC Magazine*, v. 10, no. 5 (October–November 1981), pp. 34–37.

"Carter's Mideast Muddle," *Time*, v. 114, no. 10 (September 3, 1979) pp. 12–13.

"A Case of Rape or Seduction," *Time*, v. 106, no. 4 (July 28, 1975), p. 19.

Cater, Douglass, "How the Senate Passed the Civil-Rights Bill," *The Reporter*, v. 17 (September 5, 1957), pp. 9–13.

"Challenge / Response," *New Republic*, v. 156 (March 16, 1968), pp. 5–6.

Christian Century, v. 87, (March 16, 1960), pp. 308–309.

"Civil Rights: A New Approach," *U.S. News & World Report*, v. 71, no. 8 (August 23, 1977), pp. 27–28.

"Civil Rights: Fantasy's End," *Newsweek*, v. 64, no. 7 (August 17, 1964), pp. 28–29.

Clark, Kenneth Bancroft, "The Civil Rights Movement: Momentum and Organization," *Daedalus*, v. 95, no. 1 (1966), pp. 239–267.

———, "What Business can do for the Negro," *Nation's Business*, v. 55 (October 1967), p. 66.

Clark, Mike, "Meeting the Needs of the Adult Learner," *Tennessee Adult Educator*, v. 11, no. 2 (Spring–Summer 1981), pp. 15–25.

Clark, Ramsay, "The Bakke Decision," *The Nation*, v. 227, no. 2 (July 8–15, 1978), pp. 37–38.

Clark, Septima Poinsett, "Citizenship and Gospel," *Journal of Black Studies*, v. 10, no. 4 (June 1980), pp. 461–66.

"Clues in Off-Year Elections," *U.S. News & World Report*, v. 71, no. 20 (November 15, 1971), pp. 23–24.

"The Compromise: God Help Us," *National Review*, v. 34, no. 11 (June 11, 1982), p. 673.

"Coretta King reveals What's Happening to MLK Memorial Center," *Jet*, v. 29, no. 5 (November 5, 1970), p. 12.

Cotton, Dorothy, "Conversation with Ralph Abernathy," *Journal of the Current Social Issues*, v. 9, no. 3 (1970), pp. 21–30.

The Crisis, (May 1962), p. 277; v. 68, no. 1 (January 1961), p. 11; v. 68, no. 6 (June–July, 1961), pp. 328–329; v. 70, no. 8 (October 1963), pp. 457–458; v. 71, no. 7 (August–September, 1964), pp. 432–433; v. 76, no. 7 (August–September, 1969), p. 276.

Current, Gloster B., "The Marching Convention—the 54th," *The Crisis*, v. 70, no. 7 (August–September, 1963), pp. 389–391.

———, "Why Nixon Lost the Negro Vote," *The Crisis*, v. 68, no. 1 (January 1961), pp. 5–14.

Delaney, Paul, "Middle Class Gains Create Tensions in Black Community," Part III of Series: "Two Societies; America Since the Kerner Report," *New York Times*, February 28, 1978.

"Did You Know?," *Soul Force*, v. 6, no. 12 (March–April 1973), pp. 2 and 10.

Dillin, John, "The Story of St. Augustine," *Christian Science Monitor*, July 13, 1964.

"The Dirksen Amendments," *The New Republic*, v. 150, no. 23 (June 6, 1964), pp. 3–4.

Douglas, Carlyle C., "Ralph Abernathy: the Man Who Fights to Keep King's Dream Alive," *Ebony*, v. 25 (January 1970), pp. 40–44.

Dunn, Rick, "Black Community Fights U.S. Government for Ancestral Land," *SCLC Magazine*, v. 8, no. 3 (May–June 1979), pp. 8–11.

———, "Dr. Lowery Calls Iranian Crisis Self Defeating," *SCLC Magazine*, v. 9, no. 1 (January–February 1980), pp. 34–37.

"Echoes," editorial in *New York Times*, March 1, 1978, p. 26.

"The Evolution of the Act," *Congressional Digest*, v. 60, no. 12 (December 1981), pp. 292–93.

"Expanded Role of the Black Press," *SCLC West*, v. 6, no. 2 (March 1976), pp. 31–33.

Fairclough, Adam, "The Southern Christian Leadership Conference and the Second Reconstruction, 1957–1973," *South Atlantic Quarterly*, v. 80, no. 2 (Spring 1981), pp. 177–194.

"The Fall of Andy Young," *Time*, v. 114, no. 9 (August 27, 1979), pp. 10–16.

Farris, Carl E., "The Steelworkers Strike in South Carolina," Atlanta, 1971, SCLC reprint.

Fauntroy, Walter E., "Poor People's Campaign," *Soul Force*, v. 2, no. 3 (August 13, 1969), p. 3.

Frame, Randell, "Why Black Brethren Embrace Politics," *Christianity Today*, v. 27, no. 9 (May 20, 1983), p. 34.

Gilbert, Robert E., "John F. Kennedy and Civil Rights for Black Americans," *Presidential Studies Quarterly*, v. 12, no. 3 (Summer 1982), p. 388.

Good, Paul, "No Man Can Fill Dr. King's Shoes—But Abernathy Tries," *New York Times*, May 26, 1968, pp. VI, 28ff.

———, "A White Look at Black Power," *The Nation*, v. 203, (August 8, 1966), pp. 112–115.

Goodman, George, "He Lives, Man!," *Look*, v. 33 (April 15, 1969), p. 29.

Goodwyn, Larry, "Anarchy in St. Augustine," *Harper's Magazine*, v. 230, no. 1376 (January 1965), p. 78.

"Gunfire in Greensboro," *America*, v. 141 (November 17, 1979), p. 292.

"Guns vs. Butter, Battle of the Year," *U.S. News & World Report*, v. 86, no. 3 (January 22, 1979), pp. 16–19.

Halberstam, David, "The Second Coming of Martin Luther King," *Harper's Magazine*, v. 235, no. 1407 (August 1967), pp. 47–50.

"The Hard Choice," *The New Republic*, v. 156 (February 4, 1967), pp. 7–8.

Harding, Vincent and Staughton Lynd, "Albany, Georgia," *The Crisis*, v. 70, no. 2 (February 1963), p. 76.

Harris, Louis, "The 'Backlash' Issue," *Newsweek*, v. 64, no. 2 (July 13, 1964), pp. 24–27.

Hayden, Tom, "The Future of Liberalism," *The Nation*, v. 232, no. 7 (February 21, 1981), p. 194.

Herbers, John, "Decade After Kerner Report: Division of Races Persists," Part I of Series: "Two Societies: America Since the Kerner Report," *New York Times*, February 26, 1978, p. 1.

Hill, Robert B., "The 80's: Employment," *Ebony*, v. 35, no. 3 (January 1980), pp. 27–36.

Hoffius, Steve, "I Expect I'll get a Plaque," *Southern Exposure*, v. 9, no. 2 (1979), pp. 74–76.

Hooks, Benjamin L., "The '80's: Civil Rights," in "The '80's, What's Ahead for Blacks?," *Ebony*, v. 35, no. 3 (January 1980), pp. 27–36.

464

Horton, Aimee, "The Highlander Folk School: Pioneer of Integration in the South," *Teachers College Record*, v. 68, no. 3 (December 1966).

Hughes, Emmet John, "A Curse of Confusion," *Newsweek*, v. 69 (May 1, 1967), p. 1.

Jackson, Jesse, "Dr. King Still Lives," *SCLC West*, v. 6, no. 8 (May–June 1977), p. 3.

"Joan Little's Story," *Time*, v. 106, no. 8 (August 25, 1975), p. 14.

Johnson, Thomas A., "Jesse Jackson is Rising as a Black Leader," *New York Times*, October 12, 1971, p. 14.

"Johnson, King, and Ho Chi Minh," *Christianity Today*, v. 12, no. 15 (April 26, 1968), p. 24.

Keller, Edward B., "A Changing Climate for Civil Rights: Five Key Trends," *Perspectives, A Civil Rights Quarterly*, v. 15, no. 3 (Summer 1983), pp. 10–15.

Kennedy, William S., "Highlander Praxis: Learning with Myles Horton," *Teachers College Record*, v. 83, no. 1 (Fall 1981), pp. 105–19.

King, Coretta Scott, "Twenty Years Later," *Family Weekly* (August 14, 1983), p. 5.

King, Martin Luther, Jr., "Behind the Selma March," *Saturday Review*, v. 68, no. 14 (April 3, 1965), pp. 16, 17, 57.

———, "Bold New Design for a New South," *The Nation*, v. 196 no. 13 (March 30, 1963), pp. 259–262.

———, "The Case Against Tokenism," *New York Times Magazine*, August 5, 1962, p. 11.

———, "The Casualties of the War in Vietnam," *The Nation Institute* (February 25, 1967), reprinted by Committee of Clergy and Laymen Concerned About Vietnam.

———, "Emancipation Proclamation," *Amsterdam News* (November 10, 1962), p. 1.

———, "Equality Now," *The Nation*, v. 192, no. 2 (February 4, 1961), pp. 91–95.

———, "Fumbling on the New Frontier," *The Nation*, v. 194 (March 3, 1962), pp. 190–193.

———, "The Hammer of Civil Rights," *The Nation*, v. 198, no. 11 (March 9, 1964), pp. 230–34.

———, "In a Word—Now," in "What Next?: Five Negro Leaders Reply," *New York Times Magazine*, September 29, 1963, p. 92.

———, Interview in *Playboy Magazine*, (January 1965), reprint by HMH Pub. Co. 1965, p. 4.

———, "It's a Difficult Thing to Teach a President," *Look*, v. 28 (November 17, 1964), p. 61.

———, "The Last Steep Ascent," *The Nation*, v. 202, no. 11 (March 14, 1966), pp. 288–292.

———, "Let Justice Roll Down," *The Nation*, v. 200, no. 11 (March 15, 1965), pp. 269–274.

———, "The Most Durable Power," excerpted in *Christian Century*, v. 74 (June 1957), pp. 708–709.

———, "A Need for Soul Searching," *SCLC Newsletter* (October–November, 1964), p. 7.

———, "A New Sense of Direction," *Drum Major* (August 1971), pp. 1–5.

———, "Nonviolence and Racial Justice," *Christian Century*, v. 74 (February 6, 1957), pp. 165–167.

———, "Of Riots and Wrongs Against the Jews," *SCLC Newsletter* (July–August, 1964), p. 11.

———, "Showdown for Violence," *Look*, v. 32, no. 8 (April 16, 1968), p. 24.

————, "The Terrible Cost of the Ballot," *SCLC Newsletter* (September 1962), pp. 1–2.

————, "Vietnam is Upon Us," Reprinted by Committee of Clergy and Laymen Concerned About Vietnam.

————, "Who is Their God?," *The Nation*, v. 195 (October 13, 1962), pp. 209–10.

King, Slater, "Albany, Georgia," *Freedomways* (Winter 1964), pp. 93–95.

"King Acts for Peace," *The Christian Century*, v. 82, no. 39 (September 29, 1965), pp. 1180–81.

"King Comes to Chicago," *The Christian Century*, v. 82, no. 32 (August 11, 1965), pp. 979–80.

"Klan Writes a Violent New Chapter," *U.S. News & World Report*, v. 87, no. 21 (November 19, 1979), p. 59.

Koplin, Andrew, Review of *Where Do We Go From Here?* in *New York Review of Books*, August 24, 1967, p. 1.

Kotz, Nick and Mary Lynn Kotz, "Welfare Mothers & the Civil Rights Movement," *Civil Liberties Review*, v. 4, no. 4 (April 4, 1977), pp. 74–83.

Lawrence, Charles, III, "The Bakke Case: Are Racial Quotas Defensible?", *Saturday Review*, v. 5, no. 2 (October 15, 1977), pp. 11–16.

Lester, Julius, "The Martin Luther King I Remember," *Evergreen Review*, v. 74 (January 1970), pp. 16–21.

"Let No One Be Denied: But in Resurrection City 'Someday' is Not at Hand," *Newsweek*, v. 72, no. 1 (July 1, 1968), pp. 20–21.

Love, Albert E., "We Must Save Our Children," *SCLC Magazine*, v. 9, no. 5 (November–December 1980), pp. 28–31.

Lowery, Joseph E., Address to the National Leadership Conference, Chicago, May 5–7, 1978, reprinted in *SCLC Magazine*, v. 7, no. 4 (May–June 1978), pp. 10–13.

————, "I Remember Martin," a sermon in the MLK Speaks series, April 1979, reprinted in *SCLC Magazine*, v. 10, no. 1 (January–February 1981), p. 1.

————, Statement on SCLC's contacts with the PLO, *SCLC Magazine*, v. 8, no. 6 (November–December 1979), p. 45.

————, "To Hear Somebody Pray," *SCLC Magazine*, v. 9, no. 1 (January–February, 1980), p. 23.

Maguire, Daniel C., "The Triumph of Unequal Justice," *Christian Century*, v. 95, no. 30 (September 27, 1978), pp. 882–86.

Mahajani, Usha, "Martin Luther King: The Activist Gandhian," *Indian Political Science Review*, v. 4, no. 2 (1970), pp. 171–84.

"Martyrdom of Martin Luther King, Jr.," *The Crisis*, v. 5, no. 4 (April 1968), pp. 114–15.

"Milk Fund. . .IRS. . .Bugging. . .Highlights of the Evidence," *U.S. News and World Report*, v. 77 (July 29, 1974), pp. 19–21.

"A Mission Comes to Grief in Iran," *Newsweek*, v. 95, no. 18 (May 5, 1979), pp. 24–36.

Mitchell, Clarence, "Civil Rights and Economic Rights," *The Crisis*, v. 5, no. 4 (April 1968), pp. 117–21.

————, "Mr. Ford and Civil Rights: A Mixed Record," *The Crisis*, v. 81, no. 1 (January 1974), pp. 7–11.

"The Mood of Ghetto America," *Newsweek*, v. 95, no. 22 (June 2, 1980), pp. 32–34.

Morrow, Lance, "The Gospel According to Jesse," *Horizon*, v. 21, no. 5 (1978), pp. 60–63.

"Movement—the Story of SCLC," *SCLC Magazine*, v. 10 (August–September, 1981), p. 15.

"A Nation Within a Nation," *Time*, v. 91, no. 20 (May 17, 1968) pp. 24–37.

Navasky, Victor, "The FBI's Wildest Dream," *The Nation*, v. 226, no. 23, pp. 716–718.

"Negro Leaders Ban Demonstrations," *Christian Century*, v. 81, no. 33 (August 12, 1964), p. 1005.

"Negroes Go National with Demands for Jobs," *Business Week*, no. 1981 (August 19, 1967), p. 37.

"Negroes Ponder Next Step," *New York Times*, November 24, 1963, p. 12.

Nelson, Harold A., "Whither the Civil Rights Struggle?", *The Crisis*, v. 72, no. 9 (November, 1965), pp. 556–564, 604.

"A New President: An End to a Nation's Agony," *U.S. News and World Report*, v. 77, no. 8 (August 19, 1974), p. 15.

"A New Racial Poll," *Newsweek*, v. 93, no. 9 (February 26, 1979), pp. 48–53.

Newhaus, Richard John, "Moral Leadership in Post-Secular America," *Imprimis*, v. 11, no. 7 (July 1982), pp. 1–4.

"1971 in Review," *Soul Force*, v. 5, no. 6 (November–December 1971), pp. 12–27.

"Nixon's Fight Against Hunger," *U.S. News & World Report*, v. 68, no. 3 (January 19, 1970), pp. 24–26.

"Nixon's Moves in Civil Rights," *U.S. News & World Report*, v. 66, no. 16 (April 21, 1969), p. 15.

Nordheimer, Jon, "1978 Race Relations: 3 Widely Divergent Views," Part II of Series: "Two Societies; America Since the Kerner Report," *New York Times*, February 27, 1978.

"Now in Prospect: A 'Penchpenny Congress', Survey of Freshman Lawmakers," *U.S. News & World Report*, v. 86, no. 3 (January 22, 1979), pp. 29–31.

"Old South Anti-Klan Protest in Greensboro," *Newsweek*, v. 94, no. 20 (November 12, 1979), p. 50.

"On the March," *Newsweek*, v. 61, no. 19 (September 2, 1963), p. 18.

Osborne, John, "King's Men Return to Memphis: What Will Become of His Dreams?", *New Republic*, v. 159 (August 24, 1968), pp. 12–14.

"Our New Director," *Soul Force*, v. 4, no. 5 (1971), p. 15.

Perry, David C. and Alfred J. Watkins, "Carter's Urban Policy," *The Nation*, v. 227, no. 8 (September 16, 1978), pp. 235–238.

"Politics is Power," *Drum Major* (Winter Issue 1971), pp. 6–8.

"The Politics of Austerity," *Newsweek*, v. 93, no. 5 (January 29, 1979), pp. 20–25.

"Poverty: End of the Dream," *Newsweek*, v. 72, no. 2 (July 8, 1968), p. 19.

"The President and the Preacher," editorial, *Washington Post*, May 15, 1969, p. A-18.

Raspberry, William, "Black America's Fears," *Washington Post*, July 1, 1981, p. A-25.

"Reagan's Big Win," *Time*, v. 117, no. 20 (May 18, 1981), pp. 14–16.

Reed, Roy, "Dr. King's Followers Modify His Approach in Their Continuing Pursuit of Justice," *New York Times*, January 7, 1972, p. 9.

Reinhold, Robert, "Ruling Seen as a Lift for Rights Movement," *New York Times*, (June 28, 1979), p. B-12.

"Repression in America," *Soul Force*, v. 3, no. 1 (February, 1970), pp. 2, 6.

"Reverend Martin Luther King's Diary in Jail," *Jet* (August 23, 1962), p. 18.

"Reverse Discrimination: What the Supreme Court was Told in the Bakke Case," *U.S. News & World Report*, v. 83, no. 17 (October 24, 1977), pp. 94–96.

Reynolds, Barbara A., "An Interview with the Rev. Dr. Joseph Lowery," *Dollars and Sense*, v. 7, no. 2 (June–July, 1981), pp. 102–104.

Riedman, Larry, "The Condition of Civil Rights Advocacy, Emerging from Despair with New Strategies for Progress," *Civil Rights Digest*, v. 2, no. 3 (Spring 1979), pp. 35–45.

Roberts, Pat, "Wrightsville: A Town Left Behind," *SCLC Magazine*, v. 9, no. 3 (July–August, 1980), pp. 17–23.

Rogers, Cornish, "SCLC: Faithful to Its Function," *Christian Century*, v. 88, no. 18 (May 5, 1971), p. 550.

Rowan, Carl T., "Martin Luther King's Tragic Decision," *Reader's Digest*, v. 90 (September, 1967), pp. 37–42.

Royko, Mike, *Chicago Daily News*, April 5, 1967.

"A Rush of Action to Get More Jobs for Negroes," *U.S. News and World Report*, v. 92 (September 15, 1969), p. 67.

Rustin, Bayard, "King's Dream," *SCLC Magazine*, v. 7, no. 3 (April, 1978), pp. 10–11.

———, "My Turn," *Newsweek*, v. 102, no. 9 (August 29, 1983), p. 11.

———, "To Blacks: Condemn P.L.O. Terrorism," *New York Times*, August 30, 1979, p. A-21.

"SCLC Elects Lowery President," *Atlanta Voice*, v. 12, no. 1 (August 27, 1977), pp. 1, 9.

"SCLC Officials Meet with PLO and Israeli Leaders," *SCLC Magazine*, v. 8, no. 5 (September–October 1979), pp. 31–34.

"SCLC on the Couch," *Newsweek*, v. 72, no. 24 (December 9, 1968), p. 34.

"SCLC Pledges Solidarity to Sugar Cane Workers Head," *SCLC Magazine*, v. 8, no. 3 (May–June, 1979), pp. 14–15.

SCLC West, v. 6, no. 8 (May–June, 1977), p. 26.

"SCLC's Leadership Crisis," *Christian Century*, v. 90, no. 31 (September 5, 1973), p. 844.

"Scottsboro Revisited?" *Time*, v. 112, no. 16 (October 16, 1978), p. 46.

Sheppard, Nathaniel, Jr., "Forum on Black-Jewish Relations Hears Vows for Initiatives on Ties," *New York Times*, (October 23, 1979), p. 20.

Sherry, Paul H., "Hope in a Time that Invites Despair," *United Church of Christ Journal*, v. 9, no. 3 (November–December, 1970), p. 2.

"Shootout in Greensboro: Anti-Klan Protest," *Time*, v. 114, no. 20 (November 12, 1979), p. 31.

Silberman, Charles E., "Negro Economic Gains—Impressive but Precarious," *Fortune*, v. 82, no. 1 (July 1970), pp. 74–77ff.

Sitton, Claude, "Rioting Negroes Routed by Police," *New York Times*, (May 8, 1963), p. 28.

Situation Report, *Time Magazine*, v. 95, no. 14 (April 6, 1970), p. 27.

"The 69th—The Post-Bakke Convention," *The Crisis*, v. 85, no. 8 (October, 1978), pp. 259–276.

Snyder, Dean, "Civil Disobedience: What It Means," *Christian Century*, v. 100, no. 12 (April 27, 1983), p. 404.

Soul Force, v. 2, no. 2 (June 1969).

"The South: New Black Politics," *Soul Force*, v. 3, no. 2 (December 4, 1970), pp. 1, 4.

"Special Ebony Poll," *Ebony*, v. 24, no. 7 (May, 1979), pp. 183–185.

"Split in SCLC," *Newsweek*, v. 78, no. 25 (December 20, 1971), pp. 27–28.

"Still King," *Christian Century*, v. 83 (September 7, 1966), pp. 1071–1072.

"Struggle in Gadsden Continues," *SCLC Magazine*, v. 7, no. 4 (May–June, 1978), pp. 14–15.

Suall, Irwin J., "The Ku Klux Klan Malady Lingers On," *Perspectives, The Civil Rights Quarterly*, v. 12, no. 3 (Fall–Winter, 1980–81), pp. 11–15.

Tanenbaum, Rabbi Marc H., "The Moral Legacy of Martin Luther King, Jr.," pamphlet. New York: The American Jewish Committee, 1983.

Tatel, David S., "New Riots, Old Reasons," *Washington Post*, May 24, 1980, p. A-15.

Taylor, Fred D., "Membership Drive—Why Now?", *SCLC Magazine*, v. 7, no. 5 (July–August 1978), pp. 16–17.

"Time-Louis Harris Poll," cited in *Time Magazine*, Special issue on Black America 1970, v. 95, no. 14 (April 6, 1970), pp. 28–29.

"Twenty-Five Years of SCLC Tradition," *SCLC Magazine*, v. 11, no. 3 (August–September 1982), p. 20.

"Two Societies; America Since the Kerner Report," *New York Times*, See Herbers, John; Nordheimer, Jon; and Delaney, Paul.

"Victory in Sandersville," *Soul Force*, v. 5, no. 6 (November–December 1971), pp. 4 and 10.

Walters, Ronald, "The Black Initiatives in the Middle East," *Journal of Palestine Studies*, v. 10, no. 2 (1981), pp. 3–13.

"We Still Have A Dream," *Time*, v. 122, no. 10 (September 5, 1983), pp. 8–10.

Weaver, Robert C., "Rebuilding American Cities: An Overview," *Current History*, v. 55, no. 328 (December 1968), pp. 321–326 and 364.

Welsh, James, "Welfare Reform: Born August 8, 1969, died October 4, 1972," *New York Times Magazine*, January 7, 1973, pp. 14–16ff.

"West Side Story," *Newsweek*, v. 68 (July 25, 1966), pp. 17–18.

"What Groundswell," *The Nation*, v. 235, no. 3 (June 10–17, 1982), p. 39.

"A Whig in the White House," *Time Magazine*, v. 95, no. 11 (March 16, 1970), pp. 26–27.

"Whither the Civil Rights Movement?", *New York Times*, April 9, 1979, p. 18.

Wicker, Tom, "The Perennial Klan," *New York Times*, May 20, 1979, p. A-19.

Wilkins, Roy, "Civil Rights, 1963: A Summary," *The Crisis*, v. 71, no. 2 (February 1964), pp. 69–71.

———, Letter to Congressman Diggs, May 3, 1972, reprinted in *The Crisis*, v. 79, no. 7 (August–September, 1972), p. 229.

———, "Steady as She Goes," Keynote Address to the 57th Convention of the NAACP, Los Angeles, July 5, 1966.

Williams, Hosea, "SCLC Puts Might of Its Organization Against Goldwaterism," *SCLC Newsletter* (October–November, 1964), pp. 1–2.

"With New Civil-Rights Law—How Negroes See the Future," *U.S. News and World Report*, v. 56, no. 26 (June 29, 1964), p. 39.

Woodward, Comer Vann, "What Happened to the Civil Rights Movement?", *Harper's Magazine*, v. 234 (January 1967), pp. 29–34.

"A Year of SCLC," *Soul Force*, v. 1, no. 6 (August 15, 1968), p. 21.

Yankelovich, Skelly and White, Inc. See, Keller, Edward B.

Young, Andrew J., "And Birmingham," *Drum Major* (Winter 1971), p. 21.

———, "Historic Charleston," *Soul Force*, v. 2, no. 2 (June 1969), p. 4.

"The Young Campaign," *Soul Force*, v. 3, no. 2 (December 4, 1970), pp. 2 and 4.

IV. Books

Adams, Frank. *Unearthing Seeds of Fire: The Highlander Idea*. Winston Salem: Blair Publishers, 1975.

Ahmann, Mathew. *The New Negro*. Notre Dame: Fides Publisher, 1961.

Alvarez, Joseph A. *From Reconstruction to Revolution: The Blacks' Struggle for Equality*. New York: Atheneum, 1971.

American Revolutionary Bicentennial Administration. *The Bicentinnial of the United States of America: A Final Report to the People*. 5 vols. Washington, D.C.: Government Printing Office, 1977.

Anderson, Jervis. *A. Philip Randolph: A Biographical Portrait*. New York: Harcourt, Brace, Jovanovich, 1972.

Andler, Bill. *The Wisdom of Martin Luther King in His Own Words*. New York: Lancer Books, 1968.

Ansbro, John J. *Martin Luther King, Jr.: The Making of a Mind*. Maryknoll, New York: Orbis Books, 1982.

Baldwin, James. *The Fire Next Time*. New York: Dial Press, 1963.

Barbour, Floyd B. *The Black Power Revolt*. Boston: Porter Sargent, 1968.

Bates, Daisy. *The Long Shadow of Little Rock: A Memoir*. New York: David McKay Co., 1962.

Bell, Carolyn Shaw. *The Economics of the Ghetto*. New York: Pegasus, 1970.

Bennett, Lerone. *Confrontation: Black and White*. Chicago: Johnson Publishing Company, 1965.

————. *What Manner of Man: A Biography of Martin Luther King, Jr.* 4th revised edition. Chicago: Johnson Publishing Co., 1976.

Bishop, James Alonzo. *The Days of Martin Luther King, Jr.* New York: G.P. Putnam's Sons, 1971.

Blaustein, Albert P. and Robert L. Zangrando. *Civil Rights and the American Negro*. New York: Washington Square Press, 1968.

Bockmuehl, Klaus. *The Challenge of Marxism: a Christian Response*. Downers Grove: InterVarsity Press, 1980.

Bondurant, Joan V. *Conquest of Violence: the Gandhian Philosophy of Conflict*. Berkeley: University of California Press, 1965.

Brauer, Carl M. *John F. Kennedy and the Second Reconstruction*. New York: Columbia University Press, 1977.

Breitman, George. *The Last Year of Malcolm X: The Evolution of a Revolutionary*. New York: Schocken, 1968.

Broderick, Francis L. and August Meier. *Negro Protest Thought in the Twentieth Century*. New York: Bobbs-Merrill, 1965.

Burk, Robert Frederick. *The Eisenhower Administration and Black Civil Rights*. Knoxville: University of Tennessee Press, 1984.

Carmichael, Stokely and Charles V. Hamilton. *Black Power: the Politics of Liberation in America*. New York: Random House, 1967.

Carson, Clayborne. *In Struggle: SNCC and the Black Awakening of the 1960's*. Cambridge: Harvard University Press, 1981.

Chafe, William H. *Civilities and Civil Rights: Greensboro, North Carolina and the Black Struggle for Freedom*. New York: Oxford University Press, 1980.

Citizens Review Committee Report on the Greensboro slayings in the North Carolina

Advisory Committee to the U.S. Commission on Civil Rights: *Black White Perceptions, Race Relations in Greensboro*. Greensboro, North Carolina, 1980.

Clark, Kenneth Bancroft. *Dark Ghetto*. New York: Harper and Row, 1965.

Clark, Kenneth Bancroft and Talcott Parsons, editors. *The Negro America*. Boston: Beacon Press, 1967.

Clark, Kenneth Bancroft. "The Negro in the North," in M. H. Almann, *The New Negro*. Notre Dame: Fides Publisher, 1961.

————. *The Negro Protest*. Boston: Beacon Press, 1963.

Clark, Septima Poinsett, "The Citizenship School: A Lamp Unto Their Feet," in *The SCLC Story*, p. 53.

Clayton, Edward Taylor. *Martin Luther King: The Peaceful Warrior*. Englewood Cliffs, N.J.: Prentice-Hall, 1954.

————. *The SCLC Story in Words and Pictures*. Atlanta: Southern Christian Leadership Conference, 1964.

Cleage, Albert B. *The Black Messiah*. New York: Sheed and Ward, Inc., 1971.

Cleaver, Eldridge. *Soul on Ice*, seventh edition. New York: Dell, 1972.

Colburn, David R. *Racial Change and Community Crisis: St Augustine, Florida, 1877–1980*. New York: Columbia University Press, 1985.

Committee of Clergy and Laymen Concerned About Vietnam. *Dr. Martin Luther King, Jr., Dr. John C. Bennett, Dr. Henry Steele Commanger, Rabbi Abraham Herschel Speak on the War in Vietnam*. CCLCAV, 1968.

Cone, James H. *A Black Theology of Liberation*. New York: J. B. Lippincott, 1970.

Congressional Quarterly Service. *Federal Economic Policy, 1945–1967*. Washington, D.C.: Congressional Quarterly, 1967.

DuBois, W. E. B. *Souls of Black Folk*. New York: Fawcett, 1961.

Dulles, Foster Rhea. *The Civil Rights Commission, 1957–1965*. East Lansing: Michigan State University Press, 1968.

Eisenhower, Dwight David. *The White House Years: Waging Peace, 1956–1961*. New York: Doubleday, 1965.

Ellis, Carl F. *Beyond Liberation, the Gospel in the Black American Experience*. Downers Grove: Inter Varsity Press, 1983.

Emerson, Thomas Irvin, David Haber, Norman Dorsen. *Political and Civil Rights in the United States*. 2 vols., 4th ed. Boston: Little, Brown, 1976–1979.

Encyclopedia of Black America. W. Augustus Low, editor. New York: McGraw-Hill, 1981.

Evans, Rowland and Robert Novak. *Lyndon B. Johnson: the Exercise of Power*. New York: New American Library, 1966.

————. *Nixon in the White House: The Frustration of Power*. New York: Random House, 1971.

Fager, Charles E. *Selma 1965*. New York: Charles Scribner's Sons, 1974.

Fanon, Frantz. *The Wretched of the Earth*. New York: Grove Press, 1964.

Farley, Reynolds. *Blacks and Whites Narrowing the Gap*? Cambridge, Massachusetts: Harvard University Press, 1984.

Farmer, James. *Freedom-When*? New York: Random House, 1965.

Forman, James. *The Making of Black Revolutionaries*. New York: Macmillan, 1972.

Franklin, John Hope. *From Slavery to Freedom: A History of American Negroes*, 4th ed. New York: Alfred A. Knopf, 1974.

Frazier, E. Franklin. *Black Bourgeoisie*. New York: Macmillan, 1956.

————. *Negro Church in America.* New York: Schocken, 1964.

Frazier, Thomas R., editor. *Afro-American History: Primary Sources.* New York: Harcourt, Brace, Jovanovich, 1971.

Gallup, George Horace. *The Gallup Poll: Public Opinion, 1935–1971.* 3 vols. New York: Random House, 1972.

Garrow, David J. *The FBI and Martin Luther King, Jr., From "Solo" to Memphis.* New York: W.W. Norton, 1981.

————. *Protest at Selma: Martin Luther King, Jr. and the Voting Rights Act of 1965.* New Haven: Yale University Press, 1978.

Goldman, Eric F. *The Tragedy of Lyndon Johnson.* New York: Alfred A. Knopf, 1969.

Grant, Joanne, editor. *Black Protest: History, Documents, and Analysis from 1619 to the Present.* New York: Fawcett, 1968.

Gregory, Dick. *Nigger.* New York: Dutton, 1964.

Guardini, Romano. *The Lord.* Chicago: Regnery, 1954.

Guinan, Edward. *Peace and Nonviolence: Basic writings by Prophetic Voices in the World Religions.* New York: Paulist Press, 1973.

Haley, Alex and Malcolm X. *The Autobiography of Malcolm X.* New York: The Grove Press, 1964.

Hamilton, Charles V. *The Black Preacher in America.* New York: Morrow, 1972.

Hamilton, Michael P., editor. *The Vietnam War: Christian Perspectives.* Grand Rapids: Eerdmans, 1967.

Hardwick, Elizabeth. *Bartleby in Manhattan and Other Essays.* New York: Random House, 1983.

Hayden, Thomas. *Rebellion in Newark.* New York: Random House, 1967.

Hentoff, Nat. *Peace Agitator: The Story of A. J. Muste.* New York: Macmillan, 1963.

Herring, George C. *America's Longest War: The United States and Vietnam, 1950–1975.* New York: John Wiley & Sons, 1979.

Hughes, Langston. *Fight for Freedom: The Story of the NAACP.* New York: W. W. Norton and Co., 1962.

Huie, William Bradford. *He Slew the Dreamer.* New York: Delcorte Press, 1968.

I Have a Dream: The Story of Martin Luther King in Text and Pictures. New York: Time-Life, 1968.

Johnson, Lyndon Baines. *My Hope for America.* New York: Random House, 1964.

Jones, James M. *Prejudice and Racism.* Reading: Addison-Wesley Publishing Company, 1972.

Kearns, Doris. *Lyndon Johnson and the American Dream.* New York: Harper and Row, 1976.

Killian, Lewis M. *The Impossible Revolution, Phase 2: Black Power and the American Dream.* New York: Random House, 1965.

King, Coretta Scott. *My Life With Martin Luther King, Jr.* New York: Holt, Rinehart, and Winston, 1969.

King, Martin Luther, Sr. *Daddy King: An Autobiography.* New York: Morrow, 1980.

King, Martin Luther, Jr. *The Measure of a Man.* Philadelphia: United Church Press, 1968.

————. *Strength to Love.* New York: Pocket Books, 1964.

————. *Stride Toward Freedom: The Montgomery Story.* New York: Harper and Row, 1958.

————. *The Trumpet of Conscience.* New York: Harper and Row, 1968.

————. *Where Do We Go From Here: Chaos or Community?* New York: Harper and Row, 1967.

————. *Why We Can't Wait.* New York: Harper and Row, 1964.

Koob, Kathryn. *Guest of the Revolution.* Nashville: Thomas Nelson Publishers, 1982.

Leonard, Vickie and Tom MacLean, editors. *The Continental Walk for Disarmament and Social Justice.* New York: Continental Walk for Disarmament and Social Justice Organization, 1977.

Lewis, David Levering. *King, a Biography*, second edition. Urbana: University of Illinois Press, 1978.

Lincoln, C. Eric, editor. *The Black Experience in Religion.* Garden City: Anchor, Doubleday, 1974.

————. *The Black Muslims in America.* Boston: Beacon Press, 1961.

————. *Martin Luther King, Jr.: A Profile.* New York: Hill and Wang, 1970.

Lomax, Louis E. *The Negro Revolt.* New York: Harper and Row, 1963. (Also published by New American Library.)

————. *To Kill a Black Man.* Los Angeles: Holloway House, 1968.

Lowery, Joseph E. "All Children of Abraham," in James Zogby and Jack O'Dell, *Afro-Americans Stand Up for Middle East Peace.* Washington, D.C.: Palestine Human Rights Campaign, 1980.

Lubell, Samuel. *White and Black: Test of a Nation.* New York: Harper and Row, 1964.

McCord, William. *Mississippi: The Long, Hot Summer.* New York: W. W. Norton, 1965.

Macmillan, George. *The Making of an Assassin: The Life of James Earl Ray.* New York: Little, Brown, 1976.

Malcolm X. *The Autobiography of Malcolm X* (written by Alex Haley). New York: The Grove Press, 1964.

Martin, Warren Bryan. *College of Character.* San Francisco: Jossey-Bass Publishers, 1982.

Martin Luther King, Jr., 1929–1968: An Ebony Picture Biography. Chicago: Johnson Publishing Company, 1968.

Matthews, Donald R. and James W. Prothro. *Negroes and the New Southern Politics.* New York: Harcourt, Brace and World, 1966.

Mays, Benjamin. *The Negro's God as Reflected in His Literature.* New York: Atheneum, 1968.

————. *Seeking To Be Christian in Race Relations.* New York: Friendship Press, 1964.

Meier, August and Elliott Rudwick. *CORE: A Study in the Civil Rights Movement, 1942–1968.* New York: Oxford University Press, 1973. (Also published by University of Illinois Press, 1975).

Miller, William Robert. *Martin Luther King, Jr.: His Life, Martyrdom and Meaning for the World.* New York: Weybright and Talley, 1968.

Morris, Aldon D. *The Origins of the Civil Rights Movement: Black Communities Organizing for Change.* New York: Free Press, 1984.

Murray, Charles. *Losing Ground: American Social Policy 1950–1980.* New York: Basic Books, 1984.

Newton, Huey P. *Revolutionary Suicide.* New York: Ballatine Books, 1973.

Nixon, Richard Milhous. *The Memoirs of Richard Nixon.* 2 vols. New York: Warner Books, 1978.

Novak, Michael. *Confession of a Catholic.* New York: Harper and Row, 1983.

————. *Moral Clarity in the Nuclear Age*. Nashville: Thomas Nelson Publishers, 1983.

————. *The Spirit of Democratic Capitalism*. New York: Simon and Schuster, 1982.

Novak, Robert. See Evans, Rowland and Robert Novak.

Oates, Stephen B. *Let the Trumpet Sound: The Life of Martin Luther King, Jr.* New York: Harper and Row, 1982.

Orum, Anthony M. *Black Students in Protest: A Study of the Origins of the Black Student Movement*. Washington, D.C.: American Sociological Association, 1974.

Peck, James. *Freedom Ride*. New York: Grove, 1962.

Prothro, James W. and Donald R. Matthews. *Negroes and the New Southern Politics*. New York: Harcourt, Brace and World, 1966.

Raines, Howell. *My Soul is Rested: Movement Days in the Deep South Remembered*. New York: G. P. Putnam's Sons, 1977.

Rainwater, Lee and William L. Yancey. *The Moynihan Report and Politics of Controversy*. Cambridge: MIT Press, 1967.

Rauschenbusch, Walter. *Christianizing the Social Order*. New York: Macmillan, 1919.

Reddick, Lawrence Dunbar. *Crusader Without Violence: A Biography of Martin Luther King, Jr.* New York: Harper and Brothers, 1959.

Report of the National Advisory Commission on Civil Disorders, New York Times Edition. New York: E. P. Dutton and Co., Inc. 1968.

Reynolds, Barbara A. *Jesse Jackson: the Man, the Movement, the Myth*. Chicago: Nelson-Hall, 1975.

Rowan, Carl T. *Go South to Sorrow*. New York: Random House, 1957.

Rudwick, Elliott, joint author; See Meier, August.

Rustin, Bayard. *Strategies for Freedom: The Changing Patterns of Black Protest*. New York: Columbia University Press, 1976.

Schlesinger, Arthur Meier, Jr. *History of American Presidential Elections, 1789–1968*, 4 vols. New York: McGraw-Hill Book Co., 1971.

————. *Robert Kennedy and His Times*. Boston: Houghton Mifflin, 1978.

————. *A Thousand Days: John F. Kennedy in the White House*. Boston: Houghton Mifflin, 1965.

Schuchter, Arnold. *White Power/Black Freedom*. Boston: Beacon Press, 1968.

Schulke, Flip, editor. *Martin Luther King, Jr.: A Documentary, Montgomery to Memphis*. New York: Norton, 1976.

Scott, Robert L. and Wayne Brockriede, editors. *The Rhetoric of Black Power*. New York: Harper and Row, 1969.

Selby, Earl and Mirian. *Odyssey: Journey through Black America*. New York: Putnam Sons, 1971.

Sellers, Cleveland and Robert Terrell. *The River of No Return: The Autobiography of a Black Militant and the Life and Death of SNCC*. New York: Morrow, 1973.

Smith, Kenneth L. and Ira G. Zepp, Jr. *Search for the Beloved Community: The Thinking of Martin Luther King, Jr.* Valley Forge: Judson Press, 1974.

Sobel, Lester A., editor. *Civil Rights, 1960–1966*. New York: Facts on File, 1967.

The State of the Union Messages of the Presidents, v. III: 1905–1966. New York: Chelsea House, 1966.

Tjerandsen, Carl. *Education for Citizenship: A Foundation's Experience*. Santa Cruz, California: Emil Schwarzhaupt Foundation, 1980.

To Secure These Rights: The Report of the President's Committee on Civil Rights. New York: Simon and Schuster, 1947.

United States. Commission on Civil Rights. *Report on the State of Civil Rights, 1979.* Washington, D.C.: Government Printing Office, 1980.

United States. Commission on Civil Rights. *The State of Civil Rights in 1977: a Report.* Washington, D.C.: Government Printing Office, 1978.

United States Commission on Civil Rights. *Twenty Years After Brown, A Report.* Washington, D.C.: Government Printing Office, 1975.

United States. Congress. House of Representatives. Ninety-Fifth Congress. *Hearings Before the Select Committee on Assassinations*, Second Session, vol. 1, August 14, 1978. Washington, D.C.: Government Printing Office, 1979.

United States. House of Representatives. Committee on Foreign Affairs. *Staff Report on the Assassination of Representative Leo J. Ryan and the Jonestown, Guyana Tragedy.* Washington, D.C.: Government Printing Office, 1979.

U. S. President. *Public Papers of the Presidents: 1960–1983.* Washington, D.C.: Government Printing Office, 1961–1984.

Vivian, Octavia. *Coretta: the Story of Mrs. Martin Luther King, Jr.* Philadelphia: Fortress Press, 1970.

Walker, Jack L. *Sit-ins In Atlanta.* New York: McGraw-Hill, 1964.

Walton, Hanes, Jr. *The Political Philosophy of Martin Luther King, Jr.* Westport: Greenwood Press, 1971.

Warren, Robert Penn. *Who Speaks for the Negro?* New York: Random House, 1964.

Watters, Pat and Reese Cleghorn. *Climbing Jacob's Ladder: the Arrival of Negroes in Southern Politics.* New York: Harcourt, Brace, and World, 1967.

Watters, Pat. *Down To Now, Reflections On the Southern Civil Rights Movement.* New York: Pantheon Books, 1971.

White, Theodore H. *The Making of the President, 1960.* New York: Atheneum, 1961.

———, *The Making of the President, 1972.* New York: Atheneum, 1973.

Will, Robert Erwin and Harold G. Vatter. *Poverty in Affluence: The Social, Political, and Economic Dimensions of Poverty in the United States.* New York: Harcourt, Brace, and World, 1970.

Williams, John. *The King God Didn't Save.* New York: Simon and Schuster, 1970.

Williams, Walter E. *America: A Minority Viewpoint.* Stanford: Hoover Institute Press, 1982.

———. *The State Against Blacks.* New York: McGraw-Hill, 1982.

Wolff, Miles. *Lunch at the Five and Ten, The Greensboro Sit-ins: A Contemporary History.* New York: Stein and Day, 1970.

Wortham, Anne. *The Other Side of Racism: A Philosophical Study of Black Race Consciousness.* Ohio State University Press, 1981.

Yeakey, Lamont. "Black Women in Struggle: the Montgomery Movement," *National Council for Black Studies, 6th Annual Conference: Proceedings.* Chicago, 1982, Unit III.

Young, Whitney. *To Be Equal.* New York: McGraw-Hill, 1964.

Zinn, Howard. *SNCC: The New Abolitionists.* Boston: Beacon Press, 1964.

———. *The Southern Mystique.* New York: Alfred A. Knopf, 1964.

Zogby, James and Jack O'Dell. *Afro-Americans Stand Up for Middle East Peace.* Washington, D.C.: Palestine Human Rights Campaign, 1980.

Index

485

489

490

1. One of Reverend Fred Taylor's many demonstration activities in the 1980s   (© Pamela Harvey)

2. New generations of SCLC activitists in the 1980s.

(© Pamela Harvey)

3. Candlelight march in behalf of a nuclear freeze led by SCLC officials in Washington, D.C. 1982. (©Pamela Harvey)

4. Dr. and Mrs. Lowery and Congressman Walter Fauntroy encourage voter registration in Resurrection City 1982. (©Pamela Harvey)

5. Reverend James Orange directs marchers during the 1982 Pilgrimage to Washington; North Carolina. (© Pamela Harvey)

6. Construction of Resurrection City in 1968.

(©Courtesy SCLC)

7. Montgomery Voting Rights rally 1965. Mrs. Rosa Parks at platform. (© Elaine Tomlin)

8. Dr. Ralph David Abernathy with hospital strike leaders in Charleston, S.C. 1969.　　(© Elaine Tomlin)

9. Over the Edmund Pettis Bridge on the 20th anniversary of the Selma to Montgomery March. (© Elaine Tomlin)

10. Dr. Joseph E. Lowery and SCLC staff and labor leaders announce Winn-Dixie decision to remove South African products Jan. 1986. (© Elaine Tomlin)

Unfinished Agenda:
The Case for Nonviolence in the Nuclear Age
Thomas R. Peake, General Editor
King College

A series of readable, scholarly studies of the historical roots, concepts, and strategies of nonviolence focusing on its potential in the nuclear age. Written by experts on the history and conceptual framework of nonviolent theory, these books address both the problems and the challenges of nonviolence, including its relevance to international relations. Gandhian nonviolence, the black American liberation movement, arms control, and global community-building are examined realistically and with sensitivity to the importance of moral values.

Sara H. Markham

WORKERS, WOMEN, AND AFRO-AMERICANS
Images of the United States in German Travel Literature, from 1923 to 1933

American University Studies: Series I (Germanic Languages and Literature). Vol. 45
ISBN 0-8204-0266-4   IX,317 pp.   hardcover US $ 49,90

Recommended price - alterations reserved

Sara Markham draws on interdisciplinary scholarship and a rich variety of archival sources to provide a definitive analysis of German travel literature. She examines images of the United States in a multiplicity of cultural and historical contexts. Her study delineates and assesses socially critical, women's literary, worker-oriented, socialist, and nascent anti-fascist tendencies in travel books of Weimar Germany. Markham's focus on German perceptions of U.S. workers, women, and Afro-Americans illuminates the historical dimensions of the author's contributions and limitations in regard to German cultural legacy.

Contents: This book analyzes leading progressive tendencies in travel literature of Weimar Germany – It will be of interest to scholars of literary and cultural history, women's, labor, and Afro-American studies, and German-American relations.
Deals with an extremely important, but hitherto almost totally neglected subject ... extremely well researched ... engages the reader throughout. (Jost Hermand, The University of Wisconsin – Madison)

PETER LANG PUBLISHING, INC.
62 West 45th Street
USA – New York, NY 10036

Vernessa C. White

AFRO-AMERICAN AND EAST GERMAN FICTION

A Comparative Study of Alienation, Identity and the Development of Self

American University Studies: Series III (Comparative Literature). Vol. 4
ISBN 0-8204-0016-5   186 pp.   paperback US $ 17,90

Recommended price - alterations reserved

Afro-American and East German fiction point to significant parallels in the pattern of social development among members of both groups, despite the diversities of race, culture and polemical political systems, factors tradionally viewed as barriers. This work compares the social development of contemporary Afro-American and East German counterparts by means of literary analysis.

Contents: Afro-American Literary Images – Racism, Sexism, and Black Identity – Black Identity and the Bourgeoisie – Socialist Humanism vs. Socialist Realism – Morality and Consciousness in *Renata* and *Buridans Esel*.

PETER LANG PUBLISHING, INC.
62 West 45th Street
USA – New York, NY 10036

Chester M. Hedgepeth

THEORIES OF SOCIAL ACTION IN BLACK LITERATURE

American University Studies: Series XIX (General Literature), Vol. 2
ISBN 0-8204-0311-3   VII, 158 pp.   hardcover US $ 29,60

Recommended price - alterations reserved

Theories of Social Action in Black Literature is a comparative analysis of exemplary literature that conveys the religious and secular basis of social action among Blacks during the first half of the twentieth century. The study compares and contrasts the themes of hopelessness and despair in the works of selected black novelists with the more optimistic tone of the leaders of social action movements. In the case of the novelists, the purpose is to show from an analysis of prototypical tragic literature the prominence of physical and spiritual suffering that results from the *deus absconditus* of Old Testament and selected black fiction. In particular, this section focuses on the «Samson Syndrome» as the historical and religious representation of negative self-assertion that has as its intent the transformation of a culturally repressive society.

The activists serve both individually and collectively to gain freedom. Their actions may be characterized as transcending, transforming, or accommodating. The aim of the analysis of both individual and collective leadership styles is to show the contrast in means and goals between the artists and the activists.

Contents: This study is a comparative analysis of exemplary literature that conveys the religious and secular basis of social action among Blacks during the first half of the twentieth century.

PETER LANG PUBLISHING, INC.
62 West 45th Street
USA – New York, NY 10036